Amanda Spink • Michael Zimmer

Editors

Web Search

Multidisciplinary Perspectives

 Springer

Editors
Prof. Dr. Amanda Spink
Queensland University of Technology
Faculty of Information Technology
Gardens Point Campus
2 George St.
Brisbane, QLD 4001
Australia
ah.spink@qut.edu.au

Michael Zimmer
Information Society Project
Yale Law School
127 Wall Street
New Haven, CT 06520
USA
michael.zimmer@yale.edu

ISBN: 978-3-642-09499-6   e-ISBN: 978-3-540-75829-7

Information Science and Knowledge Management ISSN: 1568-1300

ACM Codes: H.4, J.5, K.4

Cover Design: KuenkelLopka, Heidelberg, Germany

Printed on acid-free paper

5 4 3 2 1 0

springer.com

Information Science and Knowledge Management

Preface

The inspiration for this book emerged from the editors' participation in a panel discussion on Web search engines at an annual meeting of the Association of Internet Researchers. This multidisciplinary panel of Web search researches revealed the diversity of scholars interested in Web searching, coupled with a broad range of questions, attitudes, and approaches. It became clear that more "cross-fertilization" was necessary between the disciplines to ensure Web search engines (the entities) and Web searching (the user behavior) received the thorough scholarly attention they deserved. This book is a result of that realization, and an important first step in achieving new levels of awareness and collaboration across disciplines.

The book represents a core theme within the intellectual pursuits of the editors. The first editor (Spink) is an information scientist who has worked with, taught and has researched the informational dimensions of Web searching since 1997. The second editor (Zimmer) is a scholar of culture and communication who focuses on the political and ethical dimensions of new media and information technologies, and whose dissertation research focused on the value-related consequences of the quest for the "perfect" search engine.

This book is intended as a resource for researchers, educators, students, and practitioners. Researchers in the fields of social sciences, communication studies, cultural studies, information science, and related disciplines will all find the chapters presented here as a valuable source of new ideas on Web search. This book is also an appropriate text for advanced undergraduate, graduate, and doctoral level courses in areas of Web search. In addition, anyone who is interested in understanding Web search behavior and Web search engines will surely find this book a valuable read. Each section contains one or more chapters relating to the broader area of the section. Each chapter has a unique perspective and reference list. The chapters are cross-referenced where appropriate to illustrate how the different topics mesh together to form a broader expanse of Web search.

We greatly thank the chapter authors for their ground breaking and stimulating contributions. Many chapters represent the work of collaborations between researchers. We also thank those who edited sections of the book.

Amanda Spink thanks Michael Zimmer for his hard work and academic excellence during this project.

Michael Zimmer thanks Amanda Spink for her leadership, Helen Nissenbaum for her encouragement, and his wife, Rebecca, for her patience and support over the course of this project.

Amanda Spink   Michael Zimmer
Professor of Information Technology   Fellow, Information Society Project
Queensland University of Technology   Yale Law School

Contents

Part I   Introduction

1   Introduction   3
     A. Spink and M. Zimmer

Part II   Social, Cultural, and Philosophical Perspectives

2   Through the Google Goggles: Sociopolitical Bias in
     Search Engine Design   11
     A. Diaz

3   Reconsidering the Rhizome: A Textual Analysis of Web
     Search Engines as Gatekeepers of the Internet   35
     A. Hess

4   Exploring Gendered Notions: Gender, Job Hunting
     and Web Searches   51
     R.M. Martey

5   Searching Ethics: The Role of Search Engines in the
     Construction and Distribution of Knowledge   67
     L.M. Hinman

6   The Gaze of the Perfect Search Engine: Google as an
     Infrastructure of Dataveillance   77
     M. Zimmer

Part III   Political, Legal, and Economic Perspectives

7   Search Engine Liability for Copyright Infringement   103
     B. Fitzgerald, D. O'Brien, and A. Fitzgerald

8   Search Engine Bias and the Demise of Search Engine
    Utopianism   121
    E. Goldman

9   The Democratizing Effects of Search Engine Use: On Chance
    Exposures and Organizational Hubs   135
    A. Lev-On

10 'Googling' Terrorists: Are Northern Irish Terrorists Visible
    on Internet Search Engines?   151
    P. Reilly

11 The History of the Internet Search Engine: Navigational
    Media and the Traffic Commodity   177
    E. Van Couvering

Part IV   Information Behavior Perspectives

12 Toward a Web Search Information Behavior Model   209
    S.A. Knight and A. Spink

13 Web Searching for Health: Theoretical Foundations and
    Connections to Health Related Outcomes   235
    M.J. Dutta and G.D. Bodie

14 Search Engines and Expertise about Global Issues: Well-defined
    Landscape or Undomesticated Wilderness?   255
    J. Fry, S. Virkar, and R. Schroeder

15 Conceptual Models for Search Engines   277
    D.G. Hendry and E.N. Efthimiadis

16 Web Searching: A Quality Measurement Perspective   309
    D. Lewandowski and N. Höchstötter

Part V   Conclusion

17 Conclusions and Further Research   343
    A. Spink and M. Zimmer

Index   349

Contributors

Bodie, Graham D.
Department of Communication, Purdue University,
Beering Hall of Liberal Arts and Education, Room 2114
100 North University Street, Lafayette, IN 47901, USA

Diaz, Alejandro
Department of Communication, Stanford University, Building 120,
Room 110, 450 Serra Mall, Stanford, CA 94305, USA

Dutta, Mohan J., Ph.D.
Department of Communication, Purdue University,
Beering Hall of Liberal Arts and Education, Room 2114
100 North University Street, Lafayette, IN 47901, USA

Efthimiadis, Efthimis N., Ph.D.
The Information School, University of Washington, Box 352840,
Seattle, WA 98195, USA

Fitzgerald, Anne, J.D.
Faculty of Law, Queensland University of Technology Level 1,
Room 110, 126 Margaret Street, Brisbane, Qld 4000, Australia

Fitzgerald, Brian, Ph.D.
Faculty of Law, Queensland University of Technology, Level 1,
Room 110, 126 Margaret Street, Brisbane, Qld 4000, Australia

Fry, Jenny, Ph.D.
Department of Information Science, Loughborough University,
Leicester-shire, LE11 3TU, UK

Goldman, Eric, J.D.
High Tech Law Institute, Santa Clara University School of Law,
500 El Camino Real, Santa Clara, CA 95053, USA

Hendry, David G., Ph.D.
The Information School, University of Washington, Box 352840, Seattle,
WA 98195, USA

Hess, Aaron
Hugh Downs School of Human Communication, Arizona State University,
Stauffer Hall Building A, Room 412, PO Box 871205, Tempe, AZ 85287, USA

Hinman, Lawrence M., Ph.D.
Department of Philosophy, University of San Diego, 5998 Alcalá Park,
San Diego, CA 92110-2492, USA

Höchstötter, Nadine, Ph.D.
Institute for Decision Theory and Management Science, Universitaet Karlsruhe (TH),
Kaiserstrasse 12, D - 76128 Karlsruhe, Germany

Knight, Shirlee Ann
Edith Cowan University, Joondalup Campus, 100 Joondalup Drive,
Joon-dalup, 6027, Australia

Lewandowski, Dirk, Ph.D.
Department Information, Hamburg University of Applied Sciences
Berliner Tor 5, D - 20099 Hamburg, Germany

Lev-On, Azi, Ph.D.
Philosophy, Politics, and Economics Program, University of Pennsylvania
311 Logan Hall, 249 S 36th Street, Philadelphia, PA 19104, USA

Martey, Rosa Mikeal, Ph.D.
Department of Journalism & Technical Communication, Colorado State
University, Clark Building, Fort Collins, CO 80523, USA

O'Brien, Damien
Faculty of Law, Queensland University of Technology, Level 1,
Room 110, 126 Margaret Street, Brisbane Qld 4000, Australia

Reilly, Paul
Department of Politics, University of Glasgow, Adam Smith Building,
Bute Gardens, Glasgow

Schroeder, Ralph, Ph.D.
Oxford Internet Institute, University of Oxford, One St. Giles, Oxford,
OX1 3JS, UK

Spink, Amanda, Ph.D.
Faculty of Information Technology, Queensland University of Technology,
Gardens Point Campus, GPO Box 2434, Brisbane, Queensland 4001, Australia

Van Couvering, Elizabeth
Department of Media & Communications, London School of Economics
& Political Science, Houghton Street, London WC2A 2AE, UK

Virkar, Shefali
Oxford Internet Institute, University of Oxford, One St. Giles, Oxford,
OX1 3JS, UK

Zimmer, Michael, Ph.D.
Information Society Project, Yale Law School, 127 Wall Street,
New Haven, CT 06520, USA

Part I
Introduction

1
Introduction

A. Spink and M. Zimmer

1.1   Book Synopsis

Web search engines have emerged as one of the dominant technologies of modern, digital life, providing doorways to the universe of information available online. According to the Pew Internet & American Life Project, 84% of American adult Internet users have used a search engine to seek information online (Fallows 2005: 1). On any given day, more than 60 million American adults send over 200 million information requests to Web search engines, making Web searches second most popular online activity (behind using e-mail) (Rainie 2005).

More than just an indispensable tool for finding and accessing information online, Web searching has also become a defining component of the human condition. Web searching can be conceptualized as a complex behavior embedded within an individual's everyday social, cultural, political, and information-seeking activities. Following this broad impact of Web searching on daily life, the scholarly study of Web searching spans a multidisciplinary collection of researchers from the social sciences, media and cultural studies, law, information science and other related disciplines. *Web Search: Multidisciplinary Perspectives* brings together chapters that represent this range of multidisciplinary theories, models, and ideas about Web searching, drawing out and examining the various roles and impacts of Web searching on the social, cultural, political, legal, and informational spheres of our lives, such as the impact on individuals, social groups, modern and postmodern ways of knowing, and public and private life. By critically examining the issues, theories, and formations arising from, and surrounding, Web searching, *Web Search: Multidisciplinary Perspectives* represents an important contribution to the emerging multidisciplinary body of research on Web search engines.

Not surprisingly, some of the earliest research publications on Web search engines were technical in nature. Numerous computer scientists have contributed not only valuable research on improving and enhancing the underlying Web search engine technology (Brin and Page 1998; Heydon and Najork 1999; Page et al. 1998), but also technical analyses of the extent of coverage achieved by search engine products and how it relates to information access (Kleinberg and Lawrence 2001; Lawrence and Giles 1998, 2000).

A. Spink and M. Zimmer (eds.), *Web Search, Springer Series in Information Science and Knowledge Management 14.*

Social studies of Web search engines quickly emerged, typically by information scientists attempting to isolate the habits and characteristics of search engine users through the analysis of transaction log data (Jansen and Pooch 2001). These include Hoelscher's (1998) analysis of 16 million queries from the German search engine Fireball; Jansen et al. (2000) study of a sample day's worth of search activity from the Excite search engine; and Silverstein et al. (1999) detailed analysis of one billion queries submitted to the Alta Vista search engine over a 42-day period. These studies of transaction log data provide valuable information about search query structure and complexity, including insights about common search topics, query length, Boolean operator usage, search session length, and search results page viewing (Spink and Jansen 2004).

Notwithstanding the value of transaction log data analysis, these types of studies offer limited insights into the behavior of Web searchers beyond the search queries submitted. Hargittai's (2002, 2004) use of surveys and in-person observation of search engine usage helps alleviate these shortcomings, providing insights into how people find information online in the context of their other media use, their general Internet use patterns, and their social support networks. Broadening the analysis of user behavior beyond transaction logs allowed Hargittai (2004) to reveal the ways that factors such as age, gender, education level, and time spent online are relevant predictors of a user's Web searching skills. The work of Machill et al. (2004) and Hölscher and Strube (2000) also combined surveys, interviews, and transaction log analysis to characterize a number of information seeking behaviors of Web search engine users.

Recent scholarship has moved beyond the technical and individual focus of the user studies described above to include research into broader cultural, legal, and social implications of Web search engines. For example, cultural scholars (Hellsten et al. 2006; Wouters et al. 2004) have explored the ways in which search engines "re-write the past" due to the frequent updating of their indices and the corresponding loss of a historical record of content on the Web. Introna and Nissenbaum's (2000) seminal study, "Shaping the Web: Why the Politics of Search Engines Matter," was among the first to analyze search engines from the political perspective, noting how search engines have been heralded as "a democratizing force" that will

> …give voice to diverse social, economic, and cultural groups, to members of society not frequently heard in the public sphere. It will empower the traditionally disempowered, giving them access both to typically unreachable nodes of power and to previously inaccessible troves of information. (Introna and Nissenbaum 2000: 169)

Search engines, then, act as a powerful source of access and accessibility within the Web. Introna and Nissenbaum reveal, however, that search engines "systematically exclude certain sites and certain types of sites, in favor of others, systematically giving prominence to some at the expense of others" (2000: 169).

Such a critique resembles the stance that political economists take against the contemporary mass media industry (Castells 1996; Habermas 1992; McChesney 1999), a critique that has recently been extended to Web search engines. For example, Hargittai (2004) has extended her user studies to include investigations of how financial and organizational considerations within the Web search engine industry impact the way in which content is organized, presented, and distributed to users. And Van Couvering (2004) has engaged in extensive research on the political economy of the search engine industry in terms of its ownership, its revenues, the products it sells, its geographic spread, and the politics and regulations that govern it. Drawing comparisons to concerns over market consolidations in the mass media industry, Van Couvering fears that the market concentration and business practices of the search engine industry might limit its ability to serve "the public interest in the information society" (Van Couvering 2004: 25).

Extending from these social and cultural critiques, Web search engines have also recently been scrutinized from a moral or ethical perspective. A recent panel discussion at the Santa Clara University Markkula Center for Applied Ethics was one of the first to bring together ethicists, computer scientists, and social scientists for the express purpose of confronting some of the "unavoidable ethical questions about search engines," including concerns of search engine bias, censorship, trust, and privacy (Norvig et al. 2006). A special issue of the International Review of Information Ethics on "The Ethics of Search Engines" (Nagenborg 2005) brought into focus many of the particular privacy concerns with search engines.

Web Search: Multidisciplinary Perspectives contributes to this rich library of research by showcasing the latest multidisciplinary theories, models, and perspectives on Web searching. Unlike many volumes on Web search engines, our book does not provide an analysis of Web searching from computer science or other Web-related technological disciplines. Rather, *Web Search: Multidisciplinary Perspectives* is focused on investigating Web search from the non-technological perspective. The editors focused on collecting papers that broaden and deepen the framework for our understanding of Web search, and invited authors from many disciplines to contribute chapters that represented emerging research directions and ideas, in an effort to build a perspective that extends beyond traditional models and research, and provide new directions for further research. In particular, the book includes papers by outstanding, yet often less established, researchers from different disciplines who challenge the established views and paradigms of Web search research. The chapter authors – as well as the editors – are drawn from the international boundaries of Web search scholarship, and this global perspective contributed greatly to the multidisciplinary depth of the volume.

1.2 Book Outline

Web Search: Multidisciplinary Perspectives is organized into five sections. Following this introductory section, Part II presents chapters that provide social, cultural and philosophical perspectives for conceptualizing Web search. Alejandro Diaz's "Through the Google Goggles: Sociopolitical Bias in Search Engine Design" provides an opening examination based in communication and political theory on how bias in search engines – Google, in particular – might threaten the utopian and democratic ideals associated with the Web. In "Reconsidering the Rhizome: A Textual Analysis of Web Search Engines as Gatekeepers of the Internet," Aaron Hess performs a textual analysis of four major search engines to determine how they might resemble Deleuze and Guitarri's notion of the rhizome. Rosa Mikeal Martey's contribution, "Exploring Gendered Notions: Gender, Job Hunting and Web Searches," argues that the social and cultural contexts of both the search tools and the search tasks impact how these Web-based technologies serve women in their information-seeking needs. The philosopher Lawrence Hinman provides a necessary ethical analysis of Web searching in his contribution, "Searching Ethics: The Role of Search Engines in the Construction and Distribution of Knowledge," while Michael Zimmer's chapter, "The Gaze of the Perfect Search Engine: Google as an Infrastructure of Dataveillance," focuses on the particular ethical concern with the privacy and surveillance implications Web search engine practices.

Part III includes chapters that propose political, legal, and economic perspectives for understanding Web search. The first contribution, "Search Engine Liability for Copyright Infringement" by Brian Fitzgerald, Damien O'Brien, and Anne Fitzgerald, provides a broad overview of the topic of search engine liability for copyright infringement. Eric Goldman's contribution, "Search Engine Bias and the Demise of Search Engine Utopianism," provides an additional legal analysis of Web search, using legal theory to support the position that search engine bias can be a beneficial consequence of how Web search engines increasingly customize content for individual users. In "Search Engines, Chance Exposures and Emergent Organizations," Azi Lev-On relies on political theory to reveal how search engines can provide unplanned exposures to diverse viewpoints, as well as empowering what he calls "organizational hubs of collective action." Paul Reilly continues this political analysis of Web searching by discussing the relative "visibility" of organizations on search engines in his contribution, "'Googling' Terrorists: Are Northern Irish terrorists visible on Internet Search Engines?" Finally, Elizabeth Van Couvering's chapter, "The History and Geography of the Internet Search Engine: Processes of Consolidation and Processes of Expansion," provides a detailed historical and economic analysis of Web search engines, drawing out concerns over the commercialization and consolidation of the search engine industry.

Part IV presents explorations of Web searching from the information behavior perspective. The section opens with Shirlee Knight and Amanda Spink's chapter, "Towards and Integrated Information Behavior Model of Web Search," exploring the history of information retrieval research in order to propose a "macro model" of Web-based information seeking and searching behavior. In "Web Searching for Health: Theoretical Foundations and Connections to Health Related Outcomes," Mohan Dutta and Graham Bodie utilize theories of information seeking to determine how search engines might fit within an "integrative model of health information seeking." Jenny Fry, Shefali Virkar, and Ralph Schroeder follow with "Search Engines and Expertise about Global Issues: Well-defined Landscape or Undomesticated Wilderness?", an investigation of the "winner-takes-all" effect in online information resources to help determine if search engines function as facilitators in accessing expertise or as influential gatekeepers. "Conceptual Models for Search Engines," by David Hendry and Efthimis Efthimiadis, examines the conceptual and technical understanding that people have of search engines to measure levels of "literacy" of

Web search engine design and practices. Finally, Dirk Lewandowski and Nadine Höchstötter propose and evaluate various quality measures for Web search engine performance in their contribution, "Web Searching: A Quality Measurement Perspective."

In Part V the editors provide a concluding overview of the key trends, theories and models emerging these multidisciplinary studies, along with a range of new directions proposed in the chapters for further research.

References

Brin S, Page L (1998) The anatomy of a large-scale hypertextual web search engine. WWW7/ Computer Networks 30: 107–117

Castells M (1996–1998) The information age: economy, society and culture, vol. i, ii, and iii. Blackwell, Cambridge, MA

Fallows D (2005) Search engine users: Internet searchers are confident, satisfied and trusting – but they are also unaware and naïve. Pew Internet & American Life Project. Available: http://www.pewInternet.org/pdfs/PIP_Searchengine_users.pdf via the Internet.

Habermas J (1992) The structural transformation of the public sphere : an inquiry into a category of bourgeois society. Polity, Cambridge

Hargittai E (2002) Beyond logs and surveys: in-depth measures of people's web use skills. Journal of the American Society for Information Science and Technology 53: 1239–1244

Hargittai E (2004a) Informed web surfing: the social context of user sophistication. society online: the Internet in context, Thousand Oaks: Sage Publications, Inc 257–274

Hargittai E (2004b) The changing online landscape: from free-for-all to commercial gatekeeping. Available: http://www.eszter.com/research/c03-onlinelandscape.html via the Internet.

Hellsten I et al. (2006) Multiple presents: how search engines re-write the past. New Media and Society 8: 901–924

Heydon A, Najork M (1999) Mercator: a scalable, extensible web crawler. World Wide Web 2: 219–229

Hoelscher C (1998) How Internet experts search for information on the web. World Conference of the World Wide Web, Internet, and Intranet, Orlando, FL

Hölscher C, Strube G (2000) Web search behavior of Internet experts and newbies. Computer Networks 33: 337–346

Introna L, Nissenbaum H (2000) Shaping the web: why the politics of search engines matters. The Information Society 16: 169–185

Jansen BJ, Pooch U (2001) A review of web searching studies and a framework for future research. Journal of the American Society for Information Science and Technology 52: 235–246

Jansen BJ, Spink A, Saracevic T (2000) Real life, real users, and real needs: a study and analysis of user queries on the web. Information Processing and Management 36: 207–227

Kleinberg J, Lawrence S (2001) The structure of the web. Science 294: 1849–1850

Lawrence S, Giles CL (1998) Searching the world wide web. Science 280: 98–100

Lawrence S, Giles L (2000) Accessibility of information on the web. Intelligence 11: 32–39

Machill M et al. (2004) Navigating the Internet. European Journal of Communication 19: 321–347

McChesney R (1999) Rich media, poor democracy: communication politics in dubious times. University of Illinois Press, Urbana, IL

Nagenborg M (2005) The ethics of search engines (special issue). International Review of Information Ethics 3.

Norvig P et al. (2006) The ethics and politics of search engines. Panel at Santa Clara University Markkula Center for Applied Ethics. Available: http://www.scu.edu/sts/Search-Engine-Event. cfm via the Internet. Accessed Panel discussion

Page L et al. (1998) The pagerank citation ranking: bringing order to the web. Technical report

Rainie L (November 2005) Search engine use shoots up in the past year and edges towards e-mail as the primary Internet application. Pew Internet and American Life Project. Available http:// www.pewinternet.org/pdfs/ PIP_SearchData_1105.pdf via the internet

Silverstein et al. (1999) Analysis of a very large web search engine query log. SIGIR Forum 33: 6–12

Spink A, Jansen BJ (2004) Web search: public searching of the web. Kluwer Academic, New York

Van Couvering E (2004) New media? The political economy of Internet search engines. Annual Conference of the International Association of Media & Communications Researchers, Porto Alegre, Brazil, 7–14

Wouters P et al. (2004) Internet time and the reliability of search engines. First Monday. 9(10). Available: http://www.firstmonday.org/issues/issue9_10/wouters/index.html via the Internet.

Part II
Social, Cultural,
and Philosophical Perspectives

2
Through the Google Goggles: Sociopolitical Bias in Search Engine Design

A. Diaz

Summary Search engines like Google are essential to navigating the Web's endless supply of news, political information, and citizen discourse. The mechanisms and conditions under which search results are selected should therefore be of considerable interest to media scholars, political theorists, and citizens alike. In this chapter, I adopt a "deliberative" ideal for search engines and examine whether Google exhibits the "same old" media biases of mainstreaming, hypercommercialism, and industry consolidation. In the end, serious objections to Google are raised: Google may favor popularity over richness; it provides advertising that competes directly with "editorial" content; it so overwhelmingly dominates the industry that users seldom get a second opinion, and this is unlikely to change. Ultimately, however, the results of this analysis may speak less about Google than about contradictions in the deliberative ideal and the so-called "inherently democratic" nature of the Web.

2.1 Introduction

As knowledge, commerce, and politics continue move online and to the Web in particular, search engines have quickly become the "gatekeepers" of cyberspace. What's more, a *single* search engine – Google – now handles the majority of Web queries. Google directs hundreds of millions of users towards some content and not others, towards some sources and not others. As with all media gatekeepers, if we believe in the principles of deliberative democracy – and especially if we believe that the Web is an open, "democratic" medium – then we should expect our search engines to disseminate a broad spectrum of information on any given topic.

In the first section of this chapter, I describe how a "deliberative media" ideal can be used to evaluate search engine and why, as media critics have done with prior innovations, we should examine Google's content biases, its advertising policies, and consolidation in the industry as a whole. Subsequent sections will dive into each of these areas: first, we will look at the deliberative implications of the PageRank algorithm Google uses to crawl and order Web content; next,

A. Spink and M. Zimmer (eds.), *Web Search, Springer Series in Information Science and Knowledge Management 14.*
© Springer-Verlag Berlin Heidelberg 2008

we will critically examine the role advertising plays in Google's search results; lastly, we discuss the implications of a highly concentrated and commercial competitive search landscape. It is hoped that through this investigation, we might start to uncover the sociopolitics of search.

2.2   In Search of a Democratic Medium

The Supreme Court once observed that "the dissemination of the widest possible information from diverse and antagonistic sources is essential to the welfare of the public" (Associated Press v. United States 1945: 20). This goes to the heart of 'deliberative democracy,' a concept that has in recent years gained considerable currency among political scientists and media critics (Benhabib 1996; Elster 1998; Fishkin 1991; Sunstein 1997). For Benjamin Page, "In order that the public as a whole can collectively control what its government does, the public, collectively, must be well informed. Some kind of *public* deliberation is required" (Page 1996: 5). Individuals' exposure to "diverse and antagonistic views" is central to such debate, as John Stuart Mill (1859) once argued:

> He who knows only his own side of the case knows little of that. His reasons may be good … but if he is unable to refute the reasons of the opposite side, if he does not so much as know what they are, he has no ground for preferring either opinion … [H]e should hear the arguments … from the persons who actually believe them, who defend them in earnest and do their very utmost for them. He must know them in their most plausible and persuasive form. (p. 35)

For Mill, it does not matter whether arguments are popular or unpopular, correct or incorrect, offensive or pleasing; what matters is that public opinion is given the *opportunity* to "be set right when it is wrong" (p. 19). This is why "streets and parks," according to Justice Roberts, "have immemorially been held in trust for the use of the public and…have been used for purposes of assembly, communicating thoughts between citizens, and discussing public questions" (Hague et al. v. CIO et al., 1939, 515).

The deliberative model appears to capture what we usually mean by "democratic media": forums in which every corner of society is represented fairly – spaces where the debate isn't dominated by corporations, politicians, or privileged groups. Given that we are a nation too large and too distributed to engage in a singular, Habermasian debate (1990, 89) the media have an important role to play in ensuring that speakers have access to heterogeneous citizens. As Justice Kennedy observed, "minds are not exchanged in streets and parks as they once were. To an increasing degree, the more significant exchanges … occur in mass and electronic media" (DAETC et al. v. FCC 1996, 132). Given the enormous reach of radio, television, and newspapers, the media could allow citizens to access a range of perspectives they might not otherwise encounter.

2.2.1 The Traditional Media and a New Hope

But as countless critics have argued, the mass media have fallen far short of these aspirations. "[M]arket forces," writes Cooper (2003), "provide neither adequate incentives to produce the high quality media product, nor adequate incentives to distribute sufficient amounts of diverse content necessary to meet consumer and citizen needs" (p. 43). The economics of dissemination and the politics of deregulation, rather than encourage the formation of alternative outlets, have concentrated the media in fewer and fewer hands (p. 141). The scarcity of alternative channels has allowed media companies to pursue ever-greater profit margins through advertising, sponsorship, and product placement with little fear of consumer retaliation (McChesney 2000: 39–42). "The media," according to Bagdikian (1992), "have become partners in achieving the social and economic goals of their patrons" (p. 151). The value of large audiences has tended to yield "middle-of-the road," nonpolitical, mainstream content that creates a "buying mood" but fails to represent unpopular or diverse opinions. The result is a media landscape characterized by sameness, by a suppression of controversy, and by hypercommercialism.

But a new medium has recently emerged, and it has promised to change all this. Decentralized and distributed, the global Internet – and, in particular, the Web – allows anyone and everyone to make their views accessible, and to access anyone's views. It is arguably more like the printing press than radio and, indeed, information on the network is not constrained by the limits of printed matter, by delivery distances, or seemingly by time, space, and matter itself. With a click of the mouse, you can read information and opinions that have not been "filtered" by profiteering corporations or corrupt governments. At the same time, underrepresented and unheard groups can cheaply bypass the "monolithic media empire" to have a voice. The Internet is many-to-many, all-to-all, and it has for many restored faith mediated deliberation. Aspirations are expressed repeatedly, and with understandable excitement:

> The Web...breaks the traditional publishing model. ... [It] says instead, "You have something to say? Say it. You want to respond to something that's been said? Say it and link to it. ... And you never have to ask anyone's permission." (Weinberger 2002: vii–ix)

> You don't have to be writing for an organization to have a credible voice. The Net elevates those voices. What the large media were about was distribution capacity to communicate with hundreds of thousands of people. Now the Net does that. (Barlow, qtd. in Lasica 1996)

The prospects seemed so exhilarating that some jumped to label the Internet "inherently" democratic (Gilder, qtd. in Schuler 2003: 72).

And indeed, the Web has had many tangible, positive effects for diverse, democratic discussion. Access and content on the new medium has exploded; the majority of Americans now have Internet connections in their homes (Wellman and Haythornthwaite 2002: 13). Anyone with basic computer competence can now publish a Web site viewable around the globe. Activists have grown their own "grassroots" communities to pursue particular policy objectives while bloggers – self-made 'journalists' who report their findings and solicit comments in a sort of "deliberative diary" – have gained loyal followings and the attention of the mainstream media (Rodzvilla 2002). Real-world community projects have sprung up online, "evidence of an overdue renewal of interest in democracy" (Schuler 2003: 73).

And yet, over the last ten years, user traffic on the Web has gravitated around a few, large, and increasingly commercial sites. In a fascinating book, Notre Dame physicist Albert-Lásló Barabási (2002) recounts how his team of scientists mapped the Web's structure to reveal disturbing evidence about the supposed "egalitarianism" of the network. He found that a small number of pages – what he called "hubs" – are linked to by a great many other pages, while the vast majority of documents are linked to by few or no sites at all. Hubs are very easy to "come across" from anywhere on the Web; they are therefore more likely to be linked to, which further increases their discoverability (the so-called "rich get richer" phenomenon). Meanwhile, a typical page – one pointed to by only couple documents – remains almost impossible to find. It's no wonder that, by 2001, over half of users' online time was being spent at four sites; one third of the total time was spent at AOL-Time Warner properties (CNN.com 2001). On the political Web – the set of sites dealing with democratically urgent issues such the death penalty, Congress, and gun control – Hindman et al. (2003) found "strong and consistent" patterns consistent with Barabási's research: "the number of highly visible sites is small" and "almost all prominent sites are run by long-established interest groups, by government entities, by corporations, or by traditional media outlets" (p. 26). The link structure of the Web suggests the medium exhibits the same old problems: "it is hard for all but a few 'ordinary citizens' to post their views prominently – and conversely, to read the views of other ordinary citizens, unless they are highlighted by a small number of prominent sites" (p. 30). Or as Barabási put it, "The hubs are the strongest argument against the utopian vision of an egalitarian cyberspace. Yes, we all have the right to put anything we wish on the Web. But will anybody notice?" (p. 58).

2.2.2 Search Engines as Intermediaries

That so many accessible pages go unseen suggests that the Internet has done away with "spectrum scarcity" but not with *attention scarcity* (Kottke 2003). Sure, there are literally billions of pages ("channels") available on the Web. But there is a rather fixed limit to how many we, as individuals, can consume. With television, radio, and the print media, we rely on the mass media to condense the available opinions and make them easily accessible through newspapers, the evening news, radio broadcasts, and so on. And the same sort of intermediation is required online.

The key "general interest intermediaries" of the Web, I argue, are the search engines. These sites are the primary means by which Internet users are directed towards particular sources of information and are among the first and most frequently accessed pages for the vast majority of users. Consider: each one of the top 5 sites is either a portal or search engine (Burns 2007); by 2004, 84% of online Americans had used search engines, and a majority of these used them at least once a day (Fallows and Rainie 2004); search engines are the most popular way to locate medical, governmental, and religious information on the Web (Fallows 2005); fully 79% of those seeking online election information began their journeys at portals and search engines (Cornfield and Rainie 2003, p. 25).

So when Steven Levy (1995) said that "instead of a gatekeeper, users get an open invitation to the electronic world and can choose whatever they want" (p. 59), he was being less than accurate. Internet users *do* get a gatekeeper – the search engine – and they choose primarily among the sites it offers to them. As with all such intermediaries, we expect search engines to present the available information in a fair and diverse manner; we expect them, in other words, to be "democratic." We should ask about search engines like Google the same questions scholars have asked about the traditional media: *Can underrepresented voices and diverse viewpoints be heard through the filter of search engines? What role does advertising play in the returned results? Do a few players dominate the industry?* Only by answering these questions – as we will do in turn – can one assess the true "deliberativeness" of the Web itself.

2.3 The Politics of PageRank

Just as the mass media have the power and responsibility to disseminate unusual and heterodox views, so too do search engines have the capability to highlight those high-quality, out-of-the-mainstream sites that would otherwise be lost in the deafening din of the Web. Automated crawling and ranking can do what we, as individuals, cannot: find, catalog, and consider millions of poorly-linked and underrepresented pages – what Chris Anderson (2004) has called "the long tail" – and ultimately break through the link inequality that calls into question the egalitarian ideal of the Web.

2.3.1 The Mathematics of PageRank

So does Google actually promote those dissident and minority views so critical for a "well-functioning democracy"? Given the complex and propriety nature of Google's search technology its software looks at over 100 features of a page to ascertain "relevance" (Mayer 2005) – answering this question is exceedingly difficult. But we can start with what Google (2004) calls "the heart" of its software: the PageRank algorithm. PageRank estimates the "importance" of an arbitrary page by looking at how many *other* "important" pages link *to* it. Mathematically, the PageRank of your page is the weighted count of links pointing to it, with links from high-PageRank documents contributing more to your score than links from low-PageRank documents.

An analogy may be useful: an academic paper is "important" if many other papers cite it – and especially if it is referenced by other, highly cited works ("canons").

With PageRank, then, being "important" means being "popular" or "visible." PageRank actually turns out to be the precise probability that a "random surfer" clicking links from page to page will come across a given document. Thus the highly-referenced "hubs" Barabási worried about have the highest PageRanks; these tend to be the sites of large, famous, technology-oriented companies such as Amazon and eBay (Upstill et al. 2003). In contrast, the millions of "typical" pages – those we are already unlikely to "randomly" stumble across – have among the lowest PageRank values. Google apparently uses PageRank to guide its crawlers such that popular sites have a better chance of being indexed (Cho et al. 1998). Sites with high PageRank also tend to be more prominent among the search results (Diaz 2005: 81–85).

2.3.2   PageRank as a Voting Mechanism

According to Google's public relations literature (2004), PageRank is not only consonant with democratic principles; it in fact embodies the very process of democracy itself: "Google interprets a link from page A to page B as a vote, by page A, for page B." Princeton computer science professor and cyberactivist Ed Felten (2004) puts it more colorfully:

> Google is a voting scheme … not a mysterious Oracle of Truth. … It's a form of democracy – call it Googlocracy. Web authors vote by creating hyperlinks, and Google counts the votes. If we want to understand Google we need to see democracy as Google's very nature, and not as an aberration.

But what Ed Felten and other PageRank proponents fail to recognize is the important distinction between the ideal process of "democratic" *governance* and that of "democratic" *discourse*. Sure, a political democracy generally requires that the aggregated preferences of the majority be put into practice. But this does not imply that only the majority's views should be heard during deliberation, nor does it suggest that popular opinions should be preferred *ipso facto*. To the contrary, the validity of voting – of aggregating preferences – depends precisely on the dissemination of a broad spectrum of opinions, especially those put forth by unpopular or minority groups (Mill 1859: 16).

From the perspective of deliberative democrats, then, PageRank is highly problematic. Unpopular but nevertheless democratically critical voices face a double bind: search engines like Google are "biased against [these pages], ignoring them as they crawl the Web" (Barabási 2002: 58) and, even if the pages make it to the index, they may find themselves buried among the results. To the degree that Google adopts a PageRank bias, it *mirrors* rather than mitigates the Web's link inequality.

Indeed, some scholars have argued that the use of PageRank actually *magnifies* the Web's skewed distribution of links, making it increasingly difficult for new sites to be discovered (Fortunato et al. 2006; Hindman et al. 2003; Pandey et al. 2005). The problem is this: a well-linked page appears prominently on search engines like Google; this page therefore enjoys greater traffic; and, as users become even more aware of the site, they link to it on their own pages, increasing the document's PageRank and visibility even further. The result is a "vicious cycle," "entrenchment bias," or "googlearchy" wherein popular pages are, over time, increasingly likely to maintain their prominence while new pages become more difficult to discover. Cho and Roy's (2004) computer simulation indicated that "it takes 66 times longer" for a new page to become popular by means of highly PageRank-biased search engines than by pure "random surfing."

2.3.3 The "Common Case" and Majoritarian Interests

PageRank therefore seems to reproduce the same sort of "antideliberative" bias typically associated with the traditional media. To recall Cooper's (2003) remarks about big media: "In the commercial model, popular, mainstream, and middle of the road ideas will almost certainly find a voice, one that is likely to be very loud. However, the unpopular, unique, and minority points of view will not" (p. 16). Similarly, "search engines wishing to achieve greatest popularity ... tend to cater to majority interests" (Introna and Nissenaum 2000: 176). According to Google's founders, this bias was by design:

> One of the design goals of PageRank was to handle the common case for queries well. ... [T]he goal of finding a site that contains a great deal of information ... is a very different task ... There is an interesting system that attempts to find sites that discuss a topic in detail ... this results in good results for queries like "flower"; the system will return good naviga-tion pages from sites that deal with the topic of flowers in detail. Contrast that with the common case approach which might simply return a commonly used commercial site that had little information except how to buy flowers ... [W]e are concentrating only on the common case approach. (Page et al. 1999: 10–11).

PageRank, in other words, abandons the goals of actually reflecting a page's "importance" or "authoritativeness" on a given subject, and instead aims to mirror the "common" wishes of users. This, as the creators' own example illustrates, can have the problematic effect of promoting popular, commercial pages over more detailed, noncommercial sources of information.

To be sure, these problems are more or less typical of commercial search engines in general. In their groundbreaking overview of search engine bias, Introna and Nissenbaum (2000) observed that "while markets undoubtedly would force a degree of comprehensiveness and objectivity in listings, there is unlikely to be much market incentive to list sites of interest to small groups of individuals ... or, for that matter, individuals of lesser economic power" (p. 177). PageRank's "one size fits all" approach does little for the atypical, outside-the-mainstream individuals that might actually wish to see or communicate controversial content.

2.3.4   Suppression of Controversy

Susan Gerhart (2004) makes a similar point in a unique content analysis of Web search results. Gerhart queried Google, Teoma, and AllTheWeb for information on five broad topics, each of which she knew to contain some controversial subtopic that was well documented on the Web. Gerhart then recorded, in painstaking detail, whether and how such disputed perspectives were raised within the search results. She looked, for example, at whether a search for "distance learning" would return sites that shared David Noble and other academics' concern about "the loss of control over their intellectual products, as well as contact with students" and the tendency of these programs to act as "digital diploma mills." Similarly, she looked at whether the results for "Einstein" mentioned the debate over whether his first wife received appropriate credit for contributions to his work.

Her findings indicate that when a controversy was frequently discussed within a topic and widely recognized as important (e.g., the effectiveness of St. John's Wort) the disputed matters were, indeed, represented among the results. When searching for female astronauts or St. John's Wort, for example, it was possible for a user to "definitely recognize the existence of controversy, which [a result] explains in some detail." But for three of the topics – distance learning, Albert Einstein, and Belize – the respective disputes were to a great extent "suppressed," such that most surfers would not "be exposed to the controversies by [a general] search...alone." In these cases, the controversies were overrun by "organizational clout" (e.g., official Belizean tourism sites or distance learning programs) or by pages that reflected what users "wanted to see" (e.g., Einstein quotations, 'bland' biographies for term papers, etc.). In the end, the controversial viewpoints that perhaps matter most from a deliberative point of view – those antagonistic perspectives that haven't garnered widespread attention – are precisely those that are left out of the search engine's results. Gerhart concludes that

> Search technology tends to present the 'sunny side' of a topic. This bias reflects authors' links and searchers' choices. A few organizations often exert strong commercial (or nonprofit) influence through Web site investments and accrue high link counts through their off-Web prominence. ('Conclusion').

If we really believe that through "democratic media" like the Web individuals "must have the freedom to communicate radical and unpopular ideas and opinions" – and, what's more, that citizens should be exposed to what "they don't want to hear" – then search engines fall short of these aspirations when they fail to disseminate those dark, uncomfortable views on a given topic.

Of course, "Web search engines do not conspire to suppress controversy." Rather, this is direct consequence of the seemingly laudable attempt to please its users. As Gerhart suggests, "On the simplest query for a topic, a searcher expects to see the most influential organizations appear, not a bundle of dirty laundry or diatribes attacking the topic's leaders or ideas … Searchers user a particular engine because its biases give them the results they usually want." The deliberative model may ask of too much from users: pushing for them to see what they *don't* want to see because, really, it's "good for them" (Rostbøll 2005). To this extent, it conflicts with intuitive and reasonable ideas for how search engines should work.

2.3.5 Small Players (Still) Matter

Even if PageRank does, in theory, encode an antideliberative, antidemocratic bias, a few caveats are in order. First, as Dan Bricklin (2002) has pointed out, even if popular sites do get a sizeable boost for some queries, rarely do the same corporate megasites pop up across different search topics. As a result, "small players [still] matter," especially when we are conducting 'typical' searches for specialized information not easily found in the traditional media. Although it is difficult for a page to gain visibility on established topics – Microsoft," "abortion," or "flowers" – an unprecedented number of "ordinary citizens" may still be reaching sizeable publics through the Google search engine.

Second, PageRank is only one element of Google's ranking algorithm; consider, for example, that PageRank is completely *query-independent*, capturing the "importance" of a page irrespective of the user's stated interest. In practice, Google takes many other factors into account when ordering search results: whether the query appears in the page's title, what words people use to link to the page, and so forth. While it is true that PageRank predicts rank position *in the aggregate*, individual result sets exhibit at best a weak correlation (Diaz 2005: 84). For this reason, Cho and Roy's simulation – which assumed search results were strictly ordered by PageRank – may be unrealistic. Indeed, a more recent study suggests that search engines' query-dependent heuristics actually "smear out the traffic attraction of high-degree pages…counteracting the skewed distribution of links in the Web [by] directing some traffic toward sites that users would never visit otherwise" (Fortunato et al. 2006: 6). Clearly, there is a need for continued and systematic research into the many; sometimes counteracting biases of today's advanced search technology.

2.4 Commercialism, Advertising, and "Mixed Motives"

Advertising is, by and large, how the commercialized media make money. Newspapers, magazines, radio, and television outlets provide free or inexpensive content to their readers, listeners, and viewers; in exchange, they sell advertisers access to these audiences. Advertising is, however, a mixed blessing. On the one hand, it makes it viable to disseminate information to a broad audience at a low cost; on the other hand, there is the persistent threat that the wishes of sponsors will subtly work their way into the content itself, narrowing the range of opinions that can be profitably and widely expressed.

These competing forces come strongly into play in the arena of search engines. As the primary gatekeepers of the Web, search engines not only direct users to particular pages but can also direct consumers towards particular services and products. This presents an enormous opportunity for targeted advertising: search engines can "sell" access to highly segmented audiences while marketers can target individuals who are actively expressing interest in a topic or product. The money-making potential is enormous and, indeed, one industry report predicted as early as 2003 that "worldwide search revenue estimates of $7B by 2007 are conservative" (Raschtchy and Avilio 2003). By 2005, advertisements on Google *alone* brought in over $6 billion – or over 99% of the company's yearly revenue (Google 2006).

But by selling advertising, Google and its competitors have an enormous financial incentive to direct users away from the "free," "organic" results and towards the sites of its sponsors. These "mixed motives" are stated eloquently by none other than Google's founders themselves, in an appendix to their 1998 Stanford research paper:

> The goals of the advertising business model do not always correspond to providing quality search to users. For example, in our prototype search engine one of the top results for cellular phone is ... a study which explains [the] risk associated with conversing on a cell phone while driving ... It is clear that a search engine which was taking money for showing cellular phone ads would have difficulty justifying the page ... For this type of reason and historical experience with other search engines we ... expect that advertising funded search engines will be inherently biased towards the advertisers and away from the needs of the consumers. ... Since it is very difficult even for experts to evaluate search engines, search engine bias is particularly insidious ... [and] less blatant bias are likely to be tolerated by the market. (Brin and Page 1998: 17–18)

2.4.1   A Brief History of Search Advertising

When Google's founders wrote those words, the predominant form of search advertising was the so-called "banner" ad. As it turns out, these ads tended not to work well in the context of search. For one, only a few banners can reasonably be placed on each page, and searchers would often click their result before the image had finished loading (Sullivan 2003a). More importantly, users quickly developed an ability to unconsciously spot and ignore banners, focusing – with "laser beam accuracy" – on what they perceived to be the actual search results (Pagendarm and Schaumburg 2001). If sponsors wished to be noticed, their solicitations must look like, and appear amongst, the actual results. As the CEO of one search engine company put it, "The money is in the search results themselves, not the billboards on the site of that road. The question is how do you profit from the search results, when they have been given away for free" (Thornley qtd. in Pagendarm and Schaumburg 2001).

The way many of Web search engines have gone about "profiting from their results" is by offering various kinds of "paid listings." The most common scheme, called *paid placement,* allows sponsors to purchase search-result-like text ads that appear above, below, or alongside the "organic" results for their chosen keywords. Sometimes these paid results are marked as "sponsored" listings; other times, "it may be hard for the average user to distinguish" (Crowell 2003). Unsurprisingly, paid placement proved vastly more effective than previous methods at drawing users' attention towards sponsors' sites. To the degree that these "matches" walk, talk, and act like relevant results, users click them. As *Business Week* puts it, paid placements have become "the Holy Grail of Internet advertising, and no wonder" (Reinhardt 2003). These ads have caught on, in some form or another, among virtually all of Web's most popular search engines (Google, Altavista, AOL, AskJeeves, Hotbot, Google, Lycos, MSN, and Yahoo! have similar offerings). The demand for paid listings quickly became so great that, according to *The Economist* (2004), they "lead the recovery in advertising expenditure on the Internet."

While paid listings may be a bonanza for search companies, investors, and advertisers alike, their implications for online, egalitarian discourse are depressingly obvious:

> [The] concept that Web sites should be able to buy their way to the top of search listings is being copied in one way or another by every major search and portal site. As they do, the search engines, which are still the most popular gateways to the Web, are transforming themselves from infinite electronic encyclopedias to the more prosaic, if profitable, role of universal commercial directories. (Hansell 2001)

To the extent that the commercial interests of the rich dominate the results of even noncommercial queries, the practice of selling prominence can seriously distort what the Web consists of for millions of users.

But just as market forces drive search engines to paid placement, so too do market forces push back. If, as commercial listings become more numerous, the relevancy of a search engine's results decline, dissatisfied users may switch to a competitor, resulting in an overall decline in advertising revenues. From this angle, the amount of paid listings to include is a straightforward optimization problem. Economists Bhargava and Feng (2002) respond to it by proposing "a mathematical model for optimal design of a paid placement strategy" that would "give a search engine the best balance between revenues from content providers and revenues based on user base" (p. 122).

2.4.2 'Clearly Labeled'?

For search engine critics, however, such economic models are not very comforting. We might reasonably wonder – as Brin and Page did in 1998 – whether users will actually see what's missing from their search results. Although Bhargava and Feng assume "that search engines cannot hide the fact that they perform paid placement" (p. 118), it appears that many Internet users remain unaware of such practices.

In 2002, a study commissioned by Consumers Union found that *fewer than one in four* Internet users had ever heard of search engines "taking fees to list some sites more prominently than others" (Princeton Survey Research Associates 2002: 17). After being told that, in fact, most search engines do exactly this, "a solid majority (80%) say it is important for search engines to tell users about their fee details, including 44% who say it is *very* important" (p. 17). At the time of the study, several search engine companies were using remarkably vague and misleading terminology to demarcate their paid listings (e.g., "Featured Sites," "Products and Services"). So in 2001 the watchdog group Commercial Alert filed a complaint with the FTC alleging that seven search companies were engaging in "deceptive advertising" practices (Miller 2001). When FTC responded in June 2002, it did not call for immediate action against the search engines named in the complaint (Gallagher 2002), but it did agree that there was a "need for clear and conspicuous disclosures of paid placement ... to advise consumers as to when they are being solicited, as opposed to being impartially informed" (Hippsley 2002).

Google has largely avoided criticism for its AdWords paid placement program and the company was noticeably absent from the Commercial Alert complaint. While other search engines were happily crowding their search results with "Featured Links," Google insisted on drawing a line – quite literally – between "paid" and "organic" results. Algorithmically, advertising was to have no effect on the selection and ordering of the free results, and ads were "clearly marked" as "Sponsored Links." These results initially appeared only to the right of the "organic" results, but today Google includes up to three sponsored links directly above the top result. Even though these are also labeled as "sponsored," selected by relevance not price, and appear over a colored background (Sullivan 2002, AdwordsRep 2004), the fact remains: a considerable portion of Google's revenue comes from moving ads to the most prominent positions *above* the "first hit." It is unclear whether, in practice, users perceive these as ads; Google, after all, has an enormous interest in blurring that line.

In any case, disclosure alone does not solve the problems of paid listings. If we really wish to promote ideals of democratic discourse, then we should worry about any policy that allows those with money to be featured prominently among results for a given topic. This concern, it should be emphasized, is not with advertising in general. It is with a particular type of advertising competes with "organic," relevant content; it is with advertising that supplants, rather than complements, the pages individuals might otherwise see. Despite what Brin and Page say today, paid listings, even if disclosed, are not "just like" advertising in the traditional media. Industry reporter Danny Sullivan (2003a), however, disagrees:

> Think newspapers. Newspapers have both "editorial" copy, which is not supposed to be influenced by advertising, as well as ads themselves. You may read the paper primarily for the articles, but there are certainly times when you may find the advertisements useful, as well ... In "old" media ... most people can readily identify ads because they look or act so very different from "content."

But there's the rub. In the new media of search engines, paid listings (as opposed to banner ads) *don't* "look or act so very different" from normal results. Search engines with paid listings are hardly like a newspaper with lots of informative, unbiased content and obvious, product-oriented ads sprinkled here and there. They are, perhaps, more like a newspaper in which half articles on the front page are written and paid for by commercial groups and discretely labeled as "sponsored articles." Or like network television if half the primetime spots were allotted to infomercials. No wonder, despite Sullivan's claim that users will eventually "learn" to distinguish paid and unpaid content, a 2005 study continued to find that "While most consumers could easily identify the difference between TV's regular programming and its infomercials…only a little more than a third of search engine users are aware of the analogous sets of content commonly presented by search engines" (Fallows 2005: 3).

2.4.3 'Wine but not Beer' and Other Ad Policies

Although the relationship between Google's editorial and paid listings has largely escaped criticism, much controversy *has* surrounded the company's 'bias' with respect to the selection of advertisements. As Brin admits, "We don't try to put our sense of ethics into the search results, but we do when it comes to advertising" (Sheff 2004). The resulting scheme is a patchwork of proscriptions: the search engine doesn't accept ads for beer, but it does for wine (Sheff 2004); ads for pornography are fine, but ads for guns are not (Johnson 2003); you can promote T-shirts depicting the cannabis leaf and drug paraphernalia, but you may not advertise water pipes (Kopytoff 2004). Most worrisome, perhaps, is that ads have been rejected because the sponsoring site – or even a page it links to – advocates *against* an individual or group. When the nonprofit environmental advocacy group Oceana tried to run ads on Google, they were rejected because the organization's site was critical of Royal Caribbean Cruise Lines, a Google advertiser (Liedtke 2004). In August 2004, the *San Francisco Chronicle* obtained internal documents detailing the company's advertising policies (Kopytoff 2004). These policies prohibited ads for sites that bashed politicians, gave special scrutiny to ads by the Church of Scientology, and allowed sites to advertise on the keyword 'abortion' only if they made no reference to religion. Yahoo! and MSN, by many accounts, impose far fewer restrictions on the content of the ads they run.

It is not immediately clear what this bias means from the perspective of democratic discourse. Media scholars like McChesney and Bagdikian are, after all, not so much worried about biased advertising standards as they are about the dissolution of the boundary between editorial content and advertising. Google has seemingly adopted a similar position, steadfastly reminding the press, its users, and advertisers that its advertising biases in "no way affect the results [they] deliver" – as if that puts an end to the matter (Google 2005). But it is not too difficult see how advertising selectivity may have political and deliberative implications, as Lawrence Lessig (2004) suggests in his latest book:

> Say you want to run a series of ads that try to demonstrate the extraordinary collateral harm that comes from the drug war. Can you do it? Well, obviously, these ads cost lots of money. Assume you raise the money … Can you be sure your message will be heard then?

> No. You cannot. Television stations have a general policy of avoiding "controversial" ads. Ads sponsored by the government are deemed uncontroversial; ads disagreeing with the government are controversial … Thus, the major channels of commercial media will refuse one side of a crucial debate the opportunity to present its case. (p. 167)

By recognizing that advertising may be used as a tool not only for promoting products, services, political candidates but also as medium to voice antagonistic opinions about these subjects, Lessig and other scholars have argued that advertising too may serve as a kind of deliberative forum (though one largely confined to the well-heeled).

Ultimately, in newspapers or television, radio or the Internet, whenever editorial content is interspersed with paid content that deals with similar topics, the spectrum of views put forth on that subject encompasses both types of material, for better or for worse. And so, the more advertisements Google includes under the constraints of this policy the more likely it is that users will find mainstream, commercial sites promoting a particular position, product, or service, and the less likely it is that they will hit noncommercial, antagonistic, 'controversial' voices. These voices, so critical for deliberative discourse, are multiply penalized: they are less likely to appear in the 'organic' listings that tend to suppress controversy; they are less likely to have the financial means to buy a prominent advertising spot; and, even if they had the money, their message may not conform to Google's content standards. Brin and Page knew all this back in 1998; indeed, they were so uncomfortable with the "inherent bias" of commercial search engines that they declared it "crucial" to keep Google "a competitive search engine that is transparent and in the academic realm" (p. 19).

2.5   Towards 'Coke and Pepsi'? Search Engine Consolidation

Over the past few decades, concerns over media consolidation have reached a fever pitch (e.g., McChesney 1999). Media concentration allows companies to increase profit margins by leveraging economies of scale (via horizontal integration) and by developing mutually-reinforcing, cross-promotional "synergies" (through vertical conglomeration). Unfortunately, this raises the barriers of entry for newcomers who may not be able to effectively engage in wage price wars or gain access to cross-promotional outlets (Compaine and Gomery 2000: 521). To the extent that a few firms succeed in amassing control of the media, the dissemination of diverse and antagonistic views is potentially undermined.

Applying these concerns to the field of search engines, we might suppose, as Kawaguchi and Mowshowitz (2002) do in their study of variance among the search engines, that "too few intermediaries spells trouble":

> The only real way to counter the ill effects of search engine bias on the ever-expanding
> Web is to make sure a number of alternative search engines are available. Elimination of
> competition in the search engine business is just as problematic for a democratic society as
> consolidation in the news media. (p. 60)

Surprisingly, the issue of concentration in the search engine industry has received relatively little attention (exceptions include Sheu and Carley 2001, and Elizabeth van Couvering's chapter in this volume). Perhaps this is because the relatively nascent, "transitioning" state of the industry makes it difficult to distinguish long-term patterns from the normal wax and wane of competitors in new markets.

But as the dot-com dust settles, and as consistent, comparative market data become available, a fairly clear pattern of consolidation starts to emerge. Users are, first of all, increasingly converging on a smaller set of search engines. In 1998, each of the top 8 search engines was used by at least 10% of the online audience and, on average, reached about 23% of all Web users (Sullivan 1998). But today, the top three sites – Yahoo!, Microsoft, and Google – handle over four-fifths of all search traffic (Sullivan 2005), and almost half of Web users frequent a single search site (Fallows and Rainie 2004). Thus, whereas users were once distributed across many portals and individually relied on several different search engines, today they stick to a few, overwhelmingly popular sites (Diaz 2005: 130).

In addition, ownership of the various search sites has been consolidated into the hands of a decidedly smaller number of companies. These developments were predicted as early as 1996, when Jupiter Communications, an industry research firm, forecast an imminent "shake-out" in the sector. "There are simply too many players," they warned investors, "offering similar functionality and features, competing for a limited number of advertising dollars and users" (qtd. in Sullivan 2001a). Even Excite's CEO, George Bell, was pessimistic about the chances for survival: "There are a lot of 'two' examples out there ... There's Pepsi and Coke, Time and Newsweek ... the third always tends to struggle, the fourth tends to get bought. I think [Yahoo and Excite] will make it" (qtd. in Sullivan 2001a). Excite, of course, did not make it. After a steady decline in profitability and traffic, it was ultimately acquired by Ask Jeeves, which also gobbled up DirectHit, Teoma, iWon, MyWay, and MyWebSearch (Waters and Lee 2003). Yahoo! was relatively lucky, keeping a significant market share while acquiring Inktomi, AllTheWeb, Altavista, Del.icio. us, and paid listings pioneer Overture (Ostrom 2003). While Robin Kellet of MSN UK believes that the "period of consolidation is probably almost over" (qtd. in van Vark 2004), the sector is already dominated by a few, relatively large corporations, not a multitude of independent startups.

In light of these developments, it is not surprising to find many referring to the emerging 'search oligopoly' (Arnold 2003). And, economically speaking, that characterization seems apt. Under Kaysen and Turner's determination of oligopoly, for example, "type I" oligopoly is achieved when "the eight largest firms have 50% of receipts and the 20 largest at least 75%" (Compaine and Gomery 2000: 555–556) — a threshold easily exceeded regardless of whether we look at ad revenues or traffic share (Diaz 2005: 131–132). Applying the more complex Herfiendhal-Hirshman Index (HHI), which "reflects ... the number and size distribution of firms in a market, as well as concentration of the output" (Rhodes qtd. in Compaine and Gomery 2000: 558–559) we see that search achieves a level of concentration exceeding those of the much-ballyhooed traditional media sectors (Sheu and Carley 2001 14; Cooper and Cooper 2003). For Sheu and Carley, these indicators suggest that "the industry looks close to being plagued by anticompetitive practices" (p. 22). But unlike the oil, film, and music oligopolies – which "work together to … restrict the game of profit maximizing to themselves" (Compaine and Gomery 2000: 275) – there is little evidence today of a "search engine cartel," and new competitors do occasionally spring up (Grossman 2003, Hansell 2005). The situation may be in this respect more like the "loose and open oligopoly" of book publishing industry, in which "one can properly lament some concentration…[is] nowhere near as tightly controlled as movies and music" (Compaine and Gomery 2000: 517–518).

Oligopoly or not, Google is perched firm and tall at the top of the search industry. While it was certainly a latecomer – only 5% of Web users had accessed the site as of December 2000 (Sullivan 2001b) – it now handles half of all U.S. Web searches and its users are far and away the most loyal, with 56% of them using nothing else (Fallows 2005). Amazingly, Google rose to the top without the aid of mergers, acquisitions, or even a large advertising budget, and it did so amidst a stock market crash that was decimating the dot-coms. Its success was simply attributed to the quality of its results, a product of its unique and groundbreaking technologies like as PageRank. Google's algorithmic superiority clearly caught they eye of users, but it also garnered the attention of "portal" operators such as Yahoo! and AOL, who had previously ignored the importance of search and were now clamoring to license Google's technology to power its own sites (Prather 2002; Rosenberg 1998). And so, by May 2003, after Yahoo! and AOL outsourced their search technology to Google, the Web's top three search destinations were all powered by the Mountain View startup. Taken together, this meant that it was fielding a whopping 76% of all Web search queries performed in the United States (Sullivan 2003b). Although Yahoo! has since switched to in-house search technology, today Google continues to field twice as many queries as its Sunnyvale rival (Nielsen 2006).

Google's technology thus has an enormous influence on virtually all online discourse and communication. In what is perhaps the "ultimate measure of impact" on the public consciousness, its name has become a verb: potential mates "google" each other before a date, recruiters "google" job applicants, citizens "google" information on Iraq, and schoolchildren "google" for everything from encyclopedia articles to games for their graphing calculators. As Jonathan Zittrain of the Harvard Law School explains, Google has quickly become the "the traffic cop at the main intersection of the information society" (qtd. in Markoff and Zachary 2003).

If decades of media criticism are any guide, this should be a cause for concern. A dominant intermediary like Google has both the opportunity and the incentives to hypercommercialize content and to bias results in a self-interested manner. The effects of any such negative, 'antidemocratic' bias are intensified in proportion to how widely Google's search technology is diffused (McGinn 1990, p. 99). For instance, if users find Websites primarily through search engines (they do), if Google handles the vast majority of these search queries (it does), and if the use of PageRank does result in popular, mainstream opinions dominating the search results, then Google's monopoly could make it considerably more difficult for 'ordinary' sites to be seen by a significant population of Web users.

But concern over Google's dominance need not hinge on whether or not the company has illicit motives, or on whether its results are 'democratically' selected. All intermediaries, even the fairest ones, must have biases; they must all somehow choose to elevate some issues, opinions, and voices and to ignore others (Goldman 2006). But when many intermediaries can reach a sizable chunk of the public each encoding its own opinions about what is interesting, relevant, or valid – these biases can counteract each other and, taken as a whole, a broad array of opinions can be disseminated (in part, through a second step of interpersonal communication as discussed in Katz 1973). In contrast, when only one or a few outlets have any significant reach, there is enormous inequality in what is transmitted: some views garner lots attention, and those left out are not heard at all. Consequently, for Bagdikian (1992), it is consolidation – irrespective of commercialization – that is the real enemy:

> The threat does not lie in the commercial operation of the mass media. It is the best method there is and, with all its faults, it is not inherently bad. But narrow control, whether by government or corporations, is inherently bad. In the end, no small group, certainly no group with as much uniformity of outlook and as concentrated in power as the current media corporations can be sufficiently open and flexible to reflect the full richness and variety of society's values and needs. The answer is not elimination of private enterprise in the media, but the opposite. It is the restoration of genuine competition and diversity. (p. 223–224)

We should therefore worry when we hear one writer conclude, "so powerful has Google become that many ... view it as the Web itself: if you're not listed on its indexes, they say, you might as well not exist" (Olsen 2002). While the opposite extreme – a highly balkanized audience with little "common ground" – has its own problems (Sunstein 2001: 91–99), a World Wide Web that consists only of what appears at the top of Google's results is, frankly, a very attenuated sort of deliberative public forum.

2.6 Letting the Market Decide: Barriers of Entry to Search

There is an obvious retort to all this: if Google does betray the values of the Web and the needs of its users, the quality of its product will decline, and its users will just switch to another search engine. Search engines are highly substitutable commodities: users can just type in a different URL or can change their browser's start page. This is how David Zetland (2005) dismisses "naïve claims" that Google "reduces our access to dissident, minority or heterodox views": "The objection ... is groundless" because "[e]ntry is easy, and Google has major rivals" (p. 7). Or as Eric Goldman (2006) puts it, "market forces limit the scope of search engine bias" (p. 196).

Sadly, it's not so simple. First, because it is so hard to see what's "missing" from search results; users are unlikely to have the necessary knowledge to even consider a switch (Telang et al.1999). Second, bundled services such as email tend to "lock" users to a search engine. Google, for example, is building brand loyalty is through tight integration into the major browsers, through its release of the Google Toolbar (Miller 2005), and through its countless "portal-like" services including GMail, Google Calendar, and Personalized Search. These are clear – and logical – ways of increasing both switching costs for users and barriers to entry for competitors (Sheu and Carley 2001: 17–18).

Of course, our romantic visions of tech innovation – billion-dollar companies sprouting from Silicon Valley garages – suggest that the next great search engine may be just around the corner. Google, after all, began its ascent to the top, and eventually overtook multi-billion-dollar giant Yahoo!, on a 'mere' $25 million dollar investment (Marshall 2005). Since then competitors have continued to appear, though very few been able to obtain a significant market share (Hansell 2005). Thus, we may conclude that the market is, as Compaine argues, "oligopoly proof" (Compaine and Gomery: 476).

But already, companies are finding it hard to keep up with the exponential growth of the Web, which demands highly complex technical systems and enormous expertise to manage:

> Today, the wholesale search market has significant barriers to entry. Economies of scale have asserted themselves, secondary competitors have folded, and the creation of new search engines by startups is becoming prohibitively expensive. Consider: to crawl, index, and search more than eight billion pages still only a fraction of the Web – Google now operates a global infrastructure of more than 250,000 Linux-based servers of its own design … and is becoming a major consumer of electrical power, computer hardware, and telecommunications bandwidth. (Ferguson 2005)

These economic hurdles, according to an executive at Ask Jeeves, are "likely to lead to more consolidation rather than competition from new entrants" (Cox qtd. in Glover 2005). Already, the "search engine wars" are between Yahoo!, Google, and Microsoft; independent general interest search engines are few and far between, unlikely to raise the necessary capital. Even niche, "vertical" search engines seldom gain significant market share, and profitability is likely to continue inducing search engines to focus on majoritarian interests.

What about the "competitive," "academic" search engine Brin and Page promised us? Is such a search engine still possible? Probably not. As one search engine manager points out, making such a system available would "cost you a ton of money":

> This is why ever since 2000, 2001, most of the search research done at the universities is what I call Metacrawler-esque, which is people not building a search engine but doing something on top of a search engine, because they just can't afford to build their own. Which is a shame, because you're not getting these big engines coming out of academia any more. (qtd. in van Couvering 2004: 10)

The virtually insurmountable regulatory and economic challenges plaguing existing proposals for more "egalitarian" search engines suggest that the market mechanism – despite all its problems – may be, at least for now, the only practical means of getting a viable search engine off the ground. Google's founders may have abandoned their original vision for a search engine that is "competitive" and "in the academic realm" not because they sold out, but because they had come to see this as a contradiction.

2.7   Conclusion: Is Google 'Evil'?

Given the critical-analytic lens with which we have approached the sociopolitics of search, it may seem that I am promoting the view that Google is, in fact, "evil." But this is certainly not the case. It is my view that the observed tensions between the search engine and democratic aspirations are, for the most part, not the product of malicious or even profiteering intent. Instead, they stem from both the high demands of the democratic model and the inherent limitations of commercialized search. It is hard to imagine a search company staying afloat, after all, if it does not present what its users want; it is difficult to make money if it does not display advertising; it is unprofitable to operate a competitive search engine without a very significant market share.

It would be quite difficult to suggest that we are better off without Google or, for that matter, without any of the other search engines. Awash in a sea of bits, we may be tempted to look at 'democraticness' and 'bias' as binaries, as things you either have or you don't. It makes more sense to take a step back, and to think of Google as *one more way* in which people can get information. Only the most hardened cynic would think that the success of Google has resulted in a *net loss* of sources to which we are exposed. And so, as Compaine reminds,

> the questions to ask yourself are: Are there more or fewer voices available today than 15, 25 or more years ago? And, is it easier or harder, are the regulatory barriers higher or lower, is it more expensive or less expensive, to gain access, in whatever format, to a large audience … than in 1900? in 1950? in 1990? (Compaine and Gomery: 576).

I believe that the answers to all these questions are emphatically positive, and that Google – certainly more than the traditional broadcast media – is making it possible for more people to hear and contribute to a broader spectrum of opinions.

But there are a number of ways we might think about improving the deliberativeness of search engines like Google. For many, the answer is in technology – not regulation or subsidization. Cho and his colleagues, for example, have proposed two alternatives to PageRank – random selection (Pandey et. al 2005) and popularity increase rate (Cho and Adams 2003) – that arguably surface high-quality content while mitigating popularity bias and entrenchment effects. Echoing Brin and Page's (1998) footnoted musings about user-seeded PageRank computation (p. 15), Goldman (2006) has put his faith in personalized search: "Personalized algorithms mean that there are multiple 'top' search results for a particular search term … so Web publishers will not compete against each other in a zero-sum game … reducing structural biases" (p. 199). At least one search engine has already "spent a lot of R&D" on algorithms that attempt to distinguish between commercial and noncommercial searches – ensuring that paid results "only show up under paid queries" – and Yahoo! Mindset allows users to interactively bias their results according to whether they are "shopping" or "researching" (Raschtchy and Avilio 2003). Such innovative solutions are what we need to pursue if search engines are to serve the needs of both citizens and of consumers. It is what we need if Web search engines are to serve democracy, while remaining economically viable.

The purpose of this chapter has been to take a hard look at the search engine we rely on. But it is also intended to reveal the many, difficult entailments of utopian, democratic ideals associated with the Web. The deliberative standard is quite clearly an extremely difficult – some might say impossible – one to meet. And so, it's not that haven't moved forward. It's just that we aren't quite "there" yet.

References

AdWordsRep: Top position? Impossible? In: Search Engine Watch Forums. http://forums. searchenginewatch.com/showthread.php?t=2952 (2004). Cited 9 Apr 2007

Anderson C The long tail. *Wired* 12(10). http://www.wired.com/wired/archive/12.10/tail.html (2004). Cited 9 Apr 2007

Arnold S In search of clicks that make cash: three search companies are all chasing the same pool of advertising spend. World Information Review (1 Apr 2003)

Associated Press v. United States, 326 U.S. 1, US Supreme Court (1945)

Bagdikian B (1992) The media monopoly, 4th edn Beacon Press, Boston

Barabási (2002) A Linked: the new science of networks. Perseus Books, Cambridge

Benhabib S (1996) Toward a deliberative model of democratic legitimacy. In: Democracy and difference: contesting the boundaries of the political. ed by Benhabib, S. Princeton University Press, Princeton, pp 67–94

Bhargava H, Feng J (2002) Paid placement strategies for Internet search engines. In: Proceedings of the WWW2002 Conference, Honolulu, Hawaii. http://portal.acm.org/citation.cfm?id=511462 (2002). Cited 8 Apr 2007. pp 117–123

Bricklin D (2002) Why small players matter. Dan Bricklin's Web site. http://www.bricklin.com/ smallplayers.htm (2002). Cited 10 Apr 2005

Brin S, Page L (1998) The anatomy of a large-scale hypertextual web search engine. Seventh International WWW Conference, Brisbane, Australia. http://www-db.stanford.edu/pub/papers/ google.pdf (April 1998). Cited 1 May 2005

Burns E (2007) Top U.S. parent companies and stickiest brands on the Web, February 2007. Clickz Network. http://www.clickz.com/showPage.html?page=3625269 (2007). Cited 9 Apr 2007

Cho J, Adams R (2003) Page quality: in search of an unbiased web ranking. Technical report, UCLA Computer Science Department. http://oak.cs.ucla.edu/~cho/papers/cho-quality-long. pdf (2003). Cited 9 Apr 2007

Cho J, Roy S (2004) Impact of search engines on page popularity. In: Proceedings of the WWW2004 Conference, New York. http://oak.cs.ucla.edu/~cho/papers/cho-bias.pdf (May 2004). Cited 6 Aug 2006

Cho J, Garcia-Molina H, Page L (1998) Efficient crawling through URL ordering. In: Proceedings of 7th World Wide Web Conference, http://dbpubs.stanford.edu/pub/1998-51 (2000). Cited 9 Apr 2007

CNN.com: Four sites account for half of Web surfing. http://www.cnn.com/2001/TECH/Internet/06/05/Internet.consolidation/ (5 June 2001). Cited 27 Apr 2004

Compaine B, Gomery D (2000) Who owns the media? competition and concentration in the mass media industry, 3rd edn, Lawrence Erlbaum Associates, Mahwah

Cooper M (2003) Media ownership and democracy in the digital information age. http://cyberlaw.stanford.edu/blogs/cooper/archives/mediabooke.pdf (2003). Cited 15 May 2005

Cooper M, Cooper S (2003) Hope and hype v. reality: The role of the commercial Internet in democratic discourse and prospects for institutional change. Stanford Law School Center for Internet and Society. http://cyberlaw.stanford.edu/blogs/cooper/archives/HOPEALL.pdf (2003). Cited 7 May 2005

Cornfield M, Rainie L (2003) Untuned keyboards: online campaigners, citizens, and portals in the 2002 elections. In: Pew Internet and American Life Project. http://www.pewInternet.org/pdfs/PIP_IPDI_Politics_Report.pdf (2004). Cited 11 May 2005

Crowell G (2003) The "secret system" of search engine advertising. In: Search Engine Watch. http://searchenginewatch.com/_subscribers/articles/article.php/3289361 (2003). Cited 28 Apr 2004

Cunningham F (2002) Theories of democracy: a critical introduction. Routledge, New York

Denver Area Educational Telecommunications Consortium, Inc., et al. v. Federal Communications Commission et al., 518 U.S. 727, US Supreme Court(1996).

Diaz A (2005) Through the google goggles: sociopolitical bias in search engine design. Undergraduate honors thesis, Stanford University.

The Economist (2004) Spiders in the web (15 May) pp 16

Elster J (ed) (1998) Deliberative democracy. Cambridge University Press, Cambridge

Fallows D (2005) Search engine users: Internet searchers are confident, satisfied, and trusting –but they are also unaware and naïve. In: Pew Internet and American Life Project. http://www.pewInternet.org/pdfs/PIP_Searchengine_users.pdf (2005). Cited 8 Apr 2007

Fallows D, Rainie L (2004) The popularity and importance of search engines. In: Pew Internet and American Life Project. http://www.pewInternet.org/pdfs/PIP_Data_Memo_Searchengines.pdf (2004). Cited 10 May 2005

Felten E (2004) Googleocracy in action. In: Freedom to Tinker. http://freedom-to-tinker.com/archives/000509.html (2004). Cited 15 May 2005

Ferguson C (2005) What's next for google? The search firm wants to organize all digital information; that means war with Microsoft. Technology Review: MIT's Magazine of Innovation 108: 38–46

Fishkin J (1991) Democracy and deliberation: new directions for democratic reform. Yale University Press, New Haven

Fortunato S, Flammini A, Menczer F, Vespignani A (2006) The egalitarian effect of search engines. In: Proceedings of the WWW2006 Conference, Edinburgh, United Kingdom. http://arxiv.org/pdf/cs.CY/0511005 (May 2006). Cited 6 Aug 2006

Gallagher D (2002) U.S. Warns web sites to label sponsorships. The New York Times (2 July 2002)

Gerhart S (2004) Do web search engines suppress controversy? First Monday 9(1). http://firstmonday.org/issues/issue9_1/gerhart/index.html (2004). Cited 1 May 2005

Glover T (2005) Search engines power new dotcom boom. Sunday Business (27 March 2005)

Goldman E (2006) Search engine bias and the demise of search engine utopianism. Yale Journal of Law and Technology 8: 188–200

Google (2004) Our search: google technology. http://www.google.com/technology (2004). Cited 13 May 2005

Google (2005) Google adwords content policy. http://adwords.google.com/select/contentpolicy.html (2005). Cited 21 Mar 2005

Google (2006) Financial data. google investor relations. http://investor.google.com/fin_data.html (2006). Cited 6 Aug 2006

Grossman L (2003) Search and destroy: a gang of web search companies is gunning for Google. Time (22 Dec 2003) pp 46–50

Habermas J (1990) Moral consciousness and communicative action. MIT, Cambridge

Hague, Mayor et al. v. Committee for Industrial Organization et al., 307 U.S. 496, US Supreme Court (1939)

Hansell S (2001) Clicks for sale: paid placement is catching on in web searches. The New York Times (4 June 2001)

Hansell S (2005) Search sites play a game of constant catch-up. The New York Times (31 Jan 2005)

Hindman M, Tsioutsiouliklis K, Johnson J (2003) Googlearchy: how a few heavily-linked sites dominate politics on the Web. In: Annual Meeting of the Midwest Political Science Association. http://citeseer.ist.psu.edu/hindman03googlearchy.html (2003). Cited 8 Apr 2007

Hippsley H (2002) Re complaint requesting investigation of various Internet search engine companies for paid placement and paid inclusion programs. U.S. Federal Trade Commission. http://www.ftc.gov/os/closings/staff/commercialalertletter.htm (2002). Cited 20 May 2004

Introna L, Nissenbaum H (2000) Shaping the web: why the politics of search engines matters. The Information Society 16: 1–17

Johnson J (2003) Google accepts porn ads but refuses those for guns. CNSNews. http://www.cnsnews.com/Culture/archive/200310/CUL20031007c.html (2003). Cited 23 July 2003

Katz E (1973) The two-step flow of communication: an up-to-date report of a hypothesis. In: Marketing classics: a selection of influential articles, ed by Enis, B., Cox, K. Allyn and Bacon, Boston

Kopytoff V (2004) Google ad rules complex, controversial: documents reveal details about what the popular search engine accepts, rejects. San Francisco Chronicle (9 Aug 2004)

Kottke J (2003) Weblogs and power laws. http://kottke.org/03/02/weblogs-and-power-laws. Cited 1 Aug 2006

Lasica JD (1996) Interview with John Perry Barlow. http://www.jdlasica.com/interviews/barlow.html (1996). Cited 25 April 2004

Lessig L (2004) Free culture: how big media uses technology and the law to lock down culture and control creativity. Penguin, New York

Levy S (1995) How the propeller heads store the electronic future. New York Times Magazine (Sep 24) pp 58–59

Liedtke M (2004) Google bans environmental group's ads. USA Today Online. http://www.usatoday.com/tech/news/2004-02-12-google-bans-ad_x.htm (12 Feb 2004). Cited 10 June 2004

Markoff J, Zachary G (2003) In searching the web, google finds riches. The New York Times (13 Apr)

Marshall M (2005) Google founders' brashness sparks debate. San Jose Mercury News (18 Aug)

Mayer M (2005) Progress in research and ads (talk). In: Google factory tour. (Google.com, 2005), http://www.google.com/intl/en/press/factorytour.html (2005). Cited 20 May 2005

McChesney R (1999) Oligopoly: the big media game has fewer and fewer players. The Progressive (November) 1: 20–24

McChesney R (2000) Rich media, poor democracy: communication politics in dubious times. New Press, New York

McGinn R (1990) Science, technology and society. Prentice Hall, Englewood Cliffs

Mill JS (1978) On liberty, 1859, ed by Rapaport, E. Hackett, Indianapolis

Miller L (2001) How to net results in search-site seas. USA Today (13 Aug)

Miller M (2005) Broadband everywhere: Internet explorer still dominates the web, but firefox is growing fast and igniting innovation. PC Magazine. http://www.pcmag.com/article2/0,1759,1770267,00.asp (22 March 2005). Cited 9 Apr 2007

Mowshowitz A, Kawaguchi A (2002) Bias on the web. Communications of the ACM 45: 56–60

Nielsen//Netratings: Google accounts for half of all U.S. searches in April. http://www.nielsen-netratings.com/pr/pr_060525 (25 May). Cited 31 July 2006

Olsen S (2002) The google gods: does search engine's power threaten web's independence? CNet News. http://news.com.com/2009-1023-963618.html (31 Oct 2002). Cited 9 Apr 2007

Ostrom M (2003) Pasadena, calif: commercial search firm to buy web search properties. San Jose Mercury News (26 Feb)

Page B (1996) Who deliberates? University of Chicago Press, Chicago

Page L, Brin S, Motwani R, Winograd T (2007) The pagerank citation ranking: bringing order to the web. http://dbpubs.stanford.edu/pub/1999-66 (1999). Cited 8 Apr 2007

Pagendarm M, Schaumurg H (2001) Why are users banner-blind? The impact of navigation style on the perception of web banners. Journal of Digital Information 2 http://journals.tdl.org/jodi/article/view/jodi-37/38

Pandey S, Roy S, Olston C, Cho J (2005) Shuffling a stacked deck: The case for partially randomizing ranking of search engine results. http://reports-archive.adm.cs.cmu.edu/anon/2005/CMU-CS-05-116.pdf (2005). Cited 8 Apr 2007

Prather M. (2002) Ga-ga for google. Entrepreneur Magazine. http://www.entrepreneur.com/article/0,4621,297807,00.html. Cited 9 Apr 2007

Princeton Survey Research Associates: A Matter of Trust: What Users want From Web Sites. Results of a National Survey of Internet Users for Consumer WebWatch. http://www.pewtrusts.org/pdf/vf_web_watch_trust_0402.pdf. Cited 8 Apr 2007

Raschtchy S, Avilio J (2003) Industry note: search symposium shows bigger role for search in advertising. U.S. Bancorp Piper Jaffray. http://marketwatch.multexinvestor.com/download.asp?docid=29692599&sid=26. Cited 5 Feb 2005

Reinhardt A (2003) And you thought the web ad market was dead: sales of so-called 'Paid placement' listings are soaring. In: BusinessWeek Online. http://www.businessweek.com/magazine/content/03_18/b3831134_mz034.htm (2003). Cited 8 Apr 2007

Rodzvilla J (2002) (ed) We've got blog: how weblogs are changing our culture. Perseus Books, Cambridge

Rosenberg S (1998) Yes there is a better search engine: while the portal sites fiddle, Google catches fire. Salon.com. http://archive.salon.com/21st/rose/1998/12/21straight.html (1998). Cited 5 Mar 2005

Rostbøll C (2005) Preferences and paternalism: on freedom and deliberative democracy. Political Theory 33: 370–396

Schuler D (2003) Reports of the close relationship between democracy and the Internet may have been exaggerated. In: Democracy and New Media, ed by Jenkins, H., Thorbum, D. MIT, Cambridge

Sheff D (2004) Playboy interview: google guys. Playboy 51: 55–60, 142–145

Sheu T, Carley K (2001) Monopoly power on the web: a preliminary investigation of search engines. In: Proceedings of the 29th Telecommunications Policy Research Conference, Alexandria, Virginia. http://arxiv.org/as/cs.CY/0109054. Cited 7 May 2005

Sullivan D (1998) NetRatings search engine ratings, June 1998. Search Engine Watch. http://searchenginewatch.com/mhts/9806-10-netratings.mht. Cited 20 Dec 2004

Sullivan D (2001a) Nielsen NetRatings Search engine Ratings, December 2000. Search Engine Watch. http://searchenginewatch.com/mhts/9902-0012-netratings.mht. Cited 21 Dec 2004

Sullivan D (2001b) The end for search engines? Clickz Experts. http://www.clickz.com/experts/search/opt/article.php/837281. Cited 23 Dec 2004

Sullivan D (2002) FTC recommends disclosure to search engines. Search Engine Watch. http://searchenginewatch.com/sereport/article.php/2164891. Cited 20 May 2004

Sullivan D (2003a) Buying your way in search engine advertising chart. In: Search Engine Watch. http://searchenginewatch.com/wemasters/article.php/2167941. Cited 20 May 2004

Sullivan D (2003b) comScore Media Metrix search engine ratings, August 2003. Search Engine Watch. http://searchenginewatch.com/mhts/0305-mediametrix.mht. Cited 1 May 2005

Sullivan D (2005) ComScore Media Metrix search engine ratings, December 2004. Search Engine Watch. http://searchenginewatch.com/reports/article.php/2156431. Cited 8 May 2005

Sunstein C (1997) Deliberation, democracy, and disagreement. In: Justice and democracy: cross-cultural perspectives, ed by Bontekoe, R., Stepaniants, M. University of Hawaii Press, Honolulu, pp 92–117

Sunstein C (2001) Republic.com. Princeton University Press, Princeton

Telang R, Mukhopadhyay T, Wilcox R (1999) An empirical analysis of the antecedents of Internet search engine choice. Workshop on Information Systems and Economics, Charlotte, North Carolina

Upstill T, Craswell N, Hawking D (2003) Predicting fame and fortune: pagerank or indegree? In: Eighth Australasian Document Computing Symposium, Canberra, Australia. http://cs.anu.edu. au/~Trystan.Upstill/pubs/upstill_adcs03.pdf. Cited 10 May 2005

van Couvering E (2004) New media? The political economy of Internet search engines. Presented at the Annual Conference of the International Association of Media and Communications Researchers, Porto Alegre, Brazil. http://www.media.uio.no/prosjekter/ctp/papers/IAMCR-CTP04_S1-1_vanCouver.pdf. Cited 9 Apr 2007

van Vark C (2004) Search engines: search still sets the pace. Revolution (21 Apr)

Walters R, Lee A (2003) Ask jeeves to join excite Internet. The Financial Times (5 March)

Weinberger D (2002) Small pieces loosely joined: a unified theory of the web. Perseus, Cambridge

Wellman B, Haythornthwaite C (eds) The Internet in everyday life. Blackwells, Oxford

Zetland D. (2005) Is Google evil? Knowledge commodification, community and innovation. Presented at the Tenth International Kal Polanyi Conference, Istanbul (14 Oct). http://www. kysq.org/pubs/IsGoogleEvil.pdf. Cited 12 Nov 2007

3
Reconsidering the Rhizome: A Textual Analysis of Web Search Engines as Gatekeepers of the Internet

A. Hess

Summary Critical theorists have often drawn from Deleuze and Guattari's notion of the rhizome when discussing the potential of the Internet. While the Internet may structurally appear as a rhizome, its day-to-day usage by millions via search engines precludes experiencing the random interconnectedness and potential democratizing function. Through a textual analysis of four search engines, I argue that Web searching has grown hierarchies, or "trees," that organize data in tracts of knowledge and place users in marketing niches rather than assist in the development of new knowledge.

3.1 Introduction

As connections to the Internet appear more frequently as household commodities, their placement within the democratic order has become prized. Belief in the Internet's potential to radically alter the landscape of communication and democracy spread quickly through early literature about cyberspace. While some were hesitant to give the Web such power, others saw a redefinition of identity, voice, and politics. Within this body of literature, the label of "rhizome," following Deleuze and Guattari, was attached to the Web, noting its limitless expansion, random intersecting points, and abilities of rupture and re-growth. In an analysis of the more mainstream Web search engines, this chapter will question the Deleuzean notion of the rhizome as an apt metaphor for the Internet. I argue that due to the commercialization and gatekeeping functions of major Web search engines, including Google, Yahoo!, and MSN Search, the original structure of Web discourses, dissemination, and resistance has been co-opted. The consequences of the ordering of knowledge and its dissemination are threefold. First, the connections between individuals in the fight against hegemonic practices have been mitigated by the commercial restructuring of the Internet. Second, in the personalization of the digital sphere, specifically through the use of "cookies" and other digital devices, the user becomes prescribed in their experiences, which limits his or her ability to expand into new areas of learning. Finally, search engines utilize hierarchies to order knowledge and information which privileges

A. Spink and M. Zimmer (eds.), *Web Search, Springer Series in Information Science and Knowledge Management 14.*

mainstream and silences marginalized voices. Thus, what was once considered a tool for limitless knowledge and information becomes a commercial filter of packaged and priced data.

3.1.1   The Internet and the Promise of Democracy

Early theory in regard to the Internet came with great hope and promise. The medium was approached as a panacea to many of the perils of modernity. From theories of the virtual community to hacktivism to the rhizome, scholars approached the medium with varied scholarly hopes and fears. Of most importance for this chapter is the concept of the rhizome from critical theorists Gilles Deleuze and Félix Guattari. This rethinking of knowledge has been often used to describe the structure and capability of the Internet.[1] Before introducing the concept of the rhizome, I will first explore discussions of the potential of the Internet as it blossomed in the late 20th century.

Rheingold's Virtual Communities

Howard Rheingold (2000) approached the Internet as a reconceptualization of the very idea of community, remarking that the Internet has changed "the way groups of people are using CMC (computer mediated communication) to rediscover the power of cooperation, turning cooperation into a game, a way of life – a merger of knowledge capital, social capital, and communion" (p. 109). This virtual community has fostered the connection of individuals from myriad spectrums of life, including their competing interests and ideologies.

> Because we cannot see one another in cyberspace, gender, age, national origin, and physical appearance are not apparent unless a person wants to make such characteristics public. People whose physical handicaps make it difficult to form new friendships find that virtual communities treat them as they always wanted to be treated – as thinkers and transmitters of ideas and feeling beings, not carnal vessels with a certain appearance and way of thinking and talking (or not walking and not talking). (Rheingold 1993: 11)

Rheingold's earliest text (1993), and its subsequent revision (2000), follow his tales on the Internet while involved with an early online community, the Whole Earth 'Lectronic Link (WELL). He believes that cyberspace had the ability to "change our experience of the real world as individuals and communities" (p. xviii).

---

[1] It is important to note that I am approaching the theories of the Internet with a wide scope which will include theorists and areas of critical theory that have vastly different theories of epistemology (i.e. Habermas and Deleuze). While cognizant of this, my purpose here is, rather, to highlight the array of approaches to the Internet.

The WELL provided, for him, an experience of connection with other users across the globe. His anecdotes provide insight into the potential connections to be made with screen names found in multiple user domains (MUDs) and Internet Relay Chat (IRC). Rheingold's work has become known as groundbreaking in the area of theorizing about the net (Mater 2001; Resnick 1998) and has contributed, in part, to the development of a vast array of scholarly work regarding the potential of online communities.

Digital Political Activism

Parallel to Rheingold, many other theorists approach the Internet looking for the panacea to an ailing democratic order. Following the work of Jürgen Habermas, public sphere and counterpublic theorists have approached the Internet with both hope and hesitation for its potential, acknowledging the capacity of the Internet to alter the functions of democracy (Buchstein 1997; McDorman 2001; Owens and Palmer 2003; Palczewski 2001; Resnick 1998; Roper 1998; Streck 1998). At a national level, the ability for counterpublic actors to utilize new communication technology (NCT) can foster mobilization through virtual meetings and regroupings after political loss (McDorman 2001). Similarly, and on a global level, Mater (2001) argues that the increased use in new communication technology can result in "the emergence of a truly global public sphere involving all interested actors in the discussions of actions that need to be taken with regard to important global political, economic, and social problems" (p. 228). The public sphere, according to a variety of authors, becomes revitalized and invites democratic participation through the digital convergence of online actors. Additionally, new digital political arenas also invite new types of digital resistance. Hackers and hacktivism "organize 'virtual sit-ins' and recruit computer programmers to attack the World Wide Web sites of any person or company they deem responsible for oppression" (Harmon 1998 p. A1), such as those organized by Ricardo Dominguez and Stefan Wray. Hackers and hacktivists utilize mixed media and cyber resistance (Thomas 2005) to "imaginatively ally technology-based techniques with traditional and indigenous cultural resources" (Taylor 2005: 644). These uses of the Internet as a liberatory and oppositional medium highlight the democratic potential to splinter dominant ideologies.

3.1.2   The Rhizome

The above scholarship highlights the various approaches to the development of democracy within digital frameworks. While relevant to the discussion here, of more importance is the consideration of the Internet as a rhizome, specifically in the Deleuzean sense of the concept. Deleuze and Guattari (1987) introduce the concept of the rhizome as a rethinking of knowledge. Western epistemology has long relied on the metaphor of the tree, locating a unity of knowledge in primary systems of linguistics, psychoanalysis, and theology. Deleuze and Guattari (1987) argue that arborescent thought results in "binary logic and biunivocal relationships (which) still dominate psychoanalysis…, linguistics, structuralism, and even information science" (p. 5). The tree metaphor notes that at the origin of philosophic thought lies a base structure or root. For example, all languages can be traced back to an original *ur*-language. "In contradistinction to arborescent thought, rhizomatics intends to uproot philosophical trees and their first principles to deconstruct binary logic" (Best and Kellner 1991: 99). The metaphoric image of the rhizome, rather than finding a unity or beginning for knowledge, is an overlapping and intersecting system. Deleuze and Guattari (1987) argue that nature does not follow the arborescent system: "in nature, roots are taproots with a more multiple, lateral, and circular system of ramification, rather than a dichotomous one" (5). Thus, rhizomes are never beginning and never ending "non-hierarchical systems of deterrorialized lines that connect with other lines in random, unregulated relationships" (Best and Kellner 1991: 99). The concept of the rhizome has six principles which guide Deleuze and Guattari's discussion of the relationship of the metaphor to their critical project: connection, heterogeneity, multiplicity, asignifying rupture, cartography and decalcomania.

The principle of *connection* notes that "any point of a rhizome can be connected to anything other, and must be" (Deleuze and Guattari 1987: 7). The connections between nodes on a rhizome are also random in their relationship to each other which embodies the notion of *heterogeneity*, whereas arborescent structures are distinct from each other and homogenous within each tree. "A rhizome ceaselessly establishes connections between semiotic chains, organizations of power, and circumstances relative to the arts, sciences, and social struggles" (p. 7). The principle of *multiplicity* notes that: "it is only when the multiple is effectively treated as a substantive, 'multiplicity,' which it ceases to have any relation to the One as subject or object, natural or spiritual reality, image and world. Multiplicities are rhizomatic, and expose arborescent pseudomultiplicities for what they are" (p. 8). When a rhizome is broken or *ruptured*, it can still function within its remaining structure or can create new lines of growth from the ruptured area. Finally, the principles of *cartography* and *decalcomania* argue that the rhizome exists as a map and not a tracing. The structure of the tree is a self replicating and homogenous metaphor where the leaves of the tree recreate the same structure as the root. Thus, the tree grows by tracing its previous structure. The rhizome, in contrast, is a map. "A map has multiple entryways, as opposed to the tracing, which always comes back 'to the same.' The map has to do with performance, whereas the tracing always involves an alleged 'competence'" (p. 12–13). The concept is much more complex than the brief introduction here, and I will return to its implications following my analysis. However, it is important to note the central principles of the rhizome and its re-ordering of philosophic thought and knowledge. Rather than a unifying and guiding origin, rhizomatics decenter any privileging or hierarching of unity or Oneness.

Connecting Rhizomatics to Cyberspace

Critical theorists approaching the Internet have adopted the metaphor of the rhizome to approach the changing digital landscape.[2] Following these theorists, four overlapping themes emerge from the literature: structure, hypertext, epistemology, and resistance. First, on a basic level of the argument, the structure of the Internet mirrors Deleuze and Guattari's (1987) descriptions of the rhizome. "A rhizome as a subterranean stem is absolutely different from roots or radicles. Bulbs and tubers are rhizomes. Plants with roots or radicles may be rhizomorphic in other respects altogether...even some animals are, in their pack form. Rats are rhizomes" (p. 6). Van der Klei (2002) argues that, "In browsing the Web, one finds elements to be linked, in a nascent rhizome" (p. 48). The interconnectedness of the links of Web space captures the overlapping structure and limitless heterogeneity of the rhizome. A user can enter and exit from any point of the Internet and find these connections. "Computers on the Internet, using packet switching, send information to any neighboring computer on the Internet along routes that may or may not have been pre-established" (Hamman 1996). Indeed the structure of the early Internet, ARPANET, especially its military applications, was designed to sustain a possible rupture. In discussing the nature of using the Internet, the culture of cyberspace is also couched in terms of the rhizome. Lemos (1996) describes cyberculture as a self-organizing virtual space, "a sort of plateau, a 'rhizome' where the interconnections and multiplicities even change the nature of the media such that it metamorphoses into a medium of contact" (p. 46). In short, the structural level of the metaphor indicates that the Web-like nature of the Internet is much like the rhizome, which is difficult to dispute. The Internet does have multiple entry points and each one connects to many others. However, while structural arguments are sound, the experience of the Internet from a user perspective may not follow the rhizomatic image.

The second theme found in the literature discusses the nature of writing in cyberspace, specifically, the use of hypertext. Hypertext refers the linking of pages through various pathways which are written by the Web author, but chosen by the user. It is "a form of electronic text, a radically new information technology, and a mode of publication" (Landow 2006: 2). The use of this language style has been compared to the rhizome for its ability to decenter the text from a point of origin and the multiplicity of variously authored texts found in each work through the linking structure. The connection of the basic structure of the Web and hypertext is notable: "The hypertextual organization of the World Wide Web turns it into an instantiation of the concept of the rhizome whose defining attributes bear a strong affinity with those inherent in the structure of the Web" (Calleja and Schwager 2004: 7). From the linguistic organization (or lack thereof) found in cyberspace, the user becomes enmeshed in an environment which defies the use of linear logic and binary thinking.

---

[2] See Streck (1998), Moulthrop (1994) and Brande (1996) for counterarguments and reservations about applying rhizomatic theory to the Internet.

The connections found in the hypertext assist in the branching of the thought process and act in a similar manner as the performance and map argument articulated by Deleuze and Guattari (Landow 2006). The user, in the ideal hypertext, interacts by *becoming with* the text rather than overcoming or completing it.

From the interaction with hypertext, the third theme of epistemology appears. If users of the Internet engage with hypertext and its random interconnectedness, the function of the brain and use of knowledge is fundamentally different than arborescent thought. "Thus the developing episteme underlying these concerns revolves around the way these technologies of inscription are changing from linear to non-linear prosthetic extensions of thought. The gateway into exploration of the non-linear aspect of digitality can be most profitably explored through theories of hypertextuality" (Calleja and Schwager 2004: 9). In other words, brain functions follow the technology they use. If a society continues to engage with hypertextual environments, the human brain will follow in its organization. Similarly, Moulthrop (1991) sees the steps in the digital revolution as a cultural step away from the arborescent toward "a new information ecology in which the hothouse walls will come down and strange new growths will spring up across the land" (p. 255). Additionally, many authors have argued that the very identity of the hypertextual user becomes altered when on the Internet. Its use can destabilize identity (Markley 1996); or we become desiring machines (Shields 1996) or "turns us into part of the rhizome itself" (Calleja and Schwager 2004: 7). These new bodies or minds on the Internet are enabled to resist the dominant power structures and destabilize oppressive forces.

The final theme in the literature notes the use, both in theory and practice, of the Internet as a form of resistance. Again, the overlap of these themes becomes apparent as the use of hypertext and the epistemology both connect with the theory of digital resistance. Rosenberg (1994) sees the epistemology of nonlinear thinking as central to social expression and potential.

> The nomad and rhizome as concepts articulating the contingent condition of 'becoming' that enables resistance to domination. Hypertext theorists draw on these same topical oppositions to conceptualize this fuzzy micropolitical realm between determination and freedom, particularly those theorists who associate hypertext with the avant-garde thrust – the 'leading edge' in art and education. (Rosenberg 1994: 272)

Similarly, Moulthrop (1994) connects the use of both hypertext and its beneficial epistemology as able to change the nature of dominance and resistance. "Hypertext and hypermedia represent the expression of the rhizome in the social space of writing. If so, they might indeed belong in our dreams of a new culture…hypertext provides a laboratory or site of origin for a smoothly structured, nomadic alternative to the discursive space of late capitalism" (p. 304). While these theories offer the means to fight back, others have enacted the resistance through online protest and activism, similar to the hacktivists discussed above. Stefan Wray participated in the aforementioned Zapatista movement through acts of online civil disobedience. In writing about rhizomatics and resistance, Wray (1998) notes that "This movement of information through these various cyber-nets of resistance can be said to have occurred rhizomatically, moving horizontally, non-linearly, and underground." In sum, resistance from the oppressive structures of modernity is fostered through the becoming-rhizome and structural interconnectedness of the Web.

The above theorists contend that the function and use of the Internet follows the Deleuzean notion of the rhizome. From each of the four themes found in the literature, connections to the rhizomatic structure of the Internet are foundational to the ability to theorize and enact change and resistance. However, in the descriptions of hyper-text or Web space, few, if any, include the primary gateway into the Internet from a user perspective: the search engine. In response to this consideration, I offer this chapter as a phenomenological perspective regarding the daily use of the Internet. Where Wray (1998) and Palczewski (2001) note exceptional examples of online civil disobedience and hacktivism, I offer a more quotidian approach to the Internet. Felix (2006) informs us that on a typical day, 60 million adults use Internet search engines, usually Google, Yahoo!, and MSN Search. Taking into consideration the predominant usage of the Internet, then, I contend that users of the Internet are taken through tracts of knowledge rather than connecting through random intersect-ing points of the rhizome. In short, the rhizome has grown trees.

3.2 Method

To support this argument, I will analyze a set of search engines using a textual analysis including a discussion regarding the software behind the engine. In under-going this analysis, I am keeping in mind a phenomenological attitude where my experience of the Website guides my understanding of their abilities to structure the Internet. Rather than engaging the Web with a cyberactivist attitude, I approach it with a frame of mind that embodies the average user. Much of the aforementioned literature sees the Internet for its possibility, and while a valid and important approach, I believe the Internet should also be recognized for its daily and predomi-nant usage. Thus, in my analysis, I will discuss the most popular search engine Websites, Google, Yahoo! Search, and MSN Search as well as Amazon's shopping features. In my discussion of each engine, I will include details regarding their structure and function. Specifically, I will argue that through their algorithms, use of cookies, and hierarchical structure of the search engine results, users are placed the on tracts of knowledge. Thus, instead of the interconnectedness of the rhizome, where people interact in "a merger of knowledge capital, social capital, and com-munion" (Rheingold 2000: 109), the Internet becomes a place where the user becomes increasingly ingrained in their experience.

3.3 Analysis

Each of the three Web search engines is similar to the others in their construction and layout. Major differences are in style, algorithm, and extent of database. This analysis will track each of the three Websites (Google, Yahoo!, MSN) through a textual analysis of their display and search functions, their algorithms, and the use of cookies within their browsing functions. Additionally, under the heading of cookies, I will augment my analysis by examining the popular shopping site Amazon.com. Finally, while Web searching offers an expansive amount of information to the individual, the cooptation from corporate commercial activities, especially in the strategic placement of advertising, has altered the Internet's ability to promise a new type of deliberative democracy. In all, the analysis will follow the search process in a step-by-step method to highlight the actual use of search engines: approaching the engine (style and layout), searching (the algorithm), and developing a personal history of searching (cookies).

3.3.1 Style and Layout

The basic layout of search engines presents the user with a predetermined path which inherently limits the nature and number of connections to other individuals. While giving the façade of infinite choices and access, these options merely become leaves on the corporate tree. In approaching each of the three engines, the user will be faced with different layouts and paths; however, each becomes its own isolated group which dare not interact with its competitors. Both Yahoo! and MSN use colorful displays that offer the user a vast array of choices. Before the search has even begun, both sites offer information regarding the latest headlines, special offers from major commercial vendors, and company products, such as chat software and email accounts. Google, by contrast, is simple in its front page, displaying its search area prominently. The text surrounding the search area offers similar products and services, such as company products and advertising information. In the case of MSN and Yahoo!, these front pages offer key gateways into the Internet before the user begins searching. Notably, they begin the tract of knowledge where the user is given categories to guide their search process, such as Yahoo!'s "HotJobs," "Yellow Pages," and "Geocities." These categories begin the user in a direction which keeps them within the Yahoo! knowledge area. For example, a user seeking to join political organizations may approach Yahoo! to seek such information and find the category "Groups" as a place to start. In doing so, however, he or she may limit their interaction solely to other Yahoo! subscribers. Similarly, a user seeking to voice their experiences and opinions may approach MSN's "Spaces" feature, which is similar to a Weblog. Again, while this may provide the Web space necessary to write, it is mediated by the interaction with other MSN related sites and individuals. While the user can distantly interact with people, those people are simply other leaves on the same Yahoo! or MSN tree.

On a similar note to the corporate control over connectivity to other users within home pages, all three search engines frequently and persistently feature advertising within their front pages and search functions. First, Yahoo! displays to users advertising prominently within its front page which often include flashy graphics and sound to entice the casual Web surfer. Companies, such as Dell, American Express, and Ford, have been featured as sponsors of the site. When searching for items through the engine, the results are littered with advertisements, affectionately called "sponsor results," above the actual search return and in a separate column on the right side of the screen. Unfamiliar or inexperienced users may click on these links believing them to be the information requested. Additionally, the difference of the two searches is notable. In my search of the word "computer," the sponsored results included companies such as Dell, Hewlett-Packard, and Toshiba. In the actual search results, Websites included CNET.com, PC World, and ZDNet.com. Arguably, the actual search results can be considered similar in form to the sponsored results; however, on closer inspection, Websites such as CNET.com and PC World are consumer report style magazines which offer customers a wide array of choices of products other than their own. This corporate influence over search engines inherently limits the type and origin of knowledge as users seek out information over the Internet.

MSN and Yahoo! have similar advertising layouts on their search and front pages; however, again, Google's advertising is prominent only after a search is performed. MSN, on its front page, offers links and flashy advertising for an assortment of companies, including Wirefly, Circuit City, and Target. While not as prominent and colorful as Yahoo!, these advertisements are mixed with its search categories in the overall structure of the homepage, giving the appearance that they lead to information rather than product placement. Upon searching for the above search term of "computer," similar results are found to Yahoo!'s advertising, such as Dell and Toshiba. One difference, however, is in the actual results which reference the IEEE Society and Webopedia.com. Google, as argued above, is much different. The initial front page features relatively no advertising outside of Google services. Nevertheless, as the user searches, the results are surrounded by advertising, coincidently Dell, Hewlett-Packard, and Toshiba again appear as sponsored links.

If Web searching dominates the quotidian experiences of Internet behaviors, users are bombarded with advertising and corporate interests. While a comprehensive and quantitative survey of search terms, which could provide more generalizable claims, has not been conducted here, the above analysis sees that the inherent layout of the Web search engine privileges the Web space which has corporate backing rather than the individual. Other conducted searches which would not link to expected corporate sponsors are still featured in the side columns of sponsored links. Thus, the layout of search engines reflects a larger political economy of the Internet. While the digital access divide has been closing (Marriott 2006), the massive corporate control of information recreates the divide by controlling the *type* of information that users find. The Rheingold days of interacting with random users in Multiple User Domains and Internet Relay Chat have been overrun with the Web browser, which allows for marketing information through pop-up ads, sponsored Web links, and corporate self-promotion. The stylistic features of the Web, combined with a hierarchical structure which privileges corporate sponsorship over actual results of the search, create a façade of open and infinite access while only constraining the user to a limited knowledge base.

3.3.2 The Algorithm

Each search engine contains a software algorithm which sorts Webpages in its database and presents an order of return to the user after conducting a search. Inherently, the algorithms are designed to hierarchize data for the user, indicating which pages are more important than others. While style and layout indicate how the viewer receives the results of their search, the algorithm decides which data is most relevant to the search terms provided. While each search engine company hails its own algorithm, the similarities between the three are striking. MSN Search's algorithm "analyzes factors such as Web page content, the number and quality of Websites that link to (pages), and the relevance of (a) Website's content to keywords " ("Site owner help" 2006). Similarly, Yahoo! details their search algorithm process as a combination of Web crawling and indexing: "Web Results are generated from the billions of Web pages discovered, crawled, reviewed, submitted, or otherwise included in the Yahoo! Search index. More than 99% of Web pages in the Yahoo! Search index are included for free through Yahoo!'s Web crawl process" ("Yahoo! help" 2006). In addition to the basic crawling process, Yahoo! also offers a "Content Acquisition Program." This service offers Website owners, for a fee, the ability to feed content into Yahoo!'s database to facilitate searches for their site. While Yahoo! contends that the service does not guarantee placement, it arguably gives an advantage to Web masters with corporate backing and extra cash. On the whole, when combined with the layout of sponsored results, the political economy of search engines favors those with more money by placing them at the top of search results.

Google's PageRank technology is described as relying "on the uniquely democratic nature of the Web by using its vast link structure as an indicator of an individual page's value" ("Google technology" 2004). Along with a description of PageRank, Google offers an integrity statement which informs the user that their automated system is difficult to be tampered with by humans and cannot be bought into. While on the surface this may seem to be a "uniquely democratic " space, the ranking system highlights and decides "important" Websites and affords those sites with better votes for other sites. For example, if Amazon.com is considered an important Website and links to one of its product's homepages (and vice versa), each company's site receives an additional vote as important. As a result, established Web pages are privileged over infrequently visited pages. Combined with Google's "I'm Feeling Lucky" button and prefetching features, users are encouraged to utilize the primary return rather than explore further in the results. The "I'm Feeling Lucky" button sends users directly to the first page in the list and bypasses the search results. Pre-fetching is a service using Mozilla's FireFox browser which automatically begins downloading the first site returned on the search results. As Web surfers build habits in their searching, they are pushed toward using the top returned item in the search by the inherent layout and nature of the algorithm. Given the massive search returns which are impossible to navigate, the hierarchy of data becomes strengthened from the top to bottom. The first page of returns, through these services and inherent layout of the return page, will be valued far more than the second. The final page of returns will rarely be viewed.

Individual users have overcome Google's automated system by exploiting its algorithm in a process known as "Google Bombing." If pages are ranked by both content and the number of links to a specific site, then individuals can flood the links to search terms by adding anchor texts to their own sites. For example, the search term "failure" yields George W. Bush's biography from the White House Website. This is done by other individual sites connecting the URL of the biography to the word "failure" on their site. If the process is repeated by many sites (predominantly Weblogs), Google's crawler picks up on the consistent linking and accordingly ranks the search for failure in connection to the White House ("Google Bomb" 2006). The use of Google Bombs can be interpreted in two ways. First, Google Bombs can be considered a type of humorous activism, and have been effectively used in such a manner. More importantly and second, however, Google Bombs denote the failure of the objective automated algorithm of PageRank. If the system has the means of yielding false returns from searches, its claim to objective (absent of human interference) hierarchies is questionable.

The search algorithms for each of the above engines highlight multiple problems for the notion of a rhizomatic Internet. While the most obvious argument against their rhizomatic construction is the displayed results in the form of a hierarchy of data, their arboreal nature is more intricate than that. First, all of the algorithms use established pages as a tool for hierarchizing their data. As new pages are built on the Internet, the interaction between them is limited to the connection to established sites. As Internet usage continues, popular sites maintain their popularity. In other words, they become the roots for the tree which stems out in the form of hyperlinks. Second, commercial interests, with their ability to pay into services and sponsored results, are also inherently privileged in the search. This recreates the digital divide from the angle of production, where purchasing power dictates the access to personal sites. The commercially sponsored sites are more able to become the roots for other sites and dictate their construction. Finally, the promise of unbiased algorithms devoid of human corruption falls short through their ability to be manipulated. Through the exploitation of hypertext structures, search terms can provide false and politically motivated results. While promising for activism in subverting the hierarchies, the failure of software systems questions the supposed efficacy of the engine.

3.3.3 The Cookie

As software technology progressed, Web searching has included the use of the "cookie " as a means of tracking the user through their searches. Google, in their privacy policies, describes cookies as

> a small file containing a string of characters that is sent to your computer when you visit a Website. We use cookies to improve the quality of our service and to better understand how people interact with us. Google does this by storing user preferences in cookies and by tracking user trends and patterns of how people search. Most browsers are initially set up to accept cookies. ("Google Privacy Center" 2005)

The use of cookies allows search engines to track current search information in order to provide similar future searches. While the process of cookie information gathering seems invisible to the user, there are times when the cookie becomes more apparent. For example, Amazon.com uses cookies to track the types of purchases made by the user. Using two different Web browsers, Mozilla's FireFox and Microsoft's Internet Explorer, I traced the differences between visits to the Amazon.com homepage. In my initial visit with cookies enabled using FireFox, I was given a set of recommendations for purchases, including books by authors I had purchased in the past including Deleuze, Guattari, and Walter Lippmann. Conversely, using Internet Explorer, the opening page at Amazon.com highlighted purchases from various categories including women's apparel, iPods, and cellular phones. Between the two browsers, not a single product or recommendation was the same. Additionally, Amazon.com recommends specific products to the recognized user and also offers special deals in the form of the "Gold Box." The Gold Box offers a time-constrained additional discount to the user. In order to activate this feature, the user must sign in with an email address and relevant information, including name and birthday. In investigating the Gold Box with and without cookies enabled, the non-cookie browser yielded broad results without specific markings of preference, including popular books, software, and films on DVD. In the cookie enabled Gold Box, however, the results provided products suitable to my political leaning, leisure activities, and professional interests. While this analysis seems to simply highlight my shopping preferences, given that Amazon.com is the largest online retailer for literature, the ramifications for knowledge production become increasingly lucid.

Cookies, being that they invisibly exist in the background of the search, are arguably the most detrimental to the rhizome. As users seek out information, their browser settings become trained to produce results which are already attractive. If I seek out new knowledge and information to purchase from Amazon.com, I am less likely to be presented with philosophies or arguments about the world which challenge my existing belief structure. As will be discussed further, the Deleuzean notion of interference is critical to the production of knowledge. Being presented with competing interpretations and views allows the rhizome to grow in new directions. Rather than the growth of rhizomes, cookies create tracts in which the user will continue to progress through the Web. Much like the hierarchies of information with sponsorships resting on top, this knowledge tract keeps the user confined within a set of experiences and interactions. The cookie will gather data regarding literature and relevant searches and in turn produce similar results. The more often I click on Wikipedia or CNN.com, the more often that Webpage will be higher on my results. In other words, the more I search, the more limiting and defined my searching becomes. Upon reaching the massive and intersecting connections of the Internet, the user plants a seed in the form of the cookie, which grows over time to become their personal tree. While hypertextual environments continue to carry the structural features of the rhizome, where one text can link to the other in random and intersecting ways, these intersecting points begin on one plane or tree.

3.4 Implications

In their original writings regarding the rhizome and subsequent discussions of the nature of philosophy and knowledge, Deleuze and Guattari (1987) conceptualize the human brain as rhizomatic. They argue that knowledge and philosophy has remained entranced with trees. "We're tired of trees. We should stop believing in trees, roots, and radicles. They've made us suffer too much. All of arborescent culture is founded on them, from biology to linguistics" (p.15). Instead, the rhizome offers a way of approaching knowledge and the mind as possibility and potential. Schuh and Cunningham (2004) engage the notion of the rhizome as a metaphor of the mind which "prompts us to seek relationships where a researcher may typically assume that there are none. It values the connections between in-school learning and out-of-school learning as viewed by each individual based upon his/her own personal trajectories as he/she interacts in all learning situations" (p. 339). The conceptualization opens experience to becoming and interacts with other systems and disciplines in unexpected ways.

At the culmination of *What is Philosophy?*, Deleuze and Guattari (1994) implicate their construction of the planes of immanence (philosophy), reference (science), and composition (art) by arguing that the brain is a junction of the three. At this junction, the planes interfere with each other, providing the means for new knowledge. This interference, much like the interconnectedness and limitless border of the rhizome, has the potential to open new avenues of becoming. New communication technology, and the early theory surrounding it, called forth this interference. As individuals interacted at great distances in Rheingold's virtual community, they interfered with each others' beliefs, opinions, and planes. However, as search engines have become the predominant form of access to the Internet, the companies which manage these systems provide a pre-packaged experience to the user. The terms have been set; tracts already built. As the user becomes more defined through their digital ID card (cookie), she or he become rewarded for continuing on the commercial path already laid forth by their own search history. Even the ability to seek out and purchase literature at the premier vendor at Amazon.com becomes increasingly defined by purchase history and preferences.

While hypertext, as a language, may carry rhizomatic potential, the frequent use of and reliance upon search engines as a gateway into the Internet keeps this potential at bay. As Deleuze and Guattari (1987) warn: "Once a rhizome has been obstructed, arborified, it's all over, no desire stirs; for it is always by rhizome that desire moves and produces" (p. 14). If cyberspace had existed as a rhizome of possibility where random individuals interact and intersect with others, the use of search engines to impose an order upon the massive amounts of information has constrained our desire. From the early promises of a new democratic order, the Internet has become arborified. The newly grown trees are especially apparent in the algorithmic structures of Web search engines, which chart the Web under the façade of a map with many entry points, but only becomes a tracing of those who pay or play into the system. Starting a search at Yahoo! privileges those who pay entry into the Yahoo! database. As the user navigates the map, the unidirectional signs point toward those with wealth and power. If users find entry through Google, which promises results without human tampering, the flaws in the system are displayed through politically motivated manipulations. On the whole, the potential for both the interference of knowledge through competing disciplinary lines of flight and the embodiment of resistance to dominant capitalist structures, are severely mitigated as the user becomes increasingly ingrained into their own experiences.

Rather than believing that the system is bankrupt, I offer this chapter as a cautionary tale. As new media critical theorists approach the Internet for theory, examinations of the quotidian and vernacular use of the Internet rather than its ultimate potential should be considered. While individuals such as Stefan Wray have been able to utilize the Web for electronic civil disobedience, this potential is not realized by every user. If 60 million users approach search engines daily for their gateway into the Web, considerations of their experiences must be analyzed. In this chapter, through an analysis of the everyday use of the Internet, the rhizomatic structure appears to have grown trees of predetermined experiences in which knowledge itself is limited at the end of its branches. Web search engines, while convenient and technologically sophisticated, also present philosophic barriers to our growth as humans. The changes in use of the Web from Bulletin Board Systems, MUDs, and IRC, have brought forth the cooptation of the digital realm by those with more wealth and power. Recognizing the recreation of the digital divide from the angle of production is a vital step in scholarly work on cyberculture. As daily use of search engines is likely to rise, critical scholarship should engage these gateway systems to question their promise of democratic informatics.

In a similar vein, future research in to the Internet should locate and demystify the romantic notions of its promise as a democratic medium. While the potential for the Internet to have profound effects on the distribution of information to mass audiences, the commercial takeover of production, reception, and distribution has fundamentally altered the digital landscape. Research should also investigate hacktivist groups, such as the Critical Art Ensemble, as they perform acts of electronic civil disobedience. The limits upon expression, access, and production, through tools such as search engines, should be opened to critical inquiry and debate. At a fundamental level, rather than seeing the Internet as a site of radical democracy, scholars should approach new media studies to observe and deconstruct the ongoing capitalist expansion through cyberspace.

3.5   Conclusion

While the Internet continues to move and morph through technological moments, its presence and prevalence will only continue to impact the lives of millions. As fundamental functions of daily life move online, critical theorists and scholars of new media should be wary of its power and use. To believe that one device, however expansive it may be, can serve as a panacea to the ailments of democracy underestimates the power of capitalist expansion. Web searching, which provides access points to billions of documents to 60 million users daily, cannot be overlooked as a benign entry point into the Web. Rather, Web search engines have become critical gatekeepers to the vast knowledges contained within digital databases across the globe. Through the organization of the sea of Webpages, Web search engines simplify and structure information into tracts. While convenient, these tracts continue to preclude our ability to generate new means of knowing through the interaction and interference between random users of the Internet.

References

Best S, Kellner D (1991) Postmodern theory: critical interrogations. The Guiliford Press, New York

Brande D (1996) The business of cyberpunk: symbolic economy and ideology in William Gibson. In: Markley R (ed) Virtual realities and their discontents. Johns Hopkins Press, Baltimore, pp 79–106

Buchstein H (1997) Bytes that bite: the Internet and deliberative democracy. Constellations 4: 248–263

Calleja G, Schwager C (2004) Rhizomatic cyborgs: hypertextual considerations in a posthuman age. Technoetic Arts: A Journal of Speculative Research 2: 3–15

Deleuze G, Guattari F (1987) A thousand plateaus: capitalism and schizophrenia (Massumi B trans). University of Minnesota Press, Minneapolis

Deleuze G, Guattari F (1994) What is philosophy? (Tomlinson H, Burchell G trans). Columbia University Press, New York

Felix K (2006) Search engine use climbs. MultiMedia & Internet@Schools 13: 7

Google Bomb (2006) Wikipedia. http://en.wikipedia.org/wiki/Google_bomb. Cited 20 July 2006

Google Privacy Center: Privacy Policy (2005) Google.com. http://www.google.com/privacy_archive.html. Cited 7 July 2006

Google technology (2004) Google.com. http://www.google.com/technology/index.html. Cited 20 July 2006

Hamman RB (1996 May 28) Rhizome@Internet. Cybersociology Magazine. http://www.socio.demon.co.uk/rhizome.html. Cited 3 July 2006

Harmon A (1998 Oct 31) 'Hacktivists' of all persuasions take their struggle to the Web. New York Times. A1

Landow GP (2006) Hypertext 3.0: critical theory and new media in an era of globalization. Johns Hopkins University Press, Baltimore

Lemos A (1996) The labyrinth of minitel. In: Shields R (ed) Cultures of Internet: virtual spaces, real histories, living bodies. Sage Publications, London, pp 33–48

Markley R (1996) Boundaries: mathematics, alienation, and the metaphysics of cyberspace. In: Markley R (ed) Virtual realities and their discontents. Johns Hopkins Press, Baltimore, pp 55–77

Marriott M (2006 March 31) Blacks turn to Internet highway, and digital divide starts to close. New York Times. A1.

Mater MA (2001) A structural transformation for a global public sphere? the use of new communication technologies by nongovernmental organizations and the United Nations. In: Asen R, Brouwer DC (eds) Counterpublics and the state. State University of New York Press, Albany, pp 211–234

McDorman TF (2001) Crafting a virtual counterpublic: right-to-die advocates on the Internet. In: Asen R, Brouwer DC (eds) Counterpublics and the state. State University of New York Press, Albany, pp 187–211

Moulthrop S (1991) The politics of hypertext. In: Hawisher GE, Selfe CL (eds) Evolving perspectives on computers and composition studies: questions for the 1990s. National Council of Teachers of English, Urbana, IL, pp 253–274

Moulthrop S (1994) Rhizome and resistance: hypertext and the dreams of a new culture. In: Landow GP (ed) Hyper/Text/Theory. Johns Hopkins Press, Baltimore, pp 299–319

Owens L, Palmer LK (2003) Making the news: anarchist counter–public relations on the World Wide Web. Critical Studies in Media Communication, 20: 335–361

Palczewski CH (2001) Cyber-movements, new social movements, and counterpublics. In: Asen R, Brouwer DC (eds) Counterpublics and the state. State University of New York Press, Albany, pp 161–186

Resnick D (1998) Politics on the Internet: the normalization of cyberspace. In: Toulouse C, Luke T (eds) The politics of cyberspace. Routledge, New York, pp 48–68

Rheingold H (1993) The virtual community: homesteading on the electronic frontier. Addison-Wesley Pub. C., Reading, MA

Rheingold H (2000) The virtual community: homesteading on the electronic frontier. MIT, Cambridge

Roper J (1998) New Zealand political parties online: the world wide web as a tool for democratization or for political marketing? In: Toulouse C, Luke T (eds) The politics of cyberspace. Routledge, New York, pp 69–83

Rosenberg ME (1994) Physics and hypertext: liberation and complicity in art and pedagogy. In: Landow GP (ed) Hyper/Text/Theory. Johns Hopkins Press, Baltimore, pp 269–298

Schuh KL, Cunningham DJ (2004 May) Rhizome and the mind: describing the metaphor. Semiotica, 149: 325–342

Shields R (1996) Cultures of Internet: virtual spaces, real histories, living bodies. Sage Publications, London

Site owner help: about website ranking (2006) Microsoft. http://search.msn.com/docs/siteowner.aspx?t=SEARCH_WEBMASTER_CONC_AboutSiteRanking.htm. Cited 20 July 2006

Streck J (1998) Pulling the plug on electronic town meetings: participatory democracy and the reality of Usenet. In: Toulouse C, Luke T (eds) The politics of cyberspace. Routledge, New York, pp 18–47

Taylor PA (2005) From hackers to hacktivists: speed bumps on the global superhighway? New Media and Society 7: 625–646

Thomas J (2005) The moral ambiguity of social control in cyberspace: a retro-assessment of the 'Golden Age' of hacking. New Media and Society 7: 599–624

Van der Klei A (2002) Repeating the rhizome. SubStance 31: 48–55

Wray S (1998 July 7) Rhizomes, nomads, and resistant Internet use. http://www.thing.net/%7Erdom/ecd/rhizomatic.html. Cited 3 July 2006

Yahoo! help – Search (2006) Yahoo! Inc. http://help.yahoo.com/help/us/ysearch/basics/basics-03.html. Cited 20 July 2006

4
Exploring Gendered Notions:
Gender, Job Hunting and Web Searches

R.M. Martey

Summary Based on analysis of a series of interviews, this chapter suggests that in looking for jobs online, women confront gendered notions of the Internet as well as gendered notions of the jobs themselves. It argues that the social and cultural contexts of both the search tools and the search tasks should be considered in exploring how Web-based technologies serve women in a job search. For these women, the opportunities and limitations of online job-search tools were intimately related to their personal and social needs, especially needs for part-time work, maternity benefits, and career advancement. Although job-seeking services such as Monster.com were used frequently by most of these women, search services did not completely fulfill all their informational needs, and became an – often frustrating – initial starting point for a job search rather than an end-point.

4.1 Introduction

As a resource, the Internet has risen in importance in women's search for a job. The Pew Project on the Internet and American Life reports that about 42% of US women users look for jobs online, and about 48% use the Internet to look for job-related information (Fallows 2005). Women make up about half the Internet user population, and the specific issues they confront in various types of use deserve attention. The use of online job-seeking resources is influenced both by general search skills and comfort with Internet technologies, as well as by notions of gender proscriptions about those technologies and about jobs. While crucial to search experiences, skills with the Internet and with search engines are only part of the online job-seeking process. Investigations of online job seeking are enhanced by a contextualized perspective that takes into account understandings of the technology, of the specific search interface, and of the job being sought. For women job-seekers, these understandings include notions about gender proscriptions on technology use and on search options and techniques, as well as about gender divisions in the labor market.

In her decades of research on information-seeking behaviour and outcomes, Carol Kuhlthau has emphasized that the relationships among search contexts,

A. Spink and M. Zimmer (eds.), *Web Search, Springer Series in Information Science and Knowledge Management 14.*
© Springer-Verlag Berlin Heidelberg 2008

outcomes and tools should be understood from a process-oriented perspective that takes into account the perceptions users have of their goals, the search tools, and themselves. While these perceptions are surely as varied as individuals themselves, scholars have identified patterns in the use of Internet tools that differentiate some groups from others, including along racial, class, and gender lines. In particular, differences between men's and women's perceptions of the Internet have received considerable attention from scholars for the past several decades. Scholars such as Susan Herring, Sherrie Turkle, and Leslie Regen Shade have noted that women have been largely shut out of the culture, use and development of the Internet, in spite of recent increases in the proportion of women users world-wide.

From this perspective, this chapter asks, what are women's main considerations and perceptions of using the Internet as part of a job search? How do commercial online job-search services like Monster.com, CareerBuilder.com, or Hotjobs.com perform for women looking for jobs? To begin exploring these questions, this chapter approaches an online job search from two perspectives: 1) as an information-seeking activity, examining women's notions of search activities and tools; and 2) as a socio-economic activity, examining women's notions of the jobs they seek. These analyses are grounded in the literature on gendered associations with the Internet.

This investigation analyzes the results of twenty interviews with women using the Internet to look for jobs. Conducted in the major United States city of Philadelphia, PA, during the spring of 2005 with women job seekers over the age of 30, these guided interviews pursue women's specific thoughts, feelings, and perceptions of the Internet, online job-seeking, and jobs in general, in the context of being a woman. Especially because there is almost no literature on gender and online job-seeking, these interviews contribute important insights into the considerations, perceptions, and feelings women have about this process. The words of participants in the study provide evidence that gender can influence looking for a job online.

Importantly, this chapter does not assume that access to – or expert use of – new technologies is in any way a cause of socioeconomic opportunity. Rather, technology can be a resource in the pursuit of opportunity, along with a range of other resources, including educational achievement, social networks, monetary resources, marketable skills, psychological and cognitive abilities, etc. From that perspective, understanding the influence of gender on Web searches can contribute to assessments of new technologies as resources for women.

This research is part of a larger project that examines both gendered notions of the job-search process as well as a quantitative analysis of specific search behaviour. Although the present chapter does not include an exploration of the impact of specific search behaviour (e.g., patterns in search style, search moves, number of jobs found, satisfaction with a search, etc.), it is important to note that considerations of the Internet as a job-search tool are enhanced by considerations about the specific skills, experiences, and activities in which seekers engage, and are explored elsewhere by the author.

4.2 The Gendered Context of the Internet

In recent decades, theories of information-seeking have embraced process-oriented models (Detlor 2003; Kuhlthau 1993). These approaches emphasize the ways that seekers make sense of information as it is assimilated into their mental models and knowledge structures. For example, cognitive models of information-seeking argue that "any processing of information, whether perceptual or symbolic, is mediated by a system of categories or concepts that, for the information-processing device, are a model of his world." (de Mey 1977: xvi–xvii). Processes-oriented models are fundamentally concerned with achieving deeper insight into information behavior by understanding an individual's knowledge structures and personality characteristics and the effects these have on information seeking and processing (Belkin 1990). From this perspective, gendered associations of the tools individuals use in information-seeking influence the search process from its initiation throughout the tasks pursued and perceptions of the information retrieved and used. As a job-seeking tool, the Internet can be understood in the context of its gendered associations.

Feminist scholars point to the Internet as a technology strongly influenced by gender associations – a 'gendered' technology (Herring 2003; Scott et al. 2001; Shade 2004). In this view, 'gendered' things are such because their design, structure, control, and use are influenced by culture, whether intentionally or unintentionally. Since the 1980s, feminist scholars have been empirically examining the influence of gender on the culture, use, and development of Internet technologies, concluding that women were largely shut out of this domain (Herring 1994; Morhan-Martin 2000; Shade 2004; Turkle 1988; Wilder et al. 1985).

Studies have found that women have been practically and symbolically marginalized in the use and development of computer and Internet technologies. Over time, these gender messages accumulate to encourage men and women to view computing tasks as masculine in nature (Wilder et al. 1985; Williams et al. 1993). Overall, research on computing tasks has repeatedly shown that boys and men have more favorable attitudes toward computers (Durndell and Haag 2002; Ogletree and Williams 1990; Sherman et al. 2000), view computers as a career asset (Nickell et al. 1987; Venkatesh et al. 2004), and demonstrate greater interest (Krendel et al. 1989) and participation (Clark and Chambers 1989; Morhan-Martin 2000; Venkatesh and Morris 2000) than women. The current environment of the Internet also has associations with men: fears about "cyber stalking" of women and girls (Adam 2001); women's marginalization in social forums like chat rooms and bulletin boards (Herring 2003); and the predominance, importance and concerns over male-oriented pornography in content and revenue generation (Onyejekwe 2005).

Some of the concerns about gender associations with the Internet have be assuaged by a steady increase in the number of women online. With the advancement of the Web, the proportion of women Internet users rose steadily, until about half were female at the end of 2000. Chirieac et al. (2001) identified changes in gender-based perceptions toward the Internet as related technologies become more essential to the workplace, businesses, and daily life. Recent data from the Pew Internet and American Life survey (Fallows 2005) suggest that women continue to increase their involvement in a range of Internet activities, especially community-building ones like email and family-oriented services. It found that women are more likely to use the Internet for email than men are, but that men have higher overall levels of expertise and a wider breadth of knowledge of the available tools and services online (Fallows 2004).

These findings suggest gendered patterns in use and interest, even as women's access to and experience in Internet technologies become equal with men's. Howard (2004) explains that this is because, "[c]ommunication technologies became deeply embedded in personal lives very quickly, mediating our interactions with other people and the way in which we learn about our world" (2001: 2). Dervin (1998) emphasizes the importance of context in perceptions of information generally and in information-seeking tasks in specific. She notes that, "structure, culture, community, organization are created, maintained, reified, challenged, changed, resisted, and destroyed in communication and can only be understood by focusing on the individual-in-context, including social context" (Dervin 1998: 7). The intersection of women's lives and their job-seeking activities is also a deeply personal one. Understanding the constructions women have of the available tools, processes, and options in a job search is crucial to understanding relationships among gender, search technologies, and women's search processes.

4.3   Online Job Seeking as an Information-Seeking Activity

Job seeking can be viewed as an information-seeking activity, where as Kuhlthau (1993) suggests, user thoughts, feelings, beliefs, and cognition about themselves and about the search task are crucial to the process. In women's online job-search, social, cultural, psychological, and personal factors are crucial influences on the search process.

4.3.1   Gender and Information-Seeking

Although a considerable body of work is developing in the exploration of the relationships between psychological and cognitive factors and information seeking, only recently have studies exploring the relationships between gender and information-seeking styles emerged in the literature. Most of the research examines students from elementary school through college, however, and very little addresses adult populations. Some studies address gender differences from a gender/sex classification perspective (Ford et al. 2001), or from a broad Internet use perspective (Herring 1994; Kennedy et al. 2003; Shade 2004), while others examine gender roles and cognitive factors (Fan and Macredie 2006; Roy and Chi 2003).

The research on gender and information-seeking has generally found that males and females demonstrate somewhat different navigation patterns and different learning outcomes, as well has different preferences for specific interfaces (Fan and Macredie 2006; Large et al. 2002). These differences have been related to gendered associations with the medium (Ford et al. 2001) or with the software (Bhargava 2002). Reed and Oughton (1997) examined the navigation patterns of male and female graduate students at three distinct stages of search. They found that women were more linear at initial stages than men, but less linear than men overall. Roy and Chi (2003) examined search patterns among eighth-graders and found that boys tended to search more horizontally, sifting through larger number of pages, while girls searched more vertically, examining a given page or site more thoroughly. Large et al. (1999) similarly found that boys spent less time viewing individual pages and preferred a broader search strategy than girls. Large et al. (2002) later confirmed that boys were more actively engaged in browsing, jumped to more pages, and entered more searches at search engines than girls.

Although gender differences in information-seeking are not the focus of this analysis, the literature suggests that gender contextualizes the perceptions and activities of women job-seekers, especially in their search style. Borgman et al. (1996) note that "we need to understand more about which aspects of searching behaviour are universal and that are situation-specific, if we are to design information systems to serve an increasingly heterogeneous user population with increasingly diverse sets of information needs" (1996: 581).

4.3.2 Information-Seeking Online: Job-Search Tools

For the women interviewed, the Internet was an important resource in their job search. These women employed a range of techniques to use the Internet; for some, it was the focus of their search, while for others it supplemented other methods. Almost all the women in this study had used the Internet at some time to look for jobs, although their experiences with and assessment of the Internet as a job-search tool varied greatly. For some, the Internet was their primary access to job listings, while for others it was a dead end. Using a combination of newspapers, the Internet, and "pounding the pavement" with direct company inquiries was most common. A few women also used recruiters or job placement services. Two of the respondents had never used the Internet to look for jobs, even though they were comfortable online. They both explained that it was simply not their preferred way to look for jobs and that the newspaper felt more comfortable.

The themes that emerged from their descriptions of search techniques suggest that the Internet is perceived by these women in very different ways. Several women described the way the Internet opened up new worlds and provided opportunities and information they wouldn't have found otherwise. Some women explained that an important aspect of searching for jobs online was how well the

Internet fit their particular search style. Others described the ways that using the Internet made them more productive.

Many women felt the Internet opened up new possibilities in a job search, as suggested by Salaff et al. (2005), as well as Kleit (2002). Serena used the Internet to cast her resume into the waters in the hopes that someone would bite, because, "you've got to put a lot of lines out there, working on the law of averages." Freda used automatic agents to send her new job listings in specified categories, and she found new possibilities for herself and even for job-seeking friends. She found Websites dedicated to her field, Reiki healing, that helped her explore a range of possibilities and "just gave me such great hope, like wow, there's a place right here in the city, and I wouldn't have known about it". Anna explained that she was frustrated with the large commercial job-search sites, but that she could use them as starting points to explore the homepages of the organizations that interested her. Kara described the Internet as helping her find a range of possibilities, and making "the world seem so much bigger". Mary felt the Internet was the most comprehensive way to search for jobs because, "I think better companies don't advertise in the paper anymore; those are kind of low-level jobs...I really don't think there's a better way."

For Pam, the Internet was a great way to actually perform her job and "open up a lot more possibilities" for finding clients and jobs. She said, "the Internet was terrific, I couldn't have done the job [without it]." Miranda felt that because the Internet gave her access to more information about a company or a job, it gave her advantages as a woman, as well. From one company's Website, for example, she found that, "the staff is all women, so I figure my chances are probably better of working there, because they have all women, and maybe that type of place is more geared towards women."

The extent to which the Internet fit respondents' search style was important to many of them. Renata described her use of the Internet for a job search as a "love–hate relationship". She felt "kind of dependent on those Websites, like a security blanket" but also found the Internet frustrating because of the size of sites like Monster.com. She explained that, "I didn't like the fact that you have to specify categories, and that there was no other way to search it...then you have to go through it page by page." Anna, the art teacher, felt job-search sites were too general and too often outdated, and Serena, looking for a job that did not require a commute, found it difficult to specify jobs in the right location because "none of their search systems are really very good." She did note, however, that "A really big advantage of searching the Internet [with sites like Monster.com] is they do have very long ads, so instead of those four-line ads, they have [links to the companies], which is a much easier way to figure out what's going on." As a writer just starting out with a new career, Pam didn't view the major job-search sites online as good resources for someone of her experience level because, "things like Monster. com...weren't specialized enough, so they weren't really helping me out." Mary used the Internet and sites like Monster.com nearly every week because "there could be some great marketing job I didn't even know about", but she still considered large job sites a poor resource because, "there's really no filter for searching out better jobs versus almost entry level jobs."

Looking for jobs online, even with its drawbacks, helped some women feel more productive in their searches. Danielle explained that the convenience and variety of online searches Internet helped her, "Even if [I'm] not fully focused on doing the search every day, [I] can at least feel like [I'm] doing something every day when [I] check [my] e-mail." Alice described how the Internet helped her feel more accomplished in her search because it was so convenient, and, "just the fact that I'm sending out my resume, and getting it out that day, gives me a feeling of accomplishment; I got it out, and maybe I'll hear something good." Kara noted that the Internet saved her time in her search by helping her eliminate jobs she wouldn't be interested in. The downside for her, however, was that it was too large and, "it isn't personal; so they don't know who's really contacting them, they can't see you, hear you, or whatever the case may be. Sometimes there's just no response, so you don't know if it's lost out there in no man's land, if they got it, or didn't get it." Rachel felt as though the Internet could have helped her job search, but that she needed more training to be truly effective and that "my searches are hit and miss; like I try a bunch of things, and if one works, then I go for it, but I don't know what I did that made it work."

Women's considerations of the Internet as a job-search tool were varied. Some felt it increased opportunities, while others found the interface did not sufficiently accommodate their search needs. For these women, individual constructions of the Internet as a job-search resources resulted in different types of use. In particular, some women felt that services like Monster.com did not provide sufficient information for their needs, and thus use a diversity of online tools in their job search. The specific search tasks these women undertook were thus strongly related to their perceptions of how well the available tools served their needs.

4.3.3 Gender and Online Search Tools

As a job-search resource, the Internet was both a great tool and a source of frustration. When asked to consider how the Internet might or might not help women in particular with a job search, most of these respondents expressed a sense that the Internet played a special role for women. In particular, finding the right information for women's needs in a job search was a concern among respondents.

Many of the respondents described the Internet as less effective for women because of the kinds of information that was emphasized. For example, Danielle felt that the Internet did not tend to offer women as much of what they were looking for in terms of job information because of its culture. She explained,

> Just looking at stereotypes, I would say that [job-search Websites] are probably designed more for men, because when you're looking at job listings as a woman, you want to know more information about benefits. You also want to know the qualifications for the job and the background of the company up front, but it's really important, I think, for women to look at benefits; we need the health insurance. We need to know that the company is offering decent benefits there. We might need maternity benefits, or have some idea of a more comprehensive benefits package as we're looking at jobs and looking at companies.

Similarly, Miranda was frustrated with the lack of part-time positions listed online – a kind of job, she explained that was particularly important for her as a new mother. She only found a few sites that had options for her. She explained that she had to go to a range of job-search Websites just to find a few job options that would fit her needs. Monster.com in particular, she noted, was not a good place to look, because "I never expect to see anything part-time on there that's professional."

Some women felt that the Internet did offer some of the information and services women needed. Freda explains that Websites designed especially for women can be helpful, and have the kind of information women need, like:

> …things about how to address sexism in the workplace and in job hunting, questions that are legal to ask during the interviewing process, what to even ask for about different policies and procedures and benefits that are offered through companies to get a sense of how women-friendly they are, how family-friendly they are, and how updated the company is in their policies in regards to sexism and harassment, and things like that.

Freda added that by finding out "red flag" information online, women could also avoid making certain impressions like, as she put it, "uh-oh, here comes somebody who might be a potential troublemaker."

Miranda felt that because the Internet gave her access to more information about a company or a job, it gave her advantages as a woman. She explained that figuring out how many women work at a specific company gives her a sense of her chances of getting hired. She described one experience, "[I] looked at the staff. The staff is all women, so I figure my chances are probably better of working there, because they have all women, and maybe that type of place is more geared towards women"

According to, Mary, women have slightly different needs as workers than men, and companies using the Internet to post job descriptions can address those needs better. She said that, "especially for women, half of it is [matching] the skill set, but half of it is the environment, and if in that [job] description, like when a company's one of those best companies to work for, or if they talked about giving you your birthday off, or something, you would say, 'gee, there's a company that pays well, has a good job, but really cares about people.'"

Freda explained that the Internet could open up concerns that her gender would become part of the screening process in the search itself. She explained,

> Sometimes I wonder when they ask for gender, if that's going to affect the availability of listings. That's the only impression I get sometimes, is like it's not like it's not an option, like some of the information is optional, but they want to know specifically what your gender is, or it won't process the request to sign up for the search without it, so I kind of wonder.

The themes that emerged from these women's discussions of the relationships between their gender and an online job search include both advantages and disadvantages. Although many expressed notions of the Internet as a masculine space, it remained an important tool in their job search. Feelings of frustration with the search interface or a masculinized culture were off-set in many cases by notions of increased opportunities and options available online. Concerns these respondents saw as specific to women played a role in their assessment of Internet job searches, including the need for more information about job benefits and work environment.

4.4 Job-Seeking as Socio-Economic Activity

Job-seeking can also be viewed as a socio-economic activity, in which considerations of market forces and self-assessments of labor market value are relevant. In a job search, women's considerations of their employment options, necessary information, market conditions, and employability are affected by gender associations with industries, positions, and firms.

4.4.1 Gender in Jobs and Job Seeking

Considerable research has concluded that gender stereotypes in occupations exist among both employers and job-seekers (Mintz and Krymkowski 2005; Shinar 1975). Field studies have shown that gender segregation is common, even for occupations that seem to be integrated across organizations or industries (Baron et al. 1991; Reskin and Hartmann 1986). Occupational stereotyping has been found to be related to assumptions about men's and women's personality traits, including gender roles (Cejka and Eagly 1999; Lippa and Connelly 1990). Certain jobs are thought to require feminine characteristics (e.g. nurse, teacher, secretary); others are thought to require masculine ones (e.g. engineer, construction worker, doctor, mechanic) (Beggs and Doolittle 1993; Shinar 1975). These associations have an important affect on women's views of their job opportunities. For example, Mintz and Krymkowski (2005) found that women are less likely to enter occupations that are stereotyped as male, and several scholars have found that women perceive male-dominated workplaces as likely to be more discriminatory towards them (Gatton et al. 1999; Moss 2004). These findings suggest that the gender coding of a job influences women's interest in and comfort with it.

Women's perceptions of the likelihood they will be offered a job may also play a role in perceptions of job-seeking, especially given the notion that employers have definite preferences for men in the higher paying, higher prestige (i.e., male dominated) occupations (Reskin and Roos 1990), or in male-dominated workplaces (Gatton et al. 1999). Additional factors such as the social construction of job categories by firms themselves, including gender -biased wording and images in want ads, can attract or discourage women applicants (Fernandez and Sosa 2005; Gatton et al. 1999). Even the method used in a job search has been found by some to influence women's chances on the job market and their likelihood of entering female-dominated jobs, where use of social networks reinforces occupational gender segregation (Saks and Ashforth 1999). These factors contextualize women's job-seeking activities, influencing their perceptions of options. As Kuhlthau (1993) suggests, understandings of the information retrieved in a job search have an iterative effect on the approaches and processes women engage while searching.

4.4.2   Gendered Expectations in Jobs

Many of the women interviewed expressed a sense that certain jobs were more associated with men, while others were associated with women. Participants noted that especially jobs concerning engineering, computers, and manual labor were surrounded by the assumption that men are better at them, more interested in them, and more likely to work in them. Jobs that had supportive or caring roles, on the other hand, were more associated with women for participants. Teachers, secretaries, and service organizations like non-profit community services were generally dominated by women, they noted.

Alice explained that as a computer software teacher, people probably expected her to be male. She described the typical image of a computer teacher as someone young and male, and that, "the students were expecting someone different when I went in there – they weren't expecting me." She went on to explain that she thought about her gender a lot when applying for jobs because, "if they're going to hire a hardware teacher, they're going to hire a male, and I've seen that, even depending on somebody's credentials." Being female was a limitation, she noted, to performing as an instructor in a technical school.

Even for participants working in more gender neutral occupations, gendered associations with technology divided the kinds of work women did. Pam, who was beginning a career in writing, described how certain kinds of writing were still subject to gender expectations. She felt that, "if women wanted to get into really technical kinds of writing like writing about computers, writing about financial things, things that are dominated by white males, in that respect it might be a little harder [for women]." For Pam, the gendered associations with computers and finance made looking for and finding a job in those areas more of a challenge than writing about more neutral subjects like healthcare. Similarly, Mary said that companies like her former employment – an electronics equipment manufacturer – simply did not have as many women because it was largely populated by engineers who, she said, "have tended to be men, and engineers who've really [risen] to a position of management tend to be men." Mary felt that this resulted in prejudice about whether or not women would be good employees, and that even in her area of marketing, women were less likely to be hired than men.

For some participants, it was not the overall field or industry that was male dominated, but rather the level of the position. Danielle explained that there were many women at lower, but not management, positions in her field, human resources. She described human resources as highly female dominated at lower levels, but noted that in management, most positions were filled by men. She wondered, "if it's so female dominated at this lower level, why isn't it more female dominated at a higher level?" There was no question, she said, that, "the glass ceiling still exists…for not just women, but minorities, as well."

Some women noted that assumptions about women made it easier to find a job in certain areas. Mary's description of the female domination of human resources support staff was echoed by several women in other fields. Anna, the art teacher, explained that as a woman, her chances of getting a teaching job would be better than for a man, because "a large percentage of the teachers are women, and I think that the idea they had was that the position would be filled by a woman." Moreover, she commented, an art teacher is not taken very seriously. She said, "I would say that an art teacher, especially, probably brings a woman to mind...[and] somebody flaky, more laid-back, maybe spacier, not always taken as seriously."

Renata, the proposal writer, explained her profession was largely made up of women. She felt that it might be easier for a woman to find work, but not as easy to get paid well, because "grant writing is obviously mostly for social service organizations and places like that, that tend to have a lot of women involved in them." This was particularly true, she noted, because grant-writing was associated with administrative work in many organizations, and, "of course, everyone thinks of secretaries as women."

June, who worked as a "virtual" secretary after retiring from being an executive assistant for 35 years, did not believe that most people would be interested in hiring a man to be an assistant. She explained that as an executive assistant, being female was part of the expectation of the job. She felt women have an easier time getting work in secretarial jobs than men because of the service role assistants play to the largely male bosses. She noted that,

> ... most of the [secretaries] are women anyway, it's not like they're looking for a man to fulfill the role. Which, of course, brings up the interesting point, is that they're not looking for a man because they can't quite boss a man around like they'll [boss a woman].

Serena also felt that her gender fit the expectation of her position in a bank. For her, the link was related to the lower salary her position paid. She explained that, "in both of my financial [jobs], where it was mostly female, I would actually say I do kind of think it was female, but only for one reason; because the salaries were not that great, to be honest."

The conceptualizations of the jobs these women were exploring had an important influence on their job-seeking activities. Notions of gendered associations with certain jobs affected these women's view of the landscape of occupational information. They considered some jobs more accessible, while others carried substantive barriers. These assumptions affected their feelings about their search, as well as about their chances for employment in a given area. For these women, gendered associations with certain jobs were powerful cultural forces that contextualized the use of the search tools and tasks with which they engaged.

4.5 Future Directions

This chapter explores the notion that in looking for jobs online, women confront gendered notions of the Internet as well as gendered notions of the jobs themselves. It suggests that the gendered context of both the search tools and the search tasks should be considered in understanding how Web-based technologies serve women in a job search. For these women, the opportunities and limitations of online job-search tools were intimately related to their personal and social needs, especially needs for part-time work, maternity benefits, and career advancement. Although job-seeking services such as Monster.com were used frequently by most of these women, their search options and structure did not completely fulfill all their informational needs. These search services were an – often frustrating – initial starting point for a job-search rather than an end-point.

As Dervin (1998) argues, making sense of options, content, and encounters in an information search is fundamental to finding what women are seeking. Liu (1995) emphasizes the overall cultural experience of information seeking, and urges that "[information-seeking] behaviour must be viewed within the context of end-users' cultural experience" (1995: 132). Gender is one of the most pervasive and powerful social and cultural contexts in which individuals view themselves and the world around them (Bem 1993), and upon which individuals draw to guide their behaviour (Deaux and Major 1987; Eagly 1987). It is, therefore, a crucial framework for investigations of contextualized information-seeking.

More generally, notions of gender are important in other information-seeking tasks, particularly where the task itself has cultural associations with one gender over the other. The tools women use to manage the world around them necessarily involve notions of the self and of gender, and include rejecting or embracing gendered expectations and roles. For women confronting gendered notions of the knowledge, activities, behaviour, and selves they should be manifesting, adaptations of gender roles and identity form the basis for resistance to gender proscriptions. Women who are interested in engineering, for example, must confront – and counter – assumptions and associations about women's abilities in technological fields.

The findings of this project imply that we are only beginning to understand the relationships between gender and Internet technologies. Commercial services like Monster.com must continue to explore ways in which their services can encourage and enhance women's online job searches. The implications of the present study suggest that Monster.com and its competitors would do well to examine the search interface from the perspective of women job-seekers, especially with regards to the kinds of information they are looking for. The interviews performed for this project revealed women's frustration with the lack of part-time job listings, and a lack of information about benefits and other aspects of the corporate atmosphere including its opportunities for women. Less experienced women in particular might benefit from a search framework that includes search options like screening for maternity leave policies or flex-time options. Content and resources that counter women's sense that the Internet and/or certain jobs are "not for them" could help these women expand their access to job opportunities.

For scholars, the implications of this research include the notion that gender can be an important lens through which women approach online interaction. Some women, certainly, are extremely comfortable with the Internet and a range of its resources, while others feel shut out of these technologies. As Internet use increases, especially among youth, the differences between use of common services like email or online chats and more complex activities like advanced information-seeking and use of Internet software becomes a crucial distinction in tracking the benefits individuals gain. If, as the Pew study seems to suggest (Fallows 2005), women are relegating themselves to more communal activities while men take full advantage of more informational ones, social improvement via the Internet will continue to be divided in a new kind of 'haves' and 'have nots'.

Finally, for women job-seekers themselves, this research suggests that far from being a gender -neutral process, online job-seeking is embedded in gendered perceptions. Training, search techniques, and resources that take gender considerations into account may be able to enhance women's experiences using the Internet to improve their lot in life.

As online tools become an increasingly important part of today's successful job search, scholars and practitioners must incorporate an understanding of the ways in which specific groups, cultures, and individuals interact with these technologies. Future research is needed to continue exploring the relatively new area of gender in online job searches, especially in regard to identity and culture.

References

Adam A (2001) Cyberstalking: gender and computer ethics. In: Green E and Adam A (eds) Technology, consumption, and identity. London: Routledge, pp 209–224

Baron JN, Mittman BS, Newman AE (1991) Targets of opportunity: organizational and environmental determinants of gender integration within the California civil service, 1979–1985. American Journal of Sociology 96: 1362–1401

Beggs JM, Doolittle DC (1993) Perceptions of now and then of occupational sex typing: a replication of shinar's 1975 study. Journal of Applied Social Psychology 23: 1435–1453

Belkin NJ (1990) The cognitive viewpoint in information science. Journal of Information Science 16: 11–15

Bem SL (1993) The lenses of gender: transforming the debate on sexual inequality. New Haven, CT: Yale University Press

Bhargava A (2002) Gender bias in computer software programs: a checklist for teachers. Information Technology in Childhood Education Annual 1: 205–218

Borgman CL, Hirsh SG, Hiller J (1996) Rethinking online monitoring methods for information retrieval systems: from search product to search process. Journal of the American Society for Information Science 47: 568–583

Cejka MA, Eagly AH (1999) Gender-stereotypic images of occupations correspond to the sex segregation of employment. Personality and Social Psychology Bulletin 25: 413–423

Chirieac D, Burns OM, Case T (2001) The impact of gender and attitudes toward the Internet and computing technology. Proceedings of the 2001 SAIS Conference, 2–3 March, Savannah, GA

Clarke V, Chambers S (1989) Gender based factors in computing enrollments and achievement: evidence from a study of tertiary students. Journal of Educational Computing Research 5: 409–429

de Mey M (1977) The cognitive viewpoint: its development and its scope. In: CC 77: International Workshop on the Cognitive Viewpoint Ghent: Ghent University, pp xvi-xxxii

Deaux K, Major B (1987) Putting gender into context: an interactive model of gender-related behaviour. Psychological Review 94: 369–389

Dervin B (1998) Sense-making theory and practice: an overview of user interests in knowledge seeking and use. Journal of Knowledge Management 2: 36–46

Detlor B (2003) Internet-based information systems use in organizations: an information studies perspective, Information Systems Journal 13: 113–132

Durndell A, Haag Z (2002) Computer self-efficacy, computer anxiety, attitudes towards the Internet and reported experience with the Internet, by gender, in an East European sample. Computers in Human Behaviour 18: 521–535

Eagly A (1987) Sex differences in social behaviour: a social-role interpretation. Lawrence Erlbaum Associates, Hillsdale, NJ

Fallows D (2004) The Internet and daily life. Report from the Pew Internet and American Life Project, retrieved 21 June 2005, from http://wwwpewInternetorg/pdfs/PIP_Internet_and_Daily_Lifepdf

Fallows D (2005) How women and men use the Internet. Report from the from the Pew Internet and American Life Project, retrieved 11 January 2005, from http://20721232103/PPF/r/171/report_displayasp

Fan JP, Macredie RD (2006) Gender differences and hypermedia navigation: principles for adaptive hypermedia learning systems. In: Magoulas GD and Chen SY (eds) Advances in web-based education: personalized learning environments. Hershey, PA: Information Science Publishing, pp 1–20

Fernandez RM, Sosa L (2005) Gendering the job: networks and recruitment at a call center. American Journal of Sociology 111: 859–904

Ford N, Miller D, Moss N (2001) The role of individual differences in Internet searching: an empirical study. Journal of the American Society for Information Science and Technology 52: 1049–1066

Gatton DS, Dubois CLZ, Faley RH (1999) The effects of organizational context on occupational gender-stereotyping. Sex Roles 40: 567–582

Herring SC (1994) Politeness in computer culture: why women thank and men flame. In: Bucholtz M, Liang A and Sutton L (eds) Cultural performances: Proceedings of the Third Berkeley Women and Language Conference, Berkeley: Berkeley Women and Language Group, pp 278–294

Herring SC (2003) Gender and power in online communication In: Holmes J and Meyerhoff M (eds) The Handbook of Language and Gender. Oxford: Blackwell Publishers, pp 202–228

Howard PN (2004) Embedded media: who we know, what we know, and society online. In: Howard PN and Jones S (eds) Society online: the Internet in context. Sage: Thousand Oaks, pp 1–28

Kennedy T, Wellman B, Klement K (2003) Gendering the digital divide. IT and Society 1: 72–96

Kleit RG (2002) Job Search Networks and Strategies in Scattered-site Public Housing, Housing Studies 17: 83–100

Krendl K, Broihier M, & Fleetwood C (1989) Children and computers: Do sex-related differences persist? Journal of Communication 39: 85–93

Kuhlthau CC (1993) Seeking meaning: a process approach to library and information services. Journal of the American Society for Information Science 42: 361–371

Large A, Beheshti J, Moukdad H (1999) Information seeking on the web: navigational skills of grade-six primary school students. In: Woods L (ed) Proceedings of the 62nd Annual Meeting of the American Society of Information Science (ASIS), Knowledge: creation, organization and use. Washington, DC: Information Today, pp 84–97

Large A, Beheshti J, Rahman, T (2002) Design criteria for children's web portals: the users speak out. Journal for the Society for Information Science and Technology 53: 73–94

Lippa R, Connelly S (1990) Gender diagnosticity: a new bayesian approach to gender-related individual differences. Journal of Personality and Social Psychology 59: 1051–1065

Liu M (1995) Ethnicity and information seeking, The Reference Librarian 49–50: 123–134

Mintz B, Krymkowski DH (2005) What types of occupations are becoming less ethnic, race, and sex segregated? determinants of the rate of occupational sex and race integration: 1980–2000. Paper presented at the Annual Meeting of the American Sociological Association in Philadelphia

Morahan-Martin J (2000) Women and the Internet. Cyberpsychology and Behaviour 3: 747–760

Moss S (2004) Women choosing diverse workplaces: a rational preference with disturbing implications for both occupational segregation and economic analysis of law. Harvard Women;s Law Journal 27: 231–279

Nickell GS, Schmidt CR, Pinto JN (1987) Gender and sex role preferences in computer attitudes and experience. Paper presented at the annual meeting of the Southwestern Psychological Association, New Orleans, LA

Ogletree SM, Williams SW (1990) Sex and sex-typing effects on computer attitudes and aptitude. Sex Roles 23: 703–712

Onyejekwe CJ (2005) The Internet and the commercialization of sex: a gender perspective. Nebula 2: 70–81

Reed WM & Oughton JM (1997) Computer experience and interval-based linear versus nonlinear hypermedia navigation, Journal of Research on Computing in Education, 30: 38–52

Reskin BF, Hartmann HI (eds) (1986) Women's work, men's work: sex segregation on the job. National Academy, Washsington, DC

Reskin BF, Roos PA (1990) Job queues, gender queues: explaining women's inroads into male occupations. Temple University Press, Philadelphia

Roy M, Chi MTC (2003) Gender differences in patterns of searching the web. Journal of Educational Computing Research 29: 335–348

Saks AM, Ashforth BE (1999) Effects of individual differences and job search behaviors on the employment status of recent university graduates. Journal of Vocational Behavior 54: 335–349

Salaff JW, Greve A, Tao R, Chen X (2005) Can the Internet help? how immigrant women from china get jobs. In: Kuah-Pearce KE (ed) Chinese women and their cyber network. Singapore: Marshall Cavendish Academic, pp 32–41

Scott A, Semmens L, Willoughby L (2001) Women and the Internet: the natural history of a research project. In: Green E and Adam A (eds) Virtual gender: technology, consumption and identity. London: Routledge, pp 541–565

Shade L (2004) Bending gender into the net: feminizing content, corporate interests, and research strategy. In: Howard PN and Jones S (eds) Society online: the Internet in context. Sage: Thousand Oaks, pp 57–70

Sherman RC, End C, Kraan E, Cole A, Campbell J, Birchmeir Z, Klausner J (2000) The Internet gender gap among college students: forgotten but not gone? Cyberpsychology and Behaviour 3: 885–894

Shinar EH (1975) Sexual stereotypes of occupations. Journal of Vocational Behavior 7: 99–111

Turkle S (1988) Computational reticence: why women fear the intimate machine. In: Kramarae C (ed) Technology and women's voices: keeping in touch. New York, NY: Routledge, pp 41–61

Venkatesh V, Morris MG (2000) Why don't men ever stop to ask for directions? Gender, social influence, and their role in technology acceptance and usage behaviour. MIS Quarterly 24: 115–139

Venkatesh V, Morris MG, Sykes TA, Ackerman PL (2004) Individual reactions to new technologies in the workplace: the role of gender as a psychological construct. Journal of Applied Social Psychology 34: 445–467

Wilder G, Mackie D, Cooper J (1985) Gender and computers: two surveys of computer-related attitudes. Sex Roles 13: 215–229

Williams SW, Ogletree SM, Woodburn W, Raffeld P (1993) Gender roles, computer attitudes, and dyadic computer interaction performance in college students. Sex Roles 29: 515–524

5
Searching Ethics: The Role of Search Engines in the Construction and Distribution of Knowledge

L.M. Hinman

Summary Search engines play a crucial role in controlling access to information, and as such they in fact contribute significantly to the social construction of knowledge.

This paper begins with a brief survey of issues relating to access to knowledge, and places the question of search engine ethics within a wider historical and conceptual context. Peer-review in journals and for scholarly press books are one example of the way in which access to knowledge is shaped and constructed in scholarly traditions. Similarly, access to scholarly conventions was often controlled by a combination of peer-review and professional standards. In the twenty-first century, we have seen an increasing de-professionalization of knowledge, and search engines have replaced scientific and scholarly legitimation with a digital version of the *vox populi*. Increasingly they are providing a new *Rangordnung* of knowledge claims that replaces traditional legitimation structures.

The increasing importance and pervasiveness of search engines presents us with a challenge: search engines are not just providing access to knowledge, but are increasingly paying a central role in the constitution of knowledge itself. Such control of knowledge is, in a very fundamental sense, a public trust, yet it remains firmly ensconced in private hands and behind a veil of corporate secrecy intended to protect valuable algorithms from theft by competitors and from manipulation by those who would want to skew search results in their favor. Search engines are directly responsible to their paying customers, their advertisers, and not directly to the public users who are increasingly dependent on such search engines to filter through the ever-expanding universe of on-line data. These tangled lines of responsibility, combined with the opacity of the search process, suggest that public mistrust may be the more appropriate attitude, especially since we have seen cases in which this public trust has been abused for both commercial and political ends.

A. Spink and M. Zimmer (eds.), *Web Search, Springer Series in Information Science and Knowledge Management 14.*

5.1 Introduction

From the oral traditions of ancient civilizations to the contemporary Googling of scientific experiments, knowledge, both in its construction and its distribution, has always been shaped and controlled by forces external to the inner dynamic of intellectual inquiry. The library of Alexandria played a major role in forming the body of knowledge upon which the classical tradition rests. The influence of a particular work depended in part on the number of scribes charged with copying the work. Some manuscripts were copied, others destroyed, and still others were hidden until they could safely reemerge, sometimes centuries later. Scholars such as Diogenes Laërtius and Church fathers constructed a canon of significant and excluded writings. The courts of kings and lesser nobles, in both the east and the west, further shaped and extended the body of knowledge handed down to them, strengthening some currents while blocking others. Centuries later, royal societies defined and defended the halls of knowledge against obscurantism as well as interlopers and free spirits.

The second half of the twentieth century witnessed a sweeping standardization and dissemination of knowledge. Universities and research institutions opened their doors, yet granted their seal of approval only to those who had served laborious and faithful internships. Professional journals certified which ideas and authors could be taken seriously in a discipline, and textbooks standardized the body of knowledge to be transmitted to new generations of scholars. The intellectual optimist might see these developments as a steady progression of knowledge governed by its own internal dynamic, a search for truth for its own sake. More jaundiced eyes might view these same recurring developments as the professionalization of knowledge, a repetition of a recurring motif of exclusivity of knowledge workers. Both the definition of knowledge and access to it, one might argue, continues to be controlled by a comparatively small group of professionals, an intellectual guild bent as much on preserving and extending its own influence as on the pursuit of truth for its own sake. Knowledge professionals have always been intellectual gatekeepers who separate the raw from the cooked, and certify that which is suitable for intellectual consumption.

5.2 A New Millennium

We have recently witnessed the turn of a new millennium. Its technological developments strike at the very foundations of academic disciplines and traditional legitimation structures, much as the printing press did centuries earlier. The World Wide Web has dismantled the canon and given anyone with a PC and Internet access a voice that can potentially reach millions. From personal web pages to blogs, podcasts, and cooperative knowledge processes such as Wikipedia and open source disciplines, we see an ever-widening challenge to traditional epistemic authorities.

For the past century, knowledge claims were vetted by professionals – those who grant degrees, organize conferences, edit journals, award grants, publish scholarly books, and in many other ways direct the course of scholarly and scientific progress. Various inventions, beginning with the printing press and stretching through the *samizdat*, had already contributed to what could be called the democratization of knowledge, that is, the transference of the means of authentication from the hands of professionals into the hands of the people, but the World Wide Web accelerated what had been a spotty occurrence into a global force. Initially, list servers opened up the possibility of instantaneous communication among communities of scholars and scientists, but these list servers sometimes built on traditional professional affiliations. Alternative sources of knowledge claims – no longer tied to professional qualifications – sprang up across the cyberglobe almost overnight, with countless new websites representing the multifaceted *vox populi*. Unvetted knowledge claims have proliferated at an amazing rate. Recently, the movement has been accelerated with the spread of blogs, each offering an authorial opportunity to individuals on an unprecedented scale.

5.3   Search Engines and the Legitimation of Knowledge

Nowhere has the potential democratization of knowledge been more powerful than in the domain of search engines. A mere decade ago, students typically turned to scholarly journals and to books in university libraries (usually chosen by academics from university presses with academic editorial boards) when they began research projects. Now they are much more likely to turn to the web, using a search engine such as Google to find the information they seek. Vast quantities of knowledge are now available in one's own home or at a cybercafé, direct access unmediated by traditional knowledge institutions such as universities. Paradoxically, the very techniques of knowledge transmission have become the new gatekeepers of knowledge for the public in general and even for many of our students. Almost overnight search engines have come to control access to information for the majority of our citizens.

Search engines themselves are driven in part by the voice of the people, in part by the voice of advertisers. Although the precise algorithms that govern search engines such as Google are closely-guarded trade secrets, the general contours are clear enough. The ranking of sites depends on some combination its popularity and the number of other sites that link to it. Of course, there have been indexes to books and journal for many decades. Indexing systems – the Library of Congress being the model here in the United States – publications such as the *Reader's Guide to Periodical Literature* and the *International Index* have provided students and scholars with access to relevant literature for over a century. However, the criteria for inclusion were largely those shared by the scholarly community. And once included in an index, listing was alphabetical, based not on popularity, but the transparent, nonpreferential ordering of concepts. More recently, private for-fee databases such as LexisNexis have become indispensable to the professional, but once again the criteria of inclusion mirrored those of the larger professional community the database served. What makes search engines such as Google so distinctive is that they are not longer directly tethered to professional criteria. The keys to the kingdom of knowledge have been passed – to a for-profit company whose system of ranking is a closely-guarded trade secret.

This is a jarring development. As we have seen, the issue is not whether access to knowledge is controlled or not – clearly, it has always been controlled. However, the dream of the last century was that control was primarily exercised by the community of scholars and scientists themselves through the various means discussed above. Even when access was controlled by private search firms, their financial well-being depended on pleasing the community of professionals they served (as in the Lexis-Nexis), and thus they mirrored those professional standards in their searches. The new commercialization of search firms strikes a discordant note. Although traditional search options primarily served the professional communities, they were designed to provide newcomers with access to particular professional communities. Information was controlled and ordered in such a way as to facilitate entry into the community. The underlying dream was that access to knowledge was ultimately controlled by the profession itself and was structured in ways consistent with the advancement of knowledge in that profession. The assumption was that the rules governing searching, access, and control would be transparent, both within and outside the profession.

5.4   Who is the Customer?

With the rise of search engines such as Google, the factors shaping access to knowledge have radically changed. Public search engines have two types of customers. First, and more obviously, end-users are customers: they come to the site and make use of its search facilities. A company such as Google has millions of such customers. They are, however, an unusual breed of customer: they consume, but they do not pay. It is important to keep them happy and to insure that they return to the site in order to keep the second kind of customer – in many ways, the *real* customer – happy: the advertiser. Search engines such as Google survive on advertising dollars. The massive computing power at the disposal of end users is paid for by advertising dollars, and ultimately these advertising dollars are directed toward selling things. The first kind of sales are direct: the pitches are those little ads on the right-hand on your search results or the "sponsored sites" that pay the search engines to place them just before your search results. With luck, the sponsored sites will procure sales. Or, sometimes more importantly, collecting and selling information about you (this is the part you do not see: the cookies, the data gathering of surfing and buying patterns, etc.). These are the customers that search engines really have to please.

The importance of pleasing the advertisers and marketers who support Google and other search engines can hardly be underestimated. Primary marketing concerns – the desire to sell some particular product to individuals when they are searching for something – drive the enterprise in an obvious way. The more that people click and buy something as the result of a search, the more successful this type of marketing is. Yet there are secondary marketing concerns that ultimately are even more important and powerful: building a database of consumer profiles and patterns of consumer behavior. If search engines can predict what products an individual searcher is most likely to buy, then that searcher can be targeted with much more specific and more effective advertising. We have all seen such targeting at work when we return to Amazon.com and find advertisements for book similar to the ones that we bought last week. "Readers who liked Scott Turow's *Ordinary Heroes*, also bought Michael Connolly's *The Lincoln Lawyer*, John Grisham's *The Broker*, etc." Such targeted advertising is much more likely to be effective than ads for random books.

A recent offer by Google to build a free wireless network for all of San Francisco offers us a glimpse of how much money is at stake in this area. Google was willing to build and operate a completely free wi-fi network for all of San Francisco. Why? The simple answer was that Google could obtain such valuable individual and aggregate information about users, that the value of the information will outweigh the cost of the wireless network. Presumably, to use this free network, users will be asked to log on with a username and password, and this log-on will ensure that all their surfing activity (not just searches) can be tracked and analyzed. A free email account, such as gMail, can insure that one's email content is correlated with surfing activity; virtually unlimited email storage insures a far broader data set on each customer; the option of sending your gMail to your mobile phone opens up another path to information and data correlation; the option of using Google's MySearch insures that your surfing activity from any computer will be tracked and added to the database on you.. The result is tremendously sophisticated personal profiles as well as far more nuanced aggregate data, since it is possible to track each user over extended periods of time and develop much more subtle aggregate data pictures.

An additional issue now looms on the horizon as search engine companies acquire (or are acquired by) other businesses. Difficult questions of potential conflicts of interest arise when search engine companies either acquire other companies which are potential advertisers or are themselves taken over by larger companies. In the latter case, the controlling company might well have a vested interest in having their products play a more prominent role in search results. If News Corp buys Ask.com, wouldn't it like to highlight results involving its myriad subsidiary companies? Similar considerations apply when search engine companies buy out other companies who are potential advertisers. Although outright tampering with search results would probably be easily detected, subtle shifts in tightly-concealed algorithms could result in subtle biases that would be virtually impossible to prove.

The issue of subtle bias is even more complex, because it is not clear exactly what being first in a search ranking signifies. Does it mean that the site is the most popular? Well, not solely that. Does it mean that the site is the best? Certainly, this is not claimed. Does it mean that other sites link to it? Well, this is part of the picture. However, the success of a search engines such as Google lies in its ability to place very near the top the particular site(s) that the user is trying to find. This is essentially a subjective criterion of satisfaction that involves matching search terms with search results. If your site comes up first in a Google search on a particular term, that does not your site is the best or the most popular, but rather that Google's algorithms predict that users who search on that term are most likely to be satisfied when they click on the link to your site. If this is the case, there seems to be even more elasticity in the ways in which algorithms can be manipulated.

5.5   From BigBrother.gov to BigBrother.com

The furor in the United States over the National Security Agency's warrantless wire-tapping of a comparatively small number of American citizens is newsworthy, but it is ironic that there is far more surveillance of citizens within the nongovernmental sphere with little notice or outrage on the part of the public or the Congress. The real danger to privacy may come from BigBrother.com instead of BigBrother.gov. Extraordinarily powerful economic forces are pushing search engine development toward the more and more sophisticated tracking of users, and – in contrast to the governmental domain – there are economic reasons why consumers might want to be tracked. Not only do they obtain free benefits such as wireless Internet access, but they also obtain better service. They are able to find exactly the goods and services they are looking for because, using their profile data, search engines can better predict the kinds of things a particular user will find interesting and worth buying.

The detail with which companies can compile a picture of individuals is truly astounding. The history of an individual's Internet searches can provide a virtual window into that person's deepest (as well as most shallow) desires and priorities. We may be coy or circumspect in our emails and other written communications, but coyness does not work with search engines. We have to reveal exactly what we are looking for, and do so as precisely as possible. Our current medical concerns, our discontents and hopes, our future plans for travel or investment – these are but a few of the things revealed about us through our web searches. When this information is combined with other potential sources of information such as credit card purchases, cell phone activity (in the United States, it is increasingly possible to track the location of cell phones that are simply turned on, even if they are not in a call), email and IM and text messages, automotive tracking devices such as FastTrac as well as black box recorders present in cars now, and non-governmental as well as governmental CCTV tapes, we can easily create an astonishingly detailed portrait of an individual's activity – even thoughts – during a day.

5.6   The *Rangordnung* of Knowledge Claims

Once we appreciate the accelerating power and sophistication of search engines with the powerful underlying economic forces at work in this area, we can see the way in which search engines can have a tremendous influence on access to knowledge; indeed, search engines will increasingly be in a position to construct knowledge through control of access. Google already demonstrates this regarding control of information currently on the Web: through the ranking of query results, search engines orders which pages we are most likely to see, and this in turn affects our further thinking about the topic in question, thereby shaping the further development of knowledge about that issue. Over a century ago Nietzsche depicted *Rangordnung* as an expression of *Wille zur Macht*, and one cannot but wonder whether this the rank ordering done by search engines is a stealthy, virtual expression of this Nietzschean theme.

There is an obvious rejoinder to this entire line of argument – namely, while Google and other search engines may control access to information on the web, much of our accumulated knowledge exists not primarily on the web, but in traditional books, printed on paper, bound, and shelved in libraries. Yet this is precisely where Google Scholar (Google's plan to digitize the contents of several of the major libraries of the world) can play such a decisive role. The current legal battles involving Google Scholar center primarily on copyright and intellectual property issues, but these issues are of minor importance compared to the issue of control of access to the great libraries of the world. If Google succeeds in carrying out its plans to digitize these libraries, it promises on its website that, "From one place, you can search across many disciplines and sources: peer-reviewed papers, theses, books, abstracts and articles, from academic publishers, professional societies, pre-print repositories, universities and other scholarly organizations." Once that project happens, two events will probably follow in rapid succession. First, most individuals – with the exception of a handful of scholars with technical needs for examining actual manuscripts or print copy – will consult these resources on-line. Second, the books and journals will gradually be moved to remote storage sites, accessible only in unusual situations, thereby making room in libraries for ever-increasing numbers of workstations. All of this presupposes, of course, that libraries as physical centers will continue to exist at all.

Projects such as Google Scholar underscore an already increasing problem in information retrieval. Until late in the twentieth century, the most commonly experienced problem in information retrieval was not finding enough information. By the beginning of the twenty-first century, the pendulum has swung decisively: now the problem is that we have too much information, and the challenge is to find our way through mountains of data to draw out the bits of information that are most relevant to us. How do we do that? Search engines, of course.

5.7 The Potential for Abuse

The potential for abuse seems clear: as access to vital information resides firmly in the virtual hands of search engines, and as they function as for-profit corporations responsible principally to customers – advertisers, data collectors, and stockholders – and as they carry out their work behind a corporately-justified veil of secrecy, search engines will wield an extraordinary control of information. If this power falls into the hands of a single search engine company (Google is the leading contender for this position today, but several decades of experience have taught us that market dominance can change very quickly), then the extent of control of knowledge in private hands will be truly unprecedented in the history of humanity. Never before will so few have controlled so much with so little public oversight or regulation.

The potential for abuse does not, of course, mean that abuse actually will occur. However, a number of disturbing instances have already occurred that raise important questions about how adequately the current system of self-policing will be. In the early days of search engines, sites could sometimes pay to have themselves listed higher in the rankings. Fortunately, this practice has largely disappeared, and those who pay to have their listings promoted are typically included in a section under "Sponsored Sites" or some similar title, which insures that users can distinguish between paid results and results based on popularity (or something like popularity, in a more complex algorithm).

Other issues are more disturbing. Google, for example, does not want to violate local laws with its search engines. While anti-Semitic sites are easy to find in the United States on Google, they do not show up in the French (Google.fr) or German (Google.de) versions of Google. Many of us feel there is no great loss in these cases, but when we turn to China, we find that searches from within China for the Dali Lama, Fulong Gong, the Tiananmen Square massacre, and presumably most recently the uprisings in Sanshan on Guangdong province all lead only to government-approved sites. Do American-owned search engines in foreign countries follow local law and cooperate with what many would consider repressive – but legal–political censorship in those countries? In the case of China, not only does this seem to be happening with the cooperation of Google, but the hardware infrastructure which makes such censorship more efficient is being constructed in part by American companies.

In the United States, the situation is actually more opaque than it is in China, where at least we as outsiders know what is being censored. When for several months in 2004 the previously published classic photos of prisoner abuse at Abu Ghraib were not showing up in an image search in Google, Google spokespersons were unable to provide a convincing explanation of their disappearance from their search results. Either they know why they disappeared from the search results and then later reappeared in late 2004 and are not publicly divulging the reasons, or they do not know why it happened. Neither alternative is comforting.

The much-disputed Patriot Act and related legislation in the United States obligates knowledge sources upon request to give the government authority to trace various kinds of user records, including search histories. Moreover, it is a crime to divulge that the government has obtained such information from you as a library, an Internet provider, a professor, etc., so it is impossible to know how frequently such requests are made and granted. Google has resisted some of the more outlandish information requests from the United States government, while Yahoo and MSN have complied much more fully with such requests, but we have little reliable knowledge of how often even Google has cooperated with government demands for information about search histories because of the secrecy that hangs over the entire governmental project.

5.8   Conclusion

Here, then, is the challenge that faces us: search engines are not just providing access to knowledge, but are increasingly paying a central role in the constitution of knowledge itself. Such control of knowledge is, in a very fundamental sense, a *public* trust, yet it remains firmly ensconced in private hands and behind a veil of corporate secrecy intended to protect valuable algorithms from theft by competitors and from manipulation by those who would want to skew search results in their favor. Search engines are directly responsible to their paying customers, their advertisers, and not directly to the public users who are increasingly dependent on such search engines to filter through the ever-expanding universe of on-line data. These tangled lines of responsibility, combined with the opacity of the search process, suggest that public *mistrust* may be the more appropriate attitude, especially since we have seen cases in which this public trust has been abused for both commercial and political ends.

We might hope for protection against abuses from three sources. First, the proliferation of information sources such as blogs, discussion forums, instant messaging, could make the supervision and control of all information technically unfeasible; yet our experience in a variety of countries, most notably China, suggests that such control is all too feasible. Second, the free market nature of the World Wide Web might insure a healthy diversity of viewpoints and decentralization of power. Yet this offers little consolation either, since search engines themselves are quickly becoming the invisible hand that guides market economies and creates market forces. Moreover, if search engines are responsive to market forces, they are more responsive to the demands of their customers—the advertisers—than to their users. Third, we might hope that government supervision will ensure that the public trust in not violated. Such hope comes, unfortunately, at a time when major governments, most notably the United States, are themselves moving toward *less* transparency, rather than more, often under the banner of anti-terrorism.

Realizing the increasingly important role that search engines play in the construction of knowledge is an important first step toward increasing transparency, but it is only the first step. The debate that lies before us will be about how best to achieve the level of transparency necessary to guarantee that we do not become digital pawns in a game in which the search engine has become the *magister ludi* while at the same time providing sufficient financial incentives to private enterprise to guarantee the continuing improvement of search services.

References

Berger, P., Luckmann, T. The Social Construction of Reality: A Treatise in the Sociology of Knowledge (New York: Anchor, 1967)

Elgesem, Dag. Search Engines and the Problem of Transparency. In: Ethicomp 2007: Proceedings of the Ninth International Conference, edited by Bynum, T., Rogerson, S., and Murata, K. (Tokyo: Global e-SCM Research Center, Meiji University, 2007).Vol. II, 150–57

Hesse, H. The Glass Bead Game: Magister Ludi. Translated by Richard and Clara Winston. New York: Picador Press, 2002

Hinman, Lawrence M. Esse est indicato in Google: Ethical and Political Issues in Search Engines, IRIE, International Review of Information Ethics, Vol. 3 (6/2005), 19–25

Hurley, D. Pole Sstar: human rights in the information society. Montréal: International Centre for Human Rights and Democratic Development, 2003.

Introna, L. and Nissenbaum, H. (2000) Shaping the Web: why the politics of search engines matters, The Information Society, Vol. 16, No. 3, 1–17

Machill, M., Welp, C., eds. Wegweiser im Netz: Qualität und Nutzung von Suchmaschinen. Bielefeld: Verlag Bertelsman Stiftung, 2003

Nagenborg, M., Privacy and terror: some remarks from historical perspective, International Journal of Information Ethics (IJIE), Vol. 2 (11/2004), 1–5

OpenNet Initiative (ONI), Internet Filtering in China 2004–2005: A Country Study, April 14, 2005. http://opennetinitiative.net/studies/ china/ONI_China_Country_Study.pdf

OpenNet Initiative: Bulletin 005, Probing Chinese search engine filtering, August 19, 2004 http://www.opennetinitiative.net/bulletins/005/

Thompson, Dennis F. Restoring Distrust. Restoring Responsibility: Ethics in Government, Business and Healthcare. Cambridge: Cambridge University Press, 2005

Zittrain, J., Edelman, B. Empirical Analysis of Internet Filtering in China, Berkman Center for Internet and Society, Harvard Law School: http://cyber.law.harvard.edu/filtering/china/

6

The Gaze of the Perfect Search Engine: Google as an Infrastructure of Dataveillance

M. Zimmer

Summary Web search engines have emerged as a ubiquitous and vital tool for the successful navigation of the growing online informational sphere. The goal of the world's largest search engine, Google, is to "organize the world's information and make it universally accessible and useful" and to create the "perfect search engine" that provides only intuitive, personalized, and relevant results. While intended to enhance intellectual mobility in the online sphere, this chapter reveals that the quest for the perfect search engine requires the widespread monitoring and aggregation of a users' online personal and intellectual activities, threatening the values the perfect search engines were designed to sustain. It argues that these search-based infrastructures of dataveillance contribute to a rapidly emerging "soft cage" of everyday digital surveillance, where they, like other dataveillance technologies before them, contribute to the curtailing of individual freedom, affect users' sense of self, and present issues of deep discrimination and social justice.

6.1 Introduction

In January 2006 it was revealed that the U.S. Justice Department asked a federal judge to compel the Web search engine Google to turn over records on millions of its users' search queries as part of the government's effort to uphold an online pornography law (Hafner and Richtel 2006; Mintz 2006). Google resisted, but America Online, Microsoft, and Yahoo! complied with similar government subpoenas of their search records (Hafner and Richtel 2006). Later that year, America Online released over 20 million search queries from 658,000 of its users to the public in an attempt to support academic research on search engine usage (Hansell 2006). Despite AOL's attempts to anonymize the data, individual users remained identifiable based solely on their search histories, which included search terms matching users' names, social security numbers, addresses, phone numbers, and other personally identifiable information. Simple keyword analyses of the AOL database also revealed an "innumerable number of life stories ranging from the mundane to the illicit and bizarre" (McCullagh 2006b). Upon being identified by the *New York Times* based solely on her search terms in the AOL database, a Georgia woman exclaimed, "My goodness, it's my whole personal life...I had no idea somebody was looking over my shoulder" (Barbaro and Zeller Jr 2006). Together, these events brought to light the fact that search engine providers keep detailed records of users' searches, and created anxiety among searchers about the presence of such systematic monitoring of their online information-seeking activities (Barbaro and Zeller Jr 2006; Hafner 2006; Levy 2006; Maney 2006).

The freedom to move through both physical and intellectual space is a central theme of various American mythologies, such as the desire to explore unknown frontiers and acquire new knowledge, the overcoming of artificial barriers of distance for mass communication and commerce, and the ability to control one's relations and position in the world. This freedom of mobility becomes embodied in the set of values deemed vital for the success of our society, including privacy, autonomy, and liberty. The emergence of systematic modes of data surveillance – otherwise referred to as "dataveillance" (Clarke 1988) – within our spheres of mobility threatens the preservation of these fundamental values. Without the ability and opportunity to move, navigate, inquire, and explore physical, intellectual, and, increasingly, digital spaces, we cannot gain the sort of understanding of our world and develop the awareness and competencies necessary for effective participation in social, economic, cultural, and political life. This chapter will examine the particular dataveillance threats of Web search engines, paying specific attention to the dominant search engine Google, and will reveal how the aggregation of one's online information-seeking activities within the online sphere of intellectual and informational mobility contributes to the creation of a technological gaze of everyday surveillance, inflaming a growing environment of discipline and social control.

This chapter is divided into four parts. Part one builds from theories of surveillance and power to introduce the concept of dataveillance, paying particular attention to the role of information technology and data accumulation in the functioning of disciplinary power. Part two introduces the role of Web search engines as the prevailing information interface for accessing the vast amount of information available on Internet, concluding that as search engines have become the "center of gravity" for navigation within this vital sphere of information, important concerns over privacy and surveillance emerge. Part three describes the quest for the "perfect search engine" and how Google's integration of Web cookies, detailed server logs, and personal user accounts within and across its diverse product suite provides a powerful infrastructure of dataveillance to monitor, record, and aggregate information about users' online activities. Part four warns of how Google's infrastructure of dataveillance exerts its gaze, harboring concerns over its role in the exercise of disciplinary power, panoptic sorting of its users, and the challenges of resisting its "gravitational pull" in the face of default settings which require the sharing of information. The chapter concludes with a brief discussion of how an intervention in the technical design of the perfect search engine might help mitigate the effects of its disciplinary gaze.

6.2   The Gaze of Dataveillance

According to sociologist David Lyon, surveillance is the "collection and processing of personal data, whether identifiable or not, for the purposes of influencing or managing those whose data have been garnered" (Lyon 2001: 2). Surveillance "tries to make visible the identities or the behaviors of people of interest to the agency in question" (Lyon 2002: 2). Surveillance, then, encompasses a diverse range of activities and processes concerned with scrutinizing people, their actions, and the spaces they inhabit. Surveillance, of course, has existed for centuries, and its methods have been continuously refined to broaden its reach and effectiveness. One notable example is English philosopher Jeremy Bentham's model penitentiary, the Panopticon (Bentham 1995). Conceived in 1791, Bentham's Panopticon prison was designed to maintain (by allusion, if not by fact) perpetual surveillance of its inhabitants: by placing prison guards in central tower with a one-way observation system surrounded by rooms for those to be watched, the subjects were unable to determine when they were being watched. Through this unique architectural design, Bentham believed that the constant threat that one could be surveilled at any time would force the subjects to internalize the effects of surveillance:

> The more constantly the persons to be inspected are under the eyes of the persons who should inspect them, the more perfectly will the purpose of the establishment have been attained. …This being impossible, the next thing to be wished for is, that, at every instant, seeing reason to believe as much, and not being able to satisfy himself to the contrary, he [the watched] should *conceive* himself to be so. (Bentham 1995: 3)

Through such an arrangement, Bentham believed disciplinary power would be automatic, and thus exercised with minimal effort, or, as Michel Foucault later reflected, the Panopticon would "induce in the inmate a state of conscious and permanent visibility that assures the automatic functioning of power" (Foucault 1977: 197). This automatic functioning of power manifested itself through a panoptic and disciplinary gaze:

> There is no need for arms, physical violence, material constraints. Just a gaze. An inspecting gaze, a gaze which each individual under its weight will end by internalizing to the point that he is his own overseer, each individual thus exercising this surveillance over, and against, himself. A superb formula: power exercised continuously and for what turns out to be a minimal cost. (Foucault 1980: 155)

For Foucault, the Panopticon became a "generalizable model of functioning; a way of defining power relations in terms of the everyday life of men… it is in fact a figure of political technology" (Foucault 1977: 205). He viewed the Panopticon as the quintessential disciplinary apparatus of modern society, where the panoptic gaze extended beyond Bentham's specific architectural form, and manifested itself in various contexts of everyday life: the home, the school, the hospital, the workplace, and so on. The gaze of the Panopticon expands to become "a whole complex mechanism, embracing … stricter methods of surveillance [and] more efficient techniques of locating and obtaining information" (Foucault 1977: 77). By suggesting a link between the Panopticon and "more efficient techniques of locating and obtaining information," Foucault reveals a pivotal feature of the modern panoptic gaze: the functioning of power through data accumulation.

The functioning of the Panopticon depended on perpetual surveillance and the "continuous registration, perpetual assessment and classification" of those under its gaze (Foucault 1977: 220). Oscar Gandy recognized this perpetual and disciplinary gaze of personal data accumulation when he warned of the "panoptic sort" (Gandy 1993), whereby individuals are continually identified, assessed and classified for the purpose of coordinating and controlling their access to consumer goods and services, a process he insists in inherently discriminatory. Gandy's concern with panoptic sorting has been expanded beyond the consumer realm into a broader social milieu (Lyon 2003a), where the notion of "social sorting" highlights the growing drive in our modern surveillance society for identification and classification. Since classification has been shown to be closely entwined with the exercise of power (Bowker and Star 1999; Foucault 1971; Suchman 1997), the consequences of panoptic and social sorting – and the technological gaze which form their foundation – present issues of "deep discrimination...and social justice" (Lyon 2003b: 1).

The catalyst triggering both Gandy and Lyon's anxiety was the rapid emergence of a complex set of technologies and practices that involve "the collection, processing, and sharing of information about individuals and groups that is generated through their daily lives as citizens, employees, and consumers (Gandy 1993: 15). This technological apparatus represents what is referred to as dataveillance, defined as both "the massive collection and storage of vast quantities of personal data" (Bennett 1996: 237) and "the systemic use of [such] personal data...in the investigation or monitoring of one or more persons" (Clarke 1988: 499). Clarke's (1988) introduction of the term dataveillance revealed how the disciplinary gaze of the panopticon has extended from a single, centralized source (Bentham's guard tower) into the realm of advanced information technologies and computer databases that facilitate the collection and exchange of information about individuals. Yet, the resulting effect of dataveillance's technologically distributed gaze matches that of Bentham's Panopticon envisioned two hundred years before – the subversion of individual freedoms and liberties:

> An administrative apparatus that has data available to it from a wide variety of sources tends to make decisions on the person's behalf. Hence, a further, more abstract, yet scarcely less real impact of dataveillance is reduction in the meaningfulness of individual actions, and hence in self- reliance and self- responsibility. Although this may be efficient and even fair, it involves a change in mankind's image of itself, and risks sullen acceptance by the masses and stultification of the independent spirit needed to meet the challenges of the future. ... In general, mass dataveillance tends to subvert individualism and the meaningfulness of human decisions and actions. (Clarke 1988: 508)

Since Clarke's first conceptualization of dataveillance almost twenty years ago, advances in digital networking, data storage capacity and processing power have enabled previously unimaginable levels of interconnectivity, aggregation, and realtime analysis of a wide array of personal information. Increasingly, everyday interactions with health care providers, online retailers, highway tollbooths, local grocery stores and libraries result in the collection, analysis, storage and sharing of information about one's address, purchasing habits, age, education, health status, travel activity, employment history, phone numbers and much more, into what legal scholar Daniel Solove (2004) calls "digital dossiers."(Solove 2004: 2) The rising ubiquity of dataveillance in everyday life and resultant sophistication of "digital dossiers" has led to widespread concern over the social and ethical implications of this new digital panoptic gaze (Elmer 2004; Gandy 1993; Garfinkel 2000; Lyon 2003a; Lyon and Zureik, 1996; Regan 1995; Solve 2004; Staples, 2000). As Clive Norris and Gary Armstrong argue in their study of the introduction of computer databases into video surveillance systems, the pervasiveness of digital dossiers (or, using their term, "digital personas") have "more than just an electronic existence: they have concrete material effects" (Norris and Armstrong, 1999: 221). Such effects relate not only to personal privacy, but also issues of discrimination, social justice, and personal freedom. Law professor Michael Fromkin (2000) summarizes these effects best:

> Reams of data organized into either centralized or distributed databases can have substantial consequences beyond the simple loss of privacy caused by the initial data collection, especially when subject to advanced correlative techniques such as data mining. Among the possible harmful effects are various forms of discrimination, ranging from price discrimination to more invidious sorts of discrimination. Data accumulation enables the construction of personal data profiles. When the data are available to others, they can construct personal profiles for targeted marketing, and even, in rare vases, blackmail. For some, just knowing that their activities are being recorded may have a chilling effect on conduct, speech, and reading.
>
> ...A further danger is that the government or others will attempt to use the ability to construct persona profiles in order to predict dangerous or antisocial activities before they happen. People whose profiles meet the criteria will be flagged as dangerous and perhaps subjected to increased surveillance, searches, or discrimination. (Froomkin 2000: 1469–1471)

The role of modern information and communication technologies within infrastructures of dataveillance cannot be understated: frequent shopping cards connect purchasing patterns to customer databases (Ward 1998), intelligent transportation systems enable the tracking and recording of vehicles as they travel the highways (Bennett et al. 2003; Zimmer 2005), electronic key cards manage access to locations while creating a record of one's movements (Stalder and Lyon, 2003), and biometric technologies digitize one's intrinsic physical or behavioral traits for automated identification and authentication (Agre 2003; Brey 2004). Recently, the Internet has emerged as not only a revolutionary technology for communication, commerce and the distribution of information, but also as an ideal infrastructure of dataveillance, enabling the widespread monitoring and collection of personal and identifiable information about its millions of users. The privacy and surveillance concerns with various Internet technologies have been well documented and debated, ranging from the use of Web cookies and tracking bugs (Bennett 2001; Kang, 1998; Mayer-Schönberger 1997), the emergence of spyware and digital rights management systems (Cohen 1996, 2003), workplace monitoring of electronic communications (Froomkin 2000), the aggregation and data-mining of personal information available online (Garfinkel 2000; Solove 2004), and the widespread monitoring of Internet traffic by law enforcement agencies (Regan 2001; Ventura et al. 2005). The design and deployment of each of these new Internet technologies represents an expansion of the gaze of dataveillance online, which is intensified with the growing power and ubiquity of Web search engines and the larger information infrastructures on which they rely.

6.3   Web Search as the Center of Gravity

As the Internet has become increasingly important to modern citizens in their everyday lives (Horrigan and Rainie 2006), Web search engines have emerged as an indispensable tool for accessing the vast amount of information available on this global network. According to the Pew Internet & American Life Project, 84% of American adult Internet users have used a search engine to seek information online (Fallows 2005: 1). On any given day, more than 60 million American adults send over 200 million information requests to Web search engines, making searching the Web the second most popular online activity (behind using e-mail) (Rainie 2005). Originally designed to provide easy access to Internet Websites, search engines now provide gateways to online images, news reports, Usenet archives, financial information, video files, e-mail and even one's desktop files. Recently, search engine providers, such as Google, have started to digitize items in the "material" world, adding the contents of popular books, university libraries, maps, and satellite images to their growing, searchable indices. Reflecting on the rapid emergence of search-related applications, Silicon Valley venture capitalist Roger McNamee noted that "search is the new center of gravity for the computer industry" (McNamee 2005). The same can be said more generally for the role of search engines as today's dominant information interface: Search engines have become the center of gravity for people's everyday information-seeking activities.

Consider, for example, the Web search engine Google. Google has become the prevailing interface for searching and accessing virtually all information on the Web. Originating in 1996 as a Ph.D. research project by Sergey Brin and Larry Page at Stanford University (Brin and Page 1998; Page et al. 1998), Google's Web search engine now dominates the market, processing almost 3.6 billion search queries in February 2007, over half of all Web searches performed (Nielsen//NetRatings, 2007).[3] Google's mission, stated quite simply

---

[3] Nielsen/NetRatings figures represent U.S. searches only, and include local searches, image searches, news searches, shopping searches and other types of search activity from Google's various services. If only Web searches at www.google.com are considered, Google's share increases to 60% (Sullivan 2006).

and innocuously, is to "organize the world's information and make it universally accessible and useful" (Google, 2005a). In pursuit of this goal, Google has developed dozens of search-related tools and services to help users organize and use information in multiple contexts, ranging from general information inquiries to academic research, news and political information, communication and social networking, personal data management, financial data management, shopping and product research, computer file management, and enhanced Internet browsing (see Table 6.1). Consequently, users increasingly search, find, organize, and share information through Google's growing information infrastructure of search-related services and tools. They also use these tools to communicate, navigate, shop, and organize their lives. By providing a medium for various social, intellectual, and commercial activities, "Planet Google" has become a large part of people's lives, both online and off (Williams 2006).

The emerging social and cultural impacts of this increasing reliance on search engines – and the resultant rise of "Plant Google" – are being studied from a variety of disciplines. Scholars have explored the biases of search engine results (Diaz 2005; Introna and Nissenbaum 2000), the political economy of the search engine marketplace (Van Couvering 2004), the legal ramifications of search engine practices (Elkin-Koren 2001; Goldman 2005), the structure of user queries and their searching skills (Jansen et al. 2000; Hargittai 2002), the practice of paid placement of search results (Jansen and Resnick 2005; Wouters 2004; Zimmer, 2006), and general user awareness and trust in how search engines work (Fallows 2005; Marable 2003).

Scholarly attention also been paid to the particular ethical issues related to the dominant position of search engines in our lives (Nagenborg 2005; Norvig et al. 2006), including discussions of the privacy issues related to search engine practices (Hinman 2005; Tavani 2005). However, most treatments of the privacy implications of Web search engines have tended to focus on how search engines provide improved access to personal information that happens to exist online – the erosion of "security through obscurity" in the face of ever-expanding search engine indexes (Ramasastry 2005; Swidey 2003). While these particular privacy problems demand attention, we must expand the investigation of search-related privacy problems from concerns over the personal information about other people that can be *found* via search engines, to include critical exploration of the personal information that is routinely *collected* when users rely on search engines for their information-seeking activities. As we recall, the AOL searcher from Georgia mentioned above was not identifiable due to a search engine finding information about her on the Web, but rather because the Web searches *she* performed on various topics were recorded, and later released, by AOL. Of course, this dataveillance of users search queries by the search engine provider is not unique to AOL. In fact, it forms the very basis for the ultimate goal of the Web search industry: the quest for perfect search engine.

Table 6.1 Google Suite of Products and Services (partial list)

Product	Description	Notes
General Information Inquiries		
Web search	Query-based Website searches	
Personalized Homepage	Customized Google start page with content-specific modules	Use in conjunction with Google Account is encouraged
Alerts	E-mail alerts of new Google results for specific search terms	
Image Search	Query based search for Website images	
Video	Query based search for videos hosted by Google	Google Video Player available for download
Book Search	Full text searches of books scanned into Google's servers	Google Account required in order to limit the number of pages a particular user can view
Academic Research		
Scholar	Full text searches of scholarly books and journals	
News and Political Information		
News	Full text search of recent news articles	With a Google Account, users can create customized keyword-based news sections
Reader	Web-based news feed reader	Google Account required
Blog Search	Full text search of blog content	
Communication and Social Networking		
Gmail	Free Web based e-mail service with contextual advertising	Creation of Gmail account automatically results in activation of Google Account Logging into Gmail also logs user into their Google Account
Groups	Free Web based discussion forums	Includes complete Usenet archives dating back to 1981 Google Account required for creation of new Group;
Talk	Web-based instant messaging and voice calling service	Google Account and Gmail e-mail address required
Blogger	Web-based blog publishing platform	Google Account required
Orkut	Web-based social networking service	Invitation-only Google Account required
Dodgeball	Location-based social networking service for cellphones	
Personal Data Management		
Calendar	Web-based time-management tool	
Financial Data Management		
Finance	Portal providing news and financial information about stocks, mutual funds; Ability to track one's financial portfolio	Google Account required for posting to discussion board

(continued)

Table 6.1 (continued)

Product	Description	Notes
Consumer Activities		
Catalog Search	Full text search of scanned product catalogs	
Froogle	Full text search of online retailers	Google Account required for shipping lists
Local / Maps	Location specific Web searching; digital mapping	
Computer File Management		
Desktop Search	Keyword based searching of computer files	
	Ability to search files on remote computer	
Internet Browsing		
Bookmarks	Online storage of Website bookmarks	Google Account required
Notebook	Browser tool for saving notes while visiting Websites	Google Account required
Toolbar	Browser tool providing access to various Google products without visiting Google Websites	Some features require Google Account
Web Accelerator	Software to speed up page load times for faster Web browsing	

6.4 Dataveillance and the Quest for the Perfect Search Engine

Since the first search engines started to provide a way of interfacing with the content on the Web, there has been a quest for the "perfect search engine," one that has indexed all available information and provides fast and relevant results (Andrews 1999; Gussow 1999; Kushmerick, 1998). A perfect search engine would deliver intuitive results based on a user's past searches and general browsing history (Pitkow et al. 2002; Teevan et al. 2005), and deliver advertisements that are deemed useful or desirable for that particular user (Hansell 2005). Journalist John Battelle summarizes how a perfect search engine might provide a nearly perfect answer to every query:

> Imagine the ability to ask any question and get not just an accurate answer, but your perfect answer – an answer that suits the context and intent of your question, an answer that is informed by who you are and why you might be asking. The engine providing this answer is capable of incorporating all the world's knowledge to the task at hand – be it captured in text, video, or audio. It's capable of discerning between straightforward requests – who was the third president of the United States? – and more nuanced ones – under what circumstances did the third president of the United States foreswear his views on slavery?

> This perfect search also has perfect recall – it knows what you've seen, and can discern between a journey of discovery – where you want to find something new – and recovery – where you want to find something you've seen before. (Battelle 2004)

Given a search for the phrase "Paris Hilton," for example, the perfect search engine will know whether to deliver Websites about the celebrity heiress or a place to spend the night in the French capitol, and whether to provide advertisements for Parisian bistros or celebrity news sites.

The search engine company Google recognized early on the importance of designing a perfect search engine: The company's very first press release noted that "a perfect search engine will process and understand all the information in the world...That is where Google is headed" (Google 1999). Google co-founder Larry Page later reiterated the goal of achieving the perfect search: "The perfect search engine would understand exactly what you mean and give back exactly what you want" (Google 2007). When asked what a perfect search engine would be like, Brin replied quite simply, "like the mind of God" (Ferguson 2005: 40).

To attain such an omnipotent and omniscient ideal, Google must, borrowing Battelle's words, provide results that suit the "context and intent" of the search query; it must have "perfect recall" of who the searcher is and her previous search-related activities. In order to discern the context and intent of a search for "Paris Hilton," for example, the perfect search engine would know if the searcher has shown interest in European travel, or whether she spends time online searching for sites about celebrity gossip. Attaining such perfect recall requires search engine providers to collect as much information about their users as possible. To accomplish this, Google, like most Web search engines, relies on three technical strategies in order to capture the personal information necessary to fuel the perfect recall: the maintenance of server logs, the use of persistent Web cookies, and the encouragement of user registration.

Maintained by nearly all Websites, server logs help Website owners gain an understanding of who is visiting their site, the path visitors take through the Website's pages, which elements (links, icons, menu items, etc.) a visitor clicks, how much time visitors spend on each page, and from what page visitors are leaving the site. In other words, a Website owner aims to collect enough data to reconstruct the entire "episode" of a user's visit to the Website (Tec-Ed 1999). Google maintains detailed server logs recording each of the 100 million search requests processed each day (Google 2005c). While the exact contents are not publicly known, Google has provided an example of a "typical log entry" for a user who searched for the term "cars" (Google 2005b):

> 123.45.67.89 - 25/Mar/2003 10:15:32 - http://www.google.com/search?q=cars - Firefox
> 1.0.7; Windows NT 5.1 - 740674ce2123e969

In this sample entry, $123.45.67.89$ is the IP address[4] assigned to the user by the user's Internet service provider, $25/Mar/2003$ $10:15:32$ is the date and time

---

[4] An Internet Protocol (IP) address is a unique address that electronic devices use in order to identify and communicate with each other on a computer network. An IP address can be thought of as a rough equivalent of a street address or a phone number for a computer or other network device on the Internet. Just as each street address and phone number uniquely identifies a building or telephone, an IP address can uniquely identify a specific computer or other network device on a network (Wikipedia contributors 2007).

of the query, `http://www.google.com/search?q=cars` is the requested page, which also happens to identify the search query, "cars," `Firefox 1.0.7; Windows NT 5.1` is the browser and operating system being used, and `740674ce2123a969` is the unique cookie ID[5] assigned to this particular browser the first time it visited Google. To help further reconstruct a user's movements, Google also records clickstream data, including which search results or advertising links a user clicks (Google 2005b). Given Google's wide array of products and services, their server logs potentially contain much more than simply a user's Web search queries. Other searches logged by Google include those for images, news stories, videos, books, academic research, and blog posts, as well as links clicked and related usage statistics from within Google's News, Reader, Finance, Groups, and other services.

Logging this array of information – the user's IP address, cookie ID, date and time, search terms, results clicked, and so on – enhances Google's ability to attain the "perfect recall" necessary to deliver valuable search results and generally improve its search engine services. For example, by cross-referencing the IP address each request sent to the server along with the particular page being requested and other server log data, it is possible to find out which pages, and in which sequence, a particular IP address has visited. When asked, "Given a list of search terms, can Google produce a list of people who searched for that term, identified by IP address and/or Google cookie value?" and "Given an IP address or Google cookie value, can Google produce a list of the terms searched by the user of that IP address or cookie value?", Google responded in the affirmative to both questions, confirming its ability to track user activity through such logs (Battelle 2006a, 2006b).

Sole reliance on IP logging and Web cookies to reconstruct a users' browsing and searching activities completely and consistently has its limitations. Some Internet service providers frequently change the IP address assigned to a particular user's network connection. Alternatively, multiple users accessing the Internet through a university proxy server or through some ISPs (such as AOL) might share the same IP address. Privacy concerns have also led more savvy Internet users to disguise their IP address with anonymous routing services such as Tor (Zetter, 2005). Similarly, as the privacy concerns of the use of cookies to track users' online activities increases (Kristol 2001; Mayer-Schönberger, 1997; Schwartz, 2001), users increasingly take advantage of software and browser features that make it easier to view, delete and block Web cookies received from the sites they visit

---

[5] A Web cookie is a piece of text generated by a Web server and stored in the user's computer, where it waits to be sent back to the server the next time the browser accesses that particular Web address. By returning a cookie to a Web server, the browser provides the server a means of associating the current page view with prior page views in order to "remember" something about the previous page requests and events (Clarke 2001; Kristol 2001). Google's user of Web cookies allows it to identify particular browsers between sessions, even if that browser's IP address changes.

(McGann 2005; Mindlin 2006). Even in the absence of such privacy-protecting measures, cookies and IP addresses are linked only to a particular Web browser or computer, not necessarily a particular user. Neither the browser passing the cookie nor the Web server receiving it can know who is actually using the computer, or whether multiple users are using the same machine. Reliance on IP addresses and cookies might not provide necessary differentiation between users, limiting the extent of the "perfect recall" necessary for Google to deliver the most relevant results and advertising.

To overcome such limitations, Website owners frequently urge users to register with the Website and login when using the services (Ho 2005: 660–661; Tec-Ed 1999). When a user supplies a unique login identity to a Web server, that information, along with the current cookie ID is stored in each log file record for that user's subsequent activity at the site. By tying aspects of the site's functionality to being logged in, the user is compelled to accept the Web cookie for that session. Even if the user deletes the cookie or changes her IP address at the end of the session, by logging in again at the next visit, a consistent record for the user in the server log can be maintained. Logging in with a unique user name similarly reduces the variability of multiple or shielded IP addresses. Further, any personally identifiable information provided during the registration process, such as age, gender, zip code, or occupation, can be associated with the user's account and server log history, providing a more detailed profile of the user.

In early 2004, Google started experimenting with products and services that required users to register and login, including personalized search results, e-mail alerts when sites about a particular topic of interest are added to Google's index (Kopytoff 2004). Soon afterward, Google introduced products and services that required the creation of a Google Account, such as Gmail, Google Calendar, and the Reader service to organize news feeds. Other Google services can be partially used without a Google Account, but users are encouraged to create an account in order to maximize its benefits or access certain features. Examples include Google Video, with a Google Account required for certain premium content, and Book Search, in which a Google Account helps control access to copyright-protected text. When Google acquires external products and services with their own login protocols, migration to Google Accounts is typical, as the case with Blogger or Dodgeball. Internally developed products that previously utilized unique logins such as Orkut have also migrated to the universal Google Account.

Google's encouragement of the creation of Google Accounts, combined with its use of persistent Web cookies, provides the necessary architecture for the creation of detailed server logs of users' activities across Google's various products and services, ranging from the simplest of search queries to minute details of their personal lives. While the full extent of the data capturable by Google's infrastructure is difficult to estimate, Table 6.2 identifies some of the typical forms of personal information potentially stored within Google's servers.

Table 6.2 Sample of Personal Information Collected by Google's Suite of Products

Product	Information Collected	Notes
General Information Inquiries		
Web search	Web search queries	Search for own name, address, social
	Results clicked	security number, etc is common
Personalized Homepage	News preferences	
	Special interests	
	Zip code	
Alerts	News preferences	Alerts for a user's own name (vanity
	Special interests	search) are common
	E-mail address	
	Search queries	
Image Search	Results clicked	
	Search queries	
Video	Videos watched/downloaded	Google Video Player contains addi-
	Credit card information for pur-chased videos	tional DRM technology to moni-tor off-site video usage
	E-mail details for shared videos	
	Search queries	
Book Search	Results clicked	
	Pages read	
	Bookseller pages viewed	
Academic Research		
Scholar	Search queries	
	Results clicked	
	Home library (Optional)	
News and Political Information		
News	News search queries	
	Results clicked	
Reader	Feed subscriptions	
	Usage statistics	
Blog Search	Search queries	
	Results clicked	
Communication and Social Networking		
Gmail	Text of email messages	
	E-mail searches performed	
	Email address or cellphone number (used for account creation)	
Groups	Search queries	Users are encouraged to create
	User interests	detailed profiles, including name,
	Usage statistics	location, industry, homepage, etc
	Profile information	
	Contact list	
	Chat messages	
Talk	Usage statistics	
	Weblog posts and comments	
	Profile information	

(continued)

Table 6.2 (continued)

Product	Information Collected	Notes
Blogger	Usage statistics Profile information Usage statistics	Users are encouraged to create detailed profiles, including name, location, gender, birthday, etc
Orkut	E-mail address and content of invitations Profile information E-mail address Location	Users are encouraged to create detailed profiles, including name, location, gender, birthday, etc
Dodgeball	Mobile phone information Text messages sent	User location when messages sent are tracked by Google
Personal Data Management		
Calendar	Profile information Events Usage statistics	
Financial Data Management		
Finance	Financial quotes Discussion group posts Discussion group views Portfolio (optional) Profile information	Names and e-mails are displayed with discussion posts
Consumer Activities		
Catalog Search	Product search queries Results clicked	
Froogle	Product search queries Results clicked Sites visited Shopping list	
Local / Maps	Search queries	Search queries might include geographic-specific information
	Results clicked	
	Home location	Default location stored via Web cookie
Computer File Management		
Desktop Search	Search queries Computer file index (Optional)	Search queries visible to Google under certain circumstances Desktop file index is stored on Google's services if using Search Across Computers
Internet Browsing		
Bookmarks	Favorite Websites When visited	
Notebook	Notes and clippings Sites annotated	
Toolbar	Search queries	Use of some advanced features routes *all* browsing traffic through Google servers
	Websites visited	
Web Accelerator	Websites visited	*All* browsing traffic is routed through Google servers

The result is a robust infrastructure arming Google with the ability to capture and aggregate a wide array of personal and intellectual information about its users, extending beyond just the keywords for which they search, but also including the news they read, the interests they have, the blogs they follow, the books they enjoy, the stocks in their portfolio, their schedule for the coming week, and perhaps the URL of every Website they visit.

6.5 Discussion

It is easy to think of search engines like Google as one-way information interfaces: you enter a search term, and Google gives you millions of pages of information in return. You click on a link, and they direct you to a Website, a helpful map, or a news report. But there is an important feedback loop; the interface is two-way. More than just the center of gravity of information seeking online, Google's information infrastructure also acts as a black hole, to continue the metaphor, using its gravitational forces to pull as much information about its users into its domain as possible. By monitoring and aggregating the results of every Web search performed, every image result clicked, every Website bookmarked, or every page visited with the Toolbar, Google has created sophisticated infrastructure of dataveillance. The result is what John Battelle calls a "database of intentions":

> This information represents, in aggregate form, a place holder for the intentions of human-kind - a massive database of desires, needs, wants, and likes that can be discovered, sub-poenaed, archived, tracked, and exploited to all sorts of ends. Such a beast has never before existed in the history of culture, but is almost guaranteed to grow exponentially from this day forward. This artifact can tell us extraordinary things about who we are and what we want as a culture. (Battelle 2003)

While many of our day-to-day habits – such as using credit cards, ATMs, cell phones, or automated toll collection systems – leave countless "virtual footprints" of our activities, the panoptic gaze of Google's infrastructure of dataveillance tracks our search histories, e-mails, blog posts or general browsing habits, providing "an excellent source of insight into what someone is *thinking*, not just what that person is doing" (Hinman 2005: 23).

The full effects of the panoptic gaze of Google's infrastructure of dataveillance are difficult to predict, but, like most infrastructures of dataveillance, the most obvious effects of Google's infrastructure relate to the exercising of disciplinary power, panoptic sorting, and the general invisibility of both its gaze and its power. Clive Norris warns that infrastructures of dataveillance are often used to "[render] visualization meaningful for the basis of disciplinary social control" (Norris 2002: 251). Instances of how users of Google's infrastructure were made visible for the exercise of disciplinary power include a court ordering Google to provide the complete contents of a user's Gmail account, including e-mail messages he thought were deleted (McCullagh 2006a) and the introduction of evidence that a suspected murderer performed a Google search for the words "neck snap break" (Cohen 2005). While

Google appears to recognize, at least partially, the disciplinary threat of storing such robust records of its users activities when it announced it would move user data collected from its Chinese site outside of the country in order to prevent China's government from being able to access the data without Google's consent (McMillan 2006), the company recently agreed to comply with a Brazilian court order to release data on users of its Orkut social networking site to help Brazilian authorities investigate use of the site related to racism, pedophilia, and homophobia (Downie 2006). The possibility of Google providing search histories to government bodies for disciplinary action has reached new heights within the United States with the passage of the USA PATRIOT Act, greatly expanding the ability of law enforcement to access such records, while restricting the source of the records, such as Google, from disclosing any such request has even been made (Battelle 2005: 197–204).

Google's infrastructure of dataveillance also spawns instances of "panoptic sorting" where users of Google are identified, assessed and classified "to coordinate and control their access to the goods and services that define life in the modern capitalist economy" (Gandy 1993: 15). Google, like most for-profit search engine providers, is financially motivated collect as much information as possible about each user: receiving personalized search results might contribute to a user's allegiance to a particular search engine service, increasing exposure to that site's advertising partners as well as improving chances the user would use fee-based services. Similarly, search engines can charge higher advertising rates when ads are accurately placed before the eyes of users with relevant needs and interests (Hansell 2005). Through the panoptic gaze of its diverse suite of products, Google collects as much information as possible about an individual's behavior, and considers it to be potentially useful in the profiling and categorization of a user's potential economic value: recognizing that targeted advertising will be the "growth engine of Google for a very long time", Google CEO Eric Schmidt stressed the importance of collecting user information for economic gain, acknowledging that "Google knows a lot about the person surfing, especially if they have used personal search or logged into a service such as Gmail" (Miller 2006).

Perhaps the most potent aspect of the technological gaze of Google's infrastructure of dataveillance is its relative invisibility, indispensability, and apparent inescapability. The majority of Web searchers are not aware that search engines have the ability to actively track users' search behavior (Fallows 2005: 21; Kopytoff 2006), and as Google continues to expand its information infrastructure[6], it becomes arduous for everyday users to recognize the data collection threats of these services, and easier to take the design Google's infrastructure of dataveillance merely "at interface value" (Turkle 1995: 103). Greg Elmer warns of the dangers of such an

---

[6]Recent additions to Google's product suite include Web-based word processor and spreadsheet services, enterprise solutions for business use, online digital photo sharing, website authoring tools, an online database package, and the widely-popular video hosting website YouTube.

environment where the collection of personal information is a prerequisite of participation inevitably entrenches power in the hands of the technology designers:

> Ultimately, what both requesting and requiring personal information highlight is the centrality of producing, updating, and deploying consumer *profiles* – simulations or pictures of consumer likes, dislikes, and behaviors that are automated within the process of consuming goods, services, or media and that increasingly anticipate our future needs and wants based on our aggregated past choices and behaviors. And although Foucault warns of the self-disciplinary model of punishment in panoptic surveillance, computer profiling, conversely, oscillates between seemingly rewarding participation and punishing attempts to elect not to divulge personal information. (Elmer 2004: 5–6)

This blurring of punishments and rewards – subtle requests and not so subtle commands for personal information – reoccurs in Google's information interface where the default settings and arrangement of services make the collection of personal information automatic and difficult to resist, and many are willing to join "Planet Google" with only scant hesitation: "I don't know if I want all my personal information saved on this massive server in Mountain View, but it is so much of an improvement on how life was before, I can't help it" (Williams 2006). As with Bentham's panopticon, Google's infrastructure of dataveillance places its users under an almost invisible gaze, resulting in a kind of anticipatory conformity, whereby the divulgence of personal information become both routinized and internalized.

6.6   Conclusion

By amassing a tantalizing collection of, admittedly, innovative and useful tools, coupled with requiring the divulgence of personal information as a precondition for using many of its search-related products and services, Google has constructed an information-seeking environment whereby which individuals are continuously integrated into a larger infrastructure of dataveillance. Their quest for the perfect search engine has resulted in the emergence of a robust infrastructure of dataveillance that can quickly become the basis of disciplinary social control. Repeating Roger Clark's warning about the effects of dataveillance:

> [A] real impact of dataveillance is the reduction in the meaningfulness of individual actions, and hence in self- reliance and self- responsibility. Although this may be efficient and even fair, it involves a change in mankind's image of itself, and risks sullen acceptance by the masses and stultification of the independent spirit needed to meet the challenges of the future. ... In general, mass dataveillance tends to subvert individualism and the meaningfulness of human decisions and actions. (Clarke 1988: 508)

Thus a Faustian bargain emerges with the quest for the perfect search engine: The perfect search engine promises breadth, depth, efficiency, and relevancy, but enables the widespread collection of personal and intellectual information in the name of its perfect recall. If left unchecked, potential cost of this bargain is nothing less than the "individualism and the meaningfulness of human decisions and actions."

What options exist for renegotiating our Faustian bargain with the perfect search engine? One avenue for changing the terms of the Faustian bargain is to enact laws to regulate the capture and use of personal information by Web search engines. A recent gathering of leading legal scholars and industry lawyers to discuss the possibility of regulating search engines revealed, however, that viable and constitutional solutions are difficult to conceive, let alone agree upon.[7] Alternatively, the search engine industry could self-regulate, creating strict policies regarding the capture, aggregation, and use of personal data via their services. But as Chris Hoofnagle reminds us, "We now have ten years of experience with privacy self-regulation online, and the evidence points to a sustained failure of business to provide reasonable privacy protections" (2005: 1). Given search engine companies' economic interests in capturing user information for powering the perfect search engine, relying solely on self-regulation will likely be unsatisfying.

A third option is to affect the design of the technology itself. As Larry Lessig notes, "how a system is designed will affect the freedoms and control the system enables" (2001: 35), I argue that technological design is one of the *critical junctures* for society to re-negotiate its Faustian bargain with the perfect search engine in order to preserve a sense of "individualism and the meaningfulness of human decisions and actions." Potential design variables include whether default settings for new products or services automatically enroll users in data-collecting processes – or whether the process can be turned off. Or the extent to which different products should be interconnected: For example, if a user signs up to use Gmail, should the Personalized Search automatically be activated? Should the user automatically be logged in to other services? Ideally, new tools can be developed to give users access and control over the personal information collected: In the spirit of the Code of Fair Information Practices, a Google Data Privacy Center should be built to allow users to view all their personal data collected, make changes and deletions, restrict how it is used, and so on. Through such an intervention in the design of the perfect search engine, there is hope that our Faustian bargain can be re-negotiated to counter the disciplinary effects of its gaze.

References

Agre P (2003) Your face is not a bar code: arguments against automatic face recognition in public places. Retrieved July 28, 2006, from http://polaris.gseis.ucla.edu/pagre/bar-code.html
Andrews P (1999, February 7) The search for the perfect search engine. The Seattle Times, p. E1.
Barbaro M, Zeller Jr T (2006, August 9) A face is exposed for AOL searcher no. 4417749. The New York Times, p. A1.

---

[7] See "Regulating search: a symposium on search engines, law, and public policy" held in December 2005 at Yale Law School (http://islandia.law.yale.edu/isp/regulatingsearch.html).

Battelle J (2003, November 13) The database of intentions. Searchblog. Retrieved May 16, 2006, from http://battellemedia.com/archives/000063.php

Battelle J (2004, September 8) Perfect search. Searchblog. Retrieved May 16, 2006, from http://battellemedia.com/archives/000878.php

Battelle J (2005) The search: how google and its rivals rewrote the rules of business and transformed our culture. Portfolio, New York.

Battelle J (2006a, January 30). More on what google (and probably a lot of others) know. Searchblog. Retrieved May 16, 2006, from http://battellemedia.com/archives/002283.php

Battelle J (2006b, January 27) What info does google keep? Searchblog. Retrieved May 16, 2006, from http://battellemedia.com/archives/002272.php

Bennett C (1996) The public surveillance of personal data: a cross-national analysis. In D. Lyon and E. Zureik (Eds.) Computers, surveillance, and privacy (pp. 237–259) University of Minnesota Press, Minneapolis

Bennett C (2001) Cookies, web bugs, webcams and cue cats: patterns of surveillance on the world wide web. Ethics and Information Technology 3: 197–210

Bennett C, Raab C, Regan P (2003) People and place: patterns of individual identification within intelligent transport systems. In D. Lyon (Ed.) Surveillance as social sorting: privacy, risk, and digital discrimination (pp. 153–175) Routledge, London

Bentham J (1995) The Panopticon writings (M. Bozovic, Trans.). Verso, London

Bowker GC, Star SL (1999) Sorting things out: classification and its consequences. MIT, Cambridge, MA

Brey P (2004) Ethical aspects of facial recognition systems in public places. Journal of Information Communication and Ethics in Society 2: 97–109

Brin S, Page L (1998) The anatomy of a large-scale hypertextual web search engine. WWW7/ Computer Networks 30: 107–117

Clarke R (1988) Information technology and dataveillance. Communications of the ACM, 37(5), 498–512.

Clarke R (2001) Cookies. Retrieved May 5, 2006, from http://www.anu.edu.au/people/Roger.Clarke/II/Cookies.html

Cohen A (2005, November 28) What google should roll out next: a privacy upgrade. The New York Times, p. A18.

Cohen J (1996) A right to read anonymously: a closer look at 'copyright management' in cyberspace. Connecticut Law Review 28: 981–1039

Cohen J (2003). DRM and privacy. Communications of the ACM 46: 46–49

Diaz A (2005) Through the google goggles: sociopolitical bias in search engine design. Stanford University.

Downie A (2006, September 8) Google carves a middle path on privacy. The Christian Science Monitor, pp. 1.

Elkin-Koren N (2001) Let the crawlers crawl: on virtual gatekeepers and the right to exclude indexing. University of Dayton Law Review 26: 180–209

Elmer G (2004) Profiling machines: mapping the personal information economy. MIT, Cambridge, MA

Fallows D (2005) Search engine users: Internet searchers are confident, satisfied and trusting – but they are also unaware and naïve. Pew Internet & American Life Project. Retrieved October 15, 2005, from http://www.pewInternet.org/pdfs/PIP_Searchengine_users.pdf

Ferguson C (2005) That's next for google? Technology Review 108(1): 38–46.

Foucault M (1971) The order of things: an archaeology of the human sciences. Vintage, New York

Foucault M (1977) Discipline and punish: the birth of the prison (A. Sheridan, Trans. [1st American ed.] Ed.). Vintage Books, New York

Foucault M (1980) The eye of power. In: C. Gordon (Ed.) Power/knowledge: selected interviews and other writings, 1972–1977 (pp. 146–165). Pantheon, New York

Froomkin AM (2000) The death of privacy. Stanford Law Review 52: 1461–1543

Gandy (1993) The panoptic sort: a political economy of personal information. Westview, Boulder, CO

Garfinkel S (2000) Database nation: the death of privacy in the 21st century (1st ed.). O'Reilly, Sebastopol, CA

Goldman E (2005) Deregulating relevancy in Internet trademark law. Emory Law Journal 54: 507, 567–568

Google (1999, June 7) Google receives $25 million in equity funding (press release). Google Press Center. Retrieved August 18, 2006, from http://www.google.com/press/pressrel/pressrelease1. html

Google (2005a) Company overview. Retrieved May 3, 2006, from http://www.google.com/ corporate/index.html

Google (2005b) Google Privacy FAQ. Retrieved May 3, 2006, from http://www.google.com/ privacy_faq.html

Google (2005c, October 14) Google privacy policy. Retrieved May 3, 2006, from http://www. google.com/privacypolicy.html

Google (2007) Our philosophy. Retrieved March 27, 2007, from http://www.google.com/intl/en/ corporate/tenthings.html

Gussow D (1999, October 4) In search of. St. Petersburg Times, pp. 13.

Hafner K (2006, January 25) After subpoenas, Internet searches give some pause. The New York Times, pp. A1, A19.

Hafner K, Richtel M (2006, January 20) Google resists U.S. subpoena of search data. The New York Times, pp. A1, C4.

Hansell S (2005, September 26) Microsoft plans to sell search ads of its own. The New York Times, pp. C1, C8.

Hansell S (2006, August 8) AOL removes search data on vast group of web users. The New York Times, pp. C4.

Hargittai E (2002) Beyond logs and surveys: in-depth measures of people's web use skills. Journal of the American Society for Information Science and Technology 53: 1239–1244

Hinman L (2005) Esse est indicato in Google: ethical and political issues in search engines. International Review of Information Ethics 3: 19–25

Ho SY (2005) An exploratory study of using a user remote tracker to examine web users' personality traits. Proceedings of the 7th international conference on Electronic commerce, 659–665.

Hoofnagle C (2005, March 4) Privacy self regulation: a decade of disappointment. Electronic Privacy Information Center. Retrieved April 18, 2007, from http://www.epic.org/reports/ decadedisappoint.html

Horrigan J, Rainie L (2006, April 19) The Internet's growing role in life's major moments. Pew Internet and American Life Project. Retrieved May 26, 2006, from http://www.pewInternet. org/PPF/r/181/report_display.asp

Introna L, Nissenbaum H (2000) Shaping the web: why the politics of search engines matters. The Information Society 16: 169–185

Jansen BJ, Resnick M (2005) Examining searcher perceptions of and interactions with sponsored results. Paper presented at the Workshop on Sponsored Search Auctions at ACM Conference on Electronic Commerce, Vancouver, BC.

Jansen BJ, Spink A, Saracevic T (2000) Real life, real users, and real needs: a study and analysis of user queries on the web. Information Processing and Management 36: 207–227

Kang J (1998) Information privacy in cyberspace transactions. Stanford Law Review 50: 1193–1294

Kopytoff V (2004, March 30) Google tests souped-up web searches. San Francisco Chronicle, pp. C3

Kopytoff V (2006, January 24) Most web users say google should keep data private. San Francisco Chronicle, pp. C3

Kristol D (2001) HTTP cookies: standards, privacy, and politics. ACM Transactions on Internet Technology 1: 151–198.

Kushmerick N (1998, February 23). The search engineers. The Irish Times, pp. 10.

Lessig L (2001) The future of ideas: the fate of the commons in a connected world. Random House, New York

Levy S (2006, January 30) Searching for searches. Newsweek, pp. 49.

Lyon D (2001) Surveillance society: monitoring everyday life. Open University Press, Philadelphia

Lyon D (2002). Editorial. Surveillance studies: understanding visibility, mobility and the phenetic fix. Surveillance and Society 1: 1–7

Lyon D (Ed.) (2003a) Surveillance as social sorting: privacy, risk, and digital discrimination. Routledge, London

Lyon D (2003b) Introduction. In D. Lyon (Ed.) Surveillance as social sorting: Privacy, risk, and digital discrimination (pp. 1–9). Routledge, London

Lyon D, Zureik E (1996) Computers, surveillance, and privacy. University of Minnesota Press, Minneapolis

Maney K (2006, August 9) AOL's data sketch sometimes scary picture of personalities searching Net. USA Today, pp. 4B

Marable L (2003) False oracles: consumer reaction to learning the truth about how search engines work: results of an ethnographic study. http://www.consumerwebwatch.org/news/ searchengines/index.html

Mayer-Schönberger V (1997) The Internet and privacy legislation: cookies for a treat? West Virginia Journal of Law and Technology 1

McCullagh D (2006a, March 17) Police blotter: judge orders gmail disclosure. News.com. Retrieved June 20, 2006, from http://news.com.com/Police%20blotter%20Judge%20orders% 20Gmail%20disclosure/2100-1047_3-6050295.html

McCullagh D (2006b, August 7) AOL's disturbing glimpse into users' lives. CNET News.com. Retrieved December 3, 2006, from http://news.com.com/AOLs+disturbing+glimpse+into+users +lives/2100-1030_3-6103098.html?tag=st.num

McGann R (2005, March 14) Study: consumers delete cookies at surprising rate. ClickZ News. Retrieved May 15, 2006, from http://www.clickz.com/news/article.php/3489636

McMillan R (2006, March 1) Google moving search records out of china. InfoWorld. Retrieved August 20, 2006, from http://www.infoworld.com/article/06/03/01/75996_030106HNgooglechina_1.html

McNamee R (2005, February 7) Google's desktop search. The New Normal. Retrieved May 2, 2006, from http://thenewnormal.com/index.php/newnormal/googles_desktop_search/

Miller M (2006, March 17) Google's schmidt clears the air. PCMag.com. Retrieved March 17, 2006, from http://www.pcmag.com/article2/0,1895,1939257,00.asp

Mindlin A (2006, May 15) The case of the disappearing cookies. The New York Times, pp. C5.

Mintz H (2006, January 16) Feds after google data: records sought in U.S. quest to revive porn law. San Jose Mercury News. Retrieved January 19, 2006, from http://www.siliconvalley.com/ mld/siliconvalley/13657386.htm

Nagenborg M (2005) The ethics of search engines (special issue). International Review of Information Ethics. 3

Nielsen//NetRatings. (2007, March 20) Nielsen//NetRatings announces February U.S. search share rankings. Retrieved March 27, 2007, from http://www.nielsen-netratings.com/pr/ pr_070320.pdf

Norris C (2002) From personal to digital: CCTV, the panopticon, and the technological mediation of suspicion and social control. In: D. Lyon (Ed.) Surveillance as social sorting (pp. 249–281). Routledge, London

Norris C, Armstrong G (1999) The maximum surveillance society: the rise of CCTV. Oxford: Berg.

Norvig P, Winograd T, Bowker G (2006, February 27) The ethics and politics of search engines. Panel at Santa Clara University Markkula Center for Applied Ethics. Retrieved March 1, 2006, from http://www.scu.edu/sts/Search-Engine-Event.cfm

Page L, Brin S, Motwani R, Winograd T (1998) The pagerank citation ranking: bringing order to the web. Technical report. Stanford University, Stanford, CA

Pitkow J, Schütze H, Cass T, Turnbull D, Edmonds A, Adar, E (2002) Personalized search. Communications of the ACM, 45(9), 50–55

Rainie L (November 2005) Search engine use shoots up in the past year and edges towards e-mail as the primary Internet application. Pew Internet and American Life Project.

Ramasastry A (2005, May 12) Can we stop zabasearch – and similar personal information search engines? when data democratization verges on privacy invasion. FindLaw. Retrieved June 12, 2006, from http://writ.news.findlaw.com/ramasastry/20050512.html

Regan P (1995) Legislating privacy: technology, social values, and public policy. University of North Carolina Press, Chapel Hill

Regan P (2001) From clipper to carnivore: balancing privacy, law enforcement and industry interests. Paper presented at the American Political Science Association, San Francisco, CA

Schwartz J (2001, September 4) Giving the web a memory costs its users privacy. The New York Times, pp. A1

Solove D (2004) The digital person: technology and privacy in the information age (ex machina). New York University Press, New York

Stalder F, Lyon D (2003) Electronic identity cards and social classification. In D. Lyon (Ed.) Surveillance as social sorting: privacy, risk, and digital discrimination (pp. 77–93). Routledge, London

Staples WG (2000) Everyday surveillance: vigilance and visibility in postmodern life. Rowman and Littlefield, Lanham, MD

Suchman L (1997) Do categories have politics? the language/action perspective reconsidered. In: B. Friedman (Ed.) Human values and the design of computer technology (pp. 91–105). Cambridge University Press, Cambridge, UK

Sullivan D (2006, August 23) Hitwise search engine ratings. SearchEngineWatch. Retrieved August 23, 2006, from http://searchenginewatch.com/showPage.html?page=3099931

Swidey N (2003, February 2) A nation of voyeurs: how the Internet search engine google is changing what we can find out about one another – and raising questions about whether we should. The Boston Globe Sunday Magazine, pp. 10

Tavani HT (2005) Search engines, personal information and the problem of privacy in public. International Review of Information Ethics 3: 39–45

Tec-Ed (1999, December) Assessing web site usability from server log files [white paper]. Retrieved April 3, 2006, from www.teced.com/PDFs/whitepap.pdf

Teevan J, Dumais ST, Horvitz E (2005) Personalizing search via automated analysis of interests and activities. Proceedings of the 28th Annual International ACM SIGIR Conference on Research and Development in Information Retrieval, pp. 449–456.

Turkle S (1995) Life on the screen: identity in the age of the Internet. Simon and Schuster, New York

Van Couvering E (2004) New media? the political economy of Internet search engines. Annual Conference of the International Association of Media and Communications Researchers, Porto Alegre, Brazil, 7–14

Ventura HE, Miller JM, Deflem M (2005) Governmentality and the war on terror: FBI project carnivore and the diffusion of disciplinary power. Critical Criminology 13: 55–70

Ward C (1998, May 3) Grocery store shopper cards save money but cost privacy. Houston Chronicle Retrieved August 20, 2006, from http://www.chron.com/content/chronicle/business/98/05/03grocerycards.1-1.html

Wikipedia contributors (2007, April 19) IP address. Wikipedia, The Free Encyclopedia. Retrieved April 19, 2007, from http://en.wikipedia.org/w/index.php?title=IP_address&oldid=123964420

Williams A (2006, October 15) Planet google wants you. The New York Times, pp. 9.1

Wouters J (2004, November 8) Searching for disclosure: how search engines alert consumers to the presence of advertising in search results. Consumer Reports WebWatch. Retrieved September 15, 2005, from http://www.consumerwebwatch.org/news/paidsearch/finalreport.pdf

Zetter K (2005, May 17) Tor torches online tracking. Wired News. Retrieved May 28, 2006, from http://www.wired.com/news/privacy/0,1848,67542,00.html

Zimmer M (2005) Surveillance, privacy and the ethics of vehicle safety communication technolo-
    gies. Ethics and Information Technology 7: 201–210
Zimmer M (2006, January) The value implications of the practice of paid search. Bulletin of the
    American Society for Information Science and Technology. Retrieved April 3, 2006, from
    http://www.asis.org/Bulletin/Dec-05/zimmer.html

Part III
Political, Legal,
and Economic Perspectives

7
Search Engine Liability
for Copyright Infringement

B. Fitzgerald, D. O'Brien, and A. Fitzgerald

Summary The chapter provides a broad overview to the topic of search engine liability for copyright infringement. In doing so, the chapter examines some of the key copyright law principles and their application to search engines. The chapter also provides a discussion of some of the most important cases to be decided within the courts of the United States, Australia, China and Europe regarding the liability of search engines for copyright infringement. Finally, the chapter will conclude with some thoughts for reform, including how copyright law can be amended in order to accommodate and realise the great informative power which search engines have to offer society.

7.1 Introduction

The evolution and development of search engines over the past ten years to their current level of sophistication, poses a number of challenging legal issues to the area of copyright law. While search engines like Google have rapidly expanded their online services and activities, copyright law for its part, has largely failed to adequately respond to these technological developments and advances. Instead, the result has been rigid copyright laws being applied to the types of online activities, which were never contemplated when the original legislative provisions were drafted causing great ambiguity and uncertainty.

Search engines also play a vital role in ensuring the free flow of the Internet and its core purpose – access to information. However, copyright laws by their very nature, fundamentally challenge this concept of a freely accessible and flowing Internet. This conflict was alluded to in a recent decision of the United States District Court, where the Court held that the principal legal issues for search engines arise:

> out of the increasingly recurring conflict between intellectual property rights on the one hand and the dazzling capacity of Internet technology to assemble, organize, store, access and display intellectual property "content" on the one hand.[8]

---

[8] *Perfect 10 v Google Inc*, 416 F Supp 2d 828, 831 (CD Cal, 2006)

A. Spink and M. Zimmer (eds.), *Web Search, Springer Series in Information Science and Knowledge Management 14*.
© Springer-Verlag Berlin Heidelberg 2008

Indeed, it has been argued that the revolution which search engines have brought to the Internet world, has only been made possible by the fact that search engines have been able to exercise many of the exclusive rights of the copyright owner, which would not have been possible in the non-digital based world.[9]

The following chapter will provide a broad overview of the liability of search engines for copyright infringement. In doing so, the chapter will examine some of the most important cases to be decided within the United States, Australia, China and Europe regarding the liability of search engines for copyright infringement. Finally, the chapter will conclude with some thoughts for reform, including how copyright law can be amended in order to accommodate and realise the great informative power which search engines have to offer society.

7.2 Copyright Law

7.2.1 Copyright Principles

Much of the digital content distributed through the Internet, or available for viewing or downloading at Internet locations, is protected by copyright. However, the conceptual basis and core principles of copyright law were established centuries before digital era technologies, like search engines were invented. Copyright emerged in the late 15th century, in the years following the invention of the printing press. Over the ensuing centuries the scope of copyright expanded incrementally to encompass new forms of creative material, as well as new ways of distributing those materials, that have been made possible by rapid advances in technology. As new ways of expressing and exploiting creative materials have been developed, the exclusive rights conferred on creators have been reformulated and extended with the aim of ensuring that creators may reap the rewards of their efforts.[10]

Dating back to the Berne Convention on Literary and Artistic Works 1886 there have also been a variety of international treaties covering copyright law. The multilateral Agreement on Trade Related Aspects of Intellectual Property Rights 1994, World Intellectual Property Organisation Copyright Treaty 1996, World Intellectual Property Organisation Performers and Phonograms Treaty 1996 and bilateral free trade agreements, such as the Australia–United States Free Trade Agreement 2004 are also part of this landscape. These treaties which seek to harmonise copyright law across the world tend to be implemented through national or domestic law, such as the Copyright Act or Code in each country. An example of this is TRIPS, which

---

[9] Greenleaf G, (2006) Creating commons by friendly appropriate. In AIPL-Res 10 http://www.austlii.edu.au/au/other/AIPLRes/2006/10.html

[10] For an overview of the origins and evolution of copyright see (Fitzgerald and Fitzgerald 2004, p. 82-84).

requires member countries to enact copyright laws that uphold the Berne Convention and to ensure that adequate enforcement mechanisms are in place. A failure to do this can lead to the non-complying member being taken to the World Trade Organisation's Dispute Settlement Body and trade sanctions imposed.[11]

The *Berne Convention* sets up a system of copyright law where the creator or author is the copyright owner at the outset, but they can (and often do) assign their copyright to a commercialising agent, such as a publisher who then becomes the copyright owner. Copyright attaches to subject matter such as literary, musical, dramatic and artistic works (including photographs), sound recordings and film. A song for instance can be made up of a literary work (lyrics), musical work (score) and a sound recording, with the different aspects owned by different copyright owners. In most countries except the United States (where such personal rights in copyright law are very limited) creators or authors hold moral rights to be attributed as the author of copyright material and to ensure the integrity of their work (not to have it mutilated in such a manner as to cause dishonour). These rights are not usually assignable, but in some countries they can be waived or overridden with consent. However, in some countries, like France and Germany waiver is not possible.

Moral rights stay with the creator or author, while economic rights remain with the copyright owner. The key economic rights give the copyright owner power to control things such as reproduction and communication to the public. If any of these rights are exercised, the permission of the copyright owner will normally be required unless one of the exceptions under the various copyright laws that allow use of copyright material without the permission of the copyright owner applies. In the United States the fair use provision allows a broad range of uses without permission, for purposes such as parody or critique, while in other countries narrower notions, such as fair dealing allow strictly controlled use for research or study, parody or satire, news reporting and criticism or review. There may also be statutory licences (e.g., for private or educational use) that allow the use of the material without the permission of the copyright owner if compensation is paid.

In addition to liability for the primary infringement of copyright, in most jurisdictions there are also provisions, whereby third parties can be held liable for authorising (or contributing to) copyright infringement. The rationale behind such provisions are that third parties are in many cases in a better position to discourage copyright infringement, either by monitoring primary infringers or redesigning their technologies to make infringement more difficult. Generally, since authorising others to do an act in relation to copyrighted material is one of the copyright owner's exclusive rights, copyright will also be infringed by authorising another person to do the infringing act without the licence of the copyright owner.[12] However, in

---

[11] For example see the United States complaint filed against China (Montgomery and Cha 2007).

[12] For example under Australian law see *Copyright Act 1968* (Cth) ss 36(1) 101(1)

considering whether an infringement of copyright has been authorised by a third party, it is always necessary to first establish a primary act of infringement that has a causal connection to the act or acts of authorisation.

Similarly, in one of the most important jurisdictions for search engines, the United States, the Courts have also held third parties liable for copyright infringement under two long standing common law doctrines of contributory infringement[13] and vicarious liability.[14] Under the doctrine of contributory infringement, a third party can be held liable for indirectly infringing copyright where they have knowledge of the infringing activity and either induce, cause or materially contribute to the infringing conduct of another. While, under the doctrine of vicarious liability a third party can be held liable where they have the right and ability to supervise the infringing activity and have a direct financial interest in the activities.

It should also be noted that in *Metro-Goldwyn-Mayer Studios Inc v Grokster Ltd*,[15] the Supreme Court of the United States introduced an additional form of third party liability for copyright law, the doctrine of inducement. Under this doctrine the Supreme Court held that:

> one who distributes a device with the object of promoting its use to infringe copyright, as shown by clear expression or other affirmative steps taken to foster infringement, is liable for the resulting acts of infringement by third parties.[16]

Importantly, for search engines and other online intermediaries, provisions exist in most jurisdictions called 'safe harbours' which – although not always providing a complete defence to copyright infringement – act to mitigate liability by limiting the remedies available against third parties for copyright infringement in certain circumstances. In the United States, 'safe harbor' provisions exist under the *Digital Millennium Copyright Act 1998*.[17] These provisions immunise search engines, Internet access providers, telecommunication companies and other online service providers from secondary liability for copyright infringement providing these entities first satisfy a number of specific requirements which are designed to safeguard the interests of copyright holders.[18] Similarly, in other jurisdictions, like Australia, 'safe harbour' provisions also exist, although arguably their operation, at least in Australia, is much narrower than other jurisdictions.[19]

---

[13] *Shapiro, Bernstein & Co v HL Green Co*, 316 F3d 304 (2d Cir 1963)

[14] *Gershwin Publishing Corp v Columbia Artists Management Inc*, 443 F2d 1159 (2d Cir 1971)

[15] 545 US 913 (2005); Radcliffe (2006)

[16] *Metro-Goldwyn-Mayer Studios Inc v Grokster Ltd*, 545 US 913, 919 (2005)

[17] § 512(c) 17 USC

[18] See Walker (2004). While the safe harbors contain specific provisions/immunity for caching and information location tools and thereby provide search engines with some level of certainty, they are conditional upon strict requirements relating to knowledge, financial benefit and the type of caching. This serves to complicate and restrict their application. A number of the cases discussed below fall outside the safe harbors for these reasons. On the requirements of the safe harbors see *Perfect 10 Inc v CCBill LLC*, 481 F 3d 751 (9th Cir, 2007)

[19] *Copyright Act 1968* (Cth) ss 116AA-116AJ; also see O'Brien and Fitzgerald (2006)

7.2.2 *Copyright Issues for Search Engines*

Copyright law raises a number of challenging legal issues for search engines, particularly in regard to the reproduction and communication to the public of any text, images or sound recordings. Importantly, search engines do not own content, but instead organise and provide access to the vast store of material that is posted on, or to Websites and the Internet, generating revenue by selling advertising. Since much of the activity carried out by search engines involves the reproduction of copyright content that has been made available on the Internet by third parties, in many cases questions of copyright infringement are likely arise. It also should be noted, that the types of copyright issues which will arise are likely to vary to some degree depending upon the nature of the search engine and the services provided by that search engine.[20]

A series of United States cases during 2006 considered whether the 'fair use' doctrine or the notion of an 'implied licence' could protect Google from liability for copyright infringement in its day-to-day activities. The outcome of these cases has been somewhat uncertain and it is too early to predict how the law will settle in this area. However, as Google becomes one of the most valuable companies in the world by providing access and search services and as other players assume copyright interests, it is expected that further challenges will emerge in regard to the liability of search engines for copyright infringement.

7.3 Case Law

7.3.1 *United States*

The majority of decisions to have emerged from the courts involving search engine liability for copyright infringement have been from the United States, where the majority of search engines are based.

Field v Google Inc

One of the first cases to have considered the legality of caching by a search engine was *Field v Google Inc*.[21] In this case, the Nevada District Court held that Google did not infringe copyright when they copy Websites, store copies and enable them

---

[20] For example additional copyright issues may arise for video sharing websites or blogs being hosted or provided by search engines see O'Brien and Fitzgerald (2006); O'Brien D Blogs and the law: Key legal issues for the blogosphere. Media and Arts Law Review (forthcoming); Black P, Delaney H, Fitzgerald B The challenge of user-generated and peer-produced knowledge, content and culture. Murdoch e Law Journal (forthcoming)

[21] 412 F Supp 2d 1106 (District Court of Nevada, 2006)

to be downloaded by Internet users as a part of the Google cache feature.[22] The plaintiff, Field, an author and attorney brought an action for copyright infringement against the search engine Google, claming that they infringed his copyright when they automatically cached and copied a story he had posted to his Website.[23]

At issue in this case were five claims by Field that Google's caching practices breached copyright law.[24] However, the Court rejected all five of Field's claims, holding five different defences protected Google from Field's claims that their caching practices breached copyright.[25] In doing so, the Court held that:

1. Google did not directly infringe copyright when Internet users downloaded pages from the Google cache, because there was no volitional act present;[26]
2. Google was given an implied licence by the copyright owner where they know of the use and encourage it (for example, in this case despite knowing about the 'no-archive' meta-tag, Field chose not to use it);[27]
3. Google was entitled to rely upon the doctrine of estoppel;[28]
4. Google's caching practices were a fair use, as they were transformative in nature and there was no evidence that Google intended to profit from the caching;[29] and
5. Google was entitled to rely upon the 'safe harbor' provisions for intermediate and temporary storage.[30]

Parker v Google Inc

Following the decision in *Field v Google Inc*,[31] a similar action was brought against Google for direct copyright infringement in the United States District Court for the Eastern District of Pennsylvania. In *Parker v Google Inc*,[32] Parker, an author, claimed that Google had directly infringed copyright by automatically archiving a copy of his posting (a chapter of one of his e-books) he put on USENET, an online bulletin board.[33] Parker also alleged that Google directly infringed copyright by

---

[22] *Field v Google Inc*, 412 F Supp 2d 1106, 1109 (District Court of Nevada, 2006)

[23] *Field v Google Inc*, 412 F Supp 2d 1106, 1113-1114 (District Court of Nevada, 2006)

[24] See Kociubinski (2006); Bashor (2006).

[25] *Field v Google Inc*, 412 F Supp 2d 1106, 1109 (District Court of Nevada, 2006)

[26] *Field v Google Inc*, 412 F Supp 2d 1106, 1114-1115 (DC Nev, 2006)

[27] *Field v Google Inc*, 412 F Supp 2d 1106, 1115-1116 (DC Nev, 2006)

[28] *Field v Google Inc*, 412 F Supp 2d 1106, 1116-1117 (DC Nev, 2006)

[29] *Field v Google Inc*, 412 F Supp 2d 1106, 1117-1123 (DC Nev, 2006)

[30] *Field v Google Inc*, 412 F Supp 2d 1106, 1123-1125 (DC Nev, 2006)

[31] 412 F Supp 2d 1106 (DC Nev, 2006)

[32] 422 F Supp 2d 492 (ED Pa, 2006)

[33] *Parker v Google Inc*, 422 F Supp 2d 492, 495 (ED Pa, 2006)

providing users of the search engine with a list of links in response to a search query, with excerpts of his Website contained within the list of links.[34]

However, the Court rejected Parker's claims of direct copyright infringement in the archiving of his USENET posting, by holding that Google's activities fell within those of an Internet service provider and thus did not constitute copyright infringement.[35] Importantly, the Court found that Google did not have the requisite volitional conduct to support a finding of direct copyright infringement. In this regard, the Court stated:

> [w]hen an ISP automatically and temporarily stores data without human intervention so that the system can operate and transmit data to its users; the necessary element of volition is missing.'[36]

The Court also dismissed Parker's claim of direct copyright infringement through indexing and caching Websites on the basis of a failure to state a claim on which relief can be granted.[37] In briefly addressing this issue, the Court stated that s 512(b) of the *Digital Millennium Copyright Act 1998*[38] and the decision in *Field v Google Inc*,[39] meant that Google was entitled to rely upon the 'safe harbor' provisions for its system caching activities. The Court also rejected Parker's claims against Google for contributory copyright infringement and vicarious copyright infringement.[40]

Kelly v Ariba Soft Corporation

The legality of linking by search engines has also been considered in a number of recent United States cases. *Kelly v Arriba Soft Corporation*,[41] involved a dispute between a commercial photographer and a company whose visual search engine enabled Web users to search for images on the Internet. Results retrieved by the search engine were displayed in the form of thumbnail images of lower resolution and quality than the originals from which they were made. The thumbnail images contained inline links to the full-size images, so that by clicking on a thumbnail, a full-size version of the image, as it appeared on the copyright owner's Website, was displayed, as well as the Webpage from which the image originated. In other words, the use of inline linking meant that the image displayed when a Web user clicked

---

[34] Ibid.

[35] Parker v Google Inc, 422 F Supp 2d 492, 496-498 (ED Pa, 2006)

[36] *Parker v Google Inc*, 422 F Supp 2d 492, 497 (ED Pa, 2006)

[37] *Parker v Google Inc*, 422 F Supp 2d 492, 497-498 (ED Pa, 2006)

[38] § 512(c) 17 USC

[39] 412 F Supp 2d 1106 (DC Nev, 2006)

[40] *Parker v Google Inc*, 422 F Supp 2d 492, 498-500 (ED Pa, 2006)

[41] 280 F 3d 934 (9th Cir, 2002; withdrawn 9th Cir 3 July 2003)

on the thumbnail was the actual image that appeared on the copyright owner's Website. The plaintiff owned photographic images he had posted on his Website on which he sold advertising space as well as books and travel packages. When the plaintiff found that the defendant had made thumbnail images of, and links to, his photographs, he objected and commenced proceedings against the defendant for copyright infringement.

In 2002, the 9th Circuit Court of Appeals held that while the plaintiff had established a prima facie case of copyright infringement by the defendant's when they copied his photographs to create the thumbnail images, the defendant's actions were not infringing, because based on a weighing of the factors set out in s 107 of the United States *Copyright Act 1976*, they were a fair use of the copyright works.[42] This finding was based on the fact that the thumbnails were smaller, lower resolution images that served a different function to the plaintiff's original images. In other words, whereas the defendant made the copies as part of is efforts to index and improve access to images on the Web, the plaintiff used the images to portray scenery in an artistic manner and attract viewers to his Website. Users were unlikely to enlarge the thumbnails and use them for artistic purposes because they were of much lower resolution than the originals.

This meant that they were not suitable for use as substitutes for the originals and did not harm the market for the sale or licensing of the originals. By contrast, the display of the full-size version of the images as they appeared on the plaintiff's Website when a thumbnail was clicked was held to be an infringement of the plaintiff's exclusive right to publicly display the copyright work under s 106 of the United States *Copyright Act*. This was the case even though the use of inline linking meant that when a thumbnail was clicked the image that was displayed was imported directly from the plaintiff's site and did not involve any copying of the images by the defendant. The Court held that the public display of the images was not a fair use because the defendant's use of the images was not for a different purpose than the plaintiff's use of them and the defendant's use of the images was likely to divert Web users away from the plaintiff's site, thereby damaging the plaintiff's market for sales and licensing of the images.

The 9th Circuit's 2002 decision was withdrawn and superseded by a subsequent decision of the same court in July 2003, which affirmed the finding that the defendant's copying of the plaintiff's photographs to create and retrieve the thumbnail images was a non-infringing fair use.[43] However, the court avoided resolving the issue of whether the defendant's inline linking to the full-size images of the plaintiff's photographs also infringed copyright because the parties had not

---

[42] Section 107 of the United States *Copyright Act* requires a consideration of four factors: the nature of the use of the work; the nature of the copyright work itself; the amount and substantiality of the portion used; and the effect of the use upon the potential market for the copyright work

[43] *Kelly v Arriba Soft Corp* 336 F 3d 811 (9th Cir, 2003)

requested summary judgment on that point. After the parties failed to reach a settlement, default judgment was entered in favour of the plaintiff in March 2004.[44]

Perfect 10 v Google Inc

Similarly, in proceedings for an interlocutory injunction in *Perfect 10 v Google Inc*,[45] the Court concluded that the plaintiff, an adult-oriented Website, was likely to succeed in copyright infringement proceedings against the defendant, whose Google image search engine displayed thumbnail images of the plaintiff's copyright photographs.[46] When a search was conducted, each of the thumbnail images presented contained an inline link to the Web page on which the image in question had been located by Google's search engine.

The plaintiff was the owner of copyright photographs from which it derived revenue in various ways, including publication in a magazine, display on a subscription Website and the licensing of a third party to sell thumbnails of the images for downloading to mobile phones. Google's image search engine enables Web users to search for images. When a Web user conducts an image search, the Google search engine responds by presenting the user with thumbnail images created by Google from the original images it located on the Internet and which it stored on its own servers. The Court held that the plaintiff was likely to succeed in proving that Google was infringing copyright by creating and displaying the thumbnail images of the plaintiff's photographs.[47]

Furthermore, the court held that Google's actions were not likely to be exempted from infringement as a fair use of the plaintiff's copyright photographs, in light of the commercial nature of Google's use of the photographs and the likelihood that Google's activities would interfere with the market for the plaintiff's photographs, since Perfect 10 sold similar size versions of the photographs to mobile phone users.[48] The court also found that Google's practice of framing and inline linking to an image when a user conducts an image search did not infringe copyright.[49] The Court's rationale for this was that Google did not display the image within the meaning of the United States *Copyright Act* as Google only linked to the images which were available for download or viewing from a third party Website.[50]

---

[44] Judgment was entered in favour of the plaintiff in the sum of US$345,000 plus attorney fees in the sum of US$6,068.20: see http://netcopyrightlaw.com/pdf/kellyvarribasoftjudgement03182004.pdf (accessed 26 February 2007).

[45] 416 F Supp 2d 828 (CD Cal, 2006)

[46] *Perfect 10 v Google Inc*, 416 F Supp 2d 828, 858-859 (CD Cal, 2006)

[47] *Perfect 10 v Google Inc*, 416 F Supp 2d 828, 858-859 (CD Cal, 2006)

[48] *Perfect 10 v Google Inc*, 416 F Supp 2d 828, 845-851 (CD Cal, 2006)

[49] *Perfect 10 v Google Inc*, 416 F Supp 2d 828, 844-845 (CD Cal, 2006)

[50] *Perfect 10 v Google Inc*, 416 F Supp 2d 828, 838-844 (CD Cal, 2006)

In May 2007, the United States Court of Appeals for the Ninth Circuit in *Perfect 10 Inc v Amazon.com Inc and Google Inc*,[51] overturned the District Court's finding that Google's actions were an infringement and unlikely to be a fair use. The Court held:

[i]n this case, Google has put Perfect 10's thumbnail images (along with millions of other thumbnail images) to a use fundamentally different than the use intended by Perfect 10. In doing so, Google has provided a significant benefit to the public. Weighing this significant transformative use against the unproven use of Google's thumbnails for cell phone downloads, and considering the other fair use factors, all in light of the purpose of copyright, we conclude that Google's use of Perfect 10's thumbnails is a fair use. Because the district court here "found facts sufficient to evaluate each of the statutory factors ... [we] need not remand for further factfinding." *Harper & Row*, 471 U.S. at 560 (internal quotation omitted). We conclude that Perfect 10 is unlikely to be able to overcome Google's fair use defense and, accordingly, we vacate the preliminary injunction regarding Google's use of thumbnail images.[52]

Interestingly, the Court also reversed the District Court's findings on secondary liability, as it had failed to fully apply the doctrine of inducement articulated in *Metro-Goldwyn-Mayer Studios Inc v Grokster Ltd*,[53]. It is unclear what this will mean for the law of secondary liability for search engines. The Court held:

[t]he district court also erred in its secondary liability analysis because it failed to consider whether Google and Amazon.com knew of infringing activities yet failed to take reasonable and feasible steps to refrain from providing access to infringing images. Therefore we must also reverse the district court's holding that Perfect 10 was unlikely to succeed on the merits of its secondary liability claims. Due to this error, the district court did not consider whether Google and Amazon.com are entitled to the limitations on liability set forth in title II of the DMCA. The question whether Google and Amazon.com are secondarily liable, and whether they can limit that liability pursuant to title II of the DMCA, raise fact intensive inquiries, potentially requiring further fact finding, and thus can best be resolved by the district court on remand. We therefore remand this matter to the district court for further proceedings consistent with this decision.[54]

This decision will also be of interest in regard to the application of the safe harbors to search engines, as there have been some suggestions, that a strict or narrow reading of the provisions may make their potential application to some search engines problematic.[55] On this view, it is uncertain how terms like 'subscribers' 'account holders' and 'accounts', which are pre-conditions to the operation of the safe harbors, will apply to search engines. One view, is that as search engines in their strictest sense do not have subscribers or account holders, then they may

---

[51] CV-05-04753-AHM (9th Cir, 16 May 2007)

[52] CV-05-04753-AHM, 5785-5786 (9th Cir, 16 May 2007)

[53] 545 US 913, 930 (2005)

[54] CV-05-04753-AHM, 5800-5801 (9th Cir, 16 May 2007)

[55] See Walker (2004, p. 17); see for example 17 USC § 512(i); *Copyright Act 1968* (Cth) s 116AH

potentially lose their protection under the safe harbors, as they fail to satisfy the necessary pre-conditions.[56]

Agence France Presse v Google Inc

Agence France Presse and Google have recently settled a high profile media lawsuit – involving the popular Google news search – which was filed by Agence France Presse in a United States District Court for the District of Columbia in March 2005.[57] Under the agreement reached between both parties, Agence France Presse has agreed to allow Google to post Agence France Presse content, including new stories and photographs, to the Google News Website and other Google services.[58]

Agence France Presse had alleged that Google News infringed copyright by unlawfully including its photographs, headlines and excerpts from the beginning of articles (story leads) in the Google News search. Agence France Presse also alleged that Google was in breach of federal law by removing copyright management information (photo credits and copyright notices) from its copyright material. Countering these claims, Google argued that Agence France Presse's headlines were not 'original and creative' enough to be protected under copyright law.[59]

Viacom Inc v YouTube Inc and Google Inc

It also worth noting that Google owned subsidiary, YouTube Inc is currently the subject of a high profile copyright lawsuit brought by Viacom International Inc in a United States District Court.[60] In this case before the Southern District of New York, Viacom alleges six causes of action for copyright infringement against YouTube and Google, being:

1. direct copyright infringement related to the unauthorised public performance of the uploaded videos;
2. direct copyright infringement related to the unauthorised public display of the uploaded videos;
3. direct copyright infringement related to the unauthorised reproduction of the uploaded videos;
4. inducement of copyright infringement;
5. contributory copyright infringement; and

---

[56] Ibid.

[57] See McCarthy (2007)

[58] Ibid.

[59] See McCullagh and Broache (2006).

[60] *Viacom International Inc v YouTube Inc, YouTube LLC and Google Inc,* (United States District Court for the Southern District of New York, filed 13 March 2007). For a copy of the complaint see Brown E, (2007) *Viacom sues YouTube* Internet Cases http://www.Internetcases.com/archives/2007/03/viacom_sues_you.html; also see Broache and Sandoval (2007).

6. vicarious copyright infringement.

YouTube and Google's defence, essentially denies each of the allegations in Viacom's complaint and raises 12 defences in their favour. These defences include the safe harbors, licence, fair use, failure to mitigate, failure to state a claim, innocent intent, copyright misuse, estoppel, waiver, unclean hands, laches and substantial non-infringing uses.[61]

YouTube is also the subject of recent class action filed by the English Premier League and independent music publisher, Bourne Co in the United States District Court for the Southern District of New York.[62] The action essentially duplicates the claims made by Viacom in their complaint.[63]

7.3.2 Australia

In Australia there is yet to be a major decision involving the liability of search engines for copyright infringement, although there have been a number of recent related decisions, particularly in regard to the area of 'linking' and whether linking to another Website containing material that infringes copyright can amount to an authorisation of copyright infringement.[64] It is likely that these decisions will have implications for search engine liability for copyright infringement in Australia.

Universal Music Australia Pty Ltd v Cooper

In *Universal Music Australia Pty Ltd v Cooper*,[65] a decision of the Federal Court of Australia, Tamberlin J concluded that the defendant, by providing hyperlinks from his Website to thousands of sound recordings located on remote Websites, had authorised the infringement of copyright in music sound recordings, both by Internet users who accessed his Website and by the operators of the remote Websites from

---

[61] See Mills (2007)

[62] The Football Association Premier League Limited and Bourne Co v YouTube Inc, YouTube LLC and Google Inc, (United States District Court for the Southern District of New York, filed 4 May 2007); for more information see http://www.youtubeclassaction.com. Also see Tur v YouTube Inc, (CD Cal, 2006), 797

[63] See Sandoval (2007).

[64] *Copyright Act 1968* (Cth) ss 36(1), (1A), 101(1), (1A); *University of New South Wales v Moorhouse and Angus & Robertson* (1975) 133 CLR 1; *Universal City Studios Inc v Corley and 2600 Enterprises Inc*, 273 F 3d 429 (2001). Also note in Australia and a number of other jurisdictions a defence to authorisation liability exists for the mere provision of communication facilities, for example see *Copyright Act 1968* (Cth) ss 39B, 112E

[65] [2005] FCA 972

which the infringing recordings were downloaded.[66] The defendant operated a Website called MP3s4free.net Website, which did not host sound recordings, but provided hyperlinks which, when clicked, enabled users to directly access and activate the downloading of sound recordings on remote Websites. When a visitor to the defendant's Website clicked on a link on that site to an MP3 file hosted on another server, the user's browser sent a "GET" request to the server so that the MP3 file was transmitted directly on the Internet from the host server to the user's computer.[67]

The defendant's Website was designed to, and did, facilitate and enable this infringing downloading. It would have been possible for the defendant to prevent the infringements by removing the hyperlinks from his Website or by structuring the Website in such a way that the operators of the remote Websites from which MP3 files were downloaded could not automatically add hyperlinks to the defendant's Website without some supervision or control on his part. Tamberlin J explained:

> [A] Website operator is always able to control the hyperlinks on his or her Website, either by removal of the links or by requiring measures to be taken by the remote Website operator prior to adding a hyperlink. A person cannot create a hyperlink between a music file and a Website without the permission of the operator of the Website because access to the code that is required to create the link must occur at level of the Website. The Cooper Website employed a "CGI-BIN" script to accept hyperlink suggestions from visitors to the Website. By virtue of this script, such suggestions were automatically added to the Website without the intervention of Cooper. The evidence is that alternative software was in existence that would have enabled a third party to add a hyperlink to a Website but which required the consent or approval of the Website operator before such hyperlinks were added.[68]

The defendant had sufficient control over his own Website, both with regard to users accessing his Website and remote operators placing hyperlinks on his Website, that he could have taken steps to prevent the infringement.[69] However, the defendant made no attempt, when hyperlinks were submitted to his Website, to take any steps to ascertain the legality of the MP3s to which the hyperlinks related or the identity of the persons submitting the MP3s. Subsequently, it was held that the defendant had authorised the infringement of copyright in the sound recordings.[70]

The first instance decision in *Universal Music Australia Pty Ltd v Cooper*[71] by the Federal Court of Australia was upheld by the Full Court of the Federal Court of Australia in *Cooper v Universal Music Australia Pty Ltd*.[72] In this case, taking into account the elements of s 101(A) of the Australian *Copyright Act 1968* (Cth), the Court found that Cooper had authorised infringement because he:

---

[66] *Universal Music Australia Pty Ltd v Cooper* [2005] FCA 972 (Tamberlin J, 14 July 2005) [77]–[88]

[67] *Universal Music Australia Pty Ltd v Cooper* [2005] FCA 972 (Tamberlin J, 14 July 2005) [65]

[68] *Universal Music Australia Pty Ltd v Cooper* [2005] FCA 972 (Tamberlin J, 14 July 2005) [85]

[69] *Universal Music Australia Pty Ltd v Cooper* [2005] FCA 972 (Tamberlin J, 14 July 2005) [86]

[70] *Universal Music Australia Pty Ltd v Cooper* [2005] FCA 972 (Tamberlin J, 14 July 2005) [88]

[71] [2005] FCA 972 (Tamberlin J, 14 July 2005)

[72] [2006] FCAFC 187 (French, Branson and Kenny JJ, 18 December 2006)

- had the power to prevent users of his Website from infringing copyright by not making available the technical capacity for those acts to be committed;
- benefited financially and therefore had a financial relationship with users whom he attracted to his Website through sponsorship and advertising; and
- did not take reasonable steps to prevent or avoid copyright infringement by users of his Website.[73]

Importantly, from the perspective of search engine liability, one of the Judges in this case briefly considered the legal position of search engines under Australian copyright law. The appellant (Cooper) submitted that his Website was, in relevant respects, no different from a search engine, such as Google and attempted to rely upon the United States decision in *Perfect 10 Inc v Google Inc.*[74] This argument was expressly rejected by Branson J who stated:

> Mr Cooper placed considerable weight on a suggested analogy between his Website and Google. Two things may be said in this regard. First, Mr Cooper's assumption that Google's activities in Australia do not result in infringements of the [Copyright] Act is untested. *Perfect 10 Inc v Google Inc* 416 F Supp 2d 828 (CDCal 2006) upon which Mr Cooper placed reliance is a decision under the law of the United States of America which includes the doctrine of "fair use". Secondly, Google is a general purpose search engine rather than a Website designed to facilitate the downloading of music files. The suggested analogy is unhelpful in the context of Mr Cooper's appeal.[75]

7.3.3 Europe

Clearly, incorporating HTML code or content from the linked site onto the host site, may amount to a direct infringement of copyright if a substantial part of the original code or content has been taken. For example, where an Internet search engine uses a robotic spider or crawler to automatically return search results from newspapers, magazines and books, reproducing headlines, abstracts or articles or a few sentences of text from the retrieved items in a news amalgamation service, it could be argued that the newspaper publishers' copyright has been infringed, providing a 'substantial part' of the item has been reproduced.[76] In this regard, Google has been sued by a number of European newspaper publishers, who allege that the Google News service, which lists headlines and a few sentences of text from news

---

[73] *Cooper v Universal Music Australia Pty Ltd* [2006] FCAFC 187 (French, Branson and Kenny JJ, 18 December 2006) [41]–[51], [148]–[151]

[74] F Supp 2d 828 (CD Cal 2006)

[75] *Cooper v Universal Music Australia Pty Ltd* [2006] FCAFC 187 (French, Branson and Kenny JJ, 18 December 2006) [40]

[76] *Copyright Act 1968* (Cth) ss 13 (2), 36(1) and 101(1)

articles that are linked back to the publications' own Websites, infringes copyright in their online newspaper content.[77]

Copiepresse v Google Inc

In a recent case brought in Belgium by Copiepresse, an organisation that manages copyright for Belgium's French and German language newspapers, the court held that Google had infringed the newspaper publishers' copyright by caching, making automatic summaries of and reproducing the newspapers' materials on the Google News Website. In September 2006, the President of the Court of First Instance of Brussels (Tribunal de Premiere Instance de Bruxelles) ordered Google to remove the articles, photographs and graphical images from the various Belgian newspapers on Google News and Google's Belgian search Website, imposing a penalty of up to €1million per day for continued infringements. The Court rejected Google's argument that it was a non-infringing fair use to store cached copies of the newspaper articles and use short extracts from the articles on the Google News Website. Google removed links to 17 of the newspapers from the Google News Website and sought a rehearing of the case. In February 2007, the injunction was upheld but the Court reduced the penalty payable by Google (if it continued to reproduce infringing material on its Website) to a maximum daily fine of €25,000.

7.3.4   China

Seven Record Labels v Baidu.com Inc[78]

Recent litigation in the Beijing No 1 Intermediate People's Court has brought attention to the liability of search engines for copyright infringement in China. Chinese search Baidu was recently sued by seven record labels, including EMI Group Hong Kong, Sony BMG Music Hong Kong, Warner Music Hong Kong, Universal Music Hong Kong, Cinepoly Music, Go East Entertainment and Gold Label Entertainment. The record companies claimed that Baidu's act of linking songs to the public on the Internet infringed the communication right of the record companies under Chinese law.

At issue in this case was whether Baidu through their MP3 search engine service[79] had communicated MP3 songs to the public by allowing users to search and

---

[77] *Copiepresse v Google Inc* No 2006/9099/4 Tribunal de premiére instance de Bruxelles 8 September 2006; *Copiepresse v Google Inc* No 06/10.928/C Tribunal de premiére instance de Bruxelles 13 February 2007; *Agence France Presse v Google Inc*, US District Court (District of Columbia). Note in November 2006, Google reached a settlement with the Belgian copyright organisations, Sofam, representing about 3 700 photographers, and Scam, which represents journalists

[78] Note this name refers to a number of separate cases brought against Baidu

[79] See Baidu MP3 http://mp3.baidu.com

download illegal MP3 files through the Baidu MP3 search engine service. The nature of the Baidu MP3 search engine service was such that Baidu did not directly upload MP3 files to their servers, instead they only provided the links to the MP3 files stored on other servers.

The Court held that the 'sampled' and 'downloaded' MP3 files in question did not originate from the Baidu Website, instead they originated from other Web servers.[80] Thus the Court found that the communication occurs between the users downloading the MP3 files and the Website that uploaded the files.[81] The Court clearly ruled that the Website providing the links does not engage in the act of communication via the Internet under the Copyright Law of the People's Republic of China.[82]

Importantly for search engines, the Court also held that there was insufficient basis for a search engine to be held liable for the uploading and downloading of infringing sound recordings, by third party Websites. The rationale behind this finding was that search engines are unable to determine the legal status of linked Websites.

7.4   Search Engines and Copyright Law: The Future

Search engines, such as Google, Yahoo and Baidu are critical to accessing knowledge in the Internet environment. They enable Internet users to find and retrieve information and documents, trawling the Internet using 'robots' and caching material for ease of access and presentation. It is therefore essential, that copyright laws accommodate the great potential which search engines have to offer society and ensure the free flow of information on the Internet.

In many jurisdictions throughout the world there still remains uncertainty as to whether search engines can be held liable for infringing copyright. In particular, provisions regarding the caching of copyright material, the extent to which fair use or fair dealing will apply, secondary or authorisation liability and the operation of safe harbour provisions all need to be clarified from the perspectives of search engines. Compounding this uncertainty is the lack of clear judicial precedent regarding search engine liability for copyright infringement.

One example of this is under the Australian *Copyright Act 1968* (Cth), which fails to clarify whether a search engine will be entitled to the protection of the Australian 'safe harbour' provisions. Similar, ambiguity exists in regard to the potential application of the fair dealing defence for search engines and whether

---

[80] See Qian (2007)

[81] Ibid

[82] Ibid. Note that on 24 April 2007 the Beijing Second Intermediary Court reached a different conclusion, finding Yahoo! China liable for copyright infringement for links in its music search results

the practice of caching by search engines will constitute a reproduction and subsequently infringe copyright law in Australia. This example illustrates the type of uncertainty which exists under national copyright laws when considering search engines and the increasingly diverse operations which they provide.

In order to create further certainty in this area the World Intellectual Property Organisation (WIPO) through its member states should convene a conference on search engine liability. Such a conference could assess in detail the effectiveness of the current law in allowing search engines to operate without fear of being sued. A more radical proposal, which could be tabled at such a conference, would be to allow search engines the broadest possible immunity to operate in hope that they might vastly improve our ability to research, manage and process knowledge for social, cultural and economic good. An intermediate proposal would be to simply assess the series of cases discussed in this chapter and provide clarity under law in all jurisdictions about the legality of the activities of search engines.

Ultimately one of the aims of copyright law is to find a workable balance between the right to own and exploit information in the form of creative expression and the ability of users (and their intermediaries) to access and reuse informational resources especially in a knowledge economy. The complicating factor in these circumstances is that in the process of providing access to knowledge, companies like Google, Baidu and Yahoo make an enormous amount of money, at the expense, so it is argued, of the copyright owners. Some of the reproduction and communication that search engines engage in to bring us our daily fix of information clearly must be tolerated in order for the system to work. In many instances such access will also promote the interests of the copyright owner through greater profiling. The sticking point here is not so much about whether search engines should be given greater immunity from liability but about how much advertising revenue they are willing to share with copyright owners for buying such immunity.

7.5   Conclusion

This chapter has highlighted the stream of litigation that has confronted the operators of search engines in the last two years across the world. It is our suggestion that such a trend should be arrested by a closer analysis (through an international conference convened by WIPO) of the scope of immunity search engines currently possess and proposals for how and on what conditions it should be expanded. This involves the consideration of many competing interests and the resolution of difficult policy questions but the foundational importance of search engines to our 21st existence makes such a process vitally important to economic and social prosperity. In short, search engines are now a key part of our everyday lives and to this end we should ensure that their freedom to operate is clearly articulated and reinforced in law.

References

Bashor N (2006) The Cache Cow: Can Caching and Copyright Co-exist? The John Marshall Law School Review of Intellectual Property Law 6: 101–128

Broache A, Sandoval G (2007, March 13) Viacom sues google over youtube clips. CNET Newscom. Available: http://news.com.com/Viacom+sues+Google+over+YouTube+clips/2100 -1030_3-6166668.html via the Internet. Accessed May 25, 2007

Fitzgerald A, Fitzgerald B (2004) Intellectual property in principle. Lawbook, Sydney, Australia

Kociubinski B (2006) Copyright and the evolving law of Internet search: field v Google, Inc. and Perfect 10 v Google, Inc. Boston University Journal of Science and Technology Law 12

McCarthy C (2007, April 6) Agence france-presse, google settle copyright dispute. CNET Newscom. Available: http://news.com.com/Agence+France-Presse%2C+Google+settle+copyr ight+dispute/2100-1030_3-6174008.html via the Internet. Accessed May 25, 2007

McCullagh D, Broache A (2006, July 18) Judge: Google news lawsuit can proceed. CNET Newscom. Available: http://news.com.com/2100-1025_3-6095656.html via the Internet. Accessed May 25, 2007

Mills E (2007, April 30) Google denies viacom copyright charges. CNET Newscom. Available: http://news.com.com/2100-1026_3-6180387.html via the Internet. Accessed May 25, 2007

Montgomery L, Cha AE (2007, April 10) Taking a Harder Line on Piracy. The Washington Post, p D1

O'Brien D, Fitzgerald B (2006) Digital copyright law in a YouTube world. Internet Law Bulletin 9: 71,73–74

Qian W (2007) A "direct" decision vs. an "indirect" problem: a commentary on seven record labels vs. baidu.com. Journal of China Copyright 1:

Radcliffe M (2006) Grokster: the new law of third party liability for copyright infringement under United States law. Computer Law and Security Report 22: 137–149

Sandoval G (2007, May 6) Legal troubles mount for youtube. CNET Newscom. Available: http:// news.com.com/Legal+troubles+mount+for+YouTube/2100-1030_3-6181753.html via the Internet. Accessed May 25, 2007

Walker CW (2004) Application of the DMCA safe harbor provisions to search engines. Virginia Journal of Law and Technology 9: 1–23

8
Search Engine Bias and the Demise of Search Engine Utopianism

E. Goldman[83]

Summary Due to search engines' automated operations, people often assume that search engines display search results neutrally and without bias. However, this perception is mistaken. Like any other media company, search engines affirmatively control their users' experiences, which has the consequence of skewing search results (a phenomenon called "search engine bias"). Some commentators believe that search engine bias is a defect requiring legislative correction. Instead, this chapter argues that search engine bias is the beneficial consequence of search engines optimizing content for their users. The chapter further argues that the most problematic aspect of search engine bias, the "winner-take-all" effect caused by top placement in search results, will be mooted by emerging personalized search technology.

8.1 Introduction

In the past few years, search engines have emerged as a major force in our information economy, helping searchers perform hundreds of millions (or even billions) of searches per day.[84] With this broad reach, search engines have significant power to shape searcher behavior and perceptions. In turn, the choices that search engines make about how to collect and present data can have significant social implications.

---

[83] Assistant Professor, Santa Clara University School of Law and Director, High Tech Law Institute. Home page: http://www.ericgoldman.org. Email: egoldman@gmail.com. I appreciate the comments of Nico Brooks, Soumen Chakrabarti, Ben Edelman, Elizabeth Van Couvering and the participants at the Yale Law School Regulating Search Symposium and the 2005 Association of Internet Researchers (AoIR) Annual Meeting. I also am very grateful to Michael Zimmer for his help preparing this Chapter for publication.

This Chapter focuses principally on American law and consumer behavior. Consumer behavior and marketplace offerings vary by country, so this Chapter's discussion may not be readily generalizable to other jurisdictions.

[84] In 2003, search engines performed over a half-billion searches a day (Sullivan 2003).

Typically, search engines automate their core operations, including the processes that search engines use to aggregate their databases and then sort/rank the data for presentation to searchers. This automation gives search engines a veneer of objectivity and credibility (Miller 2005). Machines, not humans, appear to make the crucial judgments, creating the impression that search engines bypass the structural biases and skewed data presentations inherent in any human-edited media.[85] Search engines' marketing disclosures typically reinforce this perception of objectivity.

Unfortunately, this romanticized view of search engines does not match reality. Search engines are media companies. As explained in Part I, like other media companies, search engines make editorial choices designed to satisfy their audience (Baker 1993). As explained in Part II, these choices systematically favor certain types of content over others, producing a phenomenon called "search engine bias."

Search engine *bias* sounds scary, but Part III of this chapter explains why such bias is both necessary and desirable. Part IV will then show how emerging personalization technology will soon ameliorate many concerns about search engine bias.

8.2   Search Engines Make Editorial Choices

Search engines frequently claim that their core operations are completely automated and free from human intervention,[86] but this characterization is false. Instead, humans make numerous editorial judgments about what data to collect and how to present that data (see, generally, Mowshowitz and Kawaguchi 2002).

---

[85] There is a broad perception that search engines present search results passively and neutrally (see Marable 2003; O'Rourke 1998).

[86] *See, e.g., Does Google Ever Manipulate Its Search Results?*, Google.com, http://www.google.com/support/bin/answer.py?answer=4115&topic=368 ("The order and contents of Google search results are completely automated. No one hand picks a particular result for a given search query, nor does Google ever insert jokes or send messages by changing the order of results."); *Does Google Censor Search Results?*, Google.com, http://www.google.com/support/bin/answer.py?answer=17795&topic=368 ("Google does not censor results for any search terms. The order and content of our results are completely automated; we do not manipulate our search results by hand."); *Technology Overview*, Google.com, http://www.google.com/corporate/tech.html ("There is no human involvement or manipulation of results...."); *How Can I Improve My Site's Ranking?*, Google.com, http://www.google.com/support/webmasters/bin/answer.py?answer=34432&topic=8524 ("Sites' positions in our search results are determined automatically based on a number of factors, which are explained in more detail at http://www.google.com/technology/index.html. We don't manually assign keywords to sites, nor do we manipulate the ranking of any site in our search results.") *see also* Complaint at ¶¶ 37–38, 52–56, KinderStart.com LLC v. Google, Inc., Case No. C 06-2057 RS (N.D. Cal. Mar. 17, 2006) (giving other examples of Google's claims to be passive). Note that Google has subsequently revised some of these cited pages after its censorship controversy in China.

8.2.1 Indexing

Search engines do not index every scrap of data available on the Internet. Search engines omit (deliberately or accidentally) some Web pages entirely (Bar–Ilan 2005), or may incorporate only part of a Web page.[87]

During indexing, search engines are designed to associate third party "metadata" (data about data) with the indexed Web page. For example, search engines may use and display third party descriptions of the Website in the search results.[88] Search engines may also index "anchor text" (the text that third parties use in hyperlinking to a Website) (Pannu 2004), which can cause a Website to appear in search results for a term the Website never used (and may object to).[89]

Finally, once indexed, search engines may choose to exclude Web pages from their indexes for a variety of reasons, ranging from violations of quasi-objective search engine technical requirements[90] to simple capriciousness.[91]

8.2.2 Ranking

To determine the order of search results, search engines use complex proprietary "ranking algorithms." Ranking algorithms obviate the need for humans to make individualized ranking decisions for the millions of search terms used by searchers, but they do not lessen the role of human editorial judgment in the process. Instead, the choice of which factors to include in the ranking algorithm, and how to weight

---

[87] For example, many search engines ignore metatags (Goldman 2005). Search engines also incorporate only portions of very large files (see Bar–Ilan 2005, p. note 6; Google 2005; ResearchBuzz! 2005).

[88] Google's automated descriptions have spawned at least one lawsuit by a web publisher who believed the compilation created a false characterization (see Fineberg 2004).

[89] For example, for some time, the first search result in Google and Yahoo! for the keyword "miserable failure" was President George W. Bush's home page because so many websites have linked to the biography using the term "miserable failure" (McNichol 2004). This algorithmic vulnerability has spawned a phenomenon called "Google bombing," where websites coordinate an anchor text attack to intentionally distort search results (Hiler 2002).

[90] Google and Yahoo kicked WhenU.com out of their indexes for allegedly displaying different web pages to searchers and search engine robots, a process called "cloaking" (Olsen 2004).

[91] This was the heart of KinderStart's allegations against Google. See Complaint, KinderStart.com LLC v. Google, Inc., Case No. C 06-2057 (N.D. Cal. Mar. 17, 2006). Although the complaint's allegations about Google's core algorithmic search were not proven, Google does liberally excise sources from Google News. For example, Google claims that "news sources are selected without regard to political viewpoint or ideology" (see *Google News (Beta)*, Google.com, http://news.google.com/intl/en_us/about_google_news.html#25) but Google dropped a white supremacist news source from Google News because it allegedly promulgated "hate content" (Kuchinskas 2005).

them, reflects the search engine operator's editorial judgments about what makes content valuable. Indeed, to ensure that these judgments are produce desired results, search engines manually inspect search results[92] and make adjustments accordingly.

Additionally, search engines claim they do not modify algorithmically-generated search results, but there is some evidence to the contrary. Search engines allegedly make manual adjustments to a Web publisher's overall ranking.[93] Also, search engines occasionally modify search results presented in response to particular keyword searches. Consider the following:

- Some search engines blocked certain search terms containing the keyword "phpBB" (Gillette 2006)
- In response to the search term "Jew," for a period of time (including, at minimum November 2005 when the author observed the phenomenon), Google displayed a special result in the sponsored link, saying "Offensive Search Results: We're disturbed about these results as well. Please read our note here." The link led to a page explaining the results.[94]
- Reportedly, Ask.com blocked search results for certain terms like "pedophile," "bestiality," "sex with children" and "child sex" (Laycock 2006)[95]
- Google removed some Websites from its index in response to a 512(c)(3) takedown demand from the Church of Scientology. However, Google displayed the following legend at the bottom of affected search results pages (such as search results for "scientology site:xenu.net"): "In response to a complaint we received under the US Digital Millennium Copyright Act, we have removed 2 result(s) from this page. If you wish, you may read the DMCA complaint that caused the removal(s) at ChillingEffects.org."[96]

---

[92] For example, Google hires students to manually review search results for quality purposes. *See* Posting of Eric Goldman to Technology & Marketing Law Blog, *Google's Human Algorithm*, http://blog.ericgoldman.org/archives/2005/06/googles_human_a.htm (June 5, 2005, 14:11 EST).

[93] *See* Search King, Inc. v. Google Tech., Inc., No. CIV-02-1457-M, at 4 (W.D. Okla. Jan. 13, 2003) ("Google knowingly and intentionally decreased the PageRanks assigned to both SearchKing and PRAN."). This manual adjustment was also alleged (but not proven) in the recent *KinderStart* lawsuit. *See* Complaint, KinderStart.com L.L.C. v. Google, Inc., Case No. C 06-2057 RS (N.D. Cal. Mar. 17, 2006).

[94] *See* http://www.google.com/explanation.html.

[95] On Aug. 1, 2006, I was unable to replicate these results.

[96] *See* http://www.google.com/search?sourceid=navclient&ie=UTF-8&rls=GGLD,GGLD:2005-09,GGLD:en&q=scientology+site%3Axenu%2Enet (go to google.com, enter "scientology.site.xenu.net", then click search and scroll to the bottom of the page); see also Sherman (2002).

8.2.3 Conclusion about Editorial Control

Search engines have some duality in their self-perceptions, and this duality creates a lot of confusion (Sullivan 2006).[97] Search engines perceive themselves as objective and neutral because they let automated technology do most of the hard work. However, in practice, search engines make editorial judgments just like any other media company. Principally, these editorial judgments are instantiated in the parameters set for the automated operations, but search engines also make individualized judgments about what data to collect and how to present it. These manual interventions may be the exception and not the rule, but these exceptions only reinforce that search engines play an active role in shaping their users' experiences when necessary to accomplish their editorial goals.

8.3 Search Engine Editorial Choices Create Biases

A search result ordering has a significant effect on searchers and Web publishers. Searchers usually consider only the top few search results; the top-ranked search result gets a high percentage of searcher clicks, and clickthrough rates quickly decline from there.[98] Therefore, even if a search engine delivers hundreds or even thousands of search results in response to a searcher's query, searchers effectively ignore the vast majority of those search results. Accordingly, Web publishers desperately want to be listed among the top few search results (Totty and Mangalindan 2003).

For search engines, results placement determines how the searcher perceives the search experience. If the top few search results do not satisfy the searcher's objectives, the searcher may deem the search a failure. Therefore, to maximize searcher perceptions of search success, search engines generally tune their ranking algorithms to support majority interests (Introna and Nissenbaum 2000: 169). In turn, minority interests (and the Websites catering to them) often receive marginal exposure in search results.

---

[97] This duality, if it ends up leading to the dissemination of false information, could also create some legal liability. *See* KinderStart v. Google, No. 5:06-cv-02057-JF (N.D. Cal. motion to dismiss granted July 13, 2006) (pointing out the potential inconsistency of Google's position that PageRank is both Google's subjective opinion but an objective reflection of its algorithmic determinations).

[98] The *iProspect Search Engine User Behavior Study* reports that 62% of searchers click on a search result on the first results page (iProspect 2006); a study by Cornell professor Thorsten Joachims reports that the first search result gets 42% of clicks and the second search result gets 8%, and when the first two search results are switched, the first search result gets 34%—meaning that positioning dictated searcher behavior (Nielsen 2005); other reports indicate the first ranked search result may get ten times the quantity of clicks as the tenth ranked search result (Institute 2004).

To gauge majority interests, search engines frequently include a popularity metric in their ranking algorithm. Google's popularity metric, PageRank, treats inbound links to a Website as popularity votes, but votes are not counted equally; links from more popular Websites count more than links from lesser-known Websites.[99]

Beyond promoting search results designed to satisfy majority interests, PageRank's non-egalitarian voting structure causes search results to be biased towards Websites with economic power because these Websites get lots of links due to their marketing expenditures and general prominence (Elkin-Koren 2001; Pasquale 2006: 25; Upstill et al. 2003).

Indeed, popularity-based ranking algorithms may reinforce and perpetuate existing power structures (Hindman et al. 2003; Introna and Nissenbaum 2000). Websites that are part of the current power elite get better search result placement, which leads to greater consideration of their messages and views. Furthermore, the increased exposure attributable to better placement means that these Websites are likely to get more votes in the future, leading to a self-reinforcing process (Cho and Roy 2004; Economist 2005).[100] In contrast, minority-interest and disenfranchised Websites may have a difficult time cracking through the popularity contest, potentially leaving them perpetually relegated to the search results hinterlands (Cho and Roy 2004).[101]

A number of commentators have lamented these effects and offered some proposals in response:

8.3.1 Improve Search Engine Transparency

Search engines keep their ranking algorithms secret.[102] This secrecy hinders search engine spammers from gaining more prominence than search engines want them to have, but the secrecy also prevents searchers and commentators from accurately assessing any bias. To enlighten searchers, search engines could be required to disclose more about their practices and their algorithms (Introna and Nissenbaum 2000). This additional information has two putative benefits. First, it may improve market mechanisms by helping searchers make informed choices among search engine competitors. Second, it may help searchers determine the appropriate level of cognitive authority to assign to their search results.

---

[99] *See Our Search: Google Technology*, Google.com, http://www.google.com/technology/.

[100] For a study questioning the consequences of the "rich-gets-richer" effect see Santo Fortunato et al (2005).

[101] But see also Filippo Menczer et al (1999) providing empirical evidence suggesting that "search engines direct more traffic than expected to less popular sites".

[102] *See* Search King Inc. v. Google Tech., Inc., No. CIV-02-1457-M, at 3 n.2 (W.D. Okla. Jan. 13, 2003) ("Google's mathematical algorithm is a trade secret, and it has been characterized by the company as 'one of Google's most valuable assets.'"); See also Olsen (2003).

8.3.2 Publicly Fund Search Engines

Arguably, search engines have "public good"-like attributes, such as reducing the social costs of search behavior. If so, private actors will not incorporate these social benefits into their decision-making. In that case, public funding of search engines may be required to produce socially optimal search results (Hargittai 2000; Introna and Nissenbaum 2000; Sunstein 2001: 170–172). Indeed, there have been several proposals to create government-funded search engines (O'Brien 2006; Wearden 2005).

8.3.3 Mandate Changes to Ranking/Sorting Practices

Search engines could be forced to increase the exposure of otherwise-marginalized Websites. At least five lawsuits[103] have requested judges to force search engines to reorder search results to increase the plaintiff's visibility.[104]

In addition to plaintiffs, some academics have supported mandatory reordering of search results. For example, Pandey et al. advocate a "randomized rank promotion" scheme where obscure Websites randomly should get extra credit in ranking algorithms, appearing higher in the search results on occasion and getting additional exposure to searchers accordingly (Pandey et al. 2005; Sunstein 2001). As another example, Pasquale (2006:28–30) proposes that, when people think the search engines are providing false or misleading information, search engines should be forced to include a link to corrective information.

8.4 Search Engine Bias Is Necessary and Desirable

Before trying to solve the problem of search engine bias, we should be clear how search engine bias creates a problem that requires correction. From my perspective, search engine bias is the unavoidable consequence of search engines exercising editorial control over their databases. Like any other media company, search

---

[103] *See* Search King, Inc. v. Google Tech., Inc., No. CIV-02-1457-M (W.D. Okla. Jan. 13, 2003); KinderStart.com LLC v. Google, Inc., No. C 06-2057 RS (N.D. Cal. dismissed July 13, 2006); Langdon v. Google, Inc., No. 1:06-cv-00319-JJF (D. Del. complaint filed May 17, 2006); Roberts v. Google, No. 1-06-CV-063047 (Cal. Superior Ct. complaint filed May 5, 2006); Datner v. Yahoo! Inc, Case No. BC355217 (Cal. Superior Ct. complaint filed July 11, 2006) [note: this list updated as of July 24, 2006].

[104] As Google said in its response to the KinderStart lawsuit, "Plaintiff KinderStart contends that the judiciary should have the final say over [search engines'] editorial process. It has brought this litigation in the hopes that the Court will second-guess Google's search rankings and order Google to view KinderStart's site more favorably." Motion to Dismiss at 1, KinderStart.com LLC v. Google, Inc., No. C 06-2057 RS (N.D. Cal. May 2, 2006).

engines simply cannot passively and neutrally redistribute third party content (in this case, Web publisher content). If a search engine does not attempt to organize Web content, its system quickly and inevitably will be overtaken by spammers, fraudsters and malcontents.[105] At that point, the search engines become worthless to searchers.

Instead, searchers (like other media consumers) expect search engines to create order from the information glut. To prevent anarchy and preserve credibility, search engines unavoidably must exercise some editorial control over their systems. In turn, this editorial control necessarily will create some bias.

Fortunately, market forces limit the scope of search engine bias (Mowshowitz and Kawaguchi 2002: 60). Searchers have high expectations for search engines: they expect search engines to read their minds[106] and infer their intent based solely on a small number of search keywords.[107] Search engines that disappoint (either by failing to deliver relevant results, or by burying relevant results under too many unhelpful results) are held accountable by fickle searchers.[108] There are multiple search engines available to searchers,[109] and few barriers to switching between them.[110]

---

[105] Every Internet venue accepting user-submitted content inevitably gets attacked by unwanted content. If left untended, the venue inexorably degrades into anarchy (see, for example, Gilbert 2005; Monetize Blog 2006; Quittner 1994).

[106] See Our Philosophy, Google.com, http://www.google.com/corporate/tenthings.html ("The perfect search engine...would understand exactly what you mean and give back exactly what you want."); see also Sherman (2005).

[107] Various studies reveal that searchers routinely use a very small number of keywords to express their search interests: eighty-eight percent of search engine referrals are based on only one or two keywords (iProspect 2004). A NEC Research Institute study shows that up to 70% of searchers use only a single keyword as a search term (cited in Butler 2000). According to Jansen et al, he average keyword length was 2.35 words, while one-third of searches used one keyword and 80% used three keywords or fewer (Jansen et al. 1998). According to Nielsen, the average keyword length was 2.0 words (Nielsen 2001).

[108] MSN Search "learned that the arcane searches were the make-or-break moments for Web searchers. People weren't just happy when a search engine could find answers to their most bizarre, obscure and difficult queries. They would switch loyalties" (Peterson 2005); see also Tedeschi (2006).

[109] In addition to the recent launch of major new search engines by providers like MSN, the open-source software community is developing Nutch to allow anyone to build and customize his or her own web search engine. http://lucene.apache.org/nutch/; see also Olsen (2003).

While there are multiple major search engines, the market may still resemble an oligopoly; a few major players (Google, Yahoo, MSN, Ask Jeeves) have the lion's share of the search engine market. However, this may construe the search engine market too narrowly. Many types of search providers compete with the big mass-market search engines, ranging from specialty search engines (e.g., Technorati) to alternative types of search technology (e.g., adware) to non-search information retrieval processes (e.g., link navigation). Ultimately, every search engine competes against other search engines and these other search/retrieval options.

[110] See Rahul Telang et al., An Empirical Analysis of Internet Search Engine Choice, Aug. 2002. On file with author. For example, search engines use the same basic interface (a white search box), and searchers rarely use advanced search features that might require additional learning time at other search engines.

As a result, searchers will shop around if they do not get the results they want,[111] and this competitive pressure constrains search engine bias. If a search engine's bias degrades the relevancy of search results, searchers will explore alternatives even if searchers do not realize that the results are biased. Meanwhile, search engine proliferation means that niche search engines can segment the market and cater to underserved minority interests (Telang 2004; Silva 2003; McMurray 2006; Nielsen 2003). Admittedly, these market forces are incomplete – searchers may never consider what results they are not seeing – but they are powerful nonetheless.

In contrast, it is hard to imagine how regulatory intervention will improve the situation. First, regulatory solutions become a vehicle for normative views about what searchers should see – or should *want* to see.[112] How should we select among these normative views? What makes one bias better than the other?

Second, regulatory intervention that promotes some search results over others does not ensure that searchers will find the promoted search results useful. Determining relevancy based on very limited data (such as decontextualized keywords) is a challenging process, and search engines struggle with this challenge daily. Due to the complexity of the relevancy matching process, government regulation rarely can do better than market forces at delivering results that searchers find relevant. As a result, searchers likely will find some of the promoted results irrelevant.

The clutter of unhelpful result may hinder searchers' ability to satisfy their search objectives, undermining searchers' confidence in search engines' mind-reading abilities (Goldman 2006). In this case, regulatory intervention could counterproductively degrade search engines' value to searchers. Whatever the adverse consequences of search engine bias, the consequences of regulatory correction are probably worse.[113]

8.5 Technological Evolution Will Moot Search Engine Bias

Currently, search engines principally use "one-size-fits-all" ranking algorithms to deliver homogeneous search results to searchers with heterogeneous search objectives (Pitkow et al. 2002). One-size-fits-all algorithms exacerbate the consequences of search engine bias in two ways: (1) they create winners (Websites listed high in

---

[111] A Kelsey Research study reports that 63% of searchers used two or more search engines (Crowell 2006). According to Vividence, up to 47% of searchers try another search engine when their search expectations are not met (Vividence 2004).

[112] Gerhart (2004) argues that search engines do not adequately prioritize search results that expose controversies about the search topic. However, her argument assumes that controversy-related information has value to consumers, an assumption that deserves careful evaluation.

[113] See Crawford (2005), discussing the shortcomings of regulatory intervention in organic information systems.

the search results) and losers (those with marginal placement), and (2) they deliver suboptimal results for searchers with minority interests.[114]

These consequences will abate when search engines migrate away from one-size-fits-all algorithms towards "personalized" ranking algorithms (Pitkow et al. 2002: 50). Personalized algorithms produce search results that are custom-tailored to each searcher's interests, so searchers will see different results in response to the same search query. For example, Google offers searchers an option that "orders your search results based on your past searches, as well as the search results and news headlines you've clicked on."[115]

Personalized ranking algorithms represent the next major advance in search relevancy. One-size-fits-all ranking algorithms have inherent limits on their maximum relevancy potential, and further improvements in one-size-fits algorithms will yield progressively smaller relevancy benefits. Personalized algorithms transcend those limits, optimizing relevancy for each searcher and thus implicitly doing a better job of searcher mind-reading (see McCarthy 2005; Teevan et al. 2005).

Personalized ranking algorithms also reduce the effects of search engine bias. Personalized algorithms mean that there are multiple "top" search results for a particular search term instead of a single "winner" (Lee 2005), so Web publishers will not compete against each other in a zero-sum game. In turn, searchers will get results more influenced by their idiosyncratic preferences and less influenced by the embedded preferences of the algorithm -writers. Also, personalized algorithms necessarily will diminish the weight given to popularity-based metrics (to give more weight for searcher-specific factors), reducing the structural biases due to popularity.

Personalized ranking algorithms are not a panacea – any process where humans select and weight algorithmic factors will produce some bias[116] – but personalized algorithms will eliminate many of the current concerns about search engine bias.

8.6 Conclusion

Complaints about search engine bias implicitly reflect some disappointed expectations. In theory, search engines can transcend the deficiencies of predecessor media to produce a type of utopian media. In practice, search engines are just like every

---

[114] A Microsoft researcher has been quoted as saying "If the two of us type a query [into a search engine], we get the same thing back, and that is just brain dead. There is no way an intelligent human being would tell us the same thing about the same topic" (Kanellos 2003). See also Freedman (2006) and Personalization of Placed Content Ordering in Search Results, U.S. Patent App. 0050240580 (filed July 13, 2004).

[115] What's Personalized Search?, Google.com, http://www.google.com/support/bin/answer. py?answer=26651&topic=1593.

[116] Personalized algorithms have other potentially adverse consequences, such as creating self-reinforcing information flows (Sunstein 2001). For a critique of these consequences, see Goldman (2006).

other medium – heavily reliant on editorial control and susceptible to human biases. This fact shatters any illusions of search engine utopianism.

Fortunately, search engine bias may be largely temporal. In this respect, I see strong parallels between search engine bias and the late 1990s keyword metatag "problem" (see, generally, Goldman 2005). Web publishers used keyword metatags to distort search results, but these techniques worked only so long as search engines considered keyword metatags in their ranking algorithms. When search engines recognized the distortive effects of keyword metatags, they changed their algorithms to ignore keyword metatags (Sullivan 2002). Search result relevancy improved, and the problem was solved without regulatory intervention.

Similarly, search engines naturally will continue to evolve their ranking algorithms and improve search result relevancy – a process that, organically, will cause the most problematic aspects of search engine bias to largely disappear. To avoid undercutting search engines' quest for relevance, this effort should proceed without regulatory distortion.

References

Baker CE (1993) Advertising and a democratic press. Princeton University Press, Princeton, NJ

Bar-Ilan J (2005) Expectations versus reality–search engine features needed for web research at mid 2005. Cybermetrics 9

Butler D (2000) Souped-up search engines. Nature 405: 112–115

Cho J, Roy S (2004) Impact of search engines on page popularity. Proceedings of the 13th International Conference on World Wide Web 20–29

Crawford S (2005) Shortness of vision: regulatory ambition in the digital age. Fordham Law Review 74

Crowell G (2006, June 14) Understanding searcher behavior. Search Engine Watch. Available: http://searchenginewatch.com/showPage.html?page=3613291 via the Internet.

Economist (2005, November 17). Egalitarian Engines.

Elkin-Koren N (2001) Let the crawlers crawl: on virtual gatekeepers and the right to exclude indexing. University of Dayton Law Review 26: 180–209

Fineberg S (2004, April 16) Calif. CPA sues google over 'misleading' search results. WebCPA. Available: http://www.webcpa.com/article.cfm?articleid=193&pg-acctoday&print=yes via the Internet.

Freedman D (2006, April 6). Why Privacy Won't Matter. Newsweek,

Gerhart S (2004) Do web search engines suppress controversy? First Monday. 9(1)(1). Available: http://firstmonday.org/issues/issue9_1/gerhart/index.html via the Internet. Accessed March 15, 2006

Gilbert A (2005, November 28) Google fixes glitch that unleashed flood of porn. CNET News. com. Available: http://news.com.com/2102-1025_3-5969799.html?tag=st.util.print via the Internet.

Gillette BJ (2006, January 18) MSN blockades phpbb searchers. TrimMail's Email Battles. Available: http://www.emailbattles.com/archive/battles/vuln_aacgfbgdcb_jd/ via the Internet.

Goldman E (2005) Deregulating relevancy in Internet trademark law. Emory Law Journal 54: 507, 567–68

Goldman E (2006) A coasean analysis of marketing. Wisconsin Law Review 2006: 1151

Google (2005) Why doesn't my site have a cached copy or a description? Available: http://www.google.com/support/bin/answer.py?answer=515&topic=365 via the Internet.

Hargittai E (2000) Open portals or closed gates? channeling content on the world wide web. Poetics 27: 233–253

Hiler J (2002, March 3) Google time bomb. Microcontent News. Available: http://www.microcontentnews.com/articles/googlebombs.htm via the Internet

Hindman M et al. (2003, March 31) Googlearchy: how a few heavily-linked sites dominate politics on the web. Available: http://www.princeton.edu/~mhindman/googlearchy–hindman.pdf via the Internet.

Institute A (2004, June) The atlas rank report: how search engine rank impacts traffic. Atlas Institute Digital Marketing Highlights. Available: http://app.atlasonepoint.com/pdf/AtlasRankReport.pdf via the Internet.

Introna L, Nissenbaum H (2000) Shaping the web: why the politics of search engines matters. The Information Society 16: 169–185

iProspect (2004, November) Iprospect natural seo keyword length study. Available: http://www.iprospect.com/premiumPDFs/keyword_length_study.pdf via the Internet.

iProspect (2006, April) Iprospect search engine user behavior study. Available: http://www.iprospect.com/premiumPDFs/WhitePaper_2006_SearchEngineUserBehavior.pdf via the Internet.

Jansen BJ et al. (1998) Real life information retrieval: a study of user queries on the Web. ACM SIGIR Forum 32: 5–17

Kanellos M (2003, November 24) Microsoft aims for search on its own terms. CNET News.com. Available: http://news.com.com/2102-1008_3-5110910.html?tag=st.util.print via the Internet.

Kuchinskas S (2005, March 23) Google axes hate news. Internetnews.com. Available: http://www.Internetnews.com/xSP/article.php/3492361 via the Internet.

Laycock J (2006, June 25) Ask.Com actively censoring some search phrases. Search Engine Guide. Available: http://www.searchengineguide.com/searchbrief/senews/007837.html via the Internet.

Lee K (2005, July 15) Search personalization and ppc search marketing. Clickz News. Available: http://www.clickz.com/experts/search/strat/print.php/3519876 via the Internet.

Marable L (2003) False oracles: consumer reaction to learning the truth about how search engines work: results of an ethnographic study. Available: http://www.consumerwebwatch.org/news/searchengines/index.html via the Internet.

McCarthy T (2005, September 5). On the frontier of search. Time Magazine, p 52

McMurray J (2006, July 9) Social search promises better intelligence. Associated Press. Available: http://www.msnbc.msn.com/id/13740161/ via the Internet.

McNichol T (2004, January 22). Your message here. The New York Times, p G1

Menczer F et al. (1999, February). Googlearchy or Googlocracy. IEEE Spectrum

Miller JL (2005, May 10) Left, right, or center? Can a search engine be biased? WebProNews. com. Available: http://www.webpronews.com/insidesearch/insidesearch/wpn-56-20050510LeftRightorCenterCanaSearchEngineBeBiased.html via the Internet. Accessed May 17, 2007

Monetize Blog (2006, June 17) Step-by-step: how to get billions of pages indexed by google. Monetize blog. Available: http://merged.ca/monetize/flat/how-to-get-billions-of-pages-indexed-by-Google.html via the Internet.

Mowshowitz A, Kawaguchi A (2002) Bias on the web. Communications of the ACM 45: 56–60

Nielsen J (2001, May 13) Search: visible and simple. Jakob Nielsen's Alertbox. Available: http://www.useit.com/alertbox/20010513.html via the Internet.

Nielsen J (2003, June 16) Diversity is power for specialized sites. Jakob Nielsen's Alertbox. Available: http://www.useit.com/alertbox/20030616.html via the Internet.

Nielsen J (2005, September 26) The power of defaults. Jakob Nielsen's Alertbox. Available: http://www.useit.com/alertbox/defaults.html via the Internet.

O'Brien K (2006, January 18). Europeans weigh plan on google challenge. International Herald Tribune

O'Rourke M (1998) Defining the limits of free-riding in cyberspace: trademark liability for metatagging. Gonzaga Law Review 33: 277

Olsen S (2003, August 18) Project searches for open-source niche. CNET News.com. Available: http://news.com.com/2102-1032_3-5064913.html?tag=st_util_print via the Internet.

Olsen S (2004, May 13) Search engines delete adware company. CNET News.com. Available: http://news.com.com/2102-1024_3-5212479.html?tag=st.util.print via the Internet.

Pandey S et al. (2005) Shuffling a stacked deck: the case for partially randomized ranking of search engine results. Proceedings of the 31st International Conference on Very Large Data Bases 781–792

Pannu J (2004, April 8) Anchor text optimization. WebProNews.com. Available: http://www.webpronews.com/ebusiness/seo/wpn-4-20040408AnchorTextOptimization.html via the Internet.

Pasquale F (2006, February 25) Rankings, reductionism, and responsibility. Seton Hall Public Law Research Paper No 888327. Available: http://papers.ssrn.com/sol3/papers.cfm?abstract_id=888327 via the Internet.

Peterson K (2005, May 2). Microsoft Learns to Crawl. The Seattle Times, p A1

Pitkow J et al. (2002) Personalized search. Communications of the ACM 45: 50–55

Quittner J (1994, May). The war between alt.tasteless and rec.pets.cats. Wired, p 46

ResearchBuzz! (2005, January 31) Has google dropped their 101k cache limit? Available: http://www.researchbuzz.org/2005/01/has_google_dropped_their_101k.shtml via the Internet.

Santo F, et al. (2005, November) The egalitarian effect of search engines. Arxiv preprint csCY/0511005. Available: http://arxiv.org/pdf/cs.CY/0511005 via the Internet.

Sherman C (2002, April 15) Google makes scientology infringement demand public. Search Engine Watch. Available: http://searchenginewatch.com/searchday/article.php/2159691 via the Internet.

Sherman C (2005, May 11) If search engines could read your mind. Search Engine Watch. Available: http://searchenginewatch.com/searchday/article.php/3503931 via the Internet.

Silva MJ (2003) The case for a portuguese web search engine. Proceedings of the IADIS International Conference WWW/Internet 411–418

Sullivan D (2002, October 1) Death of a meta tag. Search Engine Watch. Available: http://www.searchenginewatch.com/sereport/print.php/34721_2165061 via the Internet.

Sullivan D (2003, February 25) Searches per day. Search Engine Watch. Available: http://searchenginewatch.com/reports/article.php/2156461 via the Internet.

Sullivan D (2006, July 14) Kinderstart becomes kinderstopped in ranking lawsuit against google. Search Engine Watch. Available: http://blog.searchenginewatch.com/blog/060714-084842 via the Internet.

Sunstein C (2001) Republic.Com. Princeton University Press, Princeton, NJ

Tedeschi B (2006, April 3). Every click you make, they'll be watching you. The New York Times, p C6

Teevan J et al. (2005) Personalizing search via automated analysis of interests and activities. Proceedings of the 28th Annual International ACM SIGIR Conference on Research and Development in Information Retrieval, pp 449–456

Telang R et al. (2004) The market structure for Internet search engines. Journal of Management Information Systems 21: 137–160

Totty M, Mangalindan M (2003, February 26) Web sites try everything to climb google rankings. Wall Street Journal Online. Available: http://online.wsj.com/article/SB1046226160884963943.html?emailf=yes via the Internet.

Upstill T et al. (2003) Predicting fame and fortune: pagerank or indegree. Proceedings of the Australasian Document Computing Symposium, ADCS2003 31–40

Vividence (2004, May 25) Google wins users' hearts, but not their ad clicks. (press release). Available: http://www.vividence.com/public/company/news+and+events/press+releases/2004-05-25+ce+rankings +search.htm via the Internet.

Wearden G (2005, December 21) Japan may create its own search engine. CNET News.com. Available: http://news.com.com/Japan+may+create+its+own+search+engine/2100-1025_3-004037.html via the Internet.

9
The Democratizing Effects of Search Engine Use: On Chance Exposures and Organizational Hubs

A. Lev-On

Summary In this paper I highlight two implications of the widespread use of search engines, which are often overlooked by commentators. In the first part of the paper I argue that search engines are conducive to unplanned exposures to diverse and even opposing views. In the second part I argue that search engines indirectly contribute to emergent political organization, since they allow large numbers of people to locate and access organizational hubs of collective action. I conclude by pointing to the democratic significance of these properties.

9.1

In late 2002 Jiang Mianheng, the son of the former Chinese president and a powerful political figure, visited the 502 research institute of the Ministry of Information Industry to see a demonstration of high-speed Internet. One of the engineers typed the name of his father, "Jiang Zemin," in the Google search engine box. Three of the top ten results were highly critical of the senior Jiang. "Evil Jiang Zemin" was the title of the first result. Shortly afterwards, according to well-informed sources, Jiang Mianheng instructed to block the search engine site (Tianliang 2005).

In a *New York Times* article from April 23, 2006 entitled *Google's China Problem (and China's Google Problem),* Clive Thompson comments that authoritarian governments and companies that provide Internet search services are strange bed-fellows. As evident from the title of his article, Thompson focuses on Google and the Chinese authorities. 'China's Google problem' refers to the authorities' discontent with the new capabilities of Chinese citizens to locate and gain access, through search engines, to websites critical of certain governmental policies. 'China's Google problem' is nicely manifest by the Jiang story above. 'Google's China problem' is Google's discontent with the authorities' demand to censor and monitor its citizens' use of the search engine. Such demands are at odds with the company's policies and, for some, cannot be reconciled with its motto of 'don't be evil.'

Google's recent policy shift and decision to comply with the authorities' demands and censor certain search results on its Chinese Website led to a public

A. Spink and M. Zimmer (eds.), *Web Search, Springer Series in Information Science and Knowledge Management 14.*
© Springer-Verlag Berlin Heidelberg 2008

uproar, and to intense and largely critical press coverage. However, in this paper I do not focus on 'Google's China problem,' but on 'China's Google problem' instead. In light of the harsh reaction of authoritarian governments against indexing and searching sites with arguably no independent political agenda, I would reflect on the dilemmas that search engines pose for authoritarian governments, and point to the democratic significance of search engine use.

This short essay is not an elaborate case study of either 'Google's China problem' or 'China's Google problem.' I utilize 'China's Google problem' to illustrate the tensions between authoritarianism and enhanced popular information-seeking capabilities. The tensions between Google and the Chinese authorities are especially interesting given Google's current dominance in the search market, and the aggressive efforts of the Chinese authorities to lock local surfers behind a 'great firewall.' But the points made in this paper equally hold for other authoritarian governments and searching and indexing services.

9.2

Undoubtedly, search engines have become a vital tool for information-seeking. Search-engine Websites consistently top the lists of popular Websites; a recent survey shows that on a given day 56% of surfers use Web search engines (Fallows 2005). In addition to search-engine sites, search boxes are embedded in countless Websites, and gradually in personal computers as well.

A common metaphor for the Internet is of a huge library, containing vast amounts of materials from great many sources. But a huge library with no efficient indexing and searching tools is essentially useless and probably counter-productive as well. Search engines effectively create an index and assist in 'making order out of chaos' and in evading information overload online. Battelle (2005) convincingly argues that we should conceptualize search engines as information intermediaries or brokers, that assist in matching information supply and demand by creating a 'marketplace' where information-providers can 'publicize' their merchandise and be located by information-seekers, and information-seekers can obtain lists of results that are potentially relevant to their queries.[117]

Famously, the algorithm behind Google, PageRank, emphasizes in-bound links when it determines the relevance of possible responses to users' queries. More precisely, the algorithm holds links from popular sites 'in greater esteem' than links from unpopular sites when determining relevance. The idea is that the linking patterns of popular sites provide a good proxy for users' needs. In other words, if according to many sites (and particularly popular sites) a particular site contains information that is relevant to your query, you are likely to find this site relevant as well.

---

[117] Battelle (2005, 47) suggests that Google "would like to provide a platform that mediates supply and demand for pretty much the entire world economy."

Search engines which utilize the linking patterns of many other users to determine relevance have, evidently, a number of advantages over human-generated indexes (where users categorize and comment on individual sites), and expert-run answering services (where users provide direct responses to other users' queries), in terms of such parameters as the efforts required from the information-broker, response times, and the number of sources upon which the answer is based. When PageRank and its cousins produce 'organic' results, which are driven by the linking decisions of individuals and not tinkered with or compromised by spammers, firms or governments, they create a rather genuine 'public choice.' PageRank and similar algorithms popularize the search function, basing it on a slightly 'filtered' public opinion.

Google and other search engines have been recently criticized for a variety of reasons. Some argue that at times there is no sufficient separation between the presentation of organic results and paid results, and consequently users may fail to clearly distinguish between the two. Other criticisms refer to biases that result from governmental intervention, as in the Chinese case. Censoring some organic search results and replacing popular items with government-approved less popular items obviously bias the search outcomes. Moreover, when search engines completely remove 'forbidden' items from the result list, without even leaving a non-functional link to the blocked result, users are unaware that such 'forbidden' results even exist.

The above critiques refer to manipulations of the *presentation* of search results. Other critiques regard the by-products of the *inherent* features of search-engine algorithms. In this regard, it has been argued that search engines assist in transforming the equality of opportunity the Internet is so much praised for, into inequality of outcome, and substantiating the dominance of a small elite of highly-linked sites over users' attention.[118] Research shows that the Web link structure is highly skewed, where a small number of sites are heavily linked to, and the overwhelming majority of sites are quite inaccessible. These skewed linking patterns hold not just for the Web as a whole, but also for thematic sites that deal with political issues as gun control, abortion, capital punishment, and general politics directories (Hindman et al. 2003). These phenomena have been explained as consequences of a 'rich get richer' dynamics, which mainly occurs due to preferential attachment of new outbound links to already salient Websites (Barabási 2002; Huberman 2001).[119] It has been argued that search engines, and especially Google-style popularity-based search engines, channel surfers primarily to already popular sites, and help substantiate

---

[118] But see Fortunato et al. (2006), who argue that search engines are "directing more traffic toward less popular sites, even in comparison to what would be expected from users randomly surfing the Web."

[119] Research shows that skewed distributions, such as power-law distributions, are ubiquitous online. In addition to the Web link structure and traffic that is correlated with it (Barabási 2002), Drezner and Farrell (2004) found that the distribution of inbound links to blogs follows a power-law distribution as well. The highly inegalitarian distributions of links and traffic have profound implications for web-based organization. The fact that a small number of sites emerge as focal sites means that users with similar tastes, economic interests or hobbies can easily converge onto a narrow set of focal sites. Such focal points serve, in essence, as organizational hubs that can be easily discerned by search engines (see later).

their centrality. But search engines not only direct people to already popular sites; assuming that the probability that users link to a particular site increases if they are routed to this site, search engines indirectly perpetuate and reinforce the highly inegalitarian distribution of links and traffic online.

Note that such critiques are reminiscent of long-standing critiques of direct democracy (that some search engines emulate) regarding its vulnerability to administrative and commercial pressures, and its tendency to lead to majority tyranny. All, or some, of these concerns may be justified to some degree or another. But they are not our main concern here. Instead, let us focus on certain advances that search engines generate in democracies, and the flip-side: the concerns they raise in authoritarian regimes. My aim here is not to deny that the uses of search-engines generate some by-products that may be at odds with our democratic sensibilities. Such potential problems coexist with the new promises that are surveyed below.

9.3

An interesting feature of search engines, which is nicely demonstrated by the Jiang incident, is that they occasionally generate unplanned and unpredictable exposures to diverse views, even to information that runs counter to searchers' prior beliefs. For example, users who want to learn about cellular phones can be directed to Websites which focus on their disadvantages and even hazards (Brin and Page 1998), but at other times can be routed to Websites which praise them. Users who champion capitalism or globalization and want to learn more about these topics can be channeled to anti-capitalist or anti-globalization sites, respectively.

Keep in mind that offline, the chances of running into opposing views, especially in political matters, are not promising. Research shows that people tend to carefully select their conversation partners, and political talk occurs mostly among friends, family and like-minded others (see Huckfeldt and Sprague 1995; Kim et al. 1999; Conover et al. 2002). Even the voluntary associations that people choose to join, evolve to become rather homogenous ideologically (Theiss-Morse and Hibbing 2005, see also Mutz 2006).

Search engines, on the other hand, enable easy access, with a click of a mouse, to vast amounts of information generated by many sources. But easy access cannot by itself counter the filtering mechanisms of everyday discourse. Let us imagine an information environment in which extensive amounts of information exist alongside refined tailoring abilities of content, i.e. people can use search engines to carefully select those items that correspond to their worldview from the massive amounts of information, and screen out all the rest. In such environments, refined search and tailoring abilities may generate exposures only to information confirming and reassuring users' prior views, consistent with users' *homophile* information-seeking patterns offline (Mutz 2006).

But I argue that, at present, search engines do not allow for such refined filtering capabilities, and at times even unintentionally expose users to opposing views.

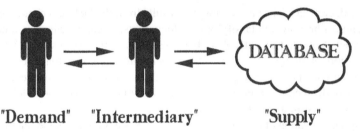

Fig. 9.1 An illustration of Mediated Database Information Retrieval Processes

While unfolding the reasoning, let us keep in mind that three 'components' are involved in the process of retrieving information through search engines: the user, the search engine, and the information available online. Figure 9.1 below shows a highly simplified version of mediated processes of searching and retrieving information from a database, where users ('demand') retrieve information from databases, using an 'intermediary.'

The 'intermediary' phase of this process is depicted in the drawing as a human and can be, for example, a family-member, a friend or an expert. But it can also be non-human; for example, the intermediary can be PageRank or another algorithm that fetches information from the database at the request of the 'demanding' person.

In an 'ideal retrieval process,' queries are perfectly framed and articulated by the users ('demand'). The intermediary does not only have access to the wording of the query, but has a 'deeper' understanding of users' intentions which enables it to ask for clarifications or suggest modifications to the query before accessing the database. The database itself is perfectly indexed, such that the intermediary can have a direct access to all the relevant information (for another account of a 'perfect search' see Battelle 2005, chap. 7). Think of an intelligent agent that can, upon command in natural language, "fetch all arguments for limiting immigration", or "provide a summary of the recent successes of pro-life efforts", or "suggest an argument why gay marriages are morally right" or wrong. Such an 'ideal search' allows users, if so they wish, to craft their own ideological universe out of the vast amounts of information available online, and effectively filter out all traces of diverse and opposing views.

But there are a number of obstacles for such an 'ideal search,' when it is carried out through search engines. Below I focus on three such obstacles involving imperfect database indexing, limited intermediary qualifications to recognize the intentions of searchers and fine-tune the query, and ill-formulations of queries. I claim that such obstacles prevent users from perfectly tailoring their 'ideological universe,' and given the massive amounts and diversity of information online, they can even facilitate exposure to diverse and opposing views. Let us review these obstacles in some detail.

Let us start with the 'supply side' of the retrieval process, and comment on the current absence of a comprehensive and reliable universal tagging system (i.e. a semantic Web) – the lack of a network of keywords that properly describe the content of online documents. The current absence results from the lack of a central authority or a 'central librarian' to classify online documents, a feature which is inherent to the Internet. Note that recently there have been some suggestions for collaborative classification of documents, where users generate keywords that are associated with individual sites. Tagging content collaboratively is an instance of what I elsewhere call second-order collaborations (Lev-On and Hardin 2007), and is increasingly used in a variety of Websites.[120]

The ill-classification of the online 'database' makes it difficult for the 'intermediary' (whether a search engine or otherwise) to locate relevant content. Moreover, it makes it difficult to discriminate content based on ideological affiliations in order to design and maintain, for example, a 'progressive universe' or a 'conservative Web' that can be queried through search engines. In other words, it makes it difficult to perfectly tailor the ideological affiliation of sites towards which users are channeled.

Where the first obstacle for an 'ideal search' is associated with the 'supply' side of the process, the second obstacle involves the interaction between the intermediary and the 'demand' side – the searcher – and regards the comparatively limited abilities of the intermediary to have a 'deep understanding' of the intentions of searchers.

Let us think of queries along the lines of 'fetch all the arguments and court rulings against stem-cell research.' one can direct such queries to an 'online answering service' composed of experts; alternatively, one can post a query to newsgroups or virtual communities with known ideological affiliations. Compared to such alternatives, the results obtained from search engines can be pale. The alternatives have clear advantages over search engines in terms of the usage of natural language, the ability to induce intentions from the context and wording of the query, and the uses of interactivity. These features allow such 'intermediaries' a fine-grained understanding of the intentions behind a formal query.

In the case of search engines, however, the interface is essentially textual and there are minimal interaction and feedback between the 'demand' side and the 'intermediary.' As a result, there are fewer opportunities for a fine-grained understanding of the intention behind a formal query when using search engines. At the current state of search engine technology, then, mapping users' intentions to relevant answers, especially for more complicated queries, can be highly imperfect (see Battelle 2005).

The third and last obstacle for an 'ideal search' process regards the searchers - the 'supply side' – and how they formulate and articulate their intentions. A number of

---

[120] By 'secondary collaborations' we refer to a 'family' of institutions that aggregate large amounts of individual selections and generate social choices. 'Secondary collaborations' can be used to produce reputations, edit and rate content, moderate discussions and provide reviews and recommendations of products and services. Note that collaborative tagging may face such problems as improper (and even malicious) tagging, and inter-personal disagreement on tagging.

studies on information-seeking behaviors online reveal that users compose very short queries, hardly use advanced searching options, view a very small number of documents per query, and almost never view more than one page of results (see Spink and Jansen 2004, Machill et al. 2004). Spelling mistakes and non-grammatical formulations are frequent (Hargittai 2006).[121]

Such information-seeking patterns limit searchers' abilities to retrieve only information tailored to their views and filter out information that opposes them, and reduce the effectiveness of searching strategies. Note that the first two obstacles for an 'ideal search' – regarding content tagging and intention guessing – can be better addressed when search technologies improve and are better able, for example, to approximate natural language or to capitalize on a comprehensive semantic Web. But improper use of searching tools and inadequate framing of search queries will continue to limit users' abilities to retrieve information, even after technological capabilities improve.

In summary, I argue that due to such factors as the absence of a comprehensive and reliable system of keywords, the difficulties of deciphering searchers' intention by intermediaries, and far-from-optimal popular search patterns, it is difficult to craft an ideal search, and searchers cannot easily limit themselves to sealed ideological spaces online. If users had the abilities to limit their horizons in such ways, they would indeed be able to efficiently craft their own ideological echo chambers and totally prevent exposure to opposing or diverse views, substantiating Sunstein's (2001) fears. But since agents can find it very difficult to limit their horizons in such ways, and given the large amount of information and the variety of sources online, when agents use search engines they can be directed to unexpected places, even to (popular) sites presenting arguments that counter their views.[122]

Earlier we commented on the role of search engines in bridging the supply and demand of information online (Battelle 2005). While search engine do make information markets more efficient, they still imperfectly bridge demand and supply. The combination of imperfect matching and tailoring abilities, with abundance and diversity of information, seems conducive to drive people to diverse and even opposing views (see Lev-On and Manin 2007).

---

[121] The somewhat paradoxical argument here is, in effect, that illiteracy has its virtues... at least in the narrow domain of generating chance exposures to diverse and opposing views while using search engines.

[122] Elsewhere we argue that occasional unplanned exposures should be seen as 'happy accidents' – that some randomness are instrumental for adequate deliberation (Lev-On and Manin 2007, Sunstein 2001). Nevertheless, we do not wish to argue that search engine should produce only random outcomes. Such search engines would attract very little traffic, and will be conducive to chance exposures of very few surfers. A necessary condition for mass exposure to opposing views through search engines is, of course, that many people actually use the search engines. And they use them, obviously, because they think that they are likely to obtain valuable information through the search engines. This is, obviously, not the case with 'random' search engines.

9.4

In the previous section I argued that search engines are conducive to chance exposures to diverse and even opposing views. In the following section I argue that search engines also assist in generating and maintaining organizational hubs that are instrumental for collective action.

Let us think of collective actions such as citizen-based campaigns to re-evaluate and reconsider public policies (i.e. Leach 2005 on such a Web-supported campaign which aimed at revising immunization policies), or orchestrated demonstrations and rallies, or community efforts to revise local development plans. Typically such collective efforts are of interest to large numbers of people, but at the absence of organizational infrastructure such causes may not attract and mobilize enough support, and may become latent (i.e. Olson 1965).

Orchestrating such collective efforts entails costs to both organizers and activists. Organizers need to make decisions about mobilization of resources, alliance formations, protest scheduling, location and coordination, and so on. Activists and sympathizers need to locate particular events, receive relevant information and forward it to relevant others, and decide where they can contribute effectively. Particularly, successful collective efforts require the existence of easily accessed focal points to which organizers, activists and sympathizers can converge to post and retrieve information in order to coordinate their efforts.

I argue that search engines contribute to such collective efforts by exposing popular organizational hubs, and directing traffic to them. The new abilities of many people to locate organizational hubs of collective action are, arguably, especially important for 'unprivileged' or 'disorganized' interests. It may be difficult – if not impossible- to find information about and join such collective efforts, that oftentimes lack a clear and easily-accessible organizational 'address', offline.

Let me note that search engines are, of course, not always successful in exposing organizational hubs. When agents rely on search engines to obtain information about collective actions, the search engines determine what the Web consists of for those seeking to contribute. If a search does not return a link for a certain site, say a grassroots effort to change public policy, then the seeker might never know that such an effort exists. On the other hand, after a site gains momentum and becomes popular, search engines make the popular effort even more noticeable for large numbers of surfers, and provide potential contributors with a powerful gateway to collective action.

Organizational hubs can have two main functions. First, they can enable intra-site communication, either in the form of documents and organizational information (about timing of protests, for example), or in the form of interactive conversations. Second, they also include links that, when followed, can easily route people to other relevant sites.[123] Search engines function *primarily in the second capacity*, i.e. they direct agents to other focal sites.

---

[123] To clarify the distinction, think of a parallel distinction between topical blogs that post information about a particular theme, and filter blogs that primarily post links to sites that post information about such a theme.

What does it mean that a site serves as an 'organizational hub' and directs traffic to other sites? To illustrate this, think of the *'Slashdot effect'*. Slashdot is one of largest virtual communities. The community is so successful that it is famous for generating a 'Slashdot effect:' right after a link to an interesting story published elsewhere becomes available, massive numbers of users flood the original site. This sudden and heavy traffic sometimes crashes the linked sites' servers (the crash is the 'Slashdot effect'). Search engines serve a similar function of revealing sites relevant for collective action to large numbers of searchers who are interested in such efforts.[124]

On the Internet it is much easier to establish such organizational hubs than offline, due to factors such as the reduction of gate keeping and setup costs.[125] Such organizational hubs can be set up by a variety of agents, such as civil society organizations, interest groups, parties, social movements, or just single individuals who take it upon themselves to initiate such collective actions. But although almost anyone can establish a Website which aims at organizing collective action, such sites get varying amounts of attention and are far from being similarly successful. Locating the sites that genuinely serve as focal points for collective action remains an intricate task.

Why do search engines efficiently expose organizational hubs? As noted above, Google and other search engines rely heavily on popularity to determine the relevance of search results. Thus, Google and its cousins serve as sensitive barometers that reveal, in our case, the sites that many people think are important access points for a certain collective effort. Typically, they channel users to popular sites that many people found relevant and important enough to link their sites to. For example, if one looks for information on a community protest against a development plan, the results obtained from the search engine are sites that, according to many people, include important information about the local protest. Search engines also enable an easy path to these access points, and direct traffic primarily (but not exclusively) to such focal sites.[126]

Think of a movement like the Falun Gong, which is now banned in China and operates from outside its borders (and, also, is blocked by the 'great firewall'.)

---

[124] Admittedly, communities are generally better able to route potential contributors to relevant collaborative projects, since they (unlike search engines) can include large pools of agents who select to join the community and have some interest or expertise relevant to the focal theme of the community. The combination of scale, self-selection and some 'local expertise' means that community members are more likely to be, as a general rule, motivated and to take an active interest in a relevant collective effort, than just an aggregation of search-engine users.

[125] Elsewhere, in a manuscript co-written with Russell Hardin, we argue that Internet communication is conducive for such large-scale collaborations. We argue that much of the success of such collaborations should be attributed to the availability of the Internet as a shared communicative and organizational platform, the large and excessive number of potential contributors attracted to focal collaborations, and the reduction of costs of both individual contributions and the social organization of production (Lev-On and Hardin 2007).

[126] A suggested above, search engines even perpetuate the popularity of such focal sites (assuming that more popular and accessible sites are linked-to more often than less popular and accessible sites).

Searching for activities organized by Falun Gong in the uncensored version of Google does not direct users to obscure sites that incidentally mention 'Falun Gong;' instead, it directs them to sites including relevant information about the movement and its activities. Many (probably most) people that use Google to look for 'Falun Gong' (or related keywords) are *routed to the same* small set of relevant destinations. Search engines, then, allow many surfers to easily distinguish popular sites from unpopular sites, and converge into a small set of focal sites.

Organizers of collective action increasingly capitalize on the centrality-enhancing property of search engines. Often they ask supporters to install links from their personal sites to the site that organizes collective action. For example, when a visitor opposed to a local development project embeds in her Website an icon that is linked to the Website of a group that arranged the opposition for the development plans, this act increases the popularity of the group's Website. Even if organizers do not think strategically when asking contributors to install such links, this practice assists in making the site more popular and, as a consequence, more easily located.[127]

Search engines, then, indirectly assist in organizational efforts by exposing focal organizational hubs and routing people there, providing a channel for people with similar interests to seamlessly coordinate their efforts.

9.5

So far I argued that search engines contribute to unintended exposure to diverse and opposing views, and indirectly contribute to the organization of collective action. Why are such contributions significant to democracy? To answer this question in a nutshell I will draw on insights from democratic theory. Space limitations will obviously make the remaining discussion somewhat sketchy.

Elsewhere I argued (with Bernard Manin, 2007) that exposure to diverse and especially opposing views contributes to the deliberative qualities of democratic discussion.[128] There is a long tradition of liberal theory praising the benefits of diverse and conflicting views for adequate deliberation (for a recent exploration see Mutz 2006, especially chap. 3). Mill (1991, 26, emphasis mine) who discusses this topic extensively in his 'On Liberty', praises the benefits that can occur when opposing views confront each other, and argues that even "[T]he most intolerant of churches, the Roman Catholic Church, even at a canonization of a saint, *admits, and patiently listens* to a 'devil's advocate'." Empirical evidence support some of the theoretic assertions, and show that exposure to opposing views is instrumental for deliberation as it generates such qualities as lack of polarization and radicalization,

---

[127] There is a notable family resemblance between such practices and practices of search-engine optimization, i.e. strategic inflation of inbound links and similar techniques which aim at pushing a site up the search-engine result list, and gaining the attention of search-engine users.

[128] The following few sections borrow from Lev-On and Manin (2007).

knowledge gains, more considered opinions, satisfaction from the deliberative process, and enhanced feelings of efficacy (Price and Cappella 2002; Iyengar et al. 2003; Muhlberger 2005).

But exposing agents to opposing views during deliberation entails a number of challenges. First, typically there are substantial opportunity costs for the deliberating agents, as deliberation takes time and cognitive resources that may be devoted to other issues, more aligned with the deliberants' interests and concerns.

Second, debates with an *adversarial* character need 'enhanced' promotion and organization, since they require participants to face conflict and generate talk across cleavages. But research shows that people tend to *avoid* the psychic discomfort of expressing opposing views and becoming involved in contentious discussions. Furthermore, as mentioned earlier, research shows that when people do talk about politics, they do so primarily with like-minded others.

Democratic deliberation, then, is a complex public good whose facilitation has to overcome a number of obstacles: opportunity costs, generating cross-cleavage communication, overcoming conflict avoidance. But organizing exposure to diversity of views, and especially to opposing views, is difficult to generate in the course of our daily lives. Mill's interpretation of the role of the *advocatus diaboli* is a mistake: the presence of a devil's advocate is *required* precisely because no one may spontaneously take the other side. This is where search engines get in. I argued that search engines can facilitate exposure to diverse and even opposing views, even against people's intentions. Widely used to seek and obtain political information, search engines can thus enrich democratic deliberation, and are a welcome addition to the few spheres in which unplanned exposures to diverse and opposing views are viable.

While exposure to diverse and opposing views may be essential for certain models of democracy, other models emphasize political organization over deliberation. Realist models of democracy propose, with Schattschneider (1960, 139), that as a general rule "conflict, competition, leadership, and organization are the essence of democratic politics," and that "the possibility of contestation by conflicting interests is sufficient to explain the dynamic of democracy" (Przeworski 1991, 10). Notably, pluralist models of democracy depict it as a process of mutual adjustments between a variety of organized partisan interests. Democratic pluralism emphasizes the importance of a variety of competitive channels to influence policy, and the need to enable multiple groups to organize and influence the policy-making process (see notably Lindblom 1965, Dahl 1967).

However, scholars realize that the competition in actually-existing democracies is highly imperfect, due to such factors as high organization and entry costs. As a result of the disparity of organizational abilities between different groups, policy areas are dominated by those groups that are better financed and organized, where unorganized interests can sink into oblivion and latency.

By now it has become common wisdom that Internet communication drastically reduces the costs of establishing organizations to promote a variety of causes that were previously squeezed out of the political marketplace. Consequently, it is much easier to generate effective voice for causes that would not otherwise be actively promoted. Internet communication supports novel intermediaries that *supplement* existing intermediaries to generate an 'advocacy explosion' (Shapiro 1999; Bimber 2003), by expanding the organizational abilities of a variety of actors to frame and articulate issues, mobilize support and effectively make political demands. Arguably, the Internet contributes to making the market for intermediaries more competitive, and hence to improving competition in democracies.

Search engines take an indirect role and make a modest contribution to the enhancement of political organization and competition, as they support the creation of focal organizational hubs that are necessary for collective action. Search engines expose those *central* sites that many agents value as organizational hubs, and allow many others an easy route to the same set of focal sites. Thus, they contribute to the reduction of organizational costs of a variety of interests.

To emphasize the importance of centrality, let us return shortly to Mill (1991, 424), who in his *Considerations on Representative Government* (in a discussion of the tensions between central and local authorities) argues that:

> Power may be localised, but knowledge, to be most useful, must be centralised; there must be somewhere a focus at which all its scattered rays are collected, that the broken and coloured lights which exist elsewhere may find there what is necessary to complete and purify them.

In the Internet, a highly decentralized environment of political information, search engines constitute such focal points for the 'scattered rays' of knowledge. They also serve as focal points to locate collaborative projects. Still, the 'purification' that search engines allow is imperfect, and hence they can generate unplanned encounters to diverse and opposing views, much more effectively than offline.

While arguably advantageous for democracies, the two properties that I surveyed (unintentional exposure to diverse and opposing views, and indirect support for political organization) may easily be perceived as threats by authoritarian regimes. Let us go back to the Chinese case I opened with. If Chinese citizens were able to seek information about Jiang Zemin in the uncensored version of Google, they could at times come upon information praising him, but at other times get exposed to information smearing the leader (as the earlier story shows), largely depending on the popularity of the sites containing the information. Note that information critical of the leader can become available not only to Jiang's opponents who seek such information to support their prior opinions but also to loyal supporters, and even to innocent elementary school students seeking information for a short presentation about the leader's legacy.

More importantly, anecdotal evidence suggest that the harsh Chinese monitoring of the Internet is also motivated, in large part, by fears from unleashing popular or factional organizations through such novel technologies. For example, the ruthless crackdown of Falun Gong was triggered by a large unauthorized gathering of between 10,000 to 15,000 supporters outside the central leadership compound in Beijing in April 25, 1999. The gathering was orchestrated primarily online. Lin (2001) argues that this has been the largest reasonable-size unauthorized gathering in the history of modern China on which the authorities failed to receive prior information. This case alerted authorities to the ability of Internet-supported movements to organize mass meetings and demonstrations while escaping the attention of the security services.[129] Clive Thompson, in his analysis of 'China's Google problem,' also points to the acuteness of fears from Web-based political organization by the Chinese authorities. Thompson (2006, 71) quotes Zhao Jing, "China's most famous political blogger" whose blog has been shut down in the time of writing, who claims that "If you talk every day online and criticize the government, they don't care… [b]ecause it's just talk. But if you organize- even if it's just three or four people- that's what they crack down on. it's not speech; it's organizing."

9.6 Conclusions

I argued that search engines indirectly advance political organization, and generate unintentional exposures to diverse and opposing views. They thus cater to the concerns of both deliberative democrats aiming at enriching the deliberative qualities of democratic discussion, and pluralist democrats who are concerned about making the political marketplace more open, inclusive and competitive.

On the other hand, Authoritarian governments aim at avoiding unpredictability and chance exposures to critical information, and at depressing emergent organization. In this, The Chinese government closely follows not Mill, but Hobbes' key advice to governments to keep a keen eye on dangers originating from dissemination of 'seditious doctrines' and coordination of anti-establishment powers (see Hardin 1991). The Internet and search engines are perceived as particularly disruptive. As argued above, at times search engines expose people to 'unwarranted' information, even against their intentions. Search engines can also be used by many people to locate and converge on organizational hubs. Sometimes search engines do both these things – they expose many people, even against their intentions, to hubs containing information that authorities disapprove of.

Authoritarian governments, then, need to monitor and regulate search engines in order to suppress exposure to 'unwarranted information' and prevent unauthorized emergent organization. The political importance of search engines is clearly demonstrated by the actions of the Chinese government. It is equally important for advocates of open and democratic societies to constantly monitor the functioning of search engines, and to verify that they continue to support and enrich the informational and organizational infrastructure of democracy.

References

Barabási AL (2002) Linked: the new science of networks. Perseus, Cambridge, MA.
Battelle J (2005) The search. Portfolio, New York.

---

[129] For extensive reviews of the movement and its uses of the Internet, see Bell and Boas 2003 and Chase and Mulvenon 2002.

Bell MR, Boas TC (2003) Falun gong and the Internet: evangelism, community, and struggle for survival. Nova Religio 6: 277–293

Bimber B (2003) Information and American democracy: technology in the evolution of political power. Cambridge University Press, New York

Brin S, Page L (1998) The anatomy of large-scale hypertextual web search engine. In: Proceedings of the Seventh World Wide Web Conference.

Chase MS, Mulvenon JC (2002) You've got dissent! chinese dissident use of the Internet and beijing's counter-strategies. RAND, Santa Monica, CA.

Conover PJ, Searing DD, Crewe IM (2002) The deliberative potential of political discussion. British Journal of Political Science 32: 21–62.

Dahl RA (1967) Pluralist democracy in the united states: conflict and consent. Rand McNally, Chicago.

Drezner D, Farrell H (2004) The power and politics of blogs. Paper presented at the Annual Meeting of the American Political Science Association, Chicago.

Fallows D (2005) Search engine users. Pew Internet and American Life Project. http://www.pewInternet.org/pdfs/PIP_Searchengine_users.pdf

Fortunato S, Flammini A, Menczer F, Vespignani A (2006) The egalitarian effect of search engines. http://arxiv.org/PS_cache/cs/pdf/0511/0511005.pdf

Hardin R (1991) Hobbesian political order. Political Theory 19: 156–180.

Hargittai E (2006) Hurdles to information seeking: Spelling and typographical mistakes during users' online behavior. Journal of the Association of Information Systems 6.

Hindman M, Tsioutsiouliklis K, Johnson JA (2003) Googlearchy: how a few heavily-linked sites dominate politics online. http://www.princeton.edu/~mhindman/googlearchy–hindman.pdf

Huberman BA (2001) The laws of the web: patterns in the ecology of information. MIT, Cambridge, MA.

Huckfeldt R, Sprague J (1995) Citizens, politics, and social communication. Cambridge University Press, New York.

Iyengar S, Luskin R, Fishkin J (2003) Facilitating informed public opinion: Evidence from face-to-face and on-line deliberative polls. http://cdd.stanford.edu/research/papers/2003/facilitating.pdf

Kim J, Wyatt RO, Katz E (1999) News, talk, opinion, participation: the part played by conversation in deliberative democracy. Political Communication 16: 361–385

Leach M (2005) MMR mobilisation: citizens and science in a British vaccine controversy. http://www.drc-citizenship.org/docs/publications/citizens_and_science/WP/wp247.pdf

Lev-On A, Manin B (2007). Happy accidents: Deliberation and online exposure to opposing views. Forthcoming. In: Davies T (ed) Online deliberation: Design, research and practice.

Lev-On A, Hardin R (2007). Internet-based collaborations and their political significance. Forthcoming in Journal of Information Technology and Politics 1.

Lin N (2001) Social capital: A theory of social structure and action. Cambridge University Press, New York.

Lindblom CE (1965) The intelligence of democracy: Decision making through mutual adjustment. Free Press, New York.

Machill M, Neuberger C, Schweiger W, Wirth W (2004). Navigating the Internet: a study of german-language search engines. European Journal of Communication 19: 321–347.

Mill JS (1991) John stuart mill: on liberty and other essays. ed. Gray J. Oxford University Press, New York.

Muhlberger P (2005) The virtual agora project: a research design for studying democratic deliberation. Journal of Public Deliberation 1: 5 http://services.bepress.com/jpd/vol1/iss1/art5

Mutz DC (2006) Hearing the other side: deliberative versus participatory democracy online. Cambridge University Press, New York.

Olson M (1965) The logic of collective action. Harvard University Press, Cambridge, MA.

Price V, Cappella JN (2002) Online deliberation and its influence: the electronic dialogue project in campaign 2000. Information Technology and Society 1: 303–328

Przeworski A (1991) Democracy and the market: political and economic reforms in eastern Europe and Latin America. Cambridge University Press, New York.

Schattschneider EE (1960) The semisovereign people: a realist's view of democracy in America. Holt, Rinehart and Winston, New York.

Shapiro A (1999) The control revolution. Public Affairs, New York.

Spink A, Jansen BJ (2004) A study of web search trends. Webology: An International Electronic Journal 1.

Sunstein CR (2001) Republic.com. Princeton University Press, Princeton, NJ.

Theiss-Morse E, Hibbing JR (2005) Citizenship and civic engagement. Annual Review of Political Science 8: 227–249

Thompson C. Google's China problem (and China's Google problem). New York Times Magazine, April 23, 2006.

Tianliang Z. Google "kowtows" to the Chinese government. Epoch Times, February 8, 2005.

10
'Googling' Terrorists: Are Northern Irish Terrorists Visible on Internet Search Engines?

P. Reilly

10.1 Introduction

In this chapter, the analysis suggests that Northern Irish terrorists are not visible on Web search engines when net users employ conventional Internet search techniques. Editors of mass media organisations traditionally have had the ability to decide whether a terrorist atrocity is 'newsworthy,' controlling the 'oxygen' supply that sustains all forms of terrorism. This process, also known as 'gatekeeping,' is often influenced by the norms of social responsibility, or alternatively, with regard to the interests of the advertisers and corporate sponsors that sustain mass media organisations. The analysis presented in this chapter suggests that Internet search engines can also be characterised as 'gatekeepers,' albeit without the ability to shape the content of Websites before it reaches net users. Instead, Internet search engines give priority retrieval to certain Websites within their directory, pointing net users towards these Websites rather than others on the Internet. Net users are more likely to click on links to the more 'visible' Websites on Internet search engine directories, these sites invariably being the highest 'ranked' in response to a particular search query. A number of factors including the design of the Website and the number of links to external sites determine the 'visibility' of a Website on Internet search engines. The study suggests that Northern Irish terrorists and their sympathisers are unlikely to achieve a greater degree of 'visibility' online than they enjoy in the conventional mass media through the perpetration of atrocities. Although these groups may have a greater degree of freedom on the Internet to publicise their ideologies, they are still likely to be speaking to the converted or members of the press. Although it is easier to locate Northern Irish terrorist organisations on Internet search engines by linking in via ideology, ideological description searches, such as 'Irish Republican' and 'Ulster Loyalist,' are more likely to generate links pointing towards the sites of research institutes and independent media organisations than sites sympathetic to Northern Irish terrorist organisations. The chapter argues that Northern Irish terrorists are only visible on search engines if net users select the correct search terms.

A. Spink and M. Zimmer (eds.), *Web Search, Springer Series in Information Science and Knowledge Management 14.*

10.2 Search Engines: Role in Computer-Mediated Communication

This section presents an analysis of the role of Internet search engines in computer-mediated communication. The 'cyber-optimist' model suggests that computer mediated communication (CMC) facilitates forms of 'communication, interaction and organisation' that undermine unequal status and power relations (Spears and Lea 1994: 428). In other words, the Internet potentially reduces social context in or around a message transmitted from a sender to a receiver (p. 431). The most likely beneficiaries of the reduction of social context in communication transactions would be the groups who are under-represented in the conventional mass media, namely marginalised sub-state political minorities and developmental nation-states. These actors receive little coverage in the conventional mass media in comparison to advanced industrialised nation-states, such as the United States. The 'cyber-optimist' model also suggests that the Internet can provide a degree of 'organisational coherence' to political actors who ordinarily are incapable of 'punching above their weight' in the international community (Hindman et al. 2003: 29). Theoretically, all sub-state political actors have equal access to the rapid low-cost communication offered by information and communication technologies, allowing them to network with like-minded actors and transmit their common values to a potential global audience. However, the 'cyber-optimist' model fails to recognise the critical role played by Internet search engines in the retrieval of information on the Internet. In theory, the Websites of groups and individuals that exist out with the political mainstream should be as accessible as any other page on the Internet (p. 4). Furthermore, Siebert's four media models [authoritarian, libertarian, social responsibility, and soviet respectively] appear to be incompatible with computer-mediated communication, as all net users are able to choose their own 'frames' for the relatively low cost of maintaining a Website. Consequently, the Internet is awash with Webmasters who behave like "primary definers" in the conventional mass media, using their Websites to issue supposedly authoritative statements on contentious issues such as terrorism (Negrine 1994: 127). Yet, sub-state political actors, such as terrorists, many of whom feel marginalised in the conventional mass media, do not achieve a greater degree of recognition or legitimacy simply through maintaining a Website. Although terrorists can manipulate mass media coverage of their atrocities to wage psychological warfare against a target audience, they are unable to compel this audience to visit their Websites. This is because net users invariably use information and communication technologies to pursue their own private purposes (Margolis and Resnick 2000: 96). "Secondary definers," such as editors that amplify the threat of terrorism in the news media, are unable to direct net users towards the Websites of terrorists and their sympathisers. Instead, net users turn to search engines, such as *Google,* to locate information online that is relevant to their private interests.

Internet search engines can be best characterised as 'digital librarians,' as opposed to the 'gatekeepers' that are employed in the conventional mass media. Internet search engines index Websites, having little or no direct influence on the tone and content of the sites in question. Nevertheless, the order of Websites within a particular search engine directory is comparable to decisions made by editorial staff in the news media. Editors have to deliberate over which stories are worthy of greater coverage in conventional media organs, such as television news bulletins or newspapers. On the one hand, they have to ensure that large numbers of media consumers access their products, particularly when advertising revenues are critical to the sustenance of their respective organisations. Advertisers are only likely to invest in media organisations that provide large numbers of readers or viewers that are able to purchase their products (Negrine 1994: 67). On the other hand, editors have to make the decision to drop news stories, as they have finite resources and space with which to give equal coverage to all events that occur within their jurisdiction. Similarly, Internet search engines are unable to give equal attention to the millions of Websites contained in their respective directories, nor index all of the sites available on the Internet. A recent study suggested that all of the major search engines combined only covered 16% of the total number of 'indexable' Websites on the Internet (Bar-Ilan 1999: 1). Consequently, by virtue of their criteria used to index a Website and their popularity with net users, search engines direct Web traffic towards certain Websites rather than others on the Internet. Net users, whether expert or non-expert, feel comfortable using Internet search engines as navigational 'tools' on the Internet. They rarely know the exact Universal Resource Locator (URL) of a Website, typically entering 'keywords' into Internet search engines to locate information relevant to their area of interest. Recent estimates suggest that as much as 90% of all traffic on the Internet comes directly from Internet search engines (Submit Corner 2004). For example, net users spend a total of 13 million hours per month interacting with the *Google* search engine alone (Ntoulas et al. 2004: 1). Furthermore, net users are unlikely to look beyond the first 25 results generated by a particular search query. This suggests that search engines can influence the choices of net users in terms of which Websites they access in order to pursue their private interests. In sum, the popularity of Internet search engines suggests that the Internet enables new forms of 'mediated interaction,' as opposed to the 'unmediated' interaction that would benefit those who receive minimal coverage in the conventional mass media (Wouters and Gerbec 2003: 4). The creation of a Website will not necessarily lead to greater levels of popular recognition for actors that lack a visible presence in the conventional mass media. Conversely, visibility on Internet search engines appears to be equally as important as visibility in the conventional mass media. The Websites of publicity-starved sub-state actors must consistently appear in the top 25 results generated by search engines, if they are to achieve a high degree of visibility online.

10.3   How Do Search Engines Work?

10.3.1   'Googlearchy'

In this section, the factors that determine whether a Website is 'visible' on Internet search engines will be analysed. Internet search engines do not behave like 'objective, well informed librarians,' each individual search engine instead having a set of protocols determining whether a Website is included in its directory and its position vis-à-vis other indexed Websites (Gerhart 1994: 3). There is little specific information available on these protocols, also known as 'algorithms.' This is because the companies behind Internet search engines are reluctant to disclose information explaining how they rank Websites to their competitors. Internet search engines compete not only to secure the patronage of net users but also to accrue revenue from companies wishing to place advertisements on their sites. *Google* remain the only search engine company to have published details of how they rank Websites in their directory. The original *Google* algorithm 'ranks' a Website in its directory through an assessment of the links pointing towards it, and an assessment of the 'standing' of these linking pages themselves (Thelwall 2001: 3). *Google* equates a link from one Website to another as an endorsement of both sites, attributing an undisclosed value to each Website. (Walker 2002: 3). For a Website to receive a high ranking in the *Google* search engine, it clearly pays to reciprocate links with other Websites, regardless of whether they share similar themes. This phenomenon of 'Googlearchy,' whereby the most heavily linked Websites received the highest ranking in the *Google* directory, would appear to militate against the cyber-optimist conception of the Internet as a political communication device open to all sections of society (Hindman et al. 2003). As small sub-state actors are unlikely to have large numbers of supporters, they are arguably unlikely to reciprocate links with large number of actors online. Therefore, the Websites of these actors are likely to be less 'visible' on search engines than the sites of extensively linked organisations, such as government agencies, research institutes, and independent news media organisations (Gerhart 2004: 22).

10.3.2   Updating Frequencies

Wouters et al. (2004) characterise Internet search engines as the 'clocks' of cyberspace, representing the updating frequency of both the Web and the underlying Internet (p.15). The maintenance of search engine directories reflects the closure of Websites, changes to the search engine algorithms, and the extent to which 'old' pages remain in their databases (p.17). Internet search engines use a combination of automated Website crawlers (or 'spiders') and human editors to index Websites and update their directories. For example, directory search engines, such as *DMOZ* (www.dmoz.org), employ as many as 50,000 human editors to decide whether a

Website should be included in their database and how it should be ranked in comparison to other sites (Search Engine Yearbook 2003). Meanwhile, the majority of commercial Internet search engines use browser like programs, such as 'spiders,' to follow the links from one Website to another, indexing everything that they find. Both human editors and automated Web crawlers look for the same information on Websites before deciding whether, or invariably where, they are to be included within their respective directories. META tags, containing information such as the name of the Webmaster and which 'keywords' best describe the content of the Website, are used to determine whether a site should be indexed by an Internet search engine (Webopedia 2004). In this respect, Meta tags arguably perform a similar function to the 'headlines' deployed by conventional news media organisations to boost public consumption of their products. The Meta tag description is critical in determining how high a Website will be 'ranked' in the results generated by 'keyword' searches on Internet search engines. Meta tags present the content of a Website - in no more than 256 characters – in an effort to attract the attention of both human editors and automated Web crawlers (Softsteel Solutions 2003). As discussed earlier, a high 'ranking' in an Internet search engine directory will in all likelihood lead to a higher degree of visibility for a particular Website. Net users will be more likely to access Websites that are visible on Internet search engines, defined in this chapter as sites that feature in the top 25 results generated in response to a particular search query. However, the visibility of Websites is subject to the constant updating of Internet search engine directories. Internet search engines have to update their databases constantly due to the high turnover of Websites on the Internet, an estimated 80% of Websites available today likely to be inaccessible after one year (Ntoulas et al. 2004: 2). Companies such as *Yahoo,* and even the market leader, *Google,* do not have the resources to index all available Websites on the Internet, or to trawl through these Websites in order to generate a list of results in response to a search query. The implication for marginalised sub-state political actors would appear stark. Failure to achieve a 'high' search engine ranking will inevitably lead to these actors remaining anonymous on the Internet, in effect replicating the paucity of coverage these actors receive in the conventional mass media. Consequently, Webmasters that seek greater visibility online must market their Websites at a target audience that not only includes net users, but also Internet search engines.

10.4 Do Search Engines 'Suppress' Information on the Internet?

This section analyses the proposition that search engines actively 'suppress' information on the Internet. As discussed earlier, search engines are more likely to direct Internet users towards the Websites of extensively linked organisations than marginalised sub-state actors. Some analysts suggest that there may be an alternative explanation for the marginalisation of small sub-state groups on Internet search engine directories. Internet search engines arguably filter information with reference to many of the norms that inform the behaviour of the conventional mass media. Each of the four media models [the authoritarian, libertarian, social responsibility and soviet models respectively] permit government censorship of the conventional mass media on the grounds that a story might endanger national security, defame character or offend public 'decency.'[130] Recent studies suggest that these norms also influence the editorial process within Internet search engines, particularly in the omission of controversial Websites from certain search engine directories. Zittrain and Edelman (2005) compared the availability of white supremacist Websites on the French and German Google sites, *google.de* and *google.fr.* The study concluded that 113 sites, such as 'Stormfront White Pride World Wide' (www.crusader.net), could not be located on both the French and German versions of *Google,* despite being listed on *google.com* (Zittrain and Edelman 2005). Government legislation forced Google to remove these Websites from their French and German portals. In December 2000, the German Supreme Court, the *Bundesgerichtshof,* had ruled that German laws against neo-Nazi propaganda would apply to Websites maintained by both German citizens and foreign nationals (Bodard 2003: 266). There is also some evidence to suggest that sub-state groups may use legal sanctions to remove controversial Websites from Internet search engine directories. In 2002, the Church of Scientology forced *Google* to remove references to Websites that were critical of its religion. The Scientologists lobbied for the removal of these Websites with reference to the US Digital Millennium Copyright Act (1998), as they contained 'copyrighted material' (Zittrain and Edelman 2005). Yet, the norms of the libertarian media model may also contribute to the predominance of 'more of the same' organisational Websites on Internet search engine directories. In the conventional mass media, advertising revenue and private investment are critical to the longevity of media organisations, particularly in the United States. Similarly, Internet search engines maintain their financial self-sufficiency through the sale of advertising space on their respective Web portals. Search engines, such as Geocities, have even sold 'priority retrieval' to companies, placing their Websites first in the results generated by a relevant 'query.' (Noveck 2000: 24). As small sub-state actors are unlikely to be able to afford priority retrieval, they are likely to be less visible on search engines directories than the Websites of extensively linked organisations, such as those of large media companies.

The 'filtering' of information by Internet search engines has implications for those Internet users who wish to research controversial political issues on the Internet. Gerhart (1994) asserts that Internet search engines reward "more of the same" organisational Websites at the expense of less popular content, 'controversy-revealing' Websites only visible in search engine results through a combination of the right search 'query' and offline experience of the relevant subject (p. 22). Internet users who lack background knowledge of a controversial political issue are

---

[130] See Siebert FS, Peterson T and Schramm W (1963) *Four theories of the Press*, Chicago: University of Illinois Press.

increasingly likely to turn to Internet search engines for links to sites of interest. As discussed above, Internet search engines are likely to direct these Internet users towards the Websites of extensively linked organisations, many of whom have the capacity to purchase 'priority retrieval.' Therefore, the predominance of 'more of the same' organisations on Internet search engines reduces the 'visibility' of 'controversy revealing' Websites online. If the Internet user is not familiar with the actor behind a controversial Website, they are likely to turn to the most 'visible' Websites on Internet search engines, principally the Website of extensively linked organisations that dominate the first page of results generated by their query. Furthermore, the algorithms of the major commercial search engines arguably perpetuate the marginalisation of 'controversy-revealing' Websites on the Internet. If these Websites do not receive a large number of 'hits' from Internet users who lack relevant background knowledge of their subject, they are likely to remain a minority interest online. Consequently, Webmasters that publish controversial opinions on their Websites are likely to be communicating with Internet users who share their views, as opposed to a potential global audience with no preconception of their particular subject. In sum, search engines filter information with reference to some of the norms of the mass media models. Extensively linked organisations are likely to populate the top 25 results generated by most search queries, often at the expense of 'controversy-revealing' Websites. These organisations are more visible on search engines because a higher volume of Web 'traffic' passes through their Websites, and, in some cases, due to the fact that they have paid companies such as *Geocities* to ensure a high search engine ranking.

10.5   Northern Irish Terrorists and Internet Search Engines

The section assesses whether Internet search engines suppress 'controversy' on the Internet from the perspective of Northern Irish terrorist organisations. The study analysed whether 'more of the same' organisational Websites dominated the search results generated by a variety of Loyalist and Republican keyword searches, using a number of high profile Internet search engines. It was anticipated that sites that expressed support for proscribed Northern Irish terrorist organisations would be vastly under-represented in the top 25 results generated by search queries, further illustrating the robustness of the analysis of 'controversy revealing' Websites presented in this chapter. The study also examined whether the ideology of the terrorist actor was a relevant factor in determining whether search engine results would provide links to Northern Irish terrorists or their sympathisers. Republican terrorist organisations, such as the Provisional Irish Republican Army (PIRA), have traditionally enjoyed a higher international profile than Loyalist terrorist organisations, such as the Ulster Volunteer Force (UVF). Irish Republicans have a long established set of international support networks, particularly amongst Irish – Catholic communities in the United States (O'Dochartaigh 2003: 1). Republican terrorists also employ more sophisticated methods of fund-raising and organisational linkage than their Loyalists counterparts (Silke 1998: 333). Since 1969, Irish-American 'solidarity' groups, such as the Irish Northern Aid Committee (NORAID), have provided resources for the Republican movement, its members even posing as tourists to transport weaponry to the Provisional IRA (Bowyer Bell 2000: 187). Conversely, Northern Ireland's Loyalist and Unionist communities have been unable to mobilise a similar emigrant population, despite a large number of people with Ulster Protestant ancestry residing in North America (O'Dochartaigh 2003: 1). Instead, groups such as the Ulster Volunteer Force have raised funds through 'domestic' activities such as extortion, video piracy, and drug dealing (Silke 1998: 336). Consequently, more 'pro-Republican' Websites were anticipated in the search results generated by Republican keyword searches, than 'pro-Loyalist' sites in the equivalent Loyalist keyword searches. Groups such as NORAID would presumably maintain a Website as part of their strategy to provide support to the Republican movement. The absence of similar Loyalist international support networks would militate against a large number of pro-Loyalist Websites featuring in the top 25 results generated by search engines. Although Republicans would appear more visible than their Loyalist counterparts on search engines, 'more of the same' organisational Websites were expected to dominate the results of the study.

10.6   Methodology

The sample selected for the study consisted of four leading Internet search engines, namely *DMOZ* (www.dmoz.org), *Google* (www.google.co.uk), *MSN* (www.msn.co.uk), and *Yahoo* (www.yahoo.co.uk). The British versions of *Google*, *MSN,* and *Yahoo* were utilised for the study as they included results from their global directories. During the period of data collection, they were the most regularly used Internet search engines across the globe.[131] The three commercial search engines were included to test the rule of 'Googlearchy.' As discussed earlier, search engines such as *Google* rank Websites within its directory in accordance with the volume of Web traffic that passes through each Website. Therefore, the study tested the hypothesis that extensively linked organisations would populate the top 25 results generated by these search engines, as opposed to 'controversy-revealing' Websites, such as those that expressed support for Northern Irish terrorists. The *DMOZ* search engine (www.DMOZ.org) was also included in the study to reflect the new generation of search engines based entirely upon human editorial, rather than automated Web crawlers. Consequently, the *DMOZ* search engine was expected to return more links to sites that could be characterised as either 'pro-Loyalist' or 'pro-Republican' than the other search engines included in the study. Human editors would presumably be less likely to provide links to Websites that had nothing to do with the terrorist organisations under analysis.

---

[131] Sullivan, D, 'Share of Searches: July 2005' www.searchenginewatch.com/reports/article.php/2156451 (accessed 20 October 2005).

A series of keyword searches were conducted using the four Internet search engines in October 2004. The names of the 14 Northern Irish terrorist organisations, proscribed under anti-terrorist legislation such as the Prevention of Terrorism Act (1984), were entered into the basic search facility of the four Internet search engines (see Table 10.1). Two ideological descriptions, 'Ulster Loyalist' and 'Irish Republican,' were also entered into the basic search facility of the four search engines. These phrases were selected as they were commonly used to describe the ideological position of Northern Irish terrorist organisations, as illustrated by the names of the 14 proscribed terrorist groups under review. It was anticipated that Webmasters that projected 'pro-Loyalist' or 'pro-Republican' propaganda on the Internet would use these words, or the name of one of the proscribed terrorist organisations, in the Meta tag descriptions of their Websites. The number of links generated by each individual search query was recorded for further analysis. These statistics provided a rudimentary method of comparing the number of sites whose Meta tags resembled Loyalist and Republican keywords. Searches conducted using the two ideological descriptions and two terrorist group names, the Irish Republican Army and the Ulster Volunteer Force, were analysed to assess whether Internet search engines produced a majority of links that were broadly in favour of Northern Irish terrorists. The top 25 results of these keyword searches were analysed as they were considered the results that closely mirrored the search terms entered in the respective Internet search engines. The sites that featured in these 25 results were then classified as one of eight categories: Official Terrorist Organisation/ Political Front, Solidarity Website, Personal Webpage/Blog, Research Institute/ University, External News Media, Opposition Website, Government, and Other. During the period of analysis, none of the 14 proscribed Northern Irish terrorist groups maintained an official Web presence under that particular name. Therefore, the category of official Website was designed to include the Websites of Loyalist and Republican political fronts in the study. The term political 'front' is used here to denote a political organisation that either is "directly under the control" or closely linked to a proscribed terrorist organisation (Richards 2001: 72). For instance, the Sinn Fein and Progressive Unionist Party sites were considered 'official' Republican and Loyalist sites with reference to the First Report of the Independent Monitoring Commission (2004). The report stated that senior members of Sinn Fein were in a position to exercise considerable influence on PIRA's major policy decisions. Similarly, the Progressive Unionist Party exercised an appreciable influence on the activities of the Ulster Volunteer Force and Red Hand Commandos.[132] Websites were categorised as 'solidarity' Websites if they appeared to exist solely to provide support for Loyalist or Republican terrorist groups. This support could take many forms, including soliciting resources for paramilitary prisoners, raising funds for political fronts or issuing propaganda in favour of one of the terrorist groups under analysis.

---

[132] Independent Monitoring Commission, First Report of the Independent Monitoring Commission, http://www.independentmonitoringcommission.org/documents/uploads/ACFA6C2.pdf (accessed 10 June 2004)

Table 10.1 Northern Irish Terrorist Groups currently proscribed in the United Kingdom

Group	Estimated Strength	Pro/Anti Good Friday Agreement	Website of Politically Linked Group	Unofficial (Solidarity) Website
Continuity Army Council[a]	Under 50 active members.	Anti	Yes (as Republican Sinn Fein)	Yes
Cumann na mBan	No Data Available	No Data Available	No	No
Fianna na hEireann	Unknown	Anti	Yes	No
Irish National Liberation Army	Under 50 active members	Anti	Yes (As Irish Republican Socialist Movement)	Yes
Irish Peoples Liberation Organisation[b]	No Data Available	No Data Available	No	No
Irish Republican Army (aka PIRA)	Several hundred active members	Pro	Yes (As Sinn Fein)	Yes
Loyalist Volunteer Force	50–150 active members, 300 supporters	Anti	No	Yes
Orange Volunteers	20 active members[c]	Anti	No	Yes
Red Hand Commandos	No Data Available	Pro	No	Yes
Red Hand Defenders	Up to 20 active members	Anti	No	No
Saor Eire	No Data Available	No Data Available	No	No
Ulster Defence Association/Ulster Freedom Fighters[d]	Few dozen active members	Pro	Yes (As Ulster Political Research Group)	Yes
Ulster Volunteer Force	Few dozen active members	Pro	Yes (As Progressive Unionist Party)	Yes

[a] Linked to Republican Sinn Fein, Continuity IRA, and according to some sources, the Real IRA
[b] The Irish Peoples Liberation Organisation (IPLO) announced its dissolution in October 1992 following an internal feud.
[c] Security sources believe that Red Hand Defenders and Orange Volunteers are served by same pool of volunteers.
[d] These two organisations are defined as autonomous terrorist organisations on the UK list of proscribed terrorist groups (2005). However, these groups are considered by many sources to be one and the same organisation.

The other six categories incorporated Websites that did not express support for Loyalist or Republican terrorist organisations. Personal Webpages and blogs were defined in the study as sites maintained by individual Internet users to express opinions on a variety of issues, such as terrorism. Although many 'bloggers' expressed opinions on Northern Irish terrorists, personal Webpages were not considered to be 'solidarity' sites dedicated to the groups under analysis. It was anticipated that these sites were set up to record the opinions of their respective authors, rather than just issue propaganda in favour of Northern Irish terrorist organisations. It was expected that 'pro-Loyalist' and 'pro-Republican' Webmasters might use their Websites to criticise the activities of their opponents. Many of these Websites might use words relating to their opponents in their Meta tag descriptions, thus making their sites visible in results generated by searches conducted using the names of the opposition groups. Subsequently, the 'Opposition Website' category was created to incorporate 'Republican' Websites in the analysis of Loyalist keyword searches and vice versa. The next three categories were designed to test the Gerhart hypothesis, namely that 'more of the same' organisational Websites dominate search engine results at the expense of less popular Websites. The sites of research institutes, external mass media organisations and government agencies were all expected to receive high search engine ratings due to the rule of 'Googlearchy.' It was anticipated that research institutes and government agencies, that analysed the Northern Irish conflict, would use keyword Meta tag descriptions on their sites that were similar to the keyword searches used in the study. External news media organisations, who reported on the activities of Northern Irish terrorists in newspaper, radio, and television formats, were expected to replicate this coverage on their Websites. The category of 'Other' was used to describe sites that did not comment specifically on contemporary Northern Irish terrorist organisations. This category included sites that promoted 'cultural' aspects of Loyalism and Republicanism but offered no 'political' analysis of contemporary Northern Irish terrorist organisations. It also included sites that did not explicitly refer to Northern Ireland, but had Meta tags that were similar to the keyword searches used in the study. For example, Websites dedicated to the Irish language, or, alternatively, Orange flute bands were considered 'cultural' rsather than political projections of the two traditions in Northern Ireland.

The data was entered into SPSS for Windows and frequency tables were created to provide a breakdown of the top 25 results by Website category. It should be noted that there had been no recorded incidents of government legal intervention to secure the exclusion of Loyalist or Republican Websites from search engine directories. Nevertheless, inferential statistics were not used to analyse the data due to doubts over the suitability of using Internet search engines for creating data sets. It was anticipated that the stability of results could not be guaranteed, as the behaviour of search engines was not transparent, the algorithms behind search engines such as *Google* being shrouded in secrecy (Thelwall 2001: 12). The top 25 results could vary from one day to another due to the updating frequency of each individual search engine, prompted by the high birth and death rates of Websites on the Internet. A second phase of data collection in October 2005 was intended to allow a comparison of the descriptive statistics over a period of a year, but these comparisons were illustrative only and no generalisations could be made based on them.

10.7   Results

10.7.1   Descriptive Statistics

The two data sets suggested that a larger number of sites featuring the ideological descriptions 'Irish Republican' than 'Ulster Loyalist' existed on Internet search engine directories (See Table 10.2). As expected, the *DMOZ* search engine produced the fewest number of search results, although they appeared more stable as there was minimal deviation between the two phases of data collection, particularly in the 'Irish Republican' keyword search. The other descriptive statistics appeared to illustrate the problem of stability in using search engines to construct data sets. There were some notable differences in the number of search results returned by the other three search engines. For example, the mean score for the number of results generated by the 'Ulster Loyalist' search rose from 32,611.8 to 216,930.8, between the two phases of data collection.

The descriptive statistics for searches by group name also cast doubt over the stability of results generated by search engines (see Table 10.3).

The *DMOZ* search engine again produced the fewest number of links in response to searches conducted using the names of Northern Irish terrorist groups. Searches conducted using names such as the Continuity Army Council generated no links on the *DMOZ* search engine. Similar to the ideological descriptions, the mean scores across all four-search engines for Republican group names varied greatly between the two phases of data collection. For instance, searches conducted using 'Saor Eire' produced mean scores of 344.75 and 4,681.25 in phases one and two respectively. Searches conducted using Loyalist terrorist group names generated larger number of links than their Republican counterparts (See Table 10.4). The search conducted using 'Orange Volunteers' as its subject received the highest mean score in both phases of data collection. However, searches conducted using Loyalist terrorist group names also showed wide variations between the two periods as data collection. For example, searches conducted using 'Ulster Freedom Fighters' produced mean scores of 8,655.25 and 52,864.75 in the two phases of data collection.

10.7.2   Analysis of Search Engine Results Using Website Categories

Irish Republican

The analysis of the type of Websites generated by the ideological descriptions suggested that official Republican organisations, such as the Irish Republican Socialist Movement (www.irsm.org), were more visible than their Loyalist counterparts on Internet search engines. The majority of links generated by the 'Irish

Table 10.2 Number of results generated by words 'Irish Republican' and 'Ulster Loyalist'

Group Name	DMOZ		Google		MSN		Yahoo		Mean	
	2004	2005	2004	2005	2004	2005	2004	2005	2004	2005
Irish Republican	50	46	404,000	3,930,000	160,883	384,124	867,000	5,040,000	357,983.32	338,542.5
Ulster Loyalist	20	12	34,200	290,000	13,127	59,711	83,100	518,000	32,611.9	216,930.8

Table 10.3 Number of results for searches conducted using Republican group names

Group Name	DMOZ		Google		MSN		Yahoo		Mean	
	2004	2005	2004	2005	2004	2005	2004	2005	2004	2005
Continuity Army Council	0	0	105,000	1,780,000	25,413	188,702	144,000	751,000	68,603.25	679,925.5
Cumann na mBan	0	0	1,860	137	405	3,648	383	2,180	662	1,491.25
Fianna na hEireann	0	0	640	9,600	570	5,434	1,690	18,900	725	6,243.5
Irish National Liberation Army	1	1	59,200	1,430,000	25,696	136,722	146,000	807,000	57,724.25	593,430.75
Irish Peoples Liberation Organisation	0	0	12,900	724,000	8,898	111,000	51,100	35,371	18,224.5	217,592.75
Irish Republican Army	0	16	148,000	2,300,000	66,197	214,159	366,000	2,430,000	145,049.3	1,236,043.75
Saor Eire	0	0	592	13,000	280	4,215	507	1,510	344.75	4,681.25

Table 10.4 Number of results for searches conducted using Loyalist group names.

Group Name	DMOZ		Google		MSN		Yahoo		Mean	
	2004	2005	2004	2005	2004	2005	2004	2005	2004	2005
Loyalist Volunteer Force	0	0	13,800	148,000	5,801	29,292	33,400	195,000	13,250.25	93,073
Orange Volunteers	0	4	328,000	5,010,000	154,339	816,841	857,000	4,790,000	334,834.8	2,654,211.3
Red Hand Commandos	0	1	53,100	1,790,000	22,157	130,969	158,000	732,000	58,314.25	663,242.5
Red Hand Defenders	0	1	130,000	1,600,000	71,007	365,944	398,000	2,100,000	149,741.8	1,016,486.25
Ulster Defence Association	0	3	48,700	423,000	9,371	53,011	58,700	307,000	29,192.75	195,753.5
Ulster Freedom Fighters	0	0	7,920	92,300	3,401	17,159	23,300	102,000	8,655.25	52,864.75
Ulster Volunteer Force	4	1	18,200	222,000	7,711	43,526	50,800	241,000	19,178.75	126,631.75

Table 10.5 'Irish Republican' search results by website category

Category	DMOZ (%)		Google (%)		MSN (%)		Yahoo (%)	
	2004	2005	2004	2005	2004	2005	2004	2005
Official Republican Organisation	32	24	36	20	16	12	52	32
Republican Solidarity Website	24	32	28	24	24	24	12	44
Personal Webpage/Blog	20	16	4	12	20	0	4	0
Research Institute/ University	4	8	20	32	8	20	16	16
External News Media	12	16	4	8	8	16	0	40
Loyalist	0	0	0	0	0	0	0	0
Government	0	0	0	0	4	8	0	0
Other	8	4	8	4	20	20	16	4
Total	100	100	100	100	100	100	100	100

Republican' search pointed towards 'pro-Republican' Websites (See Table 10.5). There was a high degree of convergence between the four search engines in terms of the results generated by this query. For example, all four of the search engines under analysis provided links pointing towards the Ireland's Own Website (www. irelandsown.net). Furthermore, the majority of sites generated by this search query could be characterised as either 'pro-Republican' or 'more of the same' organisational sites that provided analysis of Republican terrorist groups. A low percentage of links generated by the four search engines pointed towards sites that offered no political analysis of 'The Troubles.' In addition, there were no Loyalist Websites visible in the results generated by the 'Irish Republican' query.

Ulster Loyalist

The majority of links generated by the 'Ulster Loyalist' search pointed towards sites that were supportive of Loyalist terrorist organisations (see Table 10.6). However, official Loyalist organisations were less visible across the four search engines, in comparison to their Republican counterparts. The Progressive Unionist Party Website (www.pup-ni.org.uk) was the only one that was visible on the search engine results generated by this query. In contrast, Loyalist solidarity sites, such as Swansea Loyal (www.swansealoyal.co.uk), featured prominently in the results generated by all of the search engines under analysis. There was a divergence between the 'Ulster Loyalist' and 'Irish Republican' search results in a number of other categories. A larger proportion of the links generated by the Ulster Loyalist search pointed towards sites that bore little relevance to contemporary Northern Irish terrorist organisations, such as Stormfront (www.stormfront.org).[133] In addition, the Ulster Loyalist

---

[133] Stormfront is a far right group based in the United Kingdom, with loose links to Loyalist terror groups.

Table 10.6 'Ulster loyalist' results by website category

Category	DMOZ (%) 2004	DMOZ (%) 2005	Google (%) 2004	Google (%) 2005	MSN (%) 2004	MSN (%) 2005	Yahoo (%) 2004	Yahoo (%) 2005
Official Loyalist Organisation	5	0	0	0	4	0	0	0
Loyalist Solidarity Website	50	58.3	36	12	48	36	48	36
Personal Webpage/ Blog	0	0	0	8	0	0	0	0
Research Institute/ University	0	0	8	40	8	12	12	16
External News Media	0	0	4	8	12	8	16	8
Republican	0	0	0	0	0	0	0	0
Government	0	0	0	0	0	0	0	0
Other	45	41.7	52	32	28	44	24	40
Total	100	100	100	100	100	100	100	100

search was less likely to generate links pointing towards the Websites of external news media organisations or research institutes.

Irish Republican Army

Searches conducted using the 'Irish Republican Army' query generated fewer links to 'pro-Republican' sites than those conducted using the ideological description, 'Irish Republican' (see Table 10.7). It should be noted that the percentage of 'official' terrorist organisation sites generated by the 'Irish Republican Army' search query was distorted by a very small *DMOZ* sample. As expected, the *DMOZ* search engine returned fewer links than the other Internet search engines, the 'Irish Republican Army' search generating a maximum of 16 links in both phases of data collection. Nevertheless, few links generated by the other search engines pointed towards the Websites of Republican political fronts such as Sinn Fein (www.sinnfein. ie). For example, the *Google* search engine sample did not provide any links to official Republican organisations in both phases of data collection. Republican solidarity sites, such as the Irish Republican Movement (www.members.lycos.co.uk/ taaraanois), were slightly more visible in these search results than Republican political fronts. Contrary to our initial hypothesis, the majority of links generated by *DMOZ* did not point towards sites that were 'pro-Republican.' The *DMOZ* search engine was more likely to provide links pointing towards the Websites of external media organisations, such as the British Broadcasting Corporation (www. bbc.co.uk), than those of 'pro-Republican' actors. Overall, the majority of links generated by each search engine sample pointed towards the sites of research institutes, or those that offered no political analysis of Northern Irish terrorist groups. For example, the *MSN* search engine directed Internet users towards sites such as

Table 10.7 'Irish Republican Army' results by website category

Category	DMOZ (%)		Google (%)		MSN (%)		Yahoo (%)	
	2004	2005	2004	2005	2004	2005	2004	2005
Official Republican Organisation	0	18.75	0	0	8	4	8	8
Republican Solidarity Website	0	12.5	12	8	24	12	12	12
Personal Webpage/Blog	0	0	4	0	12	0	4	0
Research Institute/ University	0	56.25	40	68	12	48	28	60
External News Media	0	12.5	0	8	16	8	8	4
Loyalist	0	0	0	0	12	0	0	4
Government	0	0	0	0	0	12	4	0
Other	0	0	44	16	16	16	36	12
Total	N/A	100	100	100	100	100	100	100

Anagram Genius (www.anagramgenius.com) in response to this search. Furthermore, Loyalists received greater representation in the results generated by this search, in comparison to the results generated by the 'Irish Republican' search. Both the *MSN* and Yahoo search engines pointed Internet users seeking information on the Irish Republican Army towards Loyalist Websites.

Ulster Volunteer Force

Searches conducted using the 'Ulster Volunteer Force' query generated fewer links towards the Websites of Loyalist political fronts than the 'Ulster Loyalist' search (See Table 10.8). Only the *DMOZ* search engine generated a link that pointed towards an official Loyalist organisation, namely the site of the Progressive Unionist Party (www.pup-ni.org.uk). It should be noted that the relatively high percentage of links (25%) pointing towards official Websites on *DMOZ* was mainly due to the small number of Websites (four) generated by this search. However, this search generated a large number of links pointing towards Loyalist solidarity sites, in comparison to the number of Republican solidarity sites generated by the 'Irish Republican Army' search.[134] Once more, a large percentage of links generated by this search pointed towards sites which offered no political analysis of contemporary Northern Irish terrorism, such as the UVF Regimental Band (wwwuvfregimentalband.co.uk). There was some evidence to support the hypothesis that the *DMOZ* engine would generate a larger proportion of links to sites that dealt explicitly with Northern Irish terrorism. As expected, the *DMOZ* search engine generated fewer links than the other search engines under analysis, generating a maximum of four

---

[134] Please note that this site was no longer available as of October 2005.

Table 10.8 Ulster volunteer force' results by website category

Category	DMOZ (%)		Google (%)		MSN (%)		Yahoo (%)	
	2004	2005	2004	2005	2004	2005	2004	2005
Official Loyalist Organisation	25	0	0	0	0	0	0	0
Loyalist Solidarity Website	75	100	16	8	24	24	32	20
Personal Webpage/Blog	0	0	0	4	8	4	12	4
Research Institute/University	0	0	28	56	8	24	16	36
External News Media	0	0	8	12	12	4	8	4
Republican	0	0	0	0	0	0	0	4
Government	0	0	0	0	4	4	0	0
Other	0	0	48	20	44	40	32	32
Total	100	100	100	100	100	100	100	100

links in response to this query over both periods of data collection. However, the study found that all of the links generated by the *DMOZ* search engine pointed towards either the Websites of Loyalist political fronts or those maintained by their sympathisers.

10.8 Discussion

10.8.1 Do Search Engines Suppress the Websites of Northern Irish Terrorists?

Overall, the study provided some evidence to support the hypothesis that 'more of the same' organisational Websites are more visible on Internet search engines than 'controversy-revealing' Websites, such as 'pro-Loyalist' or 'pro-Republican' Websites.' The results generated by searches using terrorist group names would appear to illustrate the rule of Googlearchy. The Websites of extensively linked organisations, such as the British Broadcasting Corporation (www.bbc.co.uk), featured prominently in the search results, often at the expense of the Websites of Loyalist and Republican political fronts. Search engines direct Internet users who seek information relating to the two highest profile terrorist organisations in the region – the Irish Republican Army and the Ulster Volunteer Force respectively – towards the Websites of universities and media organisations, as opposed to sites that express support for these groups. These 'more of the same' organisations appear more visible on Internet search engines, by virtue of the amount of Web traffic that passes through their Website, and, in some instances, due to their prior purchase of priority retrieval. Furthermore, 'more of the same' organisational Websites are more likely to adhere to a set of informal rules that guarantee a high search engine rating for a Website. Companies such as Softsteel Solutions, who assist Webmasters who seek a high search engine rating for their Website, recommend that Webmasters implement a number of changes to their sites such as the removal of page redirects and the placement of key information about the site towards the top of the page (Softsteel Solutions 2003). The Webmasters of 'organisational' Websites are likely to possess the resources to hire companies such as Softsteel Solutions to design their sites in order to maximise their search engine rating. Although some Northern Irish terrorist organisations possess the necessary resources to purchase priority retrieval and hire Web consultants, the prospect of government sanctions against search engines that facilitate the activities of terrorists is likely to lead them to offer priority retrieval to actors who have no tangible link to these terrorist organisations. National governments can also pressurise search engines to remove terrorist Websites from their directories altogether, citing a perceived threat to national security as their justification for such censorship. In March 2005, *Google* was forced to remove an advertisement placed by the Palestinian terrorist group Hamas from its search engine following a barrage of criticism from the international media and diplomatic pressure from the US and Israeli governments (Intelligence and Terrorism Information Center 2005). These factors would appear to militate against official Loyalist and Republican terrorist organisations appearing in the top 25 results of Internet search engine results, particularly in response to searches conducted using the names of proscribed terrorist groups.

Yet, websites that expressed support for Northern Irish terrorists were visible on each of the search engines sampled. All of the searches conducted on the *DMOZ* search engine generated links to 'pro-Loyalist' or 'pro-Republican' Websites. Furthermore, the majority of links generated by the ideological description searches pointed towards sites that expressed support for Northern Irish terrorist organisations, or, alternatively, towards the sites of external agencies that studied 'The Troubles.' This suggests that Websites that support Northern Irish terrorists are visible on search engines if the Internet user enters the correct search terms, and uses a directory based search engine. In the case of the 14 proscribed terrorist organisations, an alternative search strategy may exist to enable Internet users to access the official Websites of these groups. As discussed earlier, the majority of Northern Irish terrorist organisations have developed political fronts, many of whom have established Websites of their own (see Table 10.1). Many of these political fronts, such as Sinn Fein, exert a high degree of influence over the activities of their military wing. Therefore, the Website of a political front arguably equates to the official Web presence of its respective terrorist organisation. As discussed earlier, the study examined the visibility of proscribed terrorist organisations on search engines in response to searches conducted using the names of terrorist groups, assuming that Northern Irish terrorist organisations would maintain websites in their own names. Searches conducted using the names of political fronts, such as the Irish Republican Socialist Movement, the political wing of the Irish National Liberation Army (INLA), would arguably generate more links to official Loyalist and Republican groups. In sum, the study provided some evidence to support the assertion that search engines suppress controversy-revealing Websites. The most heavily linked

Websites were prominent in the results generated by search engines during the study. However, the study also suggested that Internet users with prior knowledge of these groups could locate official terrorist Websites by altering their search terms. If an Internet user entered the name of a political front into the basic search facility of these search engines, they would be able to locate the official Web presence of a terrorist organisation much faster than using the name of the terrorist organisation itself.

10.8.2   Covert and Overt Web Activism

The study suggests that Northern Irish terrorist organizations and their political affiliates cannot assume that the existence of their Website will lead to greater numbers of people accessing their ideologies. Internet users will have to enter ideological descriptions such as 'Irish Republican' into the search facility of Internet search engines to generate links pointing towards 'pro-Loyalist' or 'pro-Republican' Websites. However, some Northern Irish terrorist organisations might not seek a high search engine rating, or to direct Internet users, with little or no knowledge of their cause, towards their Websites. A higher profile on Internet search engines will inevitably lead to increased scrutiny of the group's covert activities by intelligence agencies and the potential closure of the site by national governments. Weinmann (2004) suggests that terrorists might use the Web for a number of covert purposes such as data mining and providing tutorials on sabotaging computer networks (p.7). Consequently, dissidents on both sides might seek to avoid a higher degree of exposure on Internet search engines. These groups have continued to perpetrate acts of political violence despite the signing of the Good Friday Agreement in April 1998. Dissident Republican groups, such as the Real IRA and the Continuity IRA, have formed due to Republican discontent at concessions made by Sinn Fein during the negotiations that led to the Agreement. For example, the Real IRA broke away from the Provisional movement in November 1997, claiming that the Sinn Fein leadership had jettisoned a number of core Republican principles by declaring a ceasefire and abandoning the 'armed struggle.' (Institute for Counter-Terrorism 2004) Similarly, nearly all of the Loyalist terrorist organisations that initially supported the Good Friday Agreement have been 'specified' as 'active' terrorist organisations since 1998. Dissident Loyalist factions, such as the Loyalist Volunteer Force, have been responsible for a series of terrorist atrocities in this period, including the murder of *Sunday World* journalist Martin O'Hagan in September 2001.[135] There is already some evidence to suggest that these groups use information and communication technologies to plan and perpetrate atrocities in the offline world. For example, the Ulster Freedom Fighters have used Websites to select potential targets.

---

[135] MacDonald H (2005) A boycott that means murder, arson and terror. The Observer, 18 September 2005, p.7

In March 2001, a message posted on an 'Ulster Loyalist' Website urged UFF members to attack a named bar where it claimed members of the Irish Republican Army regularly visited.[136] For groups who use the Web covertly to support their military operations, a high degree of visibility on search engines might prove a hindrance.

Both Loyalist and Republican political fronts use the Web 'overtly' to redefine the roles of their respective terrorist organisations within society. Terrorists and their affiliates choose their own frames on their Websites, invariably making extensive use of the "language of non-violence" in an effort to counter their violent image (Weinmann 2004: 6). The Websites of Loyalist and Republican political fronts demonstrate this overt use of Web as a propaganda tool. Political fronts use the Internet to depict themselves "solely as community activists and political parties," rather than to illuminate their links with those who perpetrate political violence (Reilly 2006: 131). 'Pro-Agreement' political fronts use their Websites in a similar fashion to other political parties, namely for recruitment, fund-raising and increasing organisational coherence. As many of these political fronts participate in local and national elections, a high degree of visibility on Internet search engines might raise the profile of the group, and potentially increase the size of its vote. As such, few of these Websites make direct reference to the activities of their military wings. For example, political violence is only justified retrospectively on the Sinn Fein Website, in a section entitled 'History of the Conflict.'[137] Anti-Agreement political fronts also use their Websites to portray themselves as "legitimate members of civil society" (p.133). Once more, references to contemporary acts of political violence are conspicuous by their absence on the Websites of these groups. For example, the Website of Tullycarnet Ulster Political Research Group, linked to the Ulster Defence Association, does not define the ideology of the organisation, nor define itself as Loyalist.[138] As the Ulster Defence Association has links with both the Ulster Freedom Fighters and the Ulster Political Research Group, it is reasonable to speculate that it uses the Web covertly to plan atrocities in the offline world, while simultaneously using other Websites to establish its civil society credentials. Moreover, the Webmasters that maintain these Websites may omit material that contravenes anti-terrorist legislation in their country of origin. For example, the UK Terrorism Act (2000) defines the 'invitation of support' for a proscribed terrorist organisation as a terrorist offence.[139] Webmasters, who use their sites to incite political violence, or solicit resources on their behalf, could face prosecution under this piece of anti-terrorist legislation. Accordingly, Northern Irish terrorists have no reason to seek low visibility for their official Websites on Internet search engines.

---

[136] 'New Internet Terror Fear: Loyalists are Using Web to Pick Targets', Belfast Telegraph. 15 March 2001.

[137] Sinn Fein, www.sinnfein.ie (accessed 16/05/04).

[138] Tullycarnet Ulster Political Research Group www.tullycarnetuprg.ionichost.com (accessed 16/05/04)

[139] UK Home Office (2000) 'UK Terrorism Act' http://www.hmso.gov.uk/acts/acts2000/00011-htm. sch2. (accessed 10/05/05)

The Websites of their political fronts typically comply with the norms of acceptable behaviour online, as defined in anti-terrorist legislation such as the UK Terrorism Act (2000). The evidence of the study does support the hypothesis that search engines suppress 'controversy-revealing' Websites on the Internet. Extensively linked organisations, such as government agencies, are unlikely to define a Northern Irish terrorist organisation as a bona fide civil society actor, choosing instead to focus upon their military activities. In contrast, Northern Irish political fronts invariably use their Websites to counter this violent image. Therefore, search engines that direct Internet users towards 'more of the same' organisational Websites are in effect suppressing this information. This has implications for terrorist organisations that seek to persuade Internet users that they are committed to democratic principles. The Websites of political fronts are only likely to attract supporters from the offline world, many of whom will already be familiar with the Universal Resource Locator (URL) of their Website.

10.9   Conclusions

The study suggests that search engines suppress information regarding Northern Irish terrorists, directing Internet users towards 'more of the same' organisational Websites rather than 'pro-Loyalist' or 'pro-Republican' Websites. The rule of Googlearchy and the sale of priority retrieval militate against a high search engine ranking for Websites that express support for these terrorists. However, Northern Irish terrorists are 'visible' on search engines if an Internet user employs the correct search terms. The majority of Loyalist and Republican terrorist organisations maintain an official Web presence under the guise of their political fronts. Consequently, an Internet user can access the official Website of a Northern Irish terrorist organisation by entering the name of their respective political front into a search engine. The study also suggested that poor visibility on search engines might have a detrimental impact upon both Loyalist and Republican terrorist organisations. Although terrorists might shun publicity for their covert operations, a high degree of visibility on search engines enables them to target messages at a potential global audience, without the need to resort to political violence. Terrorist - linked political fronts use the Web 'overtly' to portray themselves as members of civil society, often denying their complicity in ongoing paramilitary activity. In addition, the Internet allows groups such as Sinn Fein to establish their democratic credentials in cyberspace, while simultaneously reaching out to potential voters. If a political front is not visible on an Internet search engine, only supporters of the group in the offline world will access their Website. In sum, Northern Irish terrorist organisations are only visible on search engines if an Internet user has background knowledge of the group in question, and is aware that these groups operate via political fronts.

References

Bar-Ilan J (1999) Search engine results over time – a case study on search engine stability. Cybermetric: International Journal of Scientometrics, Informetrics and Bibliometrics 3. Online. Available www.cybermetrics.cindoc/csic.es/pruebas/v2i191.html (accessed 23 October 2004)

Bodard K (2003) The free access to information challenged by filtering techniques. Information and Communication Technology Law 12: 263–279

Bowyer Bell J (2000) The IRA 1968–2000: analysis of a secret army. Frank Cass, London

Gerhart S (2004) Do web search engines suppress controversy? First Monday, 9 Online. Available http://www.firstmonday.org/issues/issue9_1/gerhart/index.html (accessed 10 June 2004).

Hindman M, Tsioutsiouliklis K, Johnson JA (2003) Googlearchy: how a few heavily linked sites dominate politics on the web. Online. Available www.princeton.edu/~mhindman/googlearchy–hindman.pdf (accessed 30 October 2004)

Independent Monitoring Commission, First Report of the Independent Monitoring Commission, http://www.independentmonitoringcommission.org/documents/uploads/ACFA6C2.pdf (accessed 10 June 2004)

Institute for Counter-Terrorism (2004) Terrorist group profiles. Online. Available www.ict.org.il/inter_ter/orgdat (accessed 10 June 2004)

Intelligence and Terrorism Information Center (2005) Google, the world's most popular search engine enabled Hamas to place an advertisement linking to the Izzedine al-Qassam Battalion website, Tel Aviv: Center for Special Studies

Margolis M, Resnick D (2000) Politics as usual: the cyberspace revolution. Sage, London

Negrine R (1994) Politics and the mass media in Britain. Routledge, London

Noveck BS (2000) Paradoxical partners: electronic communication and electronic democracy. In: Ferdinand, P (ed.) The Internet, democracy and democratization Frank Cass, London

Ntoulas A, Cho J, Olson C (2004) What's new on the web? the evolution of the web from a search engine perspective. Proceedings of the Thirteenth WWW Conference, New York, USA, Online. Available http://oak.cs.ucla.edu/~ntoulas/pubs/ntoulas_new.pdf (accessed 04 November 2005)

O'Dochartaigh N (2003) Building new transnational networks online: the case for ulster unionism. Development Gateway Online. Available http:// topic.developmentgateway.org/ict/rc/ItemDetail.do~346057 (accessed 17/02/2006)

Reilly P (2006) Civil society, the Internet and terrorism: case studies from northern ireland. In: Oates, S, Owen, D and Gibson, R.K The Internet and politics: citizens, voters and activists, Oxford: Routledge, pp.118–136

Richards A (2001) Terrorist groups and political fronts: the IRA, sinn fein, the peace process and democracy. Terrorism and Political Violence, 13: 72–89

Search Engine Yearbook (2003) Search engine statistics 2003, Online. Available http://www.searchengineyearbook.com/search-engines-statistics.shtml (accessed 17 October 2004)

Silke A (1998) In defense of the realm: financing loyalist terrorism in northern ireland – part one: extortion and blackmail. Studies in Conflict and Terrorism, 21: 331–361.

Softsteel Solutions (2003) Improving your search engine rating. Online. Available www.softsteel.co.uk/tutorials/search/searchIndex.html (accessed 10 June 2004)

Spears R, Lea M (1994) Panacea or panopticon: the hidden power in computer mediated communication (CMC). Communication Research 21: 427–459

Submit Corner (2004) Search engine guide. Online. Available, www.submitcorner.com/Guide/Se (accessed 14 September 2004)

Sullivan D (2005) Share of searches: July 2005. Search Engine Watch, Online. Available www.searchenginewatch.com/reports/article.php/2156451 (accessed 10 November 2005)

Thelwall M (2001) The responsiveness of search engines. Cybermetrics: International Journal of Scientometrics, Informetrics and Bibliometrics, 5. Online. Available www.cybermetrics.cindoc.csic.es/pruebos/v5i1p1.html (accessed 14 October 2004)

Walker J (2002) Links and power: the political economy of linking on the web, Baltimore: ACM Press. Online. Available www.cnc.uib.no/jill/txt/linksandpower.html (accessed 20 October 2004)

Webopedia Computer Dictionary (2004) What is a meta tag? Online. Available http://www.webopedia.com/TERM/m/Meta_tag.html (accessed 10 November 2005)

Weinmann G (2004) WWW.terror.net: how modern terrorism uses the Internet, washington DC: United States Institute of Peace. Online. Available http://www.usiporg/pubs/specialreports/sr116.html (accessed 10 October 2005).

Wouters P, Gerbec D (2003) Interactive Internet? studying mediated interaction with publicly available search engines. Journal of Computer Mediated Communication, 8. Online. Available http://jcmc.indiana.edu/vol8/issue4/wouters.html (accessed 16 November 2005)

Wouters P, Helsten K, Leydesdorff L (2004) Internet time and the reliability of search engines. First Monday 9. Online. Available www.firstmonday.org/issues/issue9_10/wouters/index.html (accessed 16 October 2004).

Zittrain J, Edelman B (2005) Localized google search result exclusions. Online. Available http://cyber.law.harvard.edu/filtering/google (accessed 10 November 2005).

11
The History of the Internet Search Engine: Navigational Media and the Traffic Commodity

E. Van Couvering

Summary This chapter traces the economic development of the search engine industry over time, beginning with the earliest Web search engines and ending with the domination of the market by Google, Yahoo! and MSN. Specifically, it focuses on the ways in which search engines are similar to and different from traditional media institutions, and how the relations between traditional and Internet media have changed over time. In addition to its historical overview, a core contribution of this chapter is the analysis of the industry using a media value chain based on audiences rather than on content, and the development of traffic as the core unit of exchange. It shows that traditional media companies failed when they attempted to create vertically integrated portals in the late 1990s, based on the idea of controlling Internet content, while search engines succeeded in creating huge "virtually integrated" networks based on control of Internet traffic rather than Internet content.

11.1 Introduction

In 1999, the political economist Dan Schiller wrote that "[W]e must locate the Internet within the evolving media economy. We must learn to see how it fits within, and how it modifies, an existing force field of institutional structures and functions." (Schiller 1999). In his early study, Schiller cites examples from Internet search engines such as Yahoo! and Infoseek among other cases. This chapter presents an investigation of the search engine market, in terms of its history, its ownership and its structure. It also examines the wider relationships between the search industry, the media industry, and the technology industry. This chapter seeks to deepen avenues of analysis suggested by Schiller by focusing specifically on the case of Internet search engines as they have developed over time. We ask: in what way are search engines similar to and different from traditional media institutions? In what ways are traditional media institutions involved in the search engine business and vice versa? Thus, how have search engines evolved over time to be part of the media economy?

This chapter uses a political economy of communication framework to investigate the centralisation of the search engine industry, which began as competitive market composed of many companies, into an oligarchic market structure composed of three dominant suppliers. It highlights the relation of those suppliers to the huge media conglomerates, telecommunications companies, and software giants who have each at times sought to take a stake in the market. It also examines the role of strategic alliances and distribution agreements in securing market position with a network and further consolidating the oligarchic structure of the market.

The chapter builds upon the insight that in order to analyse the search engine industry, we must look at the *value chain for audiences* rather than for content (e.g., news stories or television productions) as is common in analysis of media. Online, it is relatively simple to produce content – what is considerably *more* challenging is to attract audience. With the transformation of the value chain we can understand the history of search – for example, the otherwise puzzling failure of the large media conglomerates to dominate the search engine industry as they attempted to do.

The chapter takes the format of a chronology of the search business, which is divided into three periods: first, the creation of the first search engines and the period of technological entrepreneurs in the mid-1990s, resulting in a competitive market of relatively small companies; second, a period of portals and vertical integration in the late 1990s which saw many search engine acquisitions by traditional media and telecoms; and third, a period from 2001 onwards characterised by the exit of traditional media and telecoms and a period of consolidation. Today's search engines are not vertically integrated, but have developed an immense network of alliances both forward and backward along the audience value chain which form a strong, stable, and flexible base from which to defend their business position given the rapidity of technical change – a kind of "virtual" integration which nevertheless poses strong barriers to entry into navigational media.

This chapter tells the story of the emergence of navigational media as a global industry. As more and more of our global cultural heritage becomes digitized and distributed in fragmentary form, this form of media will become increasingly important. Elements of the new system – its oligarchic structure, global extent, and centralisation in the US – are familiar to students of media history. Other elements – the importance of localized innovation systems and venture capital – are familiar to technology researchers. Yet other elements, such as public service issues and the role of the state, are yet missing from the debate.

11.1.1 Internet Search Engines and Media Theory

Search engines are highly technical constructs. So, it may be appropriate, particularly in a book focusing on multidisciplinary perspectives on Web searching, to interrogate the focus on *media* rather than, for example, technology studies. Are search engines really "media" in the same way as television or radio or newspapers?

The social theorist and media John Thompson defines "mass communication" as "the institutionalized production and generalized diffusion of symbolic goods via the transmission and storage of information/communication." (Thompson 1990: 219). This definition seems clearly to contain entities such as search engines, which certainly transmit and store symbolic goods, are produced by large institutions, and are diffused not only in the United States but around the world. In fact, the search providers Google, MSN, and Yahoo! are the top three Websites worldwide, but the list of the top 15 also includes the smaller search provider Ask and major search distributors[140] AOL (Time Warner), Lycos, and Wanadoo (see Table 11.1).

But just as clearly, search engines don't produce the type of content that Thompson was considering. They don't, in effect, produce narratives or stories – as Google's CEO, Eric Schmidt, said, "Google is simply an aggregator of information," (Sullivan 2006, time 11:02). This is true, for the most part; nonetheless, search engines do mediate between the user and other Websites, sorting, classifying, and constructing a lens through which we view other content on the Web. They are also, primarily, funded through advertising, which we recognise as a core business model for media.

However, the primary reason we turn to media theory is that it offers a well-developed theory of institutional power and the relation of that power to the content of our media in the form of the political economy of communications (PEC).

A recent series of articles has highlighted the some of the deficiencies of search engines:

- They appear not to index the whole Web. In 1994, a study claimed the top six search engines together indexed only 42% of the Web (Lawrence and Giles 1999), although a more recently study put coverage at 80–90% for each of the

Table 11.1 Top 15 Online Properties Worldwide, March 2006

Property Name	Unique Visitors (000)[a]	Global Reach[b]
Worldwide Total	694,260	n/a
MSN-Microsoft Sites	538,578	77.6%
Google Sites	495,788	71.4%
Yahoo! Sites	480,228	69.2%
eBay	269,690	38.8%
Time Warner Network	241,525	34.8%
Amazon Sites	154,640	22.3%
Wikipedia Sites	131,949	19.0%
Ask Network	127,377	18.3%
Adobe Sites	115,774	16.7%
Lycos, Inc.	109,394	15.8%
CNET Networks	107,589	15.5%
Apple Computer, Inc.	98,622	14.2%
Real.com Network	78,104	11.2%
Monster Worldwide	74,152	10.7%
Wanadoo Sites	73,446	10.6%

[a] Those aged 15+ who have used the Internet during the month. Excludes traffic from public computers such as Internet cafes and, access from mobile phones or PDAs.
[b] Reach denotes percentage of unique visitors who have accessed the online property during the month
Source: adapted from comScore World Metrix

---

[140] These organisations purchase the search services they provide to their customers from one of the technology providers listed above.

major Web search engines (Vaughan 2004). Nevertheless, it is argued that most of the major Web search engines have little overlap. Also, many databases attached to the Web, sometimes called the "invisible Web," appear not to be covered (Bergman 2001). Even where protocols for interfacing with search engines exist, for example through the Open Access Initiative, the best search engine was able to find only 60% of this content (McCown et al. 2006).

• Engines do not appear to index the Web reliably. Fluctuations the documents returned have been reported for identical search terms on the same engine over both the medium term (1½ years) and the short term (10 days) (Bar-Ilan 2000; Bar-Ilan and Peritz 1999).

• Engines appear to systematically favour certain Websites. Several studies have shown that "popular" Websites – that is, sites with more links pointing to them – are favoured by search engines, creating a "rich-get-richer" effect (Kleinberg and Lawrence 2001; Lawrence and Giles 1999). Country of origin may have an effect, with American sites being favoured in a cross-national comparison of results between China, Taiwan, Singapore, and the US (Vaughan and Thelwall 2004). Language features may also result in poor results – recent studies have reported failures of search when confronted with non-English languages (Bar-Ilan and Gutman 2005; Choros 2005).

What are we to make of these deficiencies? Certainly they arise from the technology of the search engines; however, technology is not found, but made – in this case, by people working in particular institutions in a particular historical setting. Political economy suggests that the development of technology is intimately intertwined with the social, political and economic context in which it arises. In the context of capitalism, the quest for profit both directs technical development in information and is supported by them (Schiller 1992; Webster 2002). From this viewpoint, we cannot understand either the functions of search or its deficiencies without analysing and coming to terms with the context in which they have arisen.

While therefore most people, initially, reject search engines as "media", there is a strong argument to suggest that the elements that make up the search engine's content – its indexes, its crawlers, its displays of results – are influenced by its overall position in the capitalist economy. The fact that they produce lists and not narratives, in this case, is central to the analysis of their history, as we argue below.

11.2   The History of Search Consolidation

James Curran (Curran and Seaton 2003:250) argues that the Internet from the mid-1990s onwards entered a commercialised phase in which mainstream companies – in particular large media conglomerates such as Bertelsmann, Vivendi, Time Warner, News International, and Disney – began to dominate the Web, owning 3 quarters of the most visited news and entertainment sites. But in this study, we find that large media firms are conspicuously absent from the major search engine providers (which, as we have seen, are also the most highly visited Websites) in 2006, that is to say Google, Yahoo, and Microsoft. In fact, the only large media conglomerate to be represented in the top 15 properties shown in Fig. 11.1, above, is Time Warner (most likely its huge ISP and online service provider AOL).

Figure 11.1 presents in diagrammatic form the development of the major Internet search engines of the past dozen years since the invention of the Web. The chart consists of three periods: first, a period of *technical entrepreneurship* from 1994 to late 1997; second, a period which was characterised by *the development of portals and vertical integration* from late 1997 to the end of 2001, in which major media companies and network providers attempted to buy their way into the search arena; and finally a period of *consolidation and "virtual" integration* from 2002 to the present day. While presented as analytically distinct, these three periods of course overlap to a certain degree; for example, it is certainly possible to find technical entrepreneurs in the middle period (Google and Overture are excellent

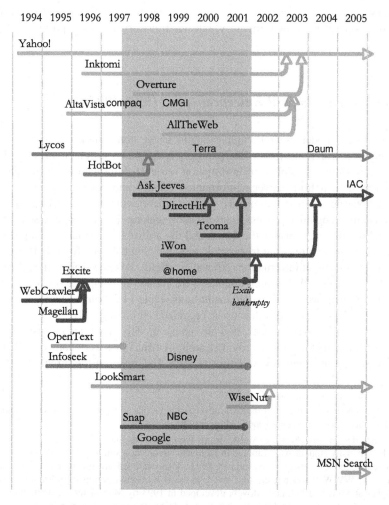

Fig. 11.1 Search engine mergers and acquisitions in the three periods of search history. Data from company Websites and press reports

examples), and attempts at consolidation in the early period (e.g., Excite's early acquisition of Magellan and WebCrawler.

The periods into which I have classified the short history of search are essentially based on shifts in revenue models and ownership, and give primacy to the economic history of search over its technological history. Clearly technological innovation is also important; and indeed, the shifts in revenue and economics closely coincide with technological developments and are related to pre-existing structures for capitalising on technology. But a history of technological "successes" is not sufficient to explain the dynamics of the search market, nor can it adequately characterise an industry likely to generate some \$12 billion in 2006.

Of the 21 search ventures listed in Fig. 11.1, only six remain independent entities. Of these, only four produce algorithmic search results of the whole Web: Yahoo, Google, MSN, and Ask. As regards the remaining two, Lycos no longer operates a Web search engine, but purchases search from Yahoo, and LookSmart no longer operates its own directory, but has transformed into a provider of paid search results.[141]

11.2.1   Technological Entrepreneurs (1994–1997)

The history of modern search engines begins in the non-commercial setting of the academy or research institution. Technologically speaking, search engines developed from the academic discipline of information retrieval. Information retrieval itself is something of a hybrid between information science and computer science. From information science, information retrieval draws theories of information categorization and the human cognitive process in information seeking. From computer science and artificial intelligence springs the desire and the ability to automate catalogue creation and information retrieval from catalogues (see Singhal 2001 for a short overview of the development of information retrieval as a field). It is no surprise, therefore, that most of the earliest Web search engines were created in computer science research laboratories, primarily in academic institutions. Table 11.2, below, shows the earliest Web search engines and their locations, organized chronologically[142].

In these early search engines, two alternative models of service provision can be seen. First, the *Web directory* provided groups of sites that were categorised and in some cases given ratings by an editorial team. Examples of the directory strategy

---

[141] In other words, they search an index of advertisements placed by website owners, rather than an independent index of results generated by crawling the web.

[142] Not included in this chart are Archie, a pre-Web search engine for FTP sites developed by McGill University student Alan Emtage in 1990 and Veronica, a similar engine for Gopher sites, developed at the University of Nevada in 1993. Also excluded are the first two Web search engines, the WWW Wanderer, the first spider to crawl the web, developed by Matthew Gray, a researcher at MIT, in 1993, and Aliweb, developed in 1993 by Martijn Koster while he worked for Nexor in Nottingham, England. Neither of these technologies was commercialised.

Table 11.2 Early period web search engine dates, institutions, and founders

Engine/ Directory	Date went live[a]	Institution (Location)	Developer(s)	Position at time of development
Yahoo (directory)	Feb 94	Stanford University (Palo Alto, CA)	Jerry Yang David Filo	Computer Science (CS) PhD students
WebCrawler (engine)	20 Apr 94	University of Washington (Seattle, WA)	Brian Pinkerton	PhD student in CS
Lycos (engine)	July 94	Carnegie Mellon University (Pittsburgh, PA)	Dr Michael Mauldin and Bob Leavitt	Postdoctoral research fellow in CS
Infoseek (engine)	13 Feb 95	n/a (Sunnyvale, CA)	Steve Kirsch	Serial technology entrepreneur – founded Frame Technology and Mouse Systems. BA and MS from MIT.
OpenText (engine)	Apr 95	n/a (Waterloo, Ontario, Canada)	(uncredited, possbly OpenText VP of Information Retrieval Larry Fitzpatrick)	Early provider of search interfaces to products such as Oxford English Dictionary
Magellan (directory)	Aug 95	n/a (Sausalito, CA)	Isabel & Christine Maxwell	Daughters of publishing magnate Richard Maxwell, originally published a print guide to the Web
Excite (engine)	29 Sep 95	Stanford University (Palo Alto, CA)	Graham Spence Joe Krausz Ben Lutch Ryan McIntyre Martin Reinfreid Mark Van Haren	Recent CS graduates (apart from Krausz who graduated in political science)
AltaVista (engine)	15 Dec 95	Digital Equipment PARC (Palo Alto, CA)	Dr Louis Monier	Research fellow
Inktomi (engine)	20 May 96	University of California at Berkeley (Berkeley, CA)	Dr Eric Brewer Paul Gaulthier	Assistant professor of CS and graduate student
LookSmart (directory)	28 Oct 96	Reader's Digest (Melbourne, Victoria, Australia)	(uncredited)	(uncredited – presumably the publishing team acting through ordinary channels?)

[a] Dates refer to when the search engine became publicly accessible.
Data derived from original press releases and news reports.

included Yahoo!, Magellan (who pioneered editorial ratings), and LookSmart. The second model was much more complex technically, and involved used automated technology to browse Websites, store them in an electronic index, and automatically retrieve them based on user queries. These were more properly called *engines*. The two main axes of technical competition at this stage were the size of the engine or directory index and the speed of retrieval.

Early search enterprises had three primary sources of revenue: venture capital, product licensing, and advertising. Later, money raised on the stock markets would help to fund the business. In particular, venture capital was absolutely crucial, since during this phase of technological entrepreneurs, no one was exactly sure how the business would be funded – that is, whether the licensing and advertising revenues would prove viable.

Just how uncertain the business model of Internet search was is emphasised in an interview with the first Chief Financial Officer (CFO) of Lycos, Ted Philip:

> "We didn't have a model to follow," Philip recalled. "There was no such thing as advertising on the Internet at that time…We had no business plan. All we had was a piece of technology." (quoted in Gavetti and Rivkin 2004:15)

Vinod Khosla, the Silicon Valley venture capitalist who gave seed funding to Excite, says the same: "I had to develop a complete business plan. Being a navigation service for the Internet wasn't originally on the list of what they wanted to do" (quoted in O'Brien 1997). The Yahoo! founders expressed similar sentiments (Battelle 2005: 59). Even those who did have a revenue plan, like Infoseek, weren't able to make it stick. Infoseek's initial $9.95/month subscription plan, which included a hundred free queries and ten cents per query after that (Infoseek, 1995a), quickly crumbled in the face of free services from Lycos, Yahoo, WebCrawler and Magellan.

The business model that most eventually decided on was a mix of advertising and licensing. Webcrawler began taking limited sponsorship on December 1, 1994 (Pinkerton 2001). On May 22, 1995, a short three months after its debut, Infoseek announced that it was introducing a new free service supported by advertisers[143] in addition to its subscription model (Infoseek 1995b). It later claimed to have introduced cost-per-thousand (CPM) advertising pricing to the Web[144] (Infoseek 1997). It certainly was the first in the search market, and it was quickly imitated. Carnegie Mellon announced in June that Lycos would become a commercial company in partnership with CMGI Ventures (a venture capitalist). It would "offer advertising space on its site and [would] license the catalog as well as key technology components" (Carnegie Mellon University 1995). Just nine days later, Yahoo! announced that it would, as founder Jerry Yang put it, "make a graceful transition from being a not-for-profit hobby into a professional commercial service" (Yahoo!

---

[143] Original advertisers were Sun Microsystems, Storage Computer and the Internet Shopping Network.

[144] CPM pricing essentially charges a fixed cost – say $10 – for every one thousand viewings of an advertisement; sponsorships, on the other hand, are typically paid at a fixed price irrespective of the numbers of people who actually view the advertisement.

1995). It debuted with five advertisers in a three-month trial. Magellan followed suit in October of 1995.

Thus by the time the second wave of search pioneers – AltaVista, Excite, Inktomi, and LookSmart – launched their services, advertising was already widespread on Web search engines. However, a second revenue stream was also clearly being developed. OpenText, one of the few companies that preceded the Web, based their plan on primarily on software licensing, as did Inktomi, which launched with a deal from Wired Digital to operate its new "HotBot" search engine.

In fact, licensing was in many ways the preferred model for many of the entrepreneurs: licensing was a known software business model, with predictable, ongoing revenue. Advertising was much more linked to Hollywood than Silicon Valley. Nevertheless, advertising predominated in the early search market, possibly because the number of companies who wanted to license search engine technology was limited. Advertising revenue, was driven by usage (especially after the introduction of cost per thousand, and later cost-per-impression[145] pricing), and the licensing model played a part here as well – many companies quickly understood that by giving or licensing their products to large traffic source – ISPs, for example – they could quickly build up usage. Distribution deals of this type proved critical, and there were no more important sources of traffic in the early days of the Web than Netscape and AOL. These two companies, while never themselves developing search technology, were crucial in the early development of the search and navigation industry. Each of the major players partnered with one or both of these companies and in so doing secured enough viewers to keep their advertising revenue high and the company solvent until their initial offerings on the stock market.

These public offerings, in turn, brought an influx of new cash to the search engines which funded their later expansion. The level of cash generated for such young businesses was unprecedented, as a contemporary account of the Yahoo IPO from the *Financial Times* shows:

"Definitive proof of the scale of the Internet craze comes in the $1.1bn market capitalisation briefly accorded last Friday to Yahoo, an electronic catalogue of the World Wide Web. So egregious is the overvaluation…that it is hard to convey in the FT's sober prose. This is a company with total revenues of around $3m since its launch in March 1995…[it] has achieved an operating profit ($62,000) in only one of its four quarters…[and is] run by Jerry Yang and David Filo…[who] have no previous business experience." (Martin 1996)

Indeed, Yahoo! was one of the defining companies of the Internet boom period, to which we now turn. However it is worthwhile noting in passing that despite the 2001 market crash in high-tech stocks, the "Internet craze" continues: as of 20 March 2006, Yahoo's market capitalisation was $46.6bn, over forty times its "egregious overvaluation" of a decade earlier.

---

[145] Cost-per-impression or CPI pricing charged a small sum (2¢ to 6¢, according to Yahoo's 1996 Annual Report) for every viewer. This was made possible by the accurate tracking of Internet servers as opposed to the more general audience measurements available for print publications.

This first period of search engine history, then, is characterised by technological innovation within research centres followed by commercialisation using advertising and licensing as business models and capitalisation through venture capital and the stock market. The market was competitive, consisting of multiple companies with different technologies.

11.2.2 Portals and Vertical Integration (1997–2001)

The middle period of the short history of search engines online comprises the heart of the dot-com boom and bust period, that is to say late 1997 to late 2001. It is characterised by the change in focus from search engines to "portals" and the involvement of traditional media and telecoms giants in the sector. If the first period of search can be characterised by technological innovation and the establishment of a vibrant, competitive marketplace for search technology, in this second period the search engines become focal points for a struggle to control the Internet as a whole on the part of traditional media companies and telecoms providers.

In general, this period in the history of search is notable for two related dynamics, which sometimes work together, and sometimes in opposition. These are: first, the growing technical opportunities for content integration; and second, the related idea that a proprietary "walled garden," or secondary Internet, could be created which might to be owned by a single company.

In order to understand these dynamics, we can use the vertical supply chain as a means of analysis. The vertical supply chain is a tool for analyzing an industry whereby activities are ordered in a sequence, which starts at the early stages of production and works its way through the various intermediaries until arriving eventually at the customer (Doyle 2002: 18). Doyle has recently defined a vertical supply chain for media as consisting of three general phases: production, packaging, and distribution. While generally useful, the supply chain is particularly helpful in understanding the dynamics of search engines at this time – but only if we change its focus, as follows.

The generic media supply chain is based upon taking *content*, that is to say, television broadcasts, news stories, pictures, etc., as the basic unit of analysis. Most traditional media companies have some element of vertical integration along this chain. So, for example, Time Warner owns production companies, networks, and cable television stations. However, it is clear that media companies operate in what is called a dual product market. On the one hand, they sell content to audiences – this is the content supply chain that Doyle is focused on. On the other hand, however, media companies sell *audiences* to advertisers. On the Internet, where audience is extremely fragmented, this turns out to be much more useful vertical supply chain to construct, since the problem is not so much getting content to your audience (a basic web page being quite easy to construct) but audience to your content. Thus, what we need is not a supply chain for media content, but a supply chain for media audiences.

To construct such a chain, we must begin by considering how audiences get on the Internet. First, they must have a computer, and the software to make it run[146]. Hardware manufacturing and software providers are therefore the first two steps in the chain. Second, they must connect to the Internet via some kind of an Internet service provider whose signal will run over telephone lines (or, possible, cable lines). The telephone or cable company and the ISP are therefore the third and fourth steps in the vertical supply chain. Fourth, they need a browser to access the Web. In the early days of the Internet, the browser was seen as the crucial point for audience aggregation. When Netscape went public, it was this insight that drove its market price sky high. Finally, in order for the audience to get to their destination Web site, they may very likely need a Web search engine, especially if this site is small and has little brand recognition of its own. Figure 11.2 presents this chain in diagrammatic form.

In general, this period of search engine history is characterized by attempts at integration – both forwards and backwards – along this audience supply chain. First, we consider attempts by Web search engines to integrate destination Websites into their products.

The development of the portal

Beginning in 1997 but accelerating in 1998, the "portal " evolved out of the navigational services (both directories and engines) developed in the technology entrepreneur phase. Portals typically had a search engine or directory service at their core, but also had many "channels" which featured content brought in directly from advertisers, including finance, shopping, travel, e-mail, music, etc.

Figures 11.3 and 11.4 show the Excite home page from October 1996 and 1997 (retrieved from the WayBack Machine at Archive.org), which illustrate this development clearly. In 1996 the page advertises that the search is "twice the power of the competition" and has content generated by the Excite/WebCrawler team, such as reviews and tours of Web content, below the search. A few services such as travel

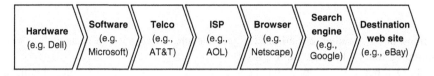

Fig. 11.2 Supply chain for search engine audiences

---

[146] Of course, today some audiences access the Internet without having a computer – for example, from mobile phones. However, during this period, the computer was by far the most important means of access.

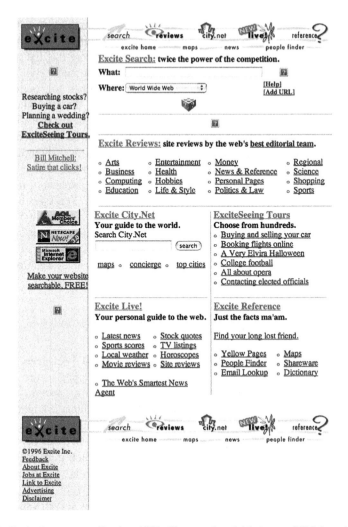

Fig. 11.3 Excite home page, October 1996. (Page retrieved 16 August 2006 from http://web. archive.org/web/19961022175004/http://www07.excite.com/)

guides, news, weather, e-mail directory, maps, etc. are also on view, as well as two shopping links – for cars and flights.

In October 1997 the page has been completely redesigned to feature channels, many of which are filled with content from partners.

These content partnerships are very interesting because they begin to give glimpses of the value that Internet traffic is beginning to take online. In an offline network such as a television network, the network pays the production company for rights to distribute the show. However, the online content partnerships were often the other way around – the content producer – for example Preview Travel – would

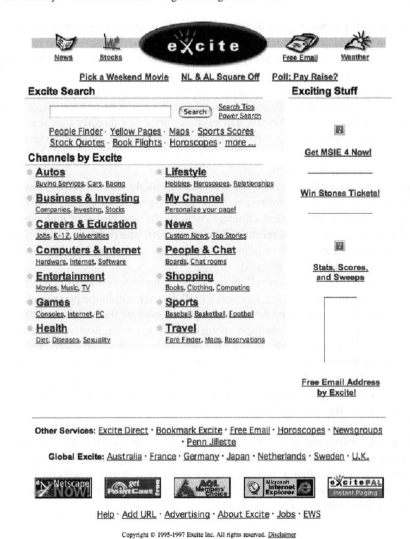

Fig. 11.4 Excite home page, October 1997 (Page retrieved 16 August 2006 from http://web. archive.org/web/19971012110114/http://www07.excite.com/)

pay Excite to be the main provider of content on its travel page, or "channel", as they began to be called.

This change requires some explanation. In television production, the network pays the production company because they need content attract an audience to sell on to an advertiser. In other words, the network acts as a packager of television content. But although a Web search engine (or portal, in this era) intuitively seems like the same kind of business, there are key differences. The Web search engine delivers not just in "impression" or view to the advertiser – although Web search engine advertisements were sold on a cost-per-thousand-impressions basis, as we have seen – but also, and much more importantly, an interaction – that is to say, an interested person who has actually taken the time to act on the content provided. A growing exploitation of the technical infrastructure of the Web made this change possible. In traditional media it is rarely possible to give advertisers the opportunity to sell directly to customers (apart from newspaper coupons and the like). But it was possible to integrate Preview Travel travel bookings directly into the Excite travel channel, and in effect for Excite to become another avenue of distribution for Preview Travel – and in a sense the Preview Travel Website became part of Excite, and vice versa (see Fig. 11.5).

Thus partnership deals with portals, while they might involve some measure of compensation for content producers, were more typically structured as a mix of direct payments by the content producer (who might now be better understood as an advertiser) and a share of revenues from customers who purchased from a portal Website. Here the producer of content becomes the customer, and the traditional value chain gets flipped on its head.

This new revenue based on selling targeted channel impressions to content providers/advertisers and allowing sponsors to sell directly within the portal pages was so successful that channels proliferated and portals became the new face of the Web search engine. The more channels available, the more high-value sponsorship opportunities could be created, and channels were even specifically created to showcase and sell partner/advertiser products and services. Deals were often long-term (several years) and multi-million dollars – one article in the *Industry Standard* magazine cites a 4-year, $89 million deal and suggests that $2 to $10 million deals were common (Werner and Helft 2000).[147]

It is important to understand that portals were not examples of vertical integration, in the traditional sense. In general, portals were not buying e-commerce companies, and e-commerce companies were not buying portals. There is no suggestion, for example, that a travel operator like Preview Travel was trying to buy a portal like Excite. But this integration of advertiser and search engine content has important implications, as we shall see later.

Vertical integration

Also, during this period many search engines were bought and sold. Dan Schiller argues that with the wide array of cross-media ownership, the increasing transnationalization of media, and the growth of commercial sponsorship as the decisive form of media patronage, the "suitable unit [for analysis] has become the diversified media conglomerate." (Schiller 1999: 36). In the second period of search

---

[147] This was also true in Europe. In late 1998, I worked for Jupiter Communications, an market research company specialising in the Internet, and documented a $10 million pan-European deal between Lycos and BOL, a book retailer (Van Couvering 1998).

Fig. 11.5 Excite Travel Channel, October 1999 (Page retrieved 16 August 2006 from http://web. archive.org/web/19991008211456/http://www.excite.com/travel). Note: question marks in the figure represent non-archived images which can no longer be displayed

engine history, portals became a natural target for media and telecoms conglomerates jockeying for position as the Internet developed commercially.

It was hoped that portals could provide a new "window" or viewing opportunity for existing media content, as well as positioning media conglomerates for control of the online operating environment, by controlling the huge audiences that visited the portals. Essentially, the strategy was one of growth through vertical integration in the content supply chain – that is to say, the conglomerates hoped to dominate

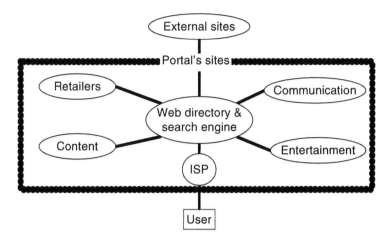

Fig. 11.6 A fully-integrated portal (adapted from Meisel and Sullivan 2000: 480)

existing portals by running their acquisitions more efficiently, exploiting economies of both scale and scope.[148]

Business texts of the time sought to promote this new kind of vertical integration, touting a concept called the "fully-integrated portal" (e.g., Meisel and Sullivan 2000, p. 484). The vision of the fully-integrated portal was to control the whole user experience online – it was envisaged that users would leave the portal only rarely to visit external sites (see Fig. 11.6). This mega-portal would have three sources of revenue: subscription fees from ISP subscribers, advertising fees, and e-commerce transactions. Economists and business pundits encouraged portals to actively to seek old media partners, develop specialised content, strengthen ties to delivery systems and expand through Europe, Asia, and Latin America.

---

[148] Economies of scale refer to the benefits that accrue for certain types of products when large numbers of them are produced. In media products, the cost of producing the first copy – for example, paying an author to write a manuscript, editing the manuscript, typesetting the book, proofreading the first copy, etc. – often far outweigh the costs of subsequent copies. This is even more true for digital content such as software, where copying and distribution costs are nearly zero. The technical definition is that economies of scale occur when marginal costs (the cost of producing a single copy of the work) are less than average costs – that is to say the average cost declines the more units are produced. Economies of scope refer to the benefits that accrue to companies who can re-use resources to produce a range of products. In media, you might see economies of scope when Harry Potter (the book) is used to provide the basis for Harry Potter (the movie) or Harry Potter (the DVD). Thus economies of scope technically occur when two (or more) products can be produced and sold more cheaply jointly rather than separately. In general, media industries tend to have large both economies of scale and economies of scope, and this in turn huge leads conglomerates such as Time Warner, Disney, Viacom, News International and Vivendi (Doyle 2002, pp. 13-15) which have holdings in radio, television, newspapers, cable television, and so on. As digitisation alters the format of media content, these media companies are increasingly also competing with the liberalised telecoms industry.

Indeed, in 1998 and 1999 the search engine industry witnessed a number of attempts at the creation of these megaportal by diversified media conglomerates. In mid-1998, Disney acquired 43% of search engine Infoseek for $70 million in cash and $240 million in Starwave stock.[149] (CNNMoney 1998a), acquiring the remainder of the engine in 1999 (CNNMoney, 1999). Infoseek was then a popular search engine in its own right, ranked 9th most visited Website overall (Harmon 1998). One week previously, NBC (owned by General Electric) had purchased 19% of C|Net's portal Snap! (CNNMoney 1998b). Both of these portals had respectable audience, although they were not the market leaders. Nonetheless, both of these high-profile acquisitions both failed and closed in 2001. AltaVista, once the most highly-regarded search engine on the Web, was sold by computer manufacturer Compaq (who had acquired its parent Digital Equipment) to media investment group CMGI (which also owned Lycos) for £2.3billion in June 1999 (Dignan 1999). In 2003 it was sold to Overture for $140 million, and later vanished into Yahoo! (see the next section, "Syndication and Consolidation").

Nor were media conglomerates the only actors seeking to dominate the online markets. Infrastructure providers, most notably telephony providers, also attempted forward-integrate along the audience value chain and enter the portal space. This was part of an overall strategy to engage with media content as digital content made convergence between telecoms and media more of a reality. Highly-rated portal Excite was acquired in January of 1999 for $6.7 billion in by broadband Internet service provision (ISP) company @Home (a joint venture of AT&T and several cable companies) (Junnarkar 1999). Similarly, Lycos was purchased for $12.5 billion in May 2000 by Terra Networks (owned by Spanish telephony operator Telefónica) (Kopytoff 2000). These acquisitions was motivated in part by a desire to emulate the enormous success of AOL, whose huge traffic, generated by a loyal base of ISP subscribers, enabled it to make some of the largest portal advertising deals. AOL, the largest ISP in the world at that time, also attempted to forward-integrate by purchasing browser manufacturer Netscape, and its NetCenter portal, in November of 1998 for $4.2b (Clark 1998).

Yet, none of these acquisitions fared well. Excite@Home went spectacularly bankrupt in 2001 (Wallack 2001), and Lycos, while still technically in existence today, stopped providing its own search in 1999 and was sold to South Korean online media company Daum Communications in 2002 for $95 million, a fraction of the price Telefónica paid (Reuters 2004). AOL still operates Netscape's Netcenter, but Netcenter no longer registers as a destination among searchers.

Certainly the nail in the coffin of many of these services was the dot-com crash. To a large extent the growth in sponsorship revenue for all the portals was funded by money from the dot-com boom that was going into start-up Internet ventures, which depended on becoming leaders in their respective markets, based on audience

---

[149] Starwave at the time operated several websites for Disney brands including abcnews.com and espn.com, as well as sites for the NFL, NBA and NASCAR.

numbers that only the search engines could bring them. When the stock market began its crash in spring of 2001, much of this money dried up. But there seem also to have been other factors.

Blevins has analysed the Disney/Infoseek deal in some detail, and accounts for the closure as a failure of "synergy" – put simply, as too much branding by Disney (Blevins 2004). This relates to a misunderstanding by the media companies about the role of the Web search engine, alluded to earlier when talking about the content supply chain versus the audience supply chain. Looking the audience supply chain for the search business, we can see that Web sites are upstream from portals, who act as distributors of audiences for other Websites like e-commerce providers. Online, however, there is not much of a distinction between the Website of an e-commerce provider or "advertiser," like Ford, and the Website of a "content provider" such as ABC. Thus, by adding more Disney content to the Go Network site (as Infoseek eventually became), Disney actually moved the portal away from its position as a distributor and instead it became merely an ordinary Website. As Blevins describes, its audience immediately began to drop, its traffic dropped, and it lost its paying customers, other advertisers. The problem of "synergy," then, as it relates to big media is as follows: search engines don't represent an economy of scope for media companies. Disney content, as it turns out, cannot be repackaged as a navigational portal. Disney is a destination site, upstream from search. A Disney portal is merely a Disney home page, with little value to audiences not interested in Disney content. In tandem, the Infoseek Web search engine was put on the back burner. In 2004, in a conference panel discussion on the history of search, Infoseek's founder, Steve Kirsch, said that around 1998 he was the only one pushing developments in search; the business people wanted to focus on the top pages, and management wanted to move towards a portal (Schwartz, 2004).

However this issue of "over-branding", if it may be termed that, seems less pertinent for infrastructure providers who should have little interest in the content of Web search engine results. Once again it is helpful to examine a particular case. The most high-profile case of failure was the acquisition of Excite by broadband cable provider @Home. This merger of a top-tier portal with an access provider backed by AT&T seemed certain to succeed and become the "AOL of broadband," but instead failed and went bankrupt within two years. Unfortunately we have no detailed academic study of this case in the way that Blevins has studied the Infoseek/Disney case. However, according to press reports at the time of the bankruptcy in 2001, the focus of Excite@Home was on developing a high-speed cable network, at the insistence of its primary shareholders, who were cable company executives. In the meantime, it began to be difficult to justify spending on developing the portal, and particularly on developing the search engine, which was seen as a necessary but unproductive part of the business – in other words, a loss-leader. Later, *Wired* magazine suggested that @Home had simply been a vehicle for off-book financing of broadband infrastructure, which AT&T bought for $307 million during the disposal of assets (Rose 2002). If that was in fact the case, the development of the Excite portal would have been irrelevant. In any case, at the time of the sale, the search technology that had built the second-largest search and directory site on the Web was deemed worthless and scrapped, and the domain name was sold for $10 million at the time.

A similar fate seems to have befallen AltaVista, this time with computer hardware rather than cable at the core of the integration strategy. At AltaVista, too, the emphasis switched from search to portals, and it became impossible to fund the development of the search engine, leading to the departure of the chief engineer and co-founder, Louis Monier, with his team (Battelle 2005: 52).

Thus an important element that characterises this phase of Web search engine development, in addition to the acquisition of may of the search engines by larger conglomerates, is the downgrading of search within the portal ; the search engine itself was no longer seen as a key competitive advantage for a portal, but rather as a simple requirement for doing business. Recall that the vision of the fully-integrated portal was that this mega-Website would be so engrossing (or "sticky," as the industry called it) that users would never want to leave. They would arrive through the Website of the service provider, browse licensed content, use branded online email, and shop for purchases all within the confines of the portal. But search, of course, is the opposite of "sticky" – the whole point of a Web search engine is that users search for something and then leave your Website. Search seemed like a giant fire hose spraying precious audience everywhere on the Web but into the portal.

Earlier we described the inclusion of partner functionality, such as flight searching from a travel provider, into portal pages. Gradually it became clear that search functionality could be conceived of in the same way. Thus, as part of the movement towards portals, which as described earlier was linked to the integration of content from advertising and technology partners, the search engine market split into those who were intent on developing media properties – for example Go – and those who focused on a more technology-led strategy, through what was called "white-labelling" or licensing of their search technology to third parties. Inktomi was perhaps the best example of this strategy. In June 2000, for example, Inktomi delivered search results to eight separate portals, including AOL, HotBot, MSN and Snap as well as smaller Websites like iWon, LookSmart, GoTo and 4Anything (Sullivan 2000).

Despite the diminution of the actual search engine from the core of the business to loss-leading commodity, there continued to be new technical innovations in search, and new Web search companies continued to be funded by venture capital. In 1998, AskJeeves debuted with a new interface to the old Magellan idea of editorially-rated sites, by letting users input natural-language questions and organising the results around the most frequently-asked questions. Search aggregation engines such as Dogpile and MetaSearch queried all the other search engines and returned a mix of results. iWon paid its audience directly in the form of a lottery in which each search submitted counted as an entry. Direct Hit began ranking by popularity rather than simply by Website content. And also in 1998, Google began a new Web search engine with a radically new ranking algorithm, backing from significant Silicon Valley venture capitalists, and a key distribution deal with Netscape (for an in-depth history of Google, see Vise and Malseed 2005).

Important as Google's technical innovations were, equally or perhaps more important for the future of the search engine industry as whole was the debut of GoTo. GoTo was a Web search engine with no pretence of searching the whole Web. The GoTo index was instead made up of people who paid to be there, and it allowed these advertisers to buy the search terms they wanted. Thus, when searching for "flight to New York" the travel agency or airline which had agreed to pay the highest advertising fee would be listed first. But GoTo knew that advertisers would not pay to be included in an unproven Web search engine, so Bill Gross, its founder, introduced the policy of charging advertisers not "per impression" as was now common practice, but rather per click. That is to say, the advertiser was only liable for the fee when someone actually clicked the ad – unclicked impressions were given away for free. The importance of this development cannot be overstated. Instead of the multi-million dollar impression and sponsorship deals based on the huge reach of the major portals, GoTo offered small, controllable deals where a few cents would get an advertiser a definite visitor for their site. It was a compelling business model, particularly because at first GoTo deliberately undercut the market (Battelle 2005: 111ff).

But it was more important than simply a brilliant business idea: it was part of a crucial shift in the search engine business. No longer would the *audience* (the traditional media commodity sold to advertisers) be at the core of the search business. Now, the online commodity of choice would be *traffic* or the flow of visitors from one Website to another. When audience was the main commodity sold, the key task of online Websites was to gather and keep as many audience members as possible, with the ultimate aim being – however unrealisable – to own the whole Internet. But as traffic emerged as a key commodity in its own right, sites which had as much traffic as possible – that is to say, as many people coming and going as possible – became the nexus of economic traffic. Web search engines were the obvious choices, and the new economic possibilities led to a resurgence of technical competence and the technically complex search product as essential elements of the large online media players we see today.

11.2.3 *Syndication and Consolidation*

The final period of the short history of search is one of consolidation and concentration, as can be seen in Fig. 11.1 at the beginning of this chapter. This is due to two interconnected dynamics. First, media and infrastructure corporations have ceded search to technology companies and are content to buy their search from search providers. Second, the revenues generated from pay-per-click search advertising have meant that the large players have been able to buy their rivals, as shown in Fig. 11.1 at the beginning of the chapter – in this period, acquisition activity of search technology is by other search providers – in fact, almost exclusively by Yahoo.

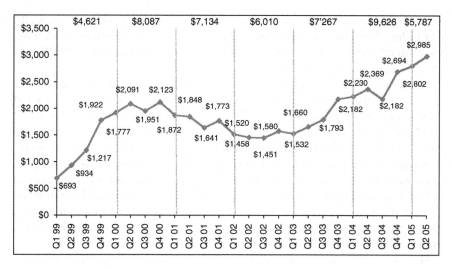

Fig. 11.7 US quarterly online ad revenue, millions of dollars, 1999–2005 (Source: Internet Advertising Bureau)

In 2001, during the dot-com crash that marks the end of the second period of search, Disney's CEO, Michael Eisner, accounted the failure of big media online by suggesting "the advertising community has abandoned the Internet" (cited in Blevins 2004: 265). At the time of writing, five years after Eisner's quote, the Internet Advertising Bureau has recorded the ninth straight quarter of advertising growth online, bringing 2004 online advertising market in the US to over $9.6 billion and the first half of 2005 to nearly $5.8 billion (the total figure for 2006 is estimated to be over $12 billion). The slump of 2001 has been revealed to be just that: a slump, as Fig. 11.7 below clearly shows. In fact, the growth in Internet advertising has outpaced the growth in television advertising in its first 10 years, according to the Internet Advertising Bureau who assemble market statistics for the industry.

This growing ad market has been increasingly funded by growth in "paid search" advertisements, that is to say the type of cost-per-click advertisements pioneered by GoTo, linked to user traffic, whether on search engine sites or syndicated to other Websites. This advertising has three key characteristics: 1) it is priced on a *cost-per click* basis; 2) it is *contextual*, linked either to page content or to the users' search term; 3) it is *syndicated* to other Websites on a revenue-sharing basis (i.e., the fee is split between the owner of the Website and the provider of the paid search service).

The market for these ads has been overwhelmingly dominated by Google and Yahoo. In November 2001, Yahoo made a deal with Overture (formerly GoTo) to launch CPC ads alongside their search results, which at that time were being provided by Google on a syndication basis (Yahoo! 2001). A year later, in December 2002, it began a transformation. Yahoo, originally a directory and always a buyer of syndicated search results, announced it would purchase Inktomi, a pure search engine company specialising in syndicated search results (Yahoo! 2002). It began serving its own search results in April 2003 (Yahoo! 2003a). Three months later in July 2003, the company announced it would acquire Overture for $1.5 billion (Yahoo!, 2003b). At the time, Overture's clients included MSN, ESPN, and CNN, as well as a staggering 88,000 other advertisers.

Meanwhile, Google had introduced its large-scale automated advertising programme, called AdWords, in October 2000 (Google 2000) – but on a CPM basis. In February 2002 it debuted its own CPC pricing programme (Google 2002). By March 2003, it announced that it had the largest advertising programme in the world, with over 100,000 advertisers (Google 2003a). In June 2003 it began to syndicate these CPC ads to partner Websites on an automated basis, through a program called AdSense (Google, 2003b). By the end of 2005, the company reported that 44% of its advertising revenue ($2.688 billion of $6.065 billion) had been made on syndicated advertising (Google 2006a). According to Google's Website, it now has "the largest online advertising network available, reaching over 80% of 30-day US Internet users," (Google 2006b).

Microsoft and Ask, the two other major providers of Web search technology, have been behind Google and Yahoo in exploiting syndicated advertising. Until 2005/6, both Web search engines simply used the syndicated services of Yahoo (in the case of Ask) or Google (in the case of MSN) (IAC Search & Media 2005; Newcomb 2006).

Google and Yahoo also aggressively pursued a syndication strategy with access providers – in Google's case primarily syndication of search results and advertising, but in Yahoo!'s case the provision of co-branded portals including e-mail, chat, news, horoscopes, etc., as well as the technical facilities for integrating partner content and other content through the RSS (Really Simple Syndication) technical standard. One such example is the BT Yahoo! Broadband portal in the UK (see Fig. 11.8), available to all BT broadband subscribers in the UK.

While such deals are too numerous to be mapped in their entirety, a review of the US market shows Web search engine deals on the homepages that ISPs provide to their customers (see Table 11.3).

It is clear from this table that Google in particular has been very effective in distributing its search engine backwards to ISPs.[150] Figure 11.9 shows that if these figures are aggregated, Google is distributed on the home pages of ISPs that account for 55.6% of the Internet subscribers in the United States.

What these very successful syndication efforts have meant is that, effectively, Google and Yahoo have achieved a situation where, without needing to purchase companies, their advertising is carried across the Web through syndicated advertising and audience is directed to them though syndicated search engine functionality.

In his recent book reviewing the state of political economy, Mosco argues for an analysis of market concentration in media markets which focuses on something more than ownership. He suggests that "networks of corporate power" might need

---

[150] Infospace, which figures several times in this table, is a provider of paid search results only – in effect, a modern GoTo.

Fig. 11.8 BT Yahoo ! personalised subscriber portal (page retrieved 18 August 2006 from http://home.bt.yahoo.com)

to be investigated through "forms of corporate interaction that build powerful relationships without actually merging businesses. These forms encompass a range of 'teaming arrangements,' including *corporate partnerships* and *strategic alliances…*" (Mosco 1996: 189 italics original).

This analysis of the Web search market seams to suggest that earlier efforts at vertical integration have been replaced by what we might term a "virtual" integration along the audience value chain. In contrast to the fully-integrated portal, the new model might be conceived as a *syndicated portal*, as in Fig. 11.10, below.

The differences with the fully-integrated portal consist not merely of the qualitative difference between ownership and partnership, but also in the quantitative differences of having multiple ISPs, multiple content providers, multiple entertainment venues and multiple retailers attached to the portal. The lines between the Web search engine and its partners are lines of both traffic and money.

By using syndication both into advertisers and also into partners who are further up the supply chain such as ISPs, the new giants of search have developed a network that extends across the Internet. No longer is it necessary to "own" the Internet, as those who dreamed of controlling a fully integrated portal did. Rather, by means of "virtual" integration using technology to achieve syndication, Google and Yahoo!, and to a lesser extent Ask (formerly AskJeeves) and MSN are able to

Table 11.3 US ISP search engine affiliations by rank and provider

Rank	ISP	Subscribers (millions)	Subscriber homepage	Search results provider
	All others	22.3		
1	AOL	18.6	aol.com	Google
2	Comcast	9	comcast.net	Google
3	SBC (AT&T)	7.4	sbc.yahoo.com	Yahoo
4	Verizon	5.7	Varies	Yahoo OR MSN Premium
5	Road Runner (TWC)	5.4	www.rr.com/publicpass/	Google
6	Earthlink	5.3	my.earthlink.net	Google
7	Cox	3.1	www.cox.net	Google
8	BellSouth	3.1	*home.bellsouth.net*	Google
9	United online	2.8	my.juno.com	Yahoo
10	Charter	2.3	www.charter.net	Google
11	Cablevision	1.8	*www.optonline.net*	Infospace
12	Qwest	1.7	qwest.msn.com	MSN
13	Sprint	0.78	my.sprint.earthlink.net	Google
14	Insight BB	0.51	*www.insightbb.com*	Infospace
15	Mediacom	0.5	e.g., suncity.mediacomtoday.com	Infospace
16	Covad	0.48	b2b lines only	not determined
17	ALLTEL	0.44	www.alltel.net	Infospace
18	Citizens	0.33	frontier.myway.com	Ask
19	CenturyTel	0.29	*www.centurytel.net*	Google
20	LocalNet	0.26	start.localnet.com	Google
21	Hughes DIRECWAY	0.26	hughesnet.myway.com	Ask
22	Cincinnati Bell	0.17	broadband.zoomtown.com	Google

Source: Author analysis Data on ISP rank and subscriber numbers from Goldman (2006) and reflect Q1 2006 status.

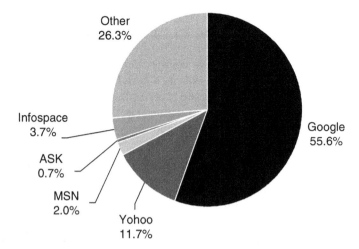

Fig. 11.9 Search affiliations of US ISPs (Source: Author analysis Data on ISP rank and subscriber numbers from Goldman (2006) and reflect Q1 2006 status)

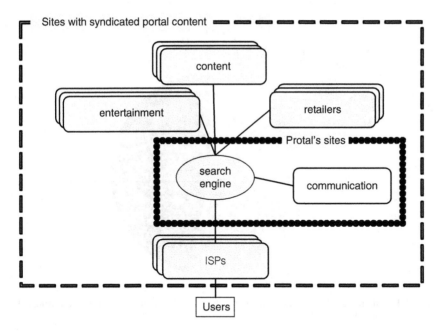

Fig. 11.10 The syndicated portal

stretch their ability to monetise (or commoditise) traffic across the Web, without
the need for ownership[151].

11.3   Conclusion

Using a theoretical framework based in the political economy of communications,
this chapter has reviewed the historical development of the Web search engine
industry. Web search engines, it has argued, are the purveyors of a new media form –
we can call it navigational media – that have taken advantage of a fragmented media
market to establish their power as distributors of traffic via the creation of flexible and
stable networks. Presently in 2006, we have a situation where the large Web search
engines overwhelmingly dominate the search market, as Fig. 11.11, below, shows.

Other smaller search engines do exist, such as Nutch (www.nutch.com) and
Gigablast (www.gigablast.com); and there are also ranges of small vertical search.
However, Fig. 11.11, above, shows that Google, Yahoo!, and MSN account for
81.2% of all searches in the US market as measured by Nielsen Net/Ratings.
Further, all the named others on the chart have search results provided by one of
these companies or by Ask. These smaller Web search engines, therefore, are dis-
regarded for the purposes of the present analysis.

---

[151] It is also worth noting that although emphasis in the industry has shifted to paid search, Yahoo
and MSN also retain more traditional "portals" with channels filled by advertiser content.

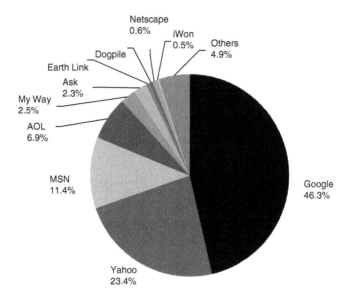

Fig. 11.11 Share of U.S. searches, November 2005 (Source: Nielsen/NetRatings for SearchEngineWatch)

As a result of the growth of paid search versus all other types of online advertising, we can also see a much more surprising result: the same four companies also account for nearly 70% of the *total* online advertising market in the US, as Fig. 11.12, below, shows. In the first half of 2005, the total online advertising market, according to the Internet Advertising Bureau (IAB), was $5.8 billion. For the first half of 2005, Google reported a US advertising income of $1.591 billion, Yahoo of $1.475 billion, MSN of $517 million, and AOL of $445 million, leaving $1.772 billion to be divided amongst all other online advertisers.

This chapter has divided the history of the search engine into three periods in order to examine this growing concentration. In the first period, many new technologies were created, and venture capital systems helped to launch the new companies into the emerging industries created out of the development of the Internet. The new companies turned to both advertising and technology licensing for revenue generation, and succeeded in gathering large audiences at least in part through significant strategic alliances with the Internet service provider AOL and the browser manufacturer Netscape, and the market was competitive, with multiple companies providing multiple search engines.

In the second period, Web search engines developed specialised content "channels" created of advertiser content where lucrative sponsorship deals became possible through the segmentation of their audiences. They were the focus of acquisition activities by both traditional media companies and telecommunications and cable companies who sought to acquire these portals with the hope of owning a large slice of the Web. However, during this period the technology of search was

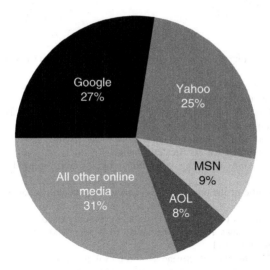

Fig. 11.12 Share of the total US online advertising market for the first half 2005 (Source: Internet Advertising Bureau, company quarterly SEC filings, author's analysis)

neglected in favour of developing channel content. There were three exceptions: first, those entrepreneurs with new technology for Web search who continued to be funded by venture capital in hopes of capitalising on the booming market for Internet stocks, such as Google and AskJeeves; second, those who developed and licensed search to other Websites, such as Inktomi; and third, those who sought to develop alternative models of payment, such as iWon and GoTo. This chapter argues that the cost-per-click model that the latter engine pioneered helped redefine the online media commodity from audience to traffic.

The third period saw the emphasis on traffic and the sale of traffic give a massive boost to search engine revenues, particularly for the early movers Overture (formerly GoTo and acquired by Yahoo during this period) and Google. Instead of seeking to acquire and control content, the engines concentrated their attention on distributing their traffic-based advertising throughout the Web. As a result, they have developed a diversified and flexible revenue base which includes hundreds of thousands of advertisers, tens of thousands of Websites on which their ads are distributed, and distribution of their search engines on most major ISPs. Microsoft, the only significant new entrant of the latter period, has so far been unable to match this "virtually-integrated" network.

The current situation, therefore, is one of oligopoly. This applies not only in the United States, upon which this chapter has focused, but all over the world. This chapter raises the very serious issue of whether or not we can now rely on competition in the marketplace, as some have urged (Goldman 2006), to assure that the provision of search to the public remains at a high quality and the deficiencies already present in search engines are remedied.

References

Bar-Ilan J (2000) Evaluating the stability of the search tools hotbot and snap: a case study. Online and CDROM Review 24: 439–449

Bar-Ilan J, Gutman T (2005) How do search engines respond to some non-english queries? Journal of Information Science 31: 13–28

Bar-Ilan J, Peritz, BC (1999) The lifespan of a specific topic on the web – The case of "informetrics": a quantitative analysis. Scientometrics 46: 371–382

Battelle J (2005) The search: how google and its rivals rewrote the rules of business and transformed our culture. Nicholas Brealey, London

Bergman MK (2001) White paper: the deep web: surfacing hidden value. Journal of Electronic Publishing 7.

Blevins JL (2004) Battle of the online brands: disney loses the portal war. Television and New Media 5: 247–271

Carnegie Mellon University (1995, 20 June) Pittsburgh company established using Lycos Internet catalog technology. News Releases Retrieved 10 March, 2006, from http://www.cs.cmu.edu/~scsnews/jun20-95.html

Choros K (2005) Testing the effectiveness of retrieval to queries using polish words with diacritics. Lecture Notes in Artificial Intelligence 3528: 101–106

Clark T (1998, 24 November) AOL buys Netscape for $4.2 billion. c|Net News.com Retrieved 21 August, 2006, from http://news.com.com/AOL+buys+Netscape+for+4.2+billion/2100-1023_3-218360.html

CNNMoney (1998a, 18 June) Disney buys infoseek stake: swaps starwave and $70M for 43% interest; will take option for control. CNNMoney News — Deals Retrieved 17 March, 2006, from http://money.cnn.com/1998/06/18/deals/infoseek

CNNMoney (1998b, 9 June) NBC enters a web portal: broadcaster buys 5 percent stake in CNET, forms venture to run Snap! CNNMoney News — Technology Retrieved 17 March, 2006, from http://money.cnn.com/1998/06/09/technology/cnet/

CNNMoney (1999, 12 July). Disney absorbs infoseek: entertainment giant, Internet search engine to expand online partnership. CNN Money News — Deals Retrieved 17 March, 2006, from http://money.cnn.com/1999/07/12/deals/disney

Curran J, Seaton, J (2003) Power without responsibility: the press, broadcasting, and new media in Britain (6th ed.). London: Routledge

Dignan L (1999, 29 June) Compaq, CMGi make AltaVista deal official. c|Net News.com Retrieved 21 August, 2006, from http://news.com.com/Compaq%2C+CMGi+make+AltaVista+deal+official/2100-12_3-258854.html

Doyle G (2002) Understanding media economics. Sage, London.

Gavetti G, Rivkin J (2004) Rationality and plasticity over time: toward a grounded theory of the origin of strategies. Retrieved 20 March, 2006, from http://www.london.edu/assets/documents/PDF/Gavetti_paper.pdf

Goldman E (2006) Search engine bias and the demise of search engine utopianism. Yale Journal of Law and Technology 8: 188–200

Google (2000, 23 October) Google launches self-service advertising program: Google's AdWrods program offers every business a fully automated, comprehensive and quick way to start an online advertising campaign. Google Press Center Retrieved 21 August, 2006, from http://www.google.com/press/pressrel/pressrelease39.html

Google (2002, 20 February) Google introduces new pricing for popular self-service online advertising program. Google Press Center Retrieved 21 August, 2006, from http://www.google.com/press/pressrel/select.html

Google (2003a, 4 March) Google builds world's largest advertising and search monetization program: company introduces automated content-targeted ads; Advertising customer base surpasses 100,000. Google Press Center Retrieved 21 August, 2006, from http://www.google.com/press/pressrel/advertising.html

Google (2003b, 18 June) Google expands advertising monetization program for websites: Google AdSense enables sites to maximize revenue potential while enhancing user experience. Google Press Center Retrieved 21 August, 2006, from http://www.google.com/press/pressrel/adsense. html

Google (2006a) Google Annual Report 2005 [online edition]. Google Investor Relations Retrieved 21 August, 2006, from http://investor.google.com/pdf/2005_Google_AnnualReport.pdf

Google (2006b) Where will my ads appear? Google help centre. Google AdWords Retrieved 2006, 18 August, from https://adwords.google.com/support/bin/answer.py?answer=6119&hl= en_GB

Harmon S (1998, 19 June) Disney buys part of Infoseek; Welcome to TomorrowWeb. InternetNews.com Retrieved 21 August, 2006, from http://www.Internetnews.com/bus-news/ article.php/21171

IAC Search & Media (2005, 1 August) Ask Jeeves launches Ask Jeeves sponsored listings: automated system replaces Ask Jeeves premier listings product, enabling access to a broader base of self-services users delivers increased ROI on Ask Jeeves advertising spend. Press Releases Retrieved 21 August, 2006, from http://www.irconnect.com/ask/pages/news_releases. html?d=83045

Infoseek (1995a, 13 February) Infoseek launches first one-stop Internet source for information. Press Releases Retrieved 21 March, 2006, from http://web.archive.org/web/19970216144951/ info.infoseek.com/doc/PressReleases/SearchLaunch.html

Infoseek (1995b, 22 May) New, fast information retrieval service sets the standard for Web searches: Infoseek, Netscape and Sun sponsor free service. Press Releases Retrieved 23 March 2006, from http://web.archive.org/web/19970216144943/info.infoseek.com/doc/PressReleases/ FreeNetSearch.html

Infoseek (1997) Company history. Company reference Retrieved 21 March, 2006, from http:// web.archive.org/web/19970216145001/info.infoseek.com/doc/Reference/History.html

Junnarkar S (1999, 19 January) @Home buys excite in $6.7 billion deal. c|Net News.com Retrieved 31 March, 2006, from http://news.com.com/Home+buys+Excite+in+6.7+billion+ deal/2100-1023_3-220281.html

Kleinberg JM, Lawrence S (2001) The structure of the web. Science 294: 1849–1850

Kopytoff V (2000, 17 May) Huge deal to buy lycos: web portal to sell for $12.5 billion. San Francisco Chronicle Retrieved 21 August, 2006, from http://www.sfgate.com/cgi-bin/article. cgi?file=/chronicle/archive/2000/05/17/BU93774.DTL

Lawrence S, Giles CL (1999) Accessibility of information on the world wide web. Nature 400: 107–109

Martin P (1996, 18 April) Land-rush in cyberspace. Financial Times FT.com Retrieved 20 March, 2006, from http://news.ft.com/msn/s/25dbb3d6-6281-11da-8dad-0000779e2340,dwp_ uuid=c2640462-6324-11da-be11-0000779e2340.html

McCown F, Nelson ML, Zubair M, Liu X (2006) Search engine coverage of the OAI-PMH corpus. IEEE Internet Computer 10: 66–73

Meisel JB, Sullivan TS (2000) Portals: the new media companies. Info — The Journal of Policy, Regulation and Strategy for Telecommunications 2: 477–486

Mosco V (1996) The political economy of communication: rethinking and renewal. Sage, London

Newcomb K (2006, 4 May) Microsoft AdCenter goes live. ClickZ News Retrieved 21 August, 2006, from http://www.clickz.com/showPage.html?page=3603746

O'Brien T (1997) The millionaires next door. Stanford Magazine Retrieved 22 March 2006, from http://www.stanfordalumni.org/news/magazine/1997/mayjun/articles/excite.html

Pinkerton B (2001) WebCrawler Timeline. WebCrawler Facts Retrieved 22 March, 2006, from http://www.thinkpink.com/bp/WebCrawler/History.html

Reuters (2004, 3 August) South Korean company buys Lycos. Wired News Retrieved 21 August, 2006, from http://www.wired.com/news/business/0,1367,64431,00.html

Rose F (2002, January). The $7 Billion Delusion. Wired Magazine Retrieved 4 April, 2006, from http://www.wired.com/wired/archive/10.01/excite_pr.html

Schiller D (1999) Deep impact: the web and the changing media economy. Info - The Journal of Policy, Regulation and Strategy for Telecommunications 1: 35–51

Schiller H (1992) *Mass Communication and American Empire* (2nd ed.). Westview Press, Boulder, CO

Schwartz B (2004, 5 August) Search memories: live from SES San Jose. SearchEngineWatch Retrieved 17 March, 2006, from http://forums.searchenginewatch.com/showthread.php?t=949

Singhal A (2001). Modern information retrieval: a brief overview. IEEE Data Engineering Bulletin 24: 35–43

Sullivan D (2000). Search engine alliances chart. Retrieved 27 April, 2006, from http://searchenginewatch.com/_subscribers/article.php/0006-alliances.mht

Sullivan D (2006, 9 August). Special edition: a conversation with google CEO Eric Schmidt. Daily SearchCast – Search Engine News Recap Retrieved 16 August, 2006, from http://media.webmasterradio.fm/episodes/audio/2006/SC080906EricSchmidt.mp3

Thompson JB (1990) *Ideology and Modern Culture*. Polity Press, London

Van Couvering E (1998, 30 November) AOL/Netscape: deal now to avoid distribution price hike. Jupiter Communications European Internet Strategies Analyst Note Retrieved 13 June, 1999, from http://www.jup.com/sps/eis/1998/57/

Vaughan L. (2004) New measurements for search engine evaluation proposed and tested. Information Processing and Management 40: 677–691

Vaughan L, Thelwall M (2004) Search engine coverage bias: evidence and possible causes. Information Processing and Management 40: 693–707

Vise DA, Malseed, M (2005) *The Google Story*. Delacorte Press, New York

Wallack T (2001, 17 December) Who killed Excite@Home: the suspects include AT&T, the Excite and @Home merger, and cable companies. San Francisco Chronicle. Retrieved 21 August, 2006, from http://www.sfgate.com/cgi-bin/article.cgi?file=/chronicle/archive/2001/12/17/BU23049.DTL

Webster F (2002) *Theories of the Information Society* (2nd ed.). Routledge, London

Werner B, Helft M (2000, 1 May) Portals start to feel the heat. The Industry Standard.

Yahoo! (1995, 29 June) Yahoo! forms marketing powerhouse to design and manage its new look: Yahoo! takes innovative approach to building powerful online advertising mechanism. Yahoo! Media relations Retrieved 20 March, 2006, from http://web.archive.org/web/20060320014607/http://docs.yahoo.com/docs/pr/release2.html

Yahoo! (2001, 13 November) Yahoo! forms alliance with Overture (formerly GoTo) to launch sponsor matches program for search results: overture as its pay-for-performance search provide until at least April 2002. Yahoo! Media Relations Retrieved 20 August, 2006, from http://yhoo.client.shareholder.com/press/ReleaseDetail.cfm?ReleaseID=173810

Yahoo! (2002) Yahoo! to acquire inktomi: create the most comprehensive search offering on the Web with largest global audience, unmatched deadth and depth of online services and world class technology. Yahoo! Media Relations Retrieved 21 August, 2006, from http://yhoo.client.shareholder.com/press/ReleaseDetail.cfm?ReleaseID=98489

Yahoo! (2003a, 7 April) Yahoo! introduces new Yahoo! Search: faster, easier search results mark latest step toward Yahoo!'s goal of providing highest-quality search experience on the Internet. Yahoo! Media Relations Retrieved 21 August, 2006, from http://yhoo.client.shareholder.com/press/ReleaseDetail.cfm?ReleaseID=105839

Yahoo! (2003b, 14 July) Yahoo! to acquire overture: acquisition positions Yahoo! as the largest global player in the rapidly growing Internet advertising market, combines leading web and commercial search services with Internet's largest global audience. Yahoo! Media Relations Retrieved 21 August, 2006, from http://yhoo.client.shareholder.com/press/ReleaseDetail.cfm?ReleaseID=113537

Part IV
Information Behavior Perspectives

12
Toward a Web Search Information Behavior Model

S.A. Knight and A. Spink

Summary Information retrieval (IR) research in the context of the Web involves a number of complex processes. Some are user-related and include cognitive processes, motivational issues, information needs, technology attitude and adoption; and some are system related and include search engine algorithms and interface design. The field currently lacks a comprehensive model of Web interaction in the information behavior context. This chapter first explores a range of information behavior, and information seeking and retrieval model. Research relating to how users seek out and retrieve information in electronic environments will be examined and these models considered for applicability to the information environment of the Web. The exploration begins at the broadest level, examining information seeking models and then interactive IR models, followed by more recent integrated models. The paper then proposes macro model of Web-based information seeking and searching behavior. Further research areas are also discussed.

12.1 Introduction

Information retrieval entails the integration of a number of complex processes within the context of three major factors or entities:

- An information Need (Broder 2002)
- An information Searcher (Kuhlthau 1991)
- An information Environment (Johnson and Meischke 1993)

Not only does each of these entities possess unique characteristics depending on the situation, they also have a considerable influence on each other. This results in a substantial number of variables in regard to the users' information seeking or searching behavior and strategies. Information behavior differs from information seeking behavior[*1] (ISB). ISB represents one component of IB which can also include components such as the nature of the information, its specific context, format, or target audience, and other variables associated with its perceived usefulness or relevancy to the searcher, and searcher characteristics such as his or her cognitive level or efficacy. The term information-seeking behavior is at times

A. Spink and M. Zimmer (eds.), *Web Search, Springer Series in Information Science and Knowledge Management 14.*
© Springer-Verlag Berlin Heidelberg 2008

mistakenly used in place of "information searching behavior", depending on the author or the system in which the user/searcher is looking for information. For example, within the context of an electronic environment, the action of seeking literally involves "search" strategies, so the seeking behavior is often described as "search behavior". This should not be confused with the term "information searching process" (ISP), which is generally used to specifically describe the cognitive processes involved in searching activities. Heinström (2000) suggests information behavior is best understood in the context of the information needs of the searcher, the inner, or cognitive, processes of the searcher, and the environmental factors relating to the information. These factors have an iterative effect on the searcher's way of responding to the information problem (Heinström, 2000).

From the decades of research into how users find and retrieve information has come a variety of proposed IB, information seeking, and searching behavior models. Wilson's (1981) notion of information need, their personality, and the environment in which they choose to look for the information are core variables that continually influence each other and the overall information seeking process.

Wilson used a framework that modeled information seeking from a "user studies" point of view. This view placed a heavy emphasis on how the user interacted with the information sought and found, rather than how the user interacted with the search system. Human computer interaction (HCI) research has typically concentrated on understanding how users feel about, interact with, and utilise technology, rather than the cognitive processes associated with the task for which they are employing that technology. This deficiency becomes particularly apparent when modeling the human/system interactive process of an activity that is largely cognitive, such as IR. Because of the noted influence of an "information environment to the information behavior of an individual searcher, the major developments in IB modeling will be considered within their historical context. Models will be compared with each other, in order to understand their influence on subsequent models, as well as to gain an understanding of the evolutionary nature of the ISB research discipline. This section will cover some of the major developments, culminating in a discussion relating to the integration of some of the common denominators into a preliminary framework of how searchers interact with Web search engines. The chapter is divided into two model types: information behavior in general and models that emphasis the interactive nature of IR and the role of system feedback in an electronic or online environment.

The historical context of the major IB model developments is closely aligned with two on-line technology revolutions. The first involved the creation of early online IR systems; used by "information professionals" who usually searched on behalf of the person who would ultimately use the found information. The second major development has been the advent of Web search engines, which have made available to any Web-user a practically immeasurable amount of information, with its own unique set of information characteristics. Research into IR, interactive IR and the resulting development of IB models has reflected this dramatic shift in both the end-user/searcher and the information environment.

12.2 Information Seeking Behavior Models

12.2.1 Wilson: Model of Information Behavior

Wilson's complex model (see Fig. 12.1) presented in 1981 and further amended in 1984, was a complicated framework that attempted to capture the information seeking process. The model included the three previously identified entities; namely (1) information user; (2) information need; and (3) information environment (see Fig. 12.1), and the iterative variables of successful (or non-successful) outcomes of specific searches, the possible involvement of other information users, and the ultimate satisfaction (or non-satisfaction) in information results or outcomes on the part of the searcher.

Central to Wilson's (1981) model was the information need – which was said to be framed by the users':

1. environment;
2. role; and
3. physiological, affective and cognitive needs. (see Fig. 12.2)

The information need was then said to influence a user's information seeking behavior, although not before it was tempered by any personal, interpersonal, and environmental barriers that the user might encounter.

Wilson's (1981) model lacked a clear description of how people interacted with an IR system in order to find and retrieve the data they sought. What Wilson labeled simply as "information seeking behavior" needed to be defined and explored

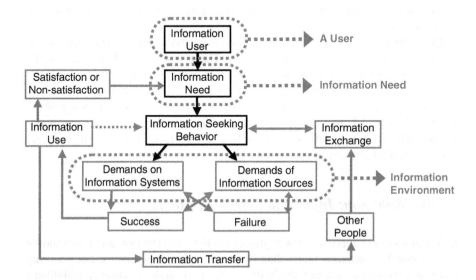

Fig. 12.1 Wilson's (1981) model of Information Behavior (emphasis, Knight 2006)

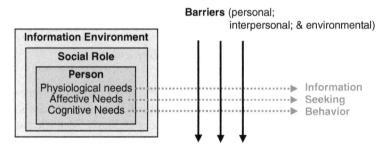

Fig. 12.2 Wilson's (1981) model of Information Seeking Behavior

further. Furthermore, a more extensive understanding of the "information systems" and "information sources" needed to be addressed in future models in order to better appreciate how the information environment – already acknowledged as a major influencing factor – impacted information seeking behavior.

12.2.2 Ellis: Behavioral Model for Information System Design

Ellis' (1989a; 1989b) research into information behavior produced a model describing six information seeking actions/strategies. The framework is illustrated and briefly described in Fig. 12.3, b.

The model was further refined with an additional two actions, verifying and ending (Ellis et al. 1993), and people's actions were described by Ellis as "features" rather than stages; indicating that the behaviors did not necessarily take place in a linear sequence, although clearly some behaviors were part of a sequence of behaviors (Fig. 12.4).

Ellis' framework was built on the observable behaviors and strategies employed by various sets of people (see Table 12.1). The extent of the description of the user's cognitive process related directly to the observable behavior being displayed by the user group in question. Although Ellis used a Grounded Theory methodological approach (Ellis 1989a) when building the model, subsequent testing of the framework using different user groups has produced similar results. It is worth noting that although the model evolves from time to time (see Table 12.1) its structure has remained largely unchanged.

12.2.3 Kuhlthau: Information-Seeking Model

Kuhlthau's (1991) approach was to model people's information seeking behavior in the context of assumed rather than observed cognitive processes. The resulting observable behaviors are not dissimilar in the two models, however Kuhlthau's presuppositions meant a framework could be developed that suggested there was a

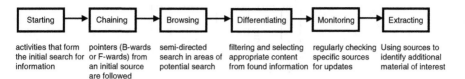

Fig. 12.3 Ellis' (1989a) Behavioral Model of Information System Design

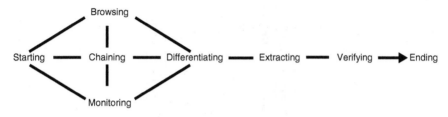

Fig. 12.4 Ellis' (1993) Behavioral Model for Information System Design

Table 12.1 Comparison of Ellis' Information Seeking Behavior Model (1989–1997)

Modelling Information Seeking Behavior (Ellis 1989a)	Info. Seeking patterns of Academic Researchers (Ellis et al. 1993)	Patterns of Engineers & Research Scientists in an Industrial Environment (Ellis and Haugan; 1997)
Starting	Starting	Surveying
Chaining	Chaining	Chaining
Browsing	Browsing	Browsing
Differentiating	Monitoring	Monitoring
Monitoring	Differentiating	Distinguishing
		Filtering
Extracting	Extracting	Extracting
	Verifying	Ending
	Ending	

logical sequence to all information seeking behavior. Each new experience is judged according to these self-made constructs, resulting in the continual reinforcement and/or development of those constructs. Kuhlthau describes an information search process (ISP) or information seeking process as a constructive activity in which the user attempts to find meaning from information (Kuhlthau 1991). The stages of Kuhlthau's model; the information seeker's feelings, thoughts, and actions; and the associated tasks are illustrated in Table 12.2.

Despite the different approaches to modeling user information seeking by Ellis (1989a) and Kuhlthau (1991), the similarities in their observed behaviors are quite remarkable (see Table 12.3), giving credence to Kuhlthau's hypothesis that there seems to be at least some information seeking strategies inbuilt into the human condition.

Table 12.2 Kuhlthau's (1991) Model

Stages		Initiation	Selection	Exploration	Formulation	Collection	Presentation
Human Experience Associated with stages	Affective (feelings)	Uncertainty	Optimism	Confusion/ Doubt	Clarity	Direction Confidence	Satisfaction or Disappointment
	Cognitive (thoughts)	General ~ Vague			Narrowed Clearer	Increased Interest	
	Physical (actions)	Seeking Background Information			Seeking Relevant Info		Focused Info
Tasks		Recognise	Identify	Investigate	Formulate	Gather	Complete

Table 12.3 Observed Information Seeking Stages/Behaviors in Ellis and Kuhlthau's Models

(Ellis (1989a)	Kuhlthau (1991)
Starting	Initiation
Chaining	Selection
Browsing	Exploration
Differentiating	Formulation
Monitoring	
Extracting	Collection
Verifying	Presentation
Ending	Ending

The weakness of both models remains their almost one-dimensional approach to the concept of the contextual variables of the observed information seeking behaviors. Ellis placed a heavy emphasis on the systems (electronic) environment context of the information being sought, while Kuhlthau concentrated on the user's cognitive predispositions towards information and learning. In contrast, Johnson suggests that a fundamental necessity of social action is that it must occur within a context (Johnson 2003), and then suggests that information seeking is a social action. Moreover, without a better understanding of the context of an information search, the information models produced lacked the flexibility to identify key components of the information environment that could trigger changes in an individual's information seeking.

12.2.4   Johnson and Meischke: Comprehensive Model of Information-Seeking

Johnson and Meischke (1991) recognised the influence of context in their research into how women diagnosed with breast cancer went about learning about their condition. They noted that an individual's seeking behavior varied depending on whether she was looking for information about breast cancer prevention, detection, treatment, or for information about dealing with the emotional issues involved with a diagnosis. They noted too that an individual's choice of information source (information-carrier factors) varied depending on the type of information required. By studying information seeking behavior within the context of that behavior, Johnson and Meischke (1993) were able to identify and validate:

1. The relationship between specific motivating factors and an individual's personal information need;
2. How the information need influenced choices relating to information environment ; and
3. The relationship(s) between information environment and individual information seeking behaviours

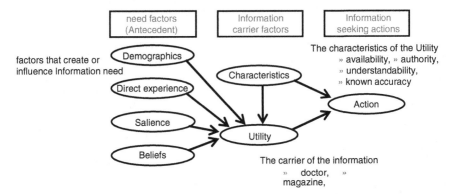

Fig. 12.5 Johnson and Meischke (1993) Comprehensive model of Information-Seeking

In the case of the initial CISM model (see Fig. 12.5) Johnson and Meischke (1993) that the information need (in this case, health-related factors relating to individual beliefs and experience of breast cancer) provided the motive for information seeking actions, which were shaped by information carrier factors. In reality however, the authors found that depending on the actual health-related factors; for example if an individual was not diagnosed with cancer, or they had never been exposed to issues relating to cancer, then the information carriers also played a motivating role in an individual's information seeking. Observations such as this can provide a significant insight regarding the impact of Web push and pull technologies, or how search engines can engage their user-base with "recommended links" or specific page relevancy algorithms.

12.3   Interactive Information Seeking Retrieval Models

The following set of models has been grouped together because of their emphasis on the dynamic interaction between the information need, searcher, and information environment. While interaction was probably always implied in previous models, its iterative affect on user search strategies, processes and outcomes was not always clearly defined.

12.3.1   Marchionini: Information Seeking in Electronic Environments Model

Like Kuhlthau, Marchionini's model (1995) is embedded in social cognitive and personal construct theories. Unlike Kuhlthau, whose primary focus was the affective and cognitive processes being experienced by individual information seekers, Marchionini took a more contextual approach, where the cognitive processes of the

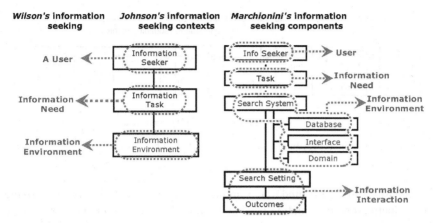

Fig. 12.6 The prominent role of the user, information need, & information environment paradigm in Wilson's (1981), Johnson and Meischke's (1993), and Brodei's (1995) information seeking models

searcher and the increasingly complex electronic information environment were considered within the scaffolding of their interactive relationship to each other. Central to Marchionini's model is the paradigm that information seeking is a natural and necessary mechanism of human existence (Marchionini 1995). It follows then, that in the context of a social science concept of human existence–seen as a series of interactions with the environment – that Marchionini defines information seeking fundamentally as an interactive process within an information environment. Understanding the information environment then, is as important as understanding the searchers cognitive processes, as it is the interaction between the two that establishes and reveals the actual information seeking strategies of the user.

Marchionini identifies eight information seeking components, which can be described as falling into four information entities (or contexts). These contexts are summarised and compared to previous information seeking model contexts in Fig. 12.6. The key difference between Marchionini's information seeking context and the previous information seeking contexts is that he adds a fourth context, namely, the interaction between the three previously considered key entities involved in information searching:

1. An information Need; (Bates 1989; Broder 2002)
2. An information Searcher; (Ellis 1989a; Kuhlthau 1991)
3. An information Environment (Johnson and Meischke 1993)
4. The various interactions between the entities of the searcher, the information need and environment (Marchionini 1995)

Marchionini's information seeking model – built on the contextual understanding developed from the information seeking contexts – is represented in Fig. 12.7.

The key supposition of Marchionini's model is that information seeking is a relatively linear process. Even with iteration taking place at the 'Reflect, iterate,

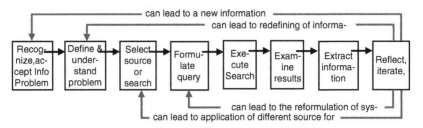

Fig. 12.7 Marchionini (1995) Information Seeking in Electronic Environments

stop' phase of the ISEE model, the implication is that the seeker is still looking and evaluating one information need at a time. The evaluation either leads to the identification of a whole new information need, or reveals possible problems in the search process, resulting in the searcher re-defining the information need, employing another electronic source, or simply formulating a new query. In reality though, information seeking and retrieval is often far more ambiguous than this. Browsing, and more specifically the concept of berry-picking (Bates 1989), is not discussed in Marchionini's model. In the early '90's the Web was still in its infancy, and virtually all participants used in prior research into IR and information search behavior still fell into the "information professional" category. These 'end-users' were, in fact, only end-users in the sense that they used the retrieval system. They were not the end-user of the information found. Moreover, they were end-users who had been specifically trained to use the systems, and so possessed a learned bias towards set strategies of searching online database systems. A second reason why Bates' model may not have been universally embraced by the early '90's ISB research status quo was that it lacked the same degree of empirical testing as other models of its day.

12.3.2 Bates: Berrypicking Model

Bates' theoretical berry-picking model, first suggested as early as 1989 but never empirical validated, is that as an end-user searches, both the information sought and the user's choices regarding what is a relevant result evolves and changes (Bates 1989). Bates argued that the berry-picking model more closely represents the actual behavior of information searchers than previous traditional linear models in that it usually begins with one feature, topic or reference; and moves through a variety of sources, with new information encountered giving new ideas and directions to the original query. The berry-picking, evolving search model of IR is shown in Fig. 12.8. The model illustrates Bates' argument that the result(s) of each query provoke a cognitive response on the part of the searcher, which can either reinforce a search query, lead to expansion or variation of a query, cause a complete overhaul, or even abandonment of a query.

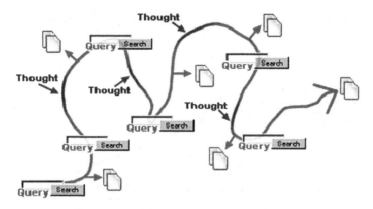

Fig. 12.8 A Berry-picking, evolving search (Bates 1989)

The four major differences noted by Bates between traditional information seeking models and the berry-picking model include, (1) The nature of the query; (2) The nature of the overall search process; (3) The range of search techniques used; and (4) The information domain (the specific data-driven environment) where the search is conducted. The fifth major difference between this model and previous models is that, implicit to the process of ISR is who will use the information. This type of evolving search can only really take place if the information searcher is also the information user, as the progression of the information sought and used is subject to the user making continual judgments regarding its relevancy and interoperability. The interactive nature of self-searchers' (end-users who were the information users) information seeking behavior became a primary focus of information behavior and IR models developed in the mid-1990's. These would become the foundation for models that would be applied to the Web.

12.3.3   Ingwersen: Cognitive IR Interaction Model

Ingwersen proposed that IR was a set of dynamic interactive processes, which occurred at multiple levels within the "cognitive space" of the user and the "information space" of the IR system. By using this poly-representation (1992; 1996) for information behavior, Ingwersen was able to at least begin to model an interactive process, said to occur not only between a user and the IR system, but also between the user and the information objects within the system with a more focused understanding of the actual information system being used, and the interactive cognitive processes that occur between the user and the system in order for information to be retrieved and ultimately used (Fig. 12.9).

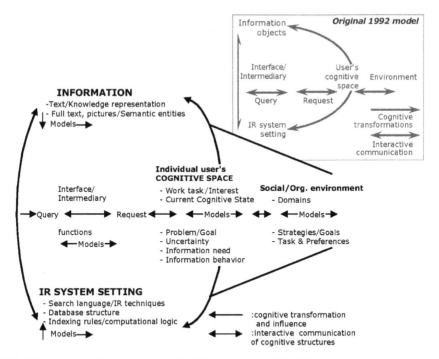

Fig. 12.9 Ingwersen's Cognitive Model of IR interaction (1992; 1996)

12.3.4 Saracevic: Stratified Interactive IR Model

The stratified interactive model (Saracevic 1996) of IR was based on an acquisition-cognition-application (A–C–A) type model of interaction. The model borrowed heavily (conceptually) from human computer interaction (HCI). The model is based on the assumption that users interact with IR systems in order to use information; that is, apply the information acquired through a cognitive process. Including "information use" as a part of the model was – like interaction – somewhat implied in previous models, but had not yet been explicitly positioned into the information seeking behavior models, perhaps because it can be safely assumed that a user would not take the time to specifically seek out information unless they were going to use it for something. Saracevic however, suggested that understanding the reason why a user sought out information was an important part of discerning the influencing factors on the interaction between the user, the IR system, and the information objects through the system.

In his stratified model, Saracevic (1996) proposed three levels, or strata, of IR interaction (Fig. 12.10):

1. A surface level of interaction – a sequence of events (interactions) between the user and the interface of the IR system.

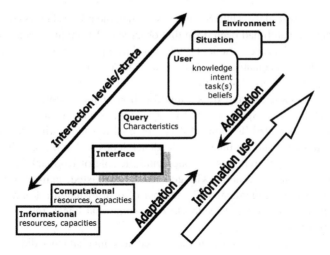

Fig. 12.10 Saracevic's Stratified Model of IR Interaction

2. A cognitive level of interaction – which identifies both the user's thinking and system's information objects as cognitive entities. At this level of interaction, the user is making judgments regarding the results (or feedback) given by the system.
3. A situational level of interaction – a context driven interaction, influenced by the original information need and how the user and/or system might categorize, or even iteratively change, the need.

The user's own pre-existing knowledge of the information, or the system, can influence the each of the levels of interaction, as well as any changes in strategies and categorizations of the information made, as the user chases the information being sought.

Saracevic acknowledged that elements within the three levels of interaction can, and in fact do, change as the process of IR is occurring. What, and how, those changes occur however, was not fully established in his model, as much of the research was still at the hypothesis stage. Empirical data was required, and needed to be analysed to establish the significant factors that influenced the interactive processes, so that that model could be tested. From the point of view of IR systems design, the strength of Saracevic's model is that it shifted the focus on IR from that of a static process to an interactive, and therefore highly dynamic one (Saracevic 1996), challenging system designers to re-consider the effectiveness of automated retrieval systems (Spink et al. 1997).

12.3.5 Spink: Search Process Model

As the importance of interaction became established in the research literature relating to ISB within a systems environment, authors began to question how the interactive process actually took place. Until Spink's research in the mid-to-late 1990s, relatively little empirical research had been done that observed IR from an interactive point of view. Spink's search process model (1997) was developed from the hypothesis that a variety of feedback mechanisms were the major influencing factors in the interactive IR process, which involved such things as the user's "evaluation of the IR system output, user's judgments, and query modification" (Spink 1997). The empirical research undertaken by Spink set out to map the types and frequency of interactive feedback during mediated IR (Spink 1997). The goal was to identify user judgments, user search strategies and the interactive feedback loops within the search process. A major focus of the research was to understand the role of feedback in the interaction. Previous models had acknowledged feedback existed; mainly in relation to (1) user relevance judgments and (2) number of result (magnitude), however this research generally considered feedback to be somewhat linear, rather than an ongoing loop process.

Spink's research confirmed that these feedback mechanisms did in fact exist within the interactive IR search process, and proposed that a further three feedback mechanisms existed. The five different types of interactive feedback identified included;

1. *Content Relevance Feedback* (CRF) consisted of a query, followed by one or more relevance judgments, resulting in a modified or reformulated query.
2. *Term Relevance Feedback* (TRF) consisted of a user utilizing a term within the retrieved objects to modify any search strategies. Spink noted that this type of interaction occurred in 60% of observed online searches.
3. *Magnitude Feedback* (MF) consisted of user using the number of results to either broaden or refine the search for information. This type of interaction occurred in 45% of the observed online searches.
4. *Tactical Review Feedback* (TCF) consisted of users choosing to use strategy-related commands, such as the display sets (DS) command, to make judgments relating to the system's output, such as viewing a search history. Tactical review feedback only occurred in 7% of observed online searches, however it would have been interesting to note whether intermediary type searchers (information professionals) represented a higher proportion of this type of feedback, as it implies a familiarity with both the IR system and specific IR system strategies.
5. *Terminology Review Feedback* (TMR) is like the tactical review feedback, in that this strategy-related interaction involved the user requesting the display of terms in the inverted file. It occurred in only 1% of observed searches.

Importantly, the feedback mechanisms listed above did not occur as an either/or manifestation. As Fig. 12.11 illustrates, each search strategy could consist of more than one cycle of user-queries, that is ~ a user session/interaction with the system could consist of multiple feedback transactions, leading to additional inputs, or queries, which could in turn lead to different feedback and new inputs.

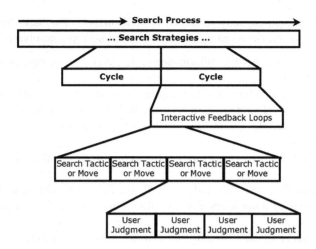

Fig. 12.11 Elements of the Interactive Search Process (Spink 1997)

12.4 Building a Web Interaction Model

The berry-picking (Bates 1989), cognitive (Ingwersen 1996), stratified (Saracevic 1997) and feedback process (Spink 1997) models provided a backdrop for the emerging "user" and "information environment " of the online IR systems of the early and mid 1990's. However, like the more linear models before them, they required a rethink and extensive testing before they could be applied to the emerging 'information environment' of the Web. Understanding the contextual makeup of IR on the Web is essential if researchers are to even begin to understand how users search and find information on/in the Web. The practical application of such research would include the design of appropriate Web search engine algorithms and interfaces, that better reflect (1) the cognitive processes of the typical Web information seeker (Spink and Jansen 2004). A big-picture focus also brings researchers back to the original supposition of information behavior models, that IR occurs in the context of an information need (or problem); an information searcher; and an information environment (Spink and Jansen 2004); and should always consider how these three contexts interact together (Marchionini 1995) in order to appreciate the extreme diversity of IR interactions.

Before the advent of the Web, the users of IR systems were largely "information professionals". These were made up of two types of individuals, those who were "intermediaries" – generally librarians who used online systems to search and retrieve information on behalf of a client who was ultimately the user of the information, and "educated professionals" – end-users who sought information directly connected with their work or profession (Ojala 1986). The enormous growth of the Web has provided an environment for a whole new user group with a vast computational capacity to search for information. This new "end-user" is different from the previous online environment end-user in a number of ways:

1. They are not necessarily the "information professionals" of the previous generation of online searchers.
2. They are unlikely to have any formal training in developing appropriate search queries or retrieval strategies. In fact, the Web has introduced an entirely new generation of people – who have never even seen an IR system–to online IR (Brooks 2003).
3. They are likely to use a wider variety of search strategies, with more inconsistent results.
4. They are usually cognitively and physically on their own – unable to directly ask intermediaries or other users how to refine a query or improve a search result (Rieh 2004).
5. They are likely to be searching for a wider variety of information type and format.
6. They are more likely to be the "information-user" of the information they are seeking.

This change in end-user profile means that new dynamic variables of different user interactions have to be considered (Spink and Saracevic 1997): user cognitive ability, personality, information task, search outcomes, and PC capabilities. These all become important variables that can influence information search behavior (Hsieh-Yee 2001). The change in the "user" has been accompanied by a dramatic change in the on-line information environment. Web search engine environments differ from traditional online library information systems in a number of key areas:

1. Open architecture – resulting in no enforceable quality standards regarding the accuracy or quality of content.
2. Open classification and meta-tagging system – resulting in Web pages failing to be indexed appropriately by search engines (Doctorow 2001).
3. Highly dynamic use of the hypertext – favouring browsing over query - making in many instances.
4. Dynamic/fluid content structure – resulting in pages being "moved" within directories of a given Website, and frequent 404 errors (where pages no longer exist as formerly known URL's).
5. Partial representation – at any one time a Search Engine can literally only provide a "snap-shot" of the Internet at one given time in history. Servers that are offline or networks that have temporarily been interrupted cannot be "indexed" by a crawling search engine (Sullivan 2002).
6. Sheer volume – the sheer size of the Internet means that the snap-shot a search engine takes of the Internet at any one time is likely to represent less than 30% of the known Web.

Understanding how these users interact with this "utility" is the key to developing sound information behavior models and ultimately to building effective Web based IR systems. Initially, applying what had been learned from the years of research into information seeking behavior in online environments seemed the logical step to understanding how users would retrieved desired information on the Web. However, early ISB studies that focused on traditional, managed, IR systems were unable to provide a rich picture of the interactions of IR on the Web (Wang et al. 2000).

In order to capture something of the heterogeneous nature of the Web, its wide variety of users and the context in which information is sought; research methodologies used in IR and ISB investigations are becoming increasingly qualitative (Martzoukou 2005). However, analysis of large data-sets (Broder 2002; Huberman et al. 1998; Spink and Jansen 2004) of user transactional data has also been applied in order to examine users' interactions with Web-based search engines. The second method (log analysis) has become more common (Spink and Jansen 2004). While analysis of keywords, results, search histories and user-logs provides an interesting picture of user actions and ultimate choices, they struggle to capture a user's cognitive processes involved with those choices. They also provide little user-related data regarding how users scan the content of Web pages or 'browse' (navigate) hypertext links. In other words, they demonstrate "how", but not "why".

Experiment-based or observational methodology will produce the most accurate results only if variables between the users' and their information interaction can be identified and accounted for or controlled. As a result, many studies relating to Web IR and seeking or searching behavior are conducted using small groups of similar users. Studies that have adopted this methodology include:

1. Navarro-Prieto et al. (1999) ~ Twenty-three University of Sussex students from the School of Cognitive and Computer Science (ten Computer Science, thirteen Psychology)
2. Hölscher and Strube (2000) ~ Twelve "expert" participants
3. Choo et al. (2000) ~ Thirty-four IT specialists, managers, and research/marketing/consulting staff from seven organisations
4. Lazonder et al. (2000) ~ Eight "expert" and seventeen "novice" participants
5. Saito and Mirva (2001) ~ Ten participants with similar knowledge and experience
6. Ford et al. (2001) ~ Sixty-nine masters students using the AltaVista for prescribed searches
7. Choo and Marton (2003) ~ Twenty four women IT professionals

12.4.1 Choo: Behavioral Model for the Web

An important aspect of IR on the Web relates to how users navigate (called browsing) the hypertext links of a Web page (including the dynamic page/results of a search engine query) in order to meet their information need.

In their behavioral model for the Web, Choo et al. (2000) propose a model of information seeking behavior to capture some of the browsing related information seeking strategies (called moves) employed by users.

Table 12.4 Information seeking behaviors and web moves

	Starting	Chaining	Browsing	Differentiating	Monitoring	Extracting
Literature Search Moves (Ellis et al. 1989a; 1993; 1997)	Identifying sources of interest	Following up references found in given material	Scanning tables of contents or headings	Assessing or restricting information according to their usefulness	Receiving regular reports or summaries from selected sources	Systematically working a source to identify material of interest
Anticipated Web Moves (Choo et al. 2000; 2003)	Identifying Web sites/ pages containing or pointing to information of interest	Following links on starting pages to other content related sites	Scanning top-level pages: lists, headings, site maps	Selecting useful pages and sites by bookmarking, printing, copying and pasting, etc.; Choosing differentiated, pre-selected site	Receiving site updates using e.g. push, agents, or profiles; Revisiting 'favorite' sites	Systematically searches a local site to extract information of interest at that site

Table 12.4 illustrates the "Web moves" identified by Choo, and their comparison to the "actions" of Ellis' behavioral model.

Any framework developed to investigate or present how users interact with and retrieve information on the Web must take both browsing type and query type behaviors into account. In doing this question relating to users' personalities and individual differences has become a key focus in much of the contemporary academic literature.

12.4.2   Ford, Millerand Moss: Individual User Differences

Ford et al. (2001, 2005) identified a number of key characteristic differences between users that affected search strategies and performance. These include such dimensions as (1) cognitive style (2) prior experience (3) Internet perceptions (4) gender, and (5) age. Information seeking behavior, and individual user and system differences were categorized into pre-existing theoretical models from multiple research disciplines. Figure 12.12 illustrates the theoretical framework in which Ford et al. (2001, 2005) examined the information seeking behavior of sixty-nine masters level students engaging the AltaVista search engine in a prescribed IR task.

In contextualizing the observed behaviors of users into pre-existing theoretical frameworks Ford et al. (2001) were able to develop initial findings regarding the

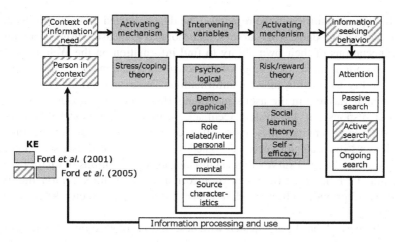

Fig. 12.12 Ford et al. (2001, 2005)

effect of identified individual differences in users on IR strategies and performance. For example, when examining Internet perceptions, it was found that poor IR performance was linked to perceptions "that the Internet is too unstructured, of not being in control, failing to keep on target, failing to find one's way around and getting lost" (Ford et al. 2001, p. 1060). A similar approach has been taken in the current research project, of which this paper is a literature review component. Pre-existing models such as the technology acceptance model (TAM) have been integrated into an interdisciplinary investigation of the impact of user perceptions of information quality on IR strategies.

Because the study investigates such cognitive processes as individual and/or groups of user perceptions, a hybrid methodology has been selected, using quantitative data collection strategies and qualitative analysis of the user results. The small sized user-groups employed in some previous qualitative studies of Web ISB – twelve 'expert' participants in Hölscher and Strube (2000), eight 'expert' and seventeen 'novice' participants in Lazonder et al. (2000), ten participants in Saito and Mirva (2001), and only five participants in Hale and Moss (1999a,b) – typically presented with limitations regarding generalisability of research findings. To address this issue, a minimum target of fifty participants was set when data collection started in March 2006. Data was collected over a thirteen month period (March 2006 to March 2007) to allow the user-group time to grow, with the final number of usable data-sets being eighty (from 123 registrations) when data collection stopped in March 2007.

For a participant's data to be considered "usable", a completed data-set of four on-line surveys had to be submitted in the specified order, and within a six-month time frame from a participant's submitted registration. With each survey designed as a stand-alone data-capturing tool however, users who only completed two or three of the four surveys have still provided valuable statistical data relating to specific topics identified in the research. The data collected includes two technology acceptance model (TAM) surveys, incorporated to measure users' perceptions and expectations of their own ability to find information on the Web, as well as their perceptions and expectations of the actual information they retrieve and the Web's ability to provide relevant information. These perceptions are seen as a fundamental variable in the user's judgments (berry-picking model, Bates 1989) and user responses to the system feedback (search process model, Spink 1997) from the search engines they most often choose to use. Data collection also includes an ISB Strategies survey designed to map out typical user/search-engine interaction, and a final survey that establishes user perceptions of quality within the context of the specific types of information they look for on the Web. Figure 12.13 provides a framework to guide the theoretical structure of the current research.

The framework has been adjusted with descriptions of specific variables as they pertain to the current research. For example; "Role" is described as "Academic Role", representing one of the user-variables upon which four sub-classes within the user-group can be identified, and results compared. In this application then, Wilson's (1994) model doesn't so much describe expected user behaviors, but provides a theoretical backdrop where synergy between the various disciplines and parts of the investigation can be identified and used to better understand the user-group results, and therefore Web-based IR behaviors. We separate information seeking behavior into information seeking and searching behavior. While the authors agree, in principle, that this is true, a significant number of Web-users begin their interaction with the Web with "search" type behaviors such as a Web search engine query, and then shift to "seeking" type moves (Choo et al. 2000, 2003) such as scanning or browsing. Essentially, in an episode such as this, it could be inferred that information seeking becomes a sub-set of the information search process. For this reason, information seeking and search behavior are classified in the current research as different user information behaviors that users can iteratively swap between.

The interdisciplinary framework (Fig. 12.13) is being used to:

1. Identify multi-disciplinary theories that can be applied to better understand human information behaviors.
2. Contextualise how and where the various identified theories contribute to the process of data collection, comparison and analysis.
3. Help map-out patterns of information behavior of the user-group, and therefore identify if relationships exist between various data-sets.

The framework is not, therefore, a predictive model for human IR on the Web, although clearly there are some predictive elements associated with it. It is a tool used to map-out patterns of participants' information behavior within multi-disciplinary constructs helping to identify what (if any) types of relationships exist between participants' data-sets. The framework is used in conjunction with a proposed theoretically-based macro information behavior model, which will be discussed in the following section.

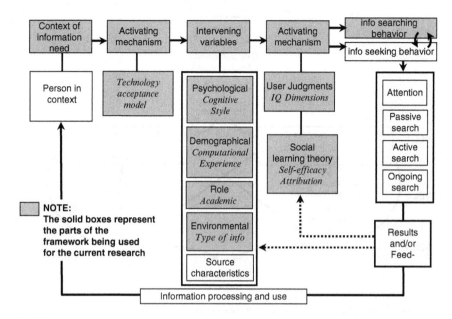

Fig. 12.13 An interdisciplinary framework for the current research project

12.4.3   Toward a Web IR Model

A theoretically-based, contextual, macro model for investigating Web-based information behavior is proposed (Fig. 12.14). The proposed model contends that user information behavior begins with an information need, which, if influenced by the user's cognitive style (Kim and Allen 2002), manifests itself in the use of specific information seeking or searching strategies. Cognitive style relates not so much to intellectual ability, but to preferred methods of operation on the part of the user. In the context of the current research, preferred modes of operation can be identified at a number of levels within the model. Research findings consistently advocate that a major influencing factor on user IR strategies is the user's pre-existing cognitive style (Ford et al. 2001; Kim 2000; Navarro-Prieto et al. 1999). In the proposed model, a user's cognitive style is seen as influencing their system-entry IR strategies, with users entering the IR process with a pre-existing preference to browse-seek (information seeking behavior) or search-seek (information searching behavior).

In this way, the two types of system interaction are classified as different sets of behavior, even though (1) there is likely to be common behaviors shared by each; and (2) users may periodically swap between the two behavior classifications. Unless a user already knows the URL of where they expect to find their target information, they are usually forced into a search-style strategy as their initial system interaction, regardless of their own cognitive preference. For this reason, user perceptions of self, the system, and expected interactions between their self and the system are also seen as having an influence on initial strategies. A better

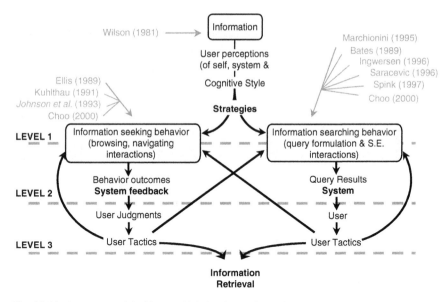

Fig. 12.14 A macro model of human IR behavior on the Web

understanding of the impact this forced step has on a user's (1) adoption of search engines, and (2) perception of the value of the search engine's results to their query is an expected outcome of the current research's data analysis.

12.5   Information Seeking and Searching Behavior

Within the next phase of the macro model (LEVEL 2) fall the many observable characteristics of previous models. Considering these models within the context of two types of IR behavior-sets allows for a measure of synergy between them not yet captured in the literature. Behavioral models such as Ellis' (1989a; Figs. 12.3 and 12.4) and Johnson and Meischke's (1993; Fig. 2.5) would fall predominantly into information seeking behavior, while the more query oriented interactive models of Spink (1997) and Bates (1989) would fall predominantly into information search behavior. The need to distinguish between information seeking and searching is recognised by researchers like Spink and Cole (2005), whose integrated information behavior model – a macro model – nests information searching behavior as a sub-set of information seeking behavior. While logically, "searching", that is, query formulation type information behaviors, is but one aspect of information seeking behavior. The problem with applying this concept to Web IR is that, more often than not, users experience the "search" and its associated tactics as their first information interaction with the system. For this reason, the current macro model seeks to classify information seeking and information searching behavior as alternative entry level strategies to IR on the Web.

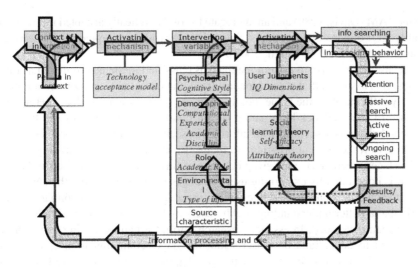

Fig. 12.15 The flow of IR (using the adapted interdisciplinary framework)

Between (LEVEL 2) and (LEVEL 3) of the macro model come any results of a user's information behavior. The result (described by some researchers as a system's "feedback") is used by the information seeker to make value judgments regarding (1) the system (search engine or Webpage) they have engaged; and (2) whether the content now presented to them will meet their information need. The value judgments of results are seen as being influenced by the intervening variables and activating mechanisms included in the adapted interdisciplinary framework (Fig. 12.13). IR is a highly iterative process, with the activating mechanisms and intervening variables imposing themselves into the IR process at any stage (see Fig. 12.15).

Generally speaking, intervening variables include such elements as users' cognitive style, level of system experience, knowledge of topic, and other "individual" characteristics associated with each user. In order for a researcher to make valid observations or develop meaningful theory in regards to those observations, a 'sample-group' of users must share a number of key intervening variables. If the user-group is large enough, then sub-groups who share different common variables can also provide a rich picture of the phenomenon being investigated. In the case of the current research, post-graduate level students and academics were identified as the target user-group. They were chosen specifically because it was assumed they would be high-end information users, and therefore posses (individually and collectively) discerning value judgments regarding the quality of any information they retrieve from the Web. The variables within the target group members that will assist in categorizing observed user information behaviors have been identified as; (1) Cognitive style; (2) Computational experience; (3) Academic discipline; (4) Academic role; and (5) Type of information most often sought. Other variables that could be investigated include age, gender, level of qualification, and geographic location. The two activating mechanisms that will be investigated most prominently are the TAM (Davis, 1989) and an aggregate list of theoretically accepted information quality (IQ) dimensions developed from nineteen widely accepted IQ frameworks (Knight and Burn 2005; Knight 2007).

The users' response to system feedback is classified in the macro model as their tactics. It is assumed that at the broadest level, the tactics chosen by users are most directly influenced by the value judgments made of the system feedback. However, because of the feedback/loop nature of the model, user tactics will see the user return to behaviors associated with information seeking, or searching; or if the user is satisfied with the content presented to them, IR. Therefore, the tactics stage is one of the stages where users may swap between or stay within classified sets of behaviors. It is hoped that by examining users' changes in behavior within the context of the activating mechanisms and intervening variables of the interdisciplinary framework, that a better understanding of why users make specific information behavior choices can developed. In essence, research into information seeking behaviors is an attempt to understand how user's link language/ communication construct to meaning. This is particularly pertinent given that the act of research itself is also an attempt to find meaning. To that end, the terminologies used to describe the various human information behaviors are themselves imposed constructs developed by researchers to help contextualize and understand the behavior being examined.

12.6   Conclusion

This chapter has provided a move towards a comprehensive model of Web interaction. Such a model needs to include the motivating human aspect (information need) that begins any Web search episode and its close connection to the cognitive make up of the individual (a searcher), and the setting (information environment) in which the individual attempts to fulfill their need. The adding of a fourth required element (to the three required elements already named) in order for Web IR to take place is the actual interaction between the user and the Web system environment, and the user and the information. Virtually all the research covered adheres to these four basic required elements of information seeking behavior, without one of them, Web IR cannot take place.

References

Bates MJ (1989) The design of browsing and berrypicking techniques for the online search interface. On-line Review 13: 407–431

Broder A (2002) A taxonomy of web search. ACM SIGIR Forum 36: 3–10

Brooks TA (2003) Web search: how the web has changed information retrieval. Information Research 8(3)

Choo CW, Marton C (2003) Information seeking on the web by women in IT professions. Internet Research 13: 267–280

Choo CW, Detlor B, Turnbull D (2000) Information seeking on the web: an integrated model of browsing and searching. First Monday 5.

Davis FD (1989) Perceived usefulness, perceived ease of use, and user acceptance of information technology. MIS Quarterly 13: 319

Doctorow C (2001) Metacrap: putting the torch to seven straw-men of the meta-utopia. http://www.well.com/~doctorow/metacrap.htm

Ellis D (1989a) A behavioral model for information retrieval system design. Journal of Information Science 15: 237–247

Ellis D (1989b) A behavioral approach to information retrieval system design. Journal of Documentation 45: 171–212

Ellis D, Cox D, Hall K (1993) A comparison of the information seeking patterns of researchers in the physical and social sciences. Journal of Documentation 49: 356–369

Ford N, Miller D, Moss N (2001) The role of individual differences in Internet searching: an empirical study. Journal of the American Society for Information Science and Technology 52.

Ford N, Miller D, Moss N (2005) Web search strategies and human individual differences: cognitive and demographic factors, Internet attitudes and approaches. Journal of the American Society for Information Science and Technology 56: 741–756

Heinström J (2000) The impact of personality and approaches to learning on information behavior. Information Research 5: 78

Hölscher C, Strube G (2000) Web search behavior of Internet experts and newbies. Proceedings of the 9th Conference on World Wide Web, pp. 81–101

Huberman B, Pirolli P, Pitkow J, Lukose R (1998) Strong regularities in world wide web surfing. Science 280: 94–97

Hsieh-Yee I (2001) Research on web search behavior. Library and Information Science Research 23: 167–185

Ingwersen P (1992) Information retrieval interaction. Taylor Graham, London

Ingwersen P (1996) Cognitive perspectives of information retrieval interaction: elements of a cognitive ir theory. Journal of Documentation 52: 3–50

Johnson JD (2003) On context of information seeking. Information Processing and Management 39: 735–760

Johnson JD, Meischke H (1991) Women's preferences for cancer information: from specific communication channels. American Behavioral Scientist 34: 742–755

Johnson JD, Meischke H (1993) A comprehensive model of cancer-related information seeking applied to magazines. Human Communications Research 19: 343–367

Kim KS (2000) Individual differences and information retrieval: implications on web design. Proceedings of RIAO.

Kim K, Allen B (2002) Cognitive and task influences on web searching behavior. Journal of the American Society for Information Science and Technology 53: 109–119

Knight SA (2007) The impact of user perceptions of information quality on world wide web information retrieval studies. Doctoral dissertation, School of MIS, Edith Cowan University

Knight SA, Burn JM (2005) Developing a framework for assessing information quality on the world wide web. Informing Science Journal 18: 159–172

Kuhlthau CC (1991) Inside the search process: information seeking from the user's perspective. Journal of the American Society for Information Science and Technology 42: 361–371

Lazonder AW, Biemans JA, Wopereis IG (2000) Differences between novice and experienced users in searching information on the world wide web. Journal of the American Society for Information Science 51: 576–581

Marchionini G (1995) Information seeking in electronic environments. Cambridge Series on human computer interaction. Cambridge University Press, Cambridge, MA

Martzoukou K (2005) A review of web information seeking research: considerations of method and foci of interest. Information Research 10: 215

Moss N, Hale G (1999b) Cognitive style and its effect on Internet searching: a quantitative investigation. ECER 99: European Conference on Educational Research, 1189

Navarro-Prieto R, Scaife M, Rogers Y (1999) Cognitive strategies in web searching. HFWEB'99: Conference on Human Factors and the Web, July 5, 1999, Washington

Ojala M (1986) Views on end-user searching. Journal of the American Society for Information Science 37: 197–203

Rieh SY (2004) On the web at home: information seeking and web searching in the home environment. Journal of the American Society for Information Science and Technology 55: 743–753

Saito H, Miwa K (2001) A cognitive study of information seeking processes in the WWW: the effects of searcher's knowledge and experience. In M.T. Özsu, H.J. Schek, K. Tanaka, Y. Zhang, Y. Kambayashi (Eds.) Proceedings of the 2nd International Conference on Web Information Systems Engineering, Kyoto, Japan (pp. 321–333)

Saracevic T (1996) Modeling interaction in information retrieval (IR): a review and proposal. Proceedings of the 59th Annual Meeting of the American Society for Information Science 33: 3–9

Spink A (1997) Study of interactive feedback during mediated information retrieval. Journal of the American Society for Information Science and Technology 48: 382–394

Spink A, Cole CB (2006) Human information behavior: integrating diverse approaches and information use. Journal of the American Society for Information Science and Technology 57: 25–35

Spink A, Jansen BJ (2004) Web search: public searching of the web. Springer

Spink A, Saracevic T (1997) Interactive information retrieval: sources and effectiveness of search terms during mediated online searching. Journal of the American Society for Information Science 48: 741–761

Sullivan D (2002) Nielsen//NetRatings search engine ratings. Search Engine Watch. http://www. searchenginewatch.com/reports/netratings.html (20 March 2003)

Wang P, Hawk WB, Tenopir C (2000) Users' interaction with world wide web resources: an exploratory study using a holistic approach. Information Processing and Management 36: 229–251

Wilson TD (1981) On user studies and information needs. Journal of Documentation 37: 3–15

Wilson TD (1994) Information needs and uses: fifty years of progress? In B.C. Vickery (Ed.) Fifty years of information progress. Journal of Documentation Review (pp. 15–51) aslib, London

13
Web Searching for Health: Theoretical Foundations and Connections to Health Related Outcomes

M.J. Dutta and G.D. Bodie

Summary Increasingly, consumers are using the Internet to seek out health information. This increasing demand for health information on the Internet has been accompanied by an increase in the number of Websites delivering health information online. This rise in online health information search calls for a theoretical approach that explains consumer health information seeking on the Internet. Based on a review of the literature related to health information seeking, this chapter introduces an integrative model of online health information seeking, arguing that the motivation and ability to seek out health information are two key constructs in predicting health information seeking. Finally, the chapter highlights the implications of adopting the integrative model of online health information seeking in understanding the health outcomes associated with new communication technologies.

13.1 Introduction

The increasing use of the Internet for seeking out health information, accompanied by the rapid rise in the number of online platforms delivering health information have led to the necessity of examining the construct of online health information seeking (Dutta-Bergman 2004a; Spink and Jansen 2004; Rice 2001). The growth in consumer usage of online health information is captured in a survey conducted by the Pew Internet and American Life Project in 2003, which reported that 66% of Internet users went online to search for health or medical information, compared to 54% of Internet users in 2000 (Fox and Fallows 2003). According to scholars investigating the role of the Internet in the healthcare industry, this dramatic rise in the use of the Internet for healthcare has been propelled by (a) increasing consumer interest in healthcare (Carlsson 2000; Dutta-Bergman 2004b; Navarro and Wilkins 2001), (b) increasing analytical sophistication of the new consumer (Mittman and Cain 2001), (c) increasing participation of healthcare consumers in decision making (Dutta-Bergman 2004a, b, c), and (d) the growing accessibility of health information on the Internet (Dutta-Bergman 2004b; Spink and Jansen 2004). Scholars

A. Spink and M. Zimmer (eds.), *Web Search, Springer Series in Information Science and Knowledge Management 14.*
© Springer-Verlag Berlin Heidelberg 2008

suggest that the Internet has brought about a paradigm shift in the healthcare industry, arguing that online health information seeking has shifted traditional patterns of consumer health information use, the dynamics of the physician-patient relationship, health services delivery, consumer participation in healthcare, and healthcare policy (Dutta-Bergman 2003b; Rice 2001).

Acknowledging the importance of adopting a consumer-centric perspective to the ways in which we study healthcare processes in general, the current state of the literature articulates the importance of developing a consumer-based framework that suggests explanatory pathways for health information seeking on the Web (Cline and Hayes 2001; Napoli 2001). Responding to this call for a theoretical framework that is driven by an emphasis on the consumer, Dutta-Bergman (2006) underscored the importance of adopting an integrative approach to e-health that theorizes the roles of motivation and ability to adopt technology for health purposes. This chapter builds on Dutta-Bergman's (2006) work to propose an integrative model of health information seeking, suggesting that the motivation and ability to seek out health information serve as critical predictors of online health information seeking. Motivation refers to the underlying interest in an issue or topic, and in this context, taps into the intrinsic consumer interest in health-related issues (Dutta-Bergman 2004b; Ferguson 1992; Napoli 2001). Ability refers to a consumer's capacity to engage in a task, and in this context, taps into the extent to which the consumer is capable of seeking out and processing health information.

The integrative model of online health information seeking makes a substantive contribution to the current literature on online health information seeking by suggesting that any form of media consumption is a heterogeneous phenomenon and that media uses ought to be approached from a segmentation-based framework (Dutta-Bergman 2006). Exploring individual and population level differences in online health information seeking equips us with an understanding of the disparities within the population in the context of online health information seeking patterns, and the varying patterns of penetration of new media technologies among consumer segments. The motivation and ability to search for health information are located in the context of broader population-level patterns such as race, ethnicity, socioeconomic status (SES), and gender. This connection between the micro and macro elements underlying online health information seeking provides a mechanism for understanding the ways in which broader social disparities shape and, in turn, are shaped by individual-level differences in motivation and ability. Furthermore, by exploring the roles of motivation and ability, the model also provides a framework for understanding the patterns underlying the non-seekers of online health information. Who are the non-seekers and why do they not use the Internet? Understanding these patterns is critical to addressing issues of digital divide and healthcare disparities within the population.

This chapter will begin with a review of the major theories of information seeking and media use, followed by a discussion of the integrative model of health information seeking. We will argue that the key components of these major theories are embedded within the integrative framework, thus capturing the essence of the online health information seeking construct. Based on the discussion of the integrative model, the chapter will then explore the ways in which online health information seeking impacts a variety of outcomes ranging from adoption of preventive behaviors, greater consumer empowerment in healthcare processes, and greater healthcare participation and civic engagement, ultimately impacting health outcomes of individuals. Finally, the chapter will connect online health information seeking to macro-level contexts, discussed in the realm of health disparities and the digital divide.

13.2   Theories of Information Seeking, Processing, and Media Use

The theories of information seeking and media use documented in this section are built on a functional approach to media use, suggesting that different media types serve different functions for different consumer segments (Dutta-Bergman 2004a, d). This perspective assumes media use is a heterogeneous process; therefore, media needs to be studied in the realm of the specific functions they serve for specific segments of the population. The function served by a particular medium emerges from the communicative needs of the audience, which in turn are determined by the disposition of the user and the specific situation that triggers the media consumption within larger systems of media access and control (see Ball-Rokeach and DeFleur 1976; DeFleur and Ball-Rokeach 1989).

More specifically in the area of online health information seeking, the medium (i.e., the Internet) needs to be studied with respect to the specific function of delivering health information to consumers, and the specific health information needs of specific consumer segments (Atkin 1993; Dutta-Bergman 2004d; Lin 1992; Lin and Jeffres 1998; Rubin 1994). In other words, online health information seeking ought to be contextualized with respect to the subtleties of the various types of health information seeking functions served by the Internet and the information needs of the consumer. For example, the Internet is sometimes used by the consumer for the purposes of finding information about a treatment, whereas at other times it is used in order to detect a condition. Ultimately, it is the consumer's need(s) that drives online health information seeking. The theories highlighted in this section capture the essence of this functional approach to online health information seeking; dual process, uses and gratifications, selective processing, and channel complementarity theories are all built on the notion of heterogeneous consumer experiences in seeking and processing information.

13.2.1   Uses and Gratifications Perspective

The uses and gratifications perspective is founded on the conceptualization of audience initiative and activity, and conceptualizes media consumption in terms of the specific functions served by the media (Rubin 1994). Uses and gratifications research examines the purposes or functions served by the medium for audiences of media programs. Located in the realm of audience choice of media stimuli, this line of research explores the purposes, functions, or uses of mass media as driven by the choice patterns of receivers (Rubin 1994, 2002). The emphasis here is on the uses of mass media in meeting the felt needs of the audience. Katz et al. (1974) outlined the following objectives for uses and gratifications research: to explain how people use media to satisfy their needs; to understand motives underlying media behavior; and to identify functions or consequences that emerge from the intersection of needs, motives, and behaviors.

The goals that consumers bring to the media landscape shape the media types that are selected and the subsequent processing of media content. According to Rubin (1994), five key points establish the framework for uses and gratifications research: (a) communication behavior is goal-directed, (b) individuals select and use communication channels to satisfy felt needs, (c) individual communication behavior is mediated by a plethora of social and psychological factors, (d) media compete with other forms of communication, and (e) although individuals are typically more influential than the media in the relationship, this is not always the case. Uses and gratifications researchers have demonstrated systematic population variances in the different uses of media types; these uses are driven by the needs felt by the consumer. The motives that have been systematically investigated under the rubric of uses and gratifications research include information, surveillance, entertainment, habit, social interaction, escape, pass time, and relaxation.

One of the functional categories that emerges from the uses and gratifications research is surveillance (Rubin 1994). Uses and gratifications researchers posit that instrumental needs involve the use of media for knowledge seeking; these needs most often are expressed in the form of environment scanning and specific information seeking (Ferguson 1992). In his categorization of media orientations, Rubin (2002) describes such information-based use of the media as instrumental use, capturing the consumer search for media content for informational reasons. This surveillance function, however, is relatively broad in scope and does not capture the variance in different kinds of information seeking. This is especially the case in the realm of health information gathering.

The Internet is used for a wide variety of information seeking purposes, and these purposes are qualitatively different from one another. For instance, it may be argued that gathering information for learning about preventative behaviors is fundamentally different from gathering health information for the purpose of detecting a disease. Gathering health information for choosing a treatment option is fundamentally different from the habitual consumption of medical news. It is important to sketch out this variance in consumer health information search on the Internet because of its possible impact on consumer information processing. Dutta-Bergman (2004d) suggested the following health-related information functions of the Internet: (a) gathering medical news, (b) looking for information about medical services, (c) searching for information about drugs and medications, (d) gathering disease specific information, (e) searching for information about healthy lifestyle, and (f) looking for and participating in discussion groups.

The cues that the consumer will attend to will perhaps differ by the different types of health information gathering in which the consumer engages. Also, consumer expectations of information quality and his or her satisfaction with the health information are likely to vary with the specific function. Dual-process theories help to explain such differences in processing.

13.2.2 Dual Process Theories

Dual process theories such as the Elaboration Likelihood Model (ELM; Petty and Cacioppo 1986) and the Heuristic Systematic Model (HSM; Chaiken 1980) posit that individuals make use of two information processing modes: *heuristic (peripheral) processing*, a fast, usually efficient mode that relies on quick decision rules (heuristics) that are typically activated by particular environmental cues, and *systematic (central) processing*, a comparatively slow, analytic process in which decisions are reached on the basis of careful scrutiny of messages and related information. When messages are processed systematically, recipients actively think about the information contained in the message, attentively compare this information to prior thoughts and beliefs, and pay comparatively close attention to the full content of a message. Although individuals are often more critical of message content when processing it systematically than heuristically, the substance of the message has the potential to have large and lasting effects on relevant outcomes when processed systematically. In contrast, when messages are processed heuristically, recipients pay comparatively little attention to the substance of the message and are more affected by peripheral features of the communicative situation (such as the physical layout of a Web page) that activate rules relevant to the interpretation and outcome of the message ("Well managed Web pages are credible").

Since the thoughtful, systematic elaboration of message content is demanding and consumes valuable (and limited) cognitive resources, the heuristic mode is generally the "default option" and depends on some environmental cue to activate a rule that guides the individual's response. More elaborated (systematic) processing of message content only occurs when individuals are motivated and able to consider this content thoughtfully. Motivational factors are those "that propel and guide people's information processing and gives it its purposive character" (Petty and Cacioppo 1986 p. 218), whereas ability factors "encompass a person's capabilities and opportunities" (Petty and Wegener 1999 p. 53). Both qualities of the individual (e.g., cognitive capacity, demographic variables) and situation (e.g., distraction) influence the motivation and ability to systematically process messages.

In the area of online health information seeking and processing, it may be argued that health-involved individuals would be more likely to consume health-oriented content on the Internet and centrally process information presented in such outlets as compared to low health-involved individuals. Therefore, involvement would be a determinant of (a) the amount of health information search, and (b) the type of health information sought. Not only would highly involved consumers look for information to fulfill their information needs in the content area, they would also be more likely to scrutinize Website content. By attending more to the quality of information presented on the Web, these individuals are more likely to reach informed decisions.

Furthermore, beyond possessing a level of involvement in a topic/issue, individuals must also possess the ability to systematically process the message (Petty and Cacioppo 1986). This suggests the relevance of exploring the role of processing capacity in understanding online health information seeking. Processing capacity here not only deals with the content of the site, but also its structure, navigability, organization, etc. Knowledge about the cognitive ability of the audience member allows health message designers to develop messages that match the cognitive level of the receiver, and respond to specific audience needs. Developers of health-related Web materials need to take into account the cognitive ability of the receiver and incorporate multiple communication channels such as graphics, photo, animations, audio and video in addition to text-based messages (Bernhardt and Cameron 2003). An increasing body of work on health information literacy focuses on the cognitive processing capabilities of the target audience in developing online health information resources. Also, knowledge about the cognitive processing capacity of the target audience would pave the way for developing effective training programs for consumers.

13.2.3   Selective Processing Theories

In line with a dual-process approach is the notion that individuals orient their attention to specific stimuli in their environment, selecting and processing information that is consistent with existing attitudes and beliefs, and avoiding information that is discrepant with their existing dispositions (Atkin, 1985; Zillman and Bryant 1985). Such "biased processing" is explained in the ELM as occurring when individuals have a certain preexisting attitude structure and/or when certain variables motivate such processing (see Petty and Cacioppo 1986, Chap. 5). Selective processing of media messages plays out in the context of selective exposure, interpretation, and memory (Oliver 2002). Selective exposure theory points out that consumers select media messages that match their existing attitudes and beliefs based on the notion that individuals seek consistency in their cognitions (Oliver 2002; Webster and Wakshlag 1985). Selective exposure effects in the area of violent television material (Atkin 1973, 1985; Atkin et al. 1979) indicate that individual aggressiveness is associated with the viewership of violent television programming (McIntyre and Teevan 1972; Robinson and Bachman 1972).

Selective exposure effects documenting the link between a particular predisposition and the exposure to media content that matches the disposition are also observed in the area of prosocial behavior, political, and moral values (Atkin 1973, 1985). Selective exposure theorists argue that consumer motivation drives the use of media outlets. For instance, Thorson (1990) identified motivation, ability, prior learning and emotion as antecedents to consumer processing of advertisements.

Selective perception theory suggests that readers and viewers ascribe meanings to and judgments of media messages that are consistent with their existing values and beliefs. Vidmar and Rokeach (1974) demonstrated that highly prejudiced individuals who watched *All in the Family* were likely to interpret the program as sympathetic to the bigoted main character whereas low-prejudiced individuals tended to interpret the program as sympathetic to the politically liberal main character. In the realm of political attitudes, similar results have been observed, with individuals being more likely to perceive their own candidates more favorably than the opponents (Bothwell and Brigham 1983). In addition to influencing message perception, pre-existing beliefs and attitudes also influence what is remembered (Oliver 2002). For instance, Eagly and Chaiken (1993) review findings that show existing beliefs and cognitions influence memory by shaping attention and elaboration at the time of encoding and by affecting retrieval and reconstruction of information subsequent to exposure.

In the context of health information processing, Dutta-Bergman (2004a, b) demonstrated that health-active individuals that are highly engaged in health-related issues are more likely to seek out health specialized media content as compared to the individuals who are not involved in issues of health. Furthermore, healthcare consumers selectively orient their attention to certain Websites that match their dispositional orientation. This is particularly the case with the Internet where its searchability allows the consumer to selectively choose those Websites that match his or her information needs. The interactivity of the Internet facilitates selective processing of information insofar as the visit to a particular site by an Internet user is dependent upon the underlying motivation of the user in the information content of the site.

Theory of Channel Complementarity

Drawing its conceptual foundation from selective exposure, uses and gratifications, and dual process theories, the theory of channel complementarity (Dutta-Bergman 2004e, g; Stempel et al. 2000) suggests that channel types that offer similar functions for the consumer exist in complementary relationships, such that the usage of one channel type is reinforced by the usage of another channel type. Supporting complementary patterns in channel usage, Stempel et al. (2000) observed that Internet users were also more likely to be newspaper readers and radio news listeners. Similarly, LaRose and Atkin (1992) observed that the use of local audiotext information services was complementary with the use of similar information technologies such as videotexts, ATMs, 800 numbers, and telephone answering services that shared the function of providing information on demand to the user.

Arguing that audience members actively participate in the channels they seek out, the theory of channel complementarity argues that channels that perform similar functions are likely to demonstrate complementarity among each other because of high consumer involvement in the content area (Dutta-Bergman 2004e; Rice 1993). In other words, the individual who feels the functional need to consume a specific channel in a certain content area is also likely to consume other, even new, channels that perform the same function in the content domain. For instance, the health-motivated consumer who is intrinsically interested in issues of health is not only likely to read health magazines such as *Prevention* and *Health*, but is also likely to watch health television, and surf health-related Websites to gather health information. In this case, the enduring consumer interest in health prompts the use of multiple media types (magazines, television, Internet) in the specific content domain of health. A recent study on the relationship among health information channels (Dutta-Bergman 2004e) found that use of the Internet for science and health information was congruent with the use of traditional media for science and health information. In addition to the role of motivation, media theories also suggest that the perceived ability to seek out and process information also plays a critical role in the consumption of media types. Social cognitive theory presents the role of self efficacy in this context.

Social Cognitive Theory

Social cognitive theory suggests that environmental, dispositional and behavioral factors operate as interacting determinants that shape each other bi-directionally, and highlights the role of self efficacy as a predictor of media consumption patterns of consumers (Bandura 2002). Self-efficacy is the amount of confidence individuals have in their ability to perform the health behavior and positively predicts the adoption of the behavior by the consumer (Bandura 1977, 1997). It is the perceived ability to exert personal control in the realm of the specific behavior under question. Self-efficacy influences the likelihood of health information seeking and systematic health informatixon processing by impacting the consumer's perception about his or her capability to seek out health information. Rimal (2001) combined perceived risk and self-efficacy to suggest a segmentation strategy for examining the differential motivations to seek information about heart disease. He observed that self-efficacy is indeed a critical factor in determining health information seeking strategies.

13.3   Integrative Model of Online Health Information Seeking

The brief review of the major information seeking and media use theories presented in the earlier section bring to surface two distinct constructs that influence online health information seeking. These constructs are (a) motivation and (b) ability. Figure 13.1 presents an integrative model of health information seeking based on a summary of the key findings of the published literature reviewed in this chapter.

Fig. 13.1 Integrative model of online health information seeking

According to this model, both motivation and ability are key contributors to online health information seeking.

Personality and situation-specific factors lead to the motivation to process health-related information on the Internet. This motivation combined with consumer efficacy shape the health uses of the medium. For instance, high perceived severity and perceived susceptibility toward a health risk are likely to trigger motivation to process health-related information (Witte 1992). Individuals who perceive themselves at great risk of HIV/AIDS are more likely to seek out and process HIV/AIDS-related information as compared to individuals who perceive themselves to be at lower risks of contracting HIV/AIDS. In addition, health orientation – an indicator of intrinsic consumer interest in issues of health – contributes to the overall motivation to search for health information. Therefore, health-oriented consumers are more likely to seek out health information on the Internet compared to their less health-oriented counterparts. Beyond the role of situational and dispositional factors, motivation is also shaped by demographic variables. For instance, Johnson and Meischke (1993) and Rice (2001) have both noted that people with lower socioeconomic status (SES) tend to report lower levels of health orientation; they are less motivated to seek out health information than those of higher SES status because of the limited learning opportunities that are available in resource-deprived contexts and because of the structurally situated absence of health capacities in underserved communities. Adding credence to these claims, Dutta-Bergman (2004f) demonstrated that motivation in health-related issues increases with education and income.

In addition to the motivation for health information seeking, the consumer needs to have access to the Internet and the ability to use this access for health information processing. The concept of efficacy taps into the consumer's belief in his or her ability to engage in a behavior. Greater the efficacy, stronger the likelihood of health information seeking under felt motivation. Efficacy is shaped by the dispositional orientation of the consumer, his or her experience with the medium

(Internet), and his or her demographic characteristics. Of particular relevance are the demographic correlates of access and efficacy, given the technology-related gaps in the population. The combination of motivation and efficacy dictates the use of the Internet for health-related purposes.

In sum, the integrative model of online health information seeking suggests that the motivation and ability to seek out health information mediate the relationship between antecedents (such as demographics, Internet use history, situation and personality) and online health information seeking. The various theories presented in the previous section reflect the idea that consumers differ in their motivation to search for health information. Furthermore, both the dual process framework and social cognitive theory underscore the role of efficacy, suggesting that there exists within-population difference in the ability of consumers to seek out, locate, and process online health information. The specific constructs of motivation and ability in the context of health information seeking are health information orientation and health information efficacy.

13.3.1 Health Information Orientation

Health information orientation reflects the underlying motivation the consumer feels in health-related topics, and therefore, taps into the degree of consumer interest in health information. The high health information oriented individual actively monitors his or her environment scanning for relevant health information to ensure that he or she is not at risk of disease or illness as compared to the low health information oriented individual who is less likely to participate in health information seeking. In other words, whereas the degree of involvement in health-related topics is fairly high in the high health information oriented segment, the level of involvement in health-related topics is low in the low health information oriented segment. Therefore, it may be argued that health information orientation would lead to the active search for health-related information, manifesting the intrinsic consumer interest in health topics. In addition, it may be argued that the health information oriented individual is more likely to learn health information from particular channels than their low health information oriented counterparts. The knowledge about the link between health information orientation and health information seeking is essential to the design, implementation, and evaluation of preventive health interventions. Also, examination of the relationship between health information orientation and health information seeking provides a theoretical framework for understanding the communication system surrounding high and low health information oriented individuals. By investigating the role of motivation in the context of health information seeking, the integrative model of health information seeking provides an explanatory pathway for articulating the process underlying the use of the Internet for purposes of health information seeking.

Uses and gratifications, selective processing theories, and the theory of channel complementarity point out that a high level of involvement in a certain issue generates issue-specific information seeking behavior. Take for instance, the case of political information processing. An individual highly interested in political issues is likely to seek out political information through a variety of communication channels such as political sections of newspapers, television news, and political Websites. Similarly, in the realm of health information seeking, it may be expected that the health information oriented individual will seek out information related to health issues from a variety of communication channels including the Internet. The intrinsic motivation to engage in health producing behaviors triggers the active search for health information through a variety of channels, including the Internet. Health information obtained from communication channels equips the health information oriented consumer with knowledge about health promoting behaviors and opportunities for enhancing health. It also reinforces existing health behaviors that are practiced by the health information oriented consumer.

The motivation to seek out and process health information is also likely to be related with information processing strategies adopted by consumers and the cues attended to by highly involved consumers as compared to those consumers who have low levels of involvement in health-related topics. Dual process theories point out that motivation triggers an individual's intrinsic interest in a particular issue or topic, leading to active engagement in cognitions, attitudes, and behaviors related to the specific issue/topic (Petty and Cacioppo 1986). In other words, motivation activates consumer engagement in information processing, decision making, and adoption of behavioral choices based on the consideration of arguments presented in messages. High levels of motivation increases the attention paid by the individual to relevant information and the comprehension of such material. It also increases the active information search for issue-based information. Therefore, a health motivated consumer actively participates in health-related issues and actively searches out relevant health information (Dutta-Bergman 2004a; MacInnis et al. 1991; Moorman and Matulich 1993; Park and Mittal 1985).

13.3.2 Health Information Efficacy

The concept of health information efficacy is built on the existing research on self-efficacy which refers to the degree of confidence individuals have in their ability to perform a health behavior and positively predicts the adoption of the preventive behavior (Bandura 2002). It is the perceived ability to exert personal control. Thus, self-efficacy should influence the likelihood of health information seeking and health information processing. Health information efficacy refers to the intrinsic consumer belief in his or her ability to search for and process health information.

In addition to the motivation for health information seeking, the consumer needs to have access to the Internet and the ability to use the Internet for health information processing. The concept of efficacy taps into the consumer's belief in his or her ability to engage in a behavior, in this case, seeking health information. Greater the efficacy, stronger the likelihood of health information seeking under states of felt motivation. Efficacy is shaped by the dispositional orientation of the consumer, his or her experience with the medium (Internet), and his or her demographic characteristics. Of particular relevance are the demographic correlates of access and efficacy, given the technology-related gaps in the population. Consumer uses of the Internet for healthcare purposes influence a variety of outcomes such as accessibility of care, quality of care, patient satisfaction, physician-patient relationship, and the effectiveness of healthcare policy. The next sections explicate one such outcome, individual health, and how our model can help to explain within population differences found in the extant literature.

13.4   Online Health Information Seeking and Health Outcomes

The literature on online health information seeking suggests that searching for health information on the Internet is correlated with a variety of outcomes that are beneficial to individual health (Murero and Rice 2006). Researchers studying the role of the Internet in the context of health suggest that searching for health information on the Internet equips consumers with the ability to engage in preventive behaviors, empowers them in the context of their ability to navigate physician-patient relationships, empowers active healthcare consumer participation in the realm of policies that impede health outcomes, and fosters community platforms for social change by presenting possible communicative spaces for engaging the health active segment of the population.

13.4.1   Online Health Information Seeking and Health Disparities

The integrative health information seeking model also offers a theoretical framework for understanding population-level healthcare disparities by suggesting mediating mechanisms through health information orientation and health information efficacy that influence online health information seeking. The motivation and perceived capacity to navigate health information tends to be lower among the marginalized communities within social systems, thus reinforcing the existing disparities within these social systems (Dutta-Bergman 2006). Health information seeking is a critical component in modern day consumer decision making processes and closely tied with a variety of health outcomes (Cline and Haynes 2001; Dutta-Bergman 2006); therefore, the extent to which certain segments of the population seek out health information significantly affects the health outcomes of these segments. In examining issues of inequity in online health information seeking, it is critical to pay attention to issues of access, patterns of usage, and evaluations of quality of online health information. We will argue that each of these components is significantly interrelated with health information orientation and health information efficacy within the population.

13.4.2 Access and Equity

The differential patterns of healthcare access are a growing area of concern for policy members, practitioners and academics working in the healthcare sector. Increasingly, scholarly articles continue to document the disparities in access to basic healthcare such that healthcare is accessible for some population segments; such care and its benefits are typically inaccessible to the marginalized segments of society (Dutta-Bergman 2004f). Healthcare access typically reflects sociodemographic differentials such that higher SES groups have significantly greater access to healthcare infrastructures as compared to lower SES groups. These patterns of inaccessibility to healthcare services are also replicated on the Web, with minimal access to healthcare structures correlated with minimal access to health information infrastructures such as health Websites (Dutta-Bergman 2006). People with preventable health problems and without insurance coverage are least likely to have access to the necessary communication technologies that would serve as repositories of health information (Eng et al. 1998). Digital divide studies attest to the significant differences between the higher and lower SES groups in the realm of access to the Internet, with the lower SES groups facing a variety of barriers such as cost, location, illiteracy, physical ability and capacity (Rice 2001). The differential demographic distribution of both health information orientation and health information efficacy between high and low SES groups further suggests differential patterns of access to health information resources on the Web.

The research on knowledge gap documents that public information campaigns typically improve overall outcome levels, and simultaneously increase the gaps between the higher and lower socioeconomic status (SES) groups of society (Viswanath and Finnegan 1995). Health information systems on the Internet are likely to contribute to such gaps. Motivation serves an important role as a mediating variable because higher SES groups are typically more health information oriented as compared to lower SES groups (Dutta-Bergman 2004d, f; Johnson and Meischke 1993). As a result, higher SES groups are more likely to seek out health information resources on the Internet, systematically process information from such resources, and adopt healthy behaviors as compared to lower SES groups (Dutta-Bergman 2004d). This suggests the need for public and governmental efforts that are specifically targeted at reducing the gaps between the health "haves" and "have nots" in society by creating sustainable technological resources for health information access and by developing initiatives for increasing awareness of such resources (Freimuth et al. 1989). Such efforts, however, need to highlight both issues of access and motivation. Eng et al. (1998) recommend steps such as providing public and residential access, increasing health and technology literacy, and integrating universal access into health planning. Technology such as multimedia kiosks, information portals, and Internet-equipped computers need to be made available in publicly accessible spaces. One such attempt in bridging the digital divide is the creation of Community Technology Centers (CTCs) that are public access computer facilities located in low income neighborhoods (Breeden et al. 1998). Furthermore, sustainable efforts need to be put into place for developing health information efficacy among the lower SES segments of the population through the development of sustainable communication skills for seeking out and processing health information.

Schools and worksites in lower SES sectors need to specifically incorporate health-oriented programs that seek to build health information orientation and health information efficacy in the underprivileged sectors of society. Such programs also need to include components of self and response efficacy to increase the perceived ability of the underprivileged segments in using the Internet for healthcare purposes. Targeted workshops and training sessions are needed that teach technology literacy skills related to the effective and efficient use of the Internet, and thus build health information efficacy in the population. Bernhardt and Cameron (2003) posit that computer literacy is a new requisite for health literacy because "people who lack adequate computer literacy are likely to have profound barriers in their ability to access information" (p. 585). For instance, Salovey et al. (2002) developed two community technology centers affiliated with two Head Start early childhood education programs in New Haven, Connecticut, one of the three poorest cities in the state of Connecticut. The program trained Head Start staff members to become technology coaches, and offered training programs for Head Start parents as well as other individuals in the neighborhood who desired training. Furthermore, health Websites may be deployed for delivering tailored health prevention campaigns that address the needs of the at-risk groups, and deliver communication messages that match the stage of change of the consumer (Rimer and Glassman 1998). Such message tailoring might be particularly relevant for the underserved sectors of the population because of the uniqueness of the barriers and the information needs experienced in such segments.

13.4.3   Patterns of Usage

Not only do consumers within the population differ in their access to communication infrastructures, but they also vary in their patterns of usage of the Internet for various functions (Dutta-Bergman 2004d). In fact, recent scholarship on the digital divide questions the simplistic notion of the digital divide being conceptualized in terms of basic access or inaccess, and calls for further exploration of the ways in which various segments of the population use the Internet (see Dutta et al. in press for a review). In other words, we ought to look beyond ownership of computer and Internet connection to explore the ways in which computer access is put to use.

Patterns of usage tap into the functions to which the Internet is put, and the ways in which it is used and navigated by consumers. Published scholarship documents critical disparities within the population in terms of patterns of usage among various consumer segments. For instance, in the area of health information seeking, individuals from the lower SES groups are significantly less health information oriented compared to their higher SES counterparts (Dutta-Bergman 2004c). The motivation to search for health information is higher among more highly educated consumers compared to consumers with lower levels of education. Individuals with lower levels of education experience greater number of barriers in using the Internet for health purposes as compared to individuals with higher levels of education. In other words, health information efficacy is also lower among lower SES groups as compared to higher SES groups.

Similarly, racial divides are significantly evident in patterns of health information usage, with African Americans being significantly less health information oriented compared to Caucasians and Asian Americans. Internet health information seeking disparities mirror the broader patterns of disparities in the population. This suggests the relevance of investing in capacity building in underserved communities that have low levels of health information orientation and health information efficacy (Dutta-Bergman 2006).

In addition to investing in infrastructures in such communities, health communicators and policy makers ought to focus on creating educational resources that foster health information orientation and health information efficacy in the communities. Specific programs addressing the barriers faced in the lower SES groups need to be put into place; also efforts need to be targeted toward building efficacy through skills training. For instance, educational programs seeking to provide training in searching, evaluating, and deciphering health information would help address some of the barriers related to the extent of overload that lower SES groups face. Similarly, design opportunities need to be created for the developers of online health information to respond to the communities that are in most need for health information.

13.4.4 Quality

The rapid growth in the use of Websites for consumer health decision-making has led to increasing concerns in the expert community about the quality of health information retrieved by patients (Dutta-Bergman 2003a, b, c; Eysenbach 2000; Rice 2001). This concern is built upon the notion that anyone can post health information on the Internet, and in the absence of a qualified gatekeeper, there really is no way to monitor the quality of what gets published. In this context, the onus of evaluating online health information and deciphering the quality of the information posted on a certain Website shifts onto the consumer. Researchers studying quality suggest that the quality of health information retrieved on the Web influences the quality, cost, and effectiveness of care received by the patient (Dutta-Bergman 2006).

Published criteria in the area of Internet use for healthcare include source credibility, accuracy, completeness, relevance, and applicability (Dutta-Bergman 2006). Applying the integrative model of health information seeking to our understanding of quality suggests that the ways in which quality of a health Website would be evaluated depends upon the motivation and ability of the consumer using the Website. From the perspective of the underlying motivation to search for health information, it may be articulated that highly health information oriented consumers will be more likely to systematic process quality criteria when evaluating a Website. In other words, the evaluation of quality is a heterogeneous process that varies with the information seeking functions of the consumer. Whereas certain quality criteria might be particularly relevant for consumer decision making in the domain of certain Internet functions, other quality criteria become critically relevant when the consumer uses the Internet for other functions. For instance, the consumer using the Internet for purchasing medicines might be more likely to evaluate the privacy policy of the Website as compared to the consumer who is simply surfing the Web for health information.

Similarly, health information efficacy also influences the quality criteria used by the consumer. Consumers who have high levels of health information efficacy are likely to pay attention to website elements that require considerable cognitive effort. Such cues might include elements such as the evaluation of the completeness and accuracy of the information on the Website. On the other hand, individuals who have low levels of health information efficacy are perhaps more likely to apply heuristic quality criteria such as Website design, the presence of visuals on the Website, and Website organization in evaluating the Website. In essence, the integrative model of health information seeking informs the current literature on health information quality by suggesting that the evaluation of quality is predicated upon health information orientation and health information efficacy of the consumer, and is hence, a heterogeneous process. Given the population-based disparities in the distribution of health information orientation and health information efficacy among the higher SES segments of the population, there is greater need of focused efforts of developing initiatives for training the low health oriented segments in the evaluation of quality of health information in patient decision-making. Sustainable educational programs need to be created that work with patients on developing quality indicators for evaluating health Websites and making healthcare decisions.

13.5 Conclusion

Based on a review of the existing literature on health information processing and media uses this chapter proposed an integrative model of online health information seeking that builds on a functional approach to health information seeking on the Web. According to this functional approach, the Internet serves a wide range of functions and meets various information processing needs of various segments of the population. The integrative model of health information seeking suggests that health information orientation and health information efficacy are two key components that determine the amount and type of health information seeking performed on the Internet. Furthermore, the differential distribution of health information orientation and health information efficacy within the population connects the individual-level approach to online health information seeking with the literature on healthcare disparities, suggesting that health information seeking on the Internet mirror broader healthcare disparities in the population, thus further reiterating these disparities. More specifically, disparities in health information seeking on the Internet are observed in the areas of access, usage patterns, and the quality criteria applied to evaluate health Websites. Finally, the chapter suggests the relevance of developing communication infrastructures, health literacy, information literacy and Internet literacy in the marginalized sectors of social systems in order to create points of accessible and sustainable health information on the Internet targeted toward underserved communities.

References

Atkin C (1973) Instrumental utilities and information seeking. In: Clarke P (ed) New models for mass communication research. Sage, Beverly Hills, CA, pp 205–242

Atkin C, Greenberg B, Korzenny F, & McDermott S (1979) Selective exposure to televised violence. Journal of Broadcasting, 23: 5–13

Atkin C (1985) Informational utility and selective exposure. In: Zillman D, Bryant J (eds) Selective exposure to communication. Lawrence Erlbaum Associates, Hillsdale, NJ, pp 63–91

Atkin D (1993) Adoption of cable amidst a multimedia environment. Telematics and Informatics 10: 51–58

Ball-Rokeach SJ, DeFleur ML (1976) A dependency model or mass-media effects. Communication Research 3: 3–21

Bandura A (1977). Social Learning Theory. New York: General Learning Press; Bandura A (1997). Self-efficacy: The exercise of control. New York: W.H. Freeman.

Bandura A (2002) Social cognitive theory of mass communication. In: Bryant J, Zillman D (eds) Media effects: advances in theory and research. Lawrence Erlbaum Associates, Hillsdale, NJ, pp 121–154

Bernhardt JM, Cameron KA (2003). Accessing, understanding, and applying health communication messages: the challenge of health literacy. In: Thompson TL, Dorsey AM, Miller KI, Parrott R (eds) Handbook of health communication Lawrence Erlbaum Associates, Mahwah, NJ, pp 583–605

Bernhardt JM, Cameron KA (2003). Television violence and deviant behavior. In G.A. Comstock & E.A. RUbinstein (Eds.) Television and social behavior, vol. 3, Television and adolescent aggressiveness. Washington, DC: United States Government Printing Office

Bothwell RK, Brigham JC (1983) Selective evaluation and recall during the 1980 Reagan–Carter debate. Journal of Applied Social Psychology 5: 427–442

Breeden L, Cisler S, Guilfoy V, Roberts M, Stone, A (1998) Computer and communications use in low-income communities: models for the neighborhood transformation and family development initiative. Annie E. Casey Foundation, Baltimore, MD

Carlsson M (2000) Cancer patients seeking information from sources outside the healthcare system. Supportive Care in Cancer: Official Journal of the Multinational Association of Supportive Care in Cancer 8: 453–457

Chaiken S (1980) Heuristic versus systematic information processing and the use of source versus message cues in persuasion. Journal of Personality and Social Psychology 39: 752–766

Cline RJ, Hayes KM (2001) Consumer health information seeking on the Internet: The state of the art. Health Education Research 16: 671–692

DeFleur ML, Ball-Rokeach S (1989) Theories of mass communication (5th ed). Longman, New York

Dutta-Bergman M (2003a) Health communication on the web: the roles of web use motivation and information completeness. Communication Monographs 70: 264–274

Dutta-Bergman M (2003b) Trusted online sources of health information: differences in demographics, health beliefs, and health-information orientation. Journal of Medical Internet Research 5, e21. Retrieved 2 June 2004 from http://www.jmir.org/2003/3/e21/index.htm

Dutta-Bergman M (2003c) Demographic and psychographic antecedents of community participation: applying a social marketing model. Social Marketing Quarterly 9: 17–31

Dutta-Bergman M (2003d) The linear interaction model of personality effects in health communication. Health Communication 15: 101–115

Dutta-Bergman M (2004a) Developing a profile of consumer intention to seek out health information beyond the doctor. Health Marketing Quarterly 21: 91–112

Dutta-Bergman M (2004b) Primary sources of health information: comparison in the domain of health attitudes, health cognitions, and health behaviors. Health Communication 16: 273–288

Dutta-Bergman M (2004c) The impact of completeness and web use motivation on the credibility of e-health information. Journal of Communication 54: 253–269

Dutta-Bergman M (2004d) Health attitudes, health cognitions and health behaviors among Internet health information seekers: Population-based survey. Journal of Medical Internet Research 6: 15. Retrieved 2 June 2004, from http://www.jmir.org/2004/2/e15/index.htm

Dutta-Bergman M (2004e) Complementarity in consumption of news types across traditional and new media. Journal of Broadcasting and Electronic Media 48: 41–60

Dutta-Bergman M (2004f) A descriptive narrative of healthy eating: a social marketing approach using psychographics. Health Marketing Quarterly 20: 81–101

Dutta-Bergman M (2004g) Idiocentrism, involvement, and health appeals: a social psychological framework. Southern Communication Journal 70: 408–417

Dutta-Bergman M (2005) Psychographic profiling of fruit and vegetable consumption: the role of health orientation. Social Marketing Quarterly 11: 1–17

Dutta-Bergman M (2006) Media use theory and Internet use for health care. In: Murero M, Rice E (eds) The Internet and health care: theory, research, and practice. Lawrence Erlbaum, Mahwah, NJ, pp 83–103

Dutta MJ, Bodie GD, Basu A (in press) Health disparity and the racial divide among the nation's youth: Internet as a site for change? In: Everett A (ed) The MacArthur Foundation series on digital media and learning: race and ethnicity

Eagly A, Chaiken S (1993) The psychology of attitudes. Harcourt Brace Jovanovich, Fort Worth, TX

Eng TR, Maxfield A, Gustafson, D (1998) Access to health information and support: a public highway or private road? Journal of the American Medical Association 280: 1371–1375

Eysenbach G (2000) Consumer health informatics. British Medical Journal 24: 1713–1716

Ferguson DA (1992) Channel repertoire in the presence of remote control devices, VCRs, and cable television. Journal of Broadcasting and Electronic Media 36: 83–91

Fox S, Fallows D (2003) Internet health resources. Pew Internet and American Life Project, Washington, DC. Retrieved 18 December 2004, from http://www.pewInternet.org/pdfs/PIP_Health_Report_July_2003.pdf

Freimuth BS, Stein JA, Kean TJ (1989) Searching for health information: the cancer information service model. University of Pennsylvania Press, Philadelphia, PA

Johnson JD, Meischke H (1993) A comprehensive model of cancer-related information seeking applied to magazines. Human Communication Research 19: 343–367

Katz E, Blumler JG, Gurevitch M (1974) Utilization of mass communication by the individual. In: Blumler JG, Katz E (eds) The uses of mass communications: current perspectives on gratifications research. Sage, Beverly Hills, CA, pp 19–32

LaRose R, Atkin D (1992) Audiotext and the reinvention of the telephone as a mass medium. Journalism Quarterly 69: 413–421

Lin CA (1992) The functions of the VCR in the home leisure environment. Journal of Broadcasting and Electronic Media 36: 345–351

Lin CA, Jeffres LW (1998) Factors influencing the adoption of multimedia cable technology. Journalism and Mass Communication Quarterly 75: 341–352

MacInnis DJ, Moorman C, Jaworski B (1991) Enhancing and measuring consumers' motivation, opportunity, and ability to process brand information from ads. Journal of Marketing 55: 32–53

McIntyre JJ, & Teevan JJ (1972) Television violence and deviant behavior. In GA Comstock & EA Rubenstein (eds), Televison and Social behavior. vol. 3: Television and adolescent aggressiveness (pp. 383–435). Washington, DC: U.S. Government Printing Office

Mittman R, Cain M (2001) The future of the Internet in healthcare: a five-year forecast. In: Rice RE, Katz J (eds) The Internet and health communication. Sage Publications, Thousand Oaks, CA, pp 47–73

Moorman C, Matulich E (1993) A model of consumers' preventive health behaviors: the role of health motivation and health ability. Journal of Consumer Research 20: 208–228

Murero M, Rice RE (2006) The Internet and health care: theory, research, and practice. Lawrence Erlbaum, Mahwah, NJ

Napoli P (2001) Consumer use of medical information from electronic and paper media: a literature review. Rice RE, Katz JE (eds) The Internet and health communication: experiences and expectations. Sage Publications, Thousand Oaks, CA, pp 79–98

Navarro FH, Wilkins ST (2001) A new perspective on consumer health web use: valuegraphic profiles of health information seekers. Managed Care Quarterly 9: 35–43

Oliver MB (2002) Individual differences in media effects. In: Bryant J, Zillman D (eds) Media effects: advances in theory and research. Lawrence Erlbaum, Mahwah, NJ, pp 507–524

Park CW, Mittal B (1985) A theory of involvement in consumer behavior: problems and issues. In: Sheth J (ed) Research in consumer behavior. JAI, Greenwich, CT, pp 201–231

Perse E, Dunn D (1998) The utility of home computers and media use: implications of multimedia and connectivity. Journal of Broadcasting and Electronic Media 42: 435–456

Petty RE, Cacioppo JT (1986) Communication and persuasion: central and peripheral routes to attitude change. Springer-Verlag, New York

Petty RE, Wegener DT (1999) The elaboration likelihood model: current status and controversies. In: Chaiken S, Trope Y (eds) Dual-process theories in social psychology. Guilford, New York, pp 41–72

Rice RE (1993) Media appropriateness: using social presence theory to compare traditional and new organizational media. Human Communication Research 19: 451–484

Rice R (2001) The Internet and health communication: a framework of experiences. In: Rice RE, Katz J (eds) The Internet and health communication. Sage Publications, Thousand Oaks, CA, pp 5–46

Rimal R (2001) Perceived risk and self-efficacy as motivators: understanding individuals' long-term use of health information. Journal of Communication 51: 633–654

Rimer BK, Glassman B (1998) Tailoring communication for primary care settings. Methods of Information in Medicine 37: 1610–1611

Robinson JP & Bachman JG (1972). Television viewing habits and aggression. In GA Comstock & EA Rubinstein (eds) Television and social behavior, vol. 3, Television and adolescent aggressiveness. Washington, DC: United States Government Printing Office

Robinson, J.P. & Bachman, J.G. (1972). Television viewing habits and aggression. In G.A. Comstock & Rubinstein (Eds.) Television and social behavior, vol. 3, Television and adolescent aggressiveness. Washington, DC: United States Government Printing Office

Rubin A (1994) Media uses and effects: a uses and gratifications perspective. In: Bryant J, Zillman D (eds) Media effects: advances in theory and research. Lawrence Erlbaum, Mahwah, NJ, pp 417–436

Rubin A (2002) The uses and gratifications perspective of media effects. In: Bryant J, Zillman D (eds) Media effects: advances in theory and research. Lawrence Erlbaum, Mahwah, NJ, pp 525–548

Salovey P, Mowad L, Pizarro J, Edlund D, Moret M (2002) Developing computer proficiency among head start parents: an in-progress case study of a New England CIS digital divide project. Electronic Journal of Communication 11: 3. Retrieved 9 October 2002 from http://www.cios.org/getfile/saolvey_v11n3

Spink A, Jansen B (2004) Web search: public searching of the web. Kluwer Academic, Boston, MA

Stempel III G, Hargrove T, Bernt J (2000) Relation of growth of use of the Internet to changes in media use from 1995 to 1999. Journalism and Mass Communication Quarterly 77: 71–79

Thorson E (1990) Consumer processing of advertising. In: Leigh JH, Martin C (eds) Current issues and research in advertising (vol 12). University of Michigan Press: Ann Arbor, MI, pp 197–230

Vidmar N & Rokeach M (1974). Archie Bunker's bigotry: A study in selective perception and exposure. Journal of Communication, 24, 36–47.

Viswanath K, Finnegan JR (1995) The knowledge gap hypothesis: twenty-five years later. In: Burleson B (ed) Communication yearbook (vol 19). Sage Publications, Thousand Oaks, CA, pp 187–227

Webster JG, Wakshlag J (1985) Measuring exposure to television. In: Zillmann D, Bryant J (eds) Selective exposure to communication. Lawrence Erlbaum Associates, Hillsdale, NJ, pp 35–62

Witte K (1992) Putting the fear back into fear appeals: the extended parallel process model. Communication Monographs 59: 329–349

Zillman D, Bryant J (1985) Selective exposure to communication. Lawrence Erlbaum Associates, Hillsdale, NJ

14
Search Engines and Expertise about Global Issues: Well-defined Landscape or Undomesticated Wilderness?

J. Fry, S. Virkar, and R. Schroeder

Summary This chapter investigates the 'winner-takes-all' hypothesis in relation to how academic researchers access online sources and resources. Some have argued that the Web provides access to a wider range of sources of information than offline resources. Others, such as Hindman et al. (2003), have shown that access to online resources is highly concentrated, particularly because of how Internet search engines are designed. With researchers increasingly using the Web and Internet search engines to disseminate and locate information and expertise, the question of whether the use of online resources enhances or diminishes the range of available sources of expertise is bound to become more pressing. To address this question four globally relevant knowledge domains were investigated using large-scale link analysis and a series of semi-structured interviews with UK-based academic researchers.

We found there to be no uniform 'winner-takes-all' effect in the use of online resources. Instead, there were different types of information gatekeepers for the four domains we examined and for the types of resources and sources that are sought. Particular characteristics of a knowledge domain's information environment appear to determine whether Google and other Internet search engines function as a *facilitator* in accessing expertise or as an *influential gatekeeper*.

14.1 Introduction

It is widely believed that the rapid diffusion of the Internet and the Web has transformed knowledge and expertise by widening access and making information available globally. Whilst there has been an exponential increase in the production and use of networked digital resources, little is known about the reach and impact of this form of distributed knowledge. Some have argued that information technology could have a 'democratizing' impact on knowledge and information (Dahl 1989), others have argued the opposite: that in the online world these resources have in fact become concentrated in a 'winner-takes-all' effect (Hindman et al. 2003), due in part to the link-based indexing algorithms of search engines and how such tools are embedded in information seeking practices. There is thus a need to

A. Spink and M. Zimmer (eds.), *Web Search, Springer Series in Information Science and Knowledge Management 14.*
© Springer-Verlag Berlin Heidelberg 2008

determine the extent to which the Internet is reshaping access to knowledge and resources world-wide (Dutton et al. 2003), particularly in science where the Internet is fast becoming the primary medium for communication and collaboration between scholars.

In this chapter, we address the issue of 'winner-takes-all' in relation to the use of online resources within four research domains: Climate Change, Internet and Society, HIV/AIDS, and Terrorism. Together these domains represent a broad mix of urgent global issues addressed by both natural and social sciences. As these topics are also arguably highly current and relevant on an international level, they provide a good case for examining whether access to scientific expertise is being reconfigured.

A popular approach for studying the dynamics of knowledge domains and the online presence of actors in those domains is Webmetric analysis (Park and Thelwall 2005). Hyperlink studies in social science research, generally referred to as Webmetric analysis, draws on techniques and frameworks from the information science field of bibliometrics. To this end, our research synthesised Webmetric data (detailed results of the Webmetric analysis are reported in Schroeder et al. 2005) with data gathered from an interview series with UK-based academic researchers. The following chapter focuses on the analysis of the interview data and the extent to which the "Google representation" of the information environment of each domain overlapped with respondents' mental models of the core institutions, people and resources in their domain. The aim of the interviews was to obtain a well-rounded understanding of how researchers use online resources, including how they combine online and offline sources of information, their use of search engines, and what kinds of sites they use most frequently.

14.2 Previous Research on How Expertise is Accessed on the Web

14.2.1 Studying the Scholarly Web

With the advent of the Internet and the Web, new online resources have become available and electronic media are becoming increasingly important channels for social interaction. In previous research, conflicting views have been argued about whether the shift to online resources democratizes or concentrates access.

A prominent argument that 'winners-take-all has been made by Barabási (2003), who has argued that power law distributions apply to online networks of hyperlinks. This concept is known in bibliometrics and the sociology of science as the 'Matthew effect' ('unto every that hath, shall be given') or cumulative advantage (Merton 1988). Pennock et al. (2002) have refined this idea by suggesting that while the winner-takes-all hypothesis may apply to the Web as a whole, the balance of competition varied by domain-specific types of pages and when distributions of links are compared for the same type of pages, they exhibit a more uniform pattern of connectivity. For example, university homepages will exhibit a more uniform pattern of connectivity to other university homepages (Thelwall et al. 2005).

The results that Web search engines yield are only partly determined by 'real' links. Ensuring that certain links rank highly among search results has also become commercially competitive, with firms specializing in 'search engine optimization' (Van Couvering 2006). High-ranking search results are valuable because they may draw customers to a site and draw them to advertising links which feature on search engine results pages (so called 'sponsored links'). One might assume that academic knowledge domains are less likely to be influenced by commercial factors affecting search results, however, the four case-study domains varied in their degree of market penetration (Walsh and Bayma 1996) and there was some overlap between commercial and non-commercial producers in their Webspheres. A Websphere being, *"a collection of dynamically defined digital resources spanning multiple Websites deemed relevant or related to a central theme or object"* (Schneider and Foot 2002). For example, pharmaceutical companies were heavily represented in the Websphere of the HIV/AIDS domain, often sponsoring sites that appeared in the top ten results of a Google search. Moreover, not-for-profit research organizations may also be engaged in competition for prominence among search results, such competition may penetrate into how the four domains are represented on the Web by Internet search engines.

14.2.2   What We Know about Online Information Practices

Although this study focuses on how domain factors influence Web searching and access to online resources amongst academic researchers, it is important to contextualise these influences within a wider understanding of the search paths and strategies that non-domain experts develop when trying to locate information and how their online search for information intersects with their offline information practices.

User studies of information seeking have shown that the Web is now a primary source of information for many people, with over 80% of Web searchers using Internet search engines to locate information. This is especially important to take into account as individuals are increasingly turning to the Internet as their primary source of expertise in critical areas of everyday life, such as health (Johnson et al. 2006).

People's attention span is brief when finding information on the Web, with Web researchers spending between 5 and 120 minutes for individual sessions (Jansen and Spink 2006). In their comparison of nine studies of Web search based on Web transaction logs, Jansen and Spink (2006) found that the average search session length is fifteen minutes and that this has remained stable from 1997–2002. Single-term queries counted for between 20–30% of all queries with an increasing trend for shorter queries. General Internet users most frequently search for people, places or things (41.5% in 2002). Most pertinently, the cross-study comparison by Jansen and Spink (2006) confirmed that the viewing of only one results page is increasing, with the percentage of searchers viewing only one results page increasing from 29% in 1997 to 73% in 2002.

There have been a number of studies that have focused specifically on users' experience with the Google Internet search engine. Granka et al. (2004), for example, used eye-tracking to study how users interact with the list of ranked results from Google. Analyzing all behaviour before a user clicks on the first link or exits the list, they found that the time spent viewing the URL abstract on the Google results page was distributed equally between the first and second ranked URLs. Users substantially more often click on the link ranked first. After the second link fixation time drops off significantly, especially after the first 5 or 6 results. This is partly because typically only the first 5 and 6 links are visible without scrolling and once a user starts scrolling then rank becomes less of an influence for attention (Granka et al. 2004).

Adams and Blandford (2005) found that academics and some clinicians preferred to use the Internet rather than specialist digital libraries for accessing information due to the lower barrier to entry in terms of ease of use. The experienced clinicians in Adams and Blandford's (2005) study reported that the Internet was an important tool for accessing authoritative and timely information sources. There was a concern, however, that new members of the domain would not be able to differentiate sufficiently between valid and non-valid sources identified through Internet search engines. In fact, Adams et al. (2005) found that the hierarchical structure of clinical settings meant that senior clinicians often acted as information gatekeepers for junior clinicians.

Johnson et al. (2006) studied of how individuals seek information about inherited cancers identified some common pathways in how people move between online and offline resources. Their findings reveal that of the seven one-step pathways where only one resource was consulted, 78 of respondents (12.1%) consulted the Internet only; of the two-step pathways 79 (12.3%) consulted the Internet then the library, 41 (6.4%) the doctor then the Internet, and 36 (5.6%) consulted the library then the Internet. There were only two common three-step pathways and these were; Internet then library then doctor 51(7.9%) of respondents, and Internet then doctor then library 38 (5.9%).

Naturalistic studies of relevance judgments have shown that relevance is shaped by the content of the user's information environment. This is particularly the case when exploring new domains as in the translation work and boundary crossing of interdisciplinary scholars (Palmer and Neumann 2002), novice domain inhabitants, or non-expert lay people. As the four domains examined here involve several disciplines, and given that people are still uncertain about what extent sources and resources are moving online, it is plausible to assume that Google will play a gatekeeper role depending on the way in which search is used and online resources are structured.

While studies of online search practice have examined query reformulation, multitasking and successive searches (Spink et al. 2001; Wang et al. 2003) they have not studied when, how and why users shift their search to a different source. In other words we know little about users' persistence with, or 'loyalty' to, a particular resource or Web-based search tool. According to the Pew Internet and American Life Survey (2005) Internet users tend to settle quickly on a single search engine and then persist with it, rather than comparing results from different search systems.

The winner-takes-all effect is therefore likely to depend on the type of Internet user, so that while domain experts are inculcated in the significance criteria that should be applied in selecting an information resource or source, non-expert information seekers will have a higher degree of uncertainty (Whitley 2000) in judging relevance, validity, authority and differentiating between various sources. The hierarchical ordering of resources and sources could have winner-takes-all ramifications in how people make sense of information and incorporate it into their decision making.

Though individual practices should not be overlooked, it is also important not to trivialize the influence that structural considerations (Solomon 1999) have in shaping information environments and practices. This is particularly the case when studying how professionals and scientists seek information as aspects of information practice such as relevance, selection of resources, sense making and decision taking will be influenced by what is considered valid, pertinent and timely by the domain community.

14.2.3 Domain Factors

There has been a strong tradition of domain analysis in human information behaviour research. This approach treats domains as discourse communities or communities of practice, rather than focusing on users in a generalized and context independent manner (Hjørland and Albrechtsen 1995). In following this approach, consideration is given to cultural aspects of domains such as knowledge structures, language, patterns of communication and cooperation and the use of information systems (Palmer and Neumann 2002).

Scholars typically rely on a core set of resources in producing knowledge. Palmer and Neumann (2002) describe how scholars extend their intellectual province through information work. They also found that in interdisciplinary domains, there is a need for translation work and boundary crossing across information environments. They argue that the imprecise language used in the humanities and social sciences is especially poor for identifying topic-based conservations across domain boundaries. This leads to what they describe as "excavating", which is the tracing of intellectual paths through sources and resources. Humanities scholars tend to refer to their research approach as detective work and descriptions of their practices show that they do follow leads to great lengths, in terms of both time and space. This practice has two important outcomes: it creates a relatively unique path of information seeking for each project and it brings scholars in contact with diverse information resources and many forms of technology, from the antiquated to the state of the art.

Related to the notion of excavating resources across domain boundaries is the concept of 'scatter': the degree to which relevant material is either concentrated within core disciplinary resources or produced and found across diverse fields and resources (Fry and Talja 2004). For example, in their study of Faculty use of electronic resources Vakkari and Talja (2005) found that in medicine 52% of respondents used publications mainly from their own field, in engineering this was 40%, and in the social sciences only 21% mainly used publications in their own field. The concept of scatter, as identified by Mote (1962), has been linked to interdisciplinary penetration although is not exclusively a symptom of it. Scatter has so far mainly been used in relation to the concentration of journals in a domain. Scholars in low scatter fields are served by a small number of highly specialized journals, whereas in high scatter fields, relevant materials are scattered across several disciplines and published in a large number of different journals (Vakkari and Talja 2005). Scatter of literature across domain information environments also influences the nature of search. For example, in high-scatter multi-disciplinary fields, where concepts are often contested, search strategies are typically developed around particular *conversations* (Tuominen et al. 2003), rather than directed searching (Fry and Talja 2004).

14.3   Approach and Methods

In order to help determine whether the winner-takes-all hypothesis applied to patterns of access to information in the four domains the interview series was used to validate[152] a subset of the Webmetric data. This sub-set comprised the 'Google representation' of each domain e.g. the most prominently indexed institutions, organizations, people and resources. It was derived by identifying the top thirty sites retrieved from searches using the following keywords :

• Climate Change	– 'Climate change'
	– 'Global warming'
	– 'Ozone depletion'
• Internet and Society	– 'Internet and society'
	– 'Internet research'
	– 'Internet Studies'
• HIV/AIDS	– 'HIV/AIDS'
	– 'HIV Infection'
	– 'HIV prevention'
• Terrorism	– 'Terrorism'
	– 'Terrorist organisation'
	– 'Terrorist network'

---

[152] The implications of the time-lag between obtaining the results of the webmetric analysis and their validation through expert interviews must be given some thought. Close to 6 months elapsed between the webmetric research and the bulk of the interviews – a fairly significant duration given that the Web is growing and changing at a rapid place.

Each of the four case-study domains was international in scope, although some had more of a national orientation in terms of resources and audiences than others. They were by and large interdisciplinary in terms of their epistemic structures and had a policy-related orientation in their outcomes. For example, the *climate change* researchers came from environmental science, biodiversity and physics. Their research interests included energy in developing countries, global energy and forecasting. The field has a strong international orientation in terms of its research concerns, institutions, information sources and patterns of dissemination.

The *Internet and Society* researchers constituted an almost trans-disciplinary topic coming from diverse disciplines such as political science, sociology, science and technology studies, public policy, media and cultural studies, and psychology. Research interests included: public identity management; e-Health; e-Learning, and the use of technology in everyday life. This area tended to be less international than Climate Change given that many of the institutions being studied have a particular national role in governance such as identity cards and health provision.

The *HIV/AIDS* domain is less interdisciplinary than the other three domains, possibly due to the greater degree of professional control over the field (Becher and Trowler 2001; Whitley 2000). Researchers came from fields such as quantitative social science and nursing science, with research areas including sexual health and health policy.

Finally, the *Terrorism* researchers came from diverse disciplines such as religious studies, political science and international relations. Their research interests ranged from religious violence to international security. In terms of geographic orientation this domain can be described as 'Global' in scope e.g. that this domain has a global dimension when the research organization is, for example, taking a world-wide approach to the topic, and local when the focus is on a particular set of organizations or similar.

In total twenty researchers were interviewed from universities in the UK, five from each domain, with a wide range of experience in the field and a range of specializations within the topic. Interviewees were asked about their research background, key institutions, groups and people in their research networks, and the variety of online resources they used. Questions also focused on their online search strategies, such as the tools they used for finding information, the keywords they used and what kind of entities they tended to search for e.g. people, groups or institutions. The interviews were recorded, transcribed in full and analysed using the Nvivo software for qualitative data analysis.

14.4 Changing Work Practices

14.4.1 Increasing Use of Online Resources

The interview participants were unanimous in their use of the Internet and Web in finding key information related to their work. They responded that they use the Web *"all the time"*, *"all the time, for everything"*, and they also described it as a *"vital tool"*. There was, nevertheless, great variation in how they used online resources and sources. They used search engines not just to find published material about their topic, but also for locating grey literature, for scoping out a new topic and finding out about the research activities of individuals.

It was interesting to observe that discussions about what kind of information could be gathered about *other* researchers or research groupings in their domains were also reflected in researchers' perceptions about their *own* Web presence. One of the Climate Change researchers, for example, noted the large amount of work required for 'showcasing' his group's research online and that generating visibility by posting on message boards also required effort and constant maintenance. This was also corroborated by two of the Internet and society researchers who agreed that *"it has really become quite a task, a chore that everybody hates"* (IS03) to create and maintain one's Website. Further, the variable amount of information about researchers or research groups also limited the helpfulness of online resources, with some people and groups having much more information available than others. Consistency, in terms of what types of information and material was made available on individual and group Web pages varied by domain. For example, Climate Change researchers in particular commented on such variability, whereas the Internet and Society researchers took it for granted that they could go to personal home pages to download articles.

14.4.2   Decreasing Use of Libraries

With one exception (an Internet and society researcher who said he still uses libraries as he always has done), researchers registered a decline in the use of libraries. This ranged from those who now almost never use libraries:

> I don't use any offline material ... so if I can't get a journal online I don't use it ... I hardly ever use books; I don't have the time now. (IS 03)

To others who simply noted that more material is available online now *"I find myself going less and less to the library ... it has really changed my way of doing research"* (IS 02). Researchers appeared embarrassed to admit that they very rarely go to a physical library anymore.

14.4.3   Combining Online and Offline Resources
in Various Ways

There are a variety of ways in which researchers combined online and offline resources. This varied according to the stage they were at in their search for relevant material as well as according to the currency of available information sources. This variation, however, needs to be put into the context that domains varied in the extent to which all of the relevant material is available online (Törmä and Vakkari 2004).

One of the Internet and Society researchers who was intellectually closer to the computer science, rather than the social science, aspect of the domain said that *'the ACM portal ... contains almost everything in computing'*, so going to individual journals is no longer necessary'. In this case we see that some domains have highly centralized gateways to information. Even in domains where key sources may not be centrally organized under a single online resource researchers still tend to start their search online, "I used to go from offline to online ... and now I go online first." (TM02).

A further point made by one of the Internet and Society researchers is the problem of publication lag in their domain, whereby printed sources come too late to be useful:

> ... nobody really reads the [print] papers and the journals anymore at all. If you get it in a journal, you've waited too late (IS 01).

Despite the importance of the availability of online articles in this researcher's topic area, rather than creating a personal collection of digital sources on his local computer this researcher used Google as a tool for re-finding resources that he uses regularly:

> I have to use the Web for primary and secondary sources because I lose them all! It's quicker to find them again than to store them that's the amazing fact. (IS 01).

There may also be differences in what type of online material is sought depending on the task in hand. For one Internet and Society researcher policy documents needed to simply to be *"tracked down online"*, as a pre-defined source for the project, whereas for another project, it was a case of *"looking online for things to build up material"* in the first place.

The researchers also needed different materials at different times. For example, one of the Terrorist researchers sometimes locates journal articles and books online (secondary materials), and at other times is mainly looking for speeches (primary material). Within the domain of Terrorism research, differences in the type of material sought may be determined by whether the topic is current or historical. For example, legal cases in Terrorism will not be available *"until the draft has been approved and becomes law"*, therefore printed papers and books are necessary. This is also the case for historians of Terrorism, whereas *"for those who are studying current trends of movements...current responses and reactions by government ... the [Internet] is an absolutely vital source"* (TM03).

14.5 Validation of Cybermetric Results

Despite the communitarian view often held of scholarly communities, a large body of research that focuses on the dynamics of scholarly communication and collaboration has found that there is a strong winner-take-all or cumulative advantage effect in science, whereby over time researchers with an initial advantage in a domain obtain even greater advantage in the reputation of their research and control over that domain. The same has arguably happened with regard to the Web presence of individuals, groups, organizations and institutions, with some Websites becoming increasingly central and dominant as information resources. Online hierarchies, however, do not necessarily represent offline status (Caldas 2005).

Findings from our Webmetric results indicated that a small number of cliques comprising of the most highly-linked sites existed within each of the four domains. These cliques were located at the top of a steep curve of the most highly linked sites (Schroeder et al. 2005), demonstrating a power-law distribution or *power law* tail for each of the domains. The presence of such a distribution mathematically indicated the 'winner-take-all' hypothesis, and implied that for each topic area, some sites are exponentially better connected within the network, with only a small share of Web nodes receiving or providing many links while the bulk of the nodes have only a few in-links or out-links each.

A limitation of large-scale Webmetric analysis, however, is that the social and institutional phenomena underlying hyperlink patterns are difficult to interpret (Thelwall 2006). It was necessary, therefore, to validate the Webmetric findings with active researchers in each of the domains by asking them about their information practices and characteristics of the information environment at the domain level. In addition, participants were presented with the 'Google representation' derived from the keywords listed in Sect. 3. Respondents were asked how well the Google representation mapped onto their own mental model of the domain – their individual perception of what constitutes the core set of resources and sources (It is important to note that this is different to a mental model they may have at any one time in relation to a situational information need).

Any overlaps or inconsistencies between the Google representation of each domain and the participants' own mental model was further validated by coding the Websites, institutions, organizations, people and other resources they reported using throughout the interview transcripts and then comparing this list with their responses to the Google representation. For example, a comparison was made between how the URLs within the Google representation were distributed across top level domain and top level country code domain names, and the institutional and geographical dimensions of the self-reported model of participants' information environments. The top ten URLs in each of the Google representations tended to be dominated by the large US-based Top-level country code domain names: .org, .com, .gov, and .edu. The break-down of top level domain names for the top 30 Google results across each of the four cases are shown in Table 14.1:

In general, participants recognised, but tolerated, the U.S. bias in the Google representation. Not only was this bias accepted, but it was also anticipated based on their experiences of using Internet search engines to locate sources and resources. To counter this bias some participants reported tailoring their searches or made use of Google's country specific indexes, depending on the geographic orientation of their research.

We found that the extent to which the two domain views, Webmetric versus inhabitants, mapped onto one another was determined by the geographic orientation of the domain, characteristics in networks of excellence and individual perceptions of Google's effectiveness.

Table 14.1 Break down of Google representation by top-level country code domain name

	Top-level country code domain name				
	.org	.com	.gov	.edu	Other
Climate change	13	3	5	1	.co (1)
					.ca (1)
					.ac (1)
					.ch (1)
					.int (2)
					.net (2)
Internet and society	6	10	0	14	
HIV/AIDS	12	4	7	2	.ca (3)
					.int (2)
Terrorism	12	5	5	3	.mil (2)
					.net (1)
					.gov.uk (1)
					tr (1)

14.5.1 Geographic Orientation of Field

The interviews revealed that there was only a limited overlap between the Google representation of each of the case study domains and the researchers' mental models of key networks, structures and organizations. Researchers reported that many of the key online resources in their domain were missing from the Google representation. The extent of the overlap appears to be domain dependent, with those researchers working within a more nationally orientated information environment reporting less of an overlap. For example, the HIV/AIDS researchers reported using national sources and resources, such as the *British Journal of Sexual Health*, UK-based charity organizations, such as the Terrence Higgins Trust, and national statistics, such as those distributed by the Office of National Statistics, and public sector organizations, such as the Health Protection Agency, but none of these appear in the top thirty Google results for generic domain keywords (even when the search was repeated using Google.co.uk). Climate Change researchers, on the other hand, for whom the geographical boundaries of research were far more 'international', were able to recognise many more Google results on the Climate Change validation sheet.

14.5.2 Networks of Excellence

In addition to the gaps that participants identified in response to the direct validation of the Webmetric data there was also a discrepancy between the organizations, institutions, people and resources that they reported using during the course of the interview and the Google representation. This was particularly true for the Web pages of academics and academic institutions that the respondents frequently used.

In the cases where participants recognised some of the top sites from the list, or named key institutions, groups or people that did appear in the top thirty results, those identified were unlikely to appear in the top 10 results. The low ranking of some of the institutions, resources and people they perceived to be core in their domain's information environment surprised some participants, such as this HIV/ AIDs researcher, *"I'm surprised that the W.H.O. [World Health Organization] doesn't figure higher!"* (HA03).

One of the Terrorism researchers, on the other hand, accepted the low ranking of one of the top resources in their domain:

> ... you've got the M.I.P.T. [Memorial Institute for the Prevention of Terrorism] database on here – absolutely crucial – halfway down the left column ... The M.I.P.T. database is really outstanding! (TM 02).

The M.I.P.T database is branded by its producers as the 'Terrorism Knowledge Base' and is a non-profit organization with a remit to prevent terrorism in the U.S. and provides access to statistics about global terrorist incidents. It is interesting to note that if a Google search is run using the keyword 'Terrorism', the M.I.P.T. database appears as the 11th result, and typically this would be the first link on the second page of results. Such a difference between perception and actual Web-presence could be crucial in terms of online visibility.

Respondents from all four domains reported that they did not go beyond the first page or first ten links of Google results. The number of links that respondents typically viewed was dependent upon whether or not they were multi-tasking and how much time they had available:

> It depends if I've got a lot on ice and depends on time. Say I know I've got to search for a lot of things and I've got this session, I might make a decision after the first 10 [results] to stop. If I've got a bit more time, then that's 20. If I've got a lot more time I go to the first 30. I won't go beyond the first 30. And if you ask out of those three what happens the most, I'd probably say 10 because I'm always busy. (IS05)

Persistence with a particular set of results also depended on whether the researchers believed it was worth sifting through a large volume of irrelevant material to unearth 'gems'. The Terrorism researchers were more likely to persist with a particular set of search results, 'excavating' links in a similar way to the interdisciplinary humanities scholars observed by Palmer and Neumann (2002):

> ... there's a great deal of rather boring work in culling and identifying sources, but you can't afford to not do it in case you miss some outstanding new input, and this is rather expensive in time and the resources of researchers, but there's no alternative to actually looking hard through what's available on the Net. (TM03)

This search behaviour was different to that described by the Internet and Society researchers who described more directed searching:

> [I search] for very specific things. I try to be as specific as possible otherwise you get too much nonsense. (IS03)

Fry and Talja (2007) have linked directed searching to scatter of relevant material across domain boundaries and the comparative findings reported here seem to corroborate their argument.

14.5.3 Preconceptions of Google Effectiveness and Tolerating Irrelevance in Search Results

Despite recognition by respondents that Google is a blunt instrument in terms of seeking information, and UK-based researchers' recognition of a persistent US bias in its indexes, it was still the main tool for finding sources and resources on the Web. As Fallows (2005) has argued, trust in Internet search engines amongst Internet users tends to be high and users often persist with a particular engine. When asked what alternate strategies they used if Google failed to retrieve relevant results, most respondents preferred to change the keywords or phrases they had used for a search and persist with Google, rather than change search engine.

> No, not another search engine - I stick with Google, but what I sometimes do is change the keywords. For example, what I typed in second I put in first place, which may also make a difference. Also I use other keywords, or when I get too many hits specify more and use a third or fourth keyword (IS02)

There was a general perception that the source they were looking for was available through Google if only they could 'hack' the indexes in the correct way:

> I'll start again, but as they say 'modify your search'... I assume that I can actually get it out of Google if only I've got the wit to get the search right. (IS01)

Respondents generally had preconceived notions about the effectiveness of Google. For example, they were aware that not all the results obtained in a Google search were going to be relevant. In fact, all of them expected the search engine to come up with what one researcher termed 'slash-and-burn kinds of pages' (TM02). Despite this, however, they preferred Google for its clean interface and perceived ease of use, and appeared convinced that Google could give them the results they were looking for should they only persist and tailor their searches through altering key words and narrowing down search terms.

Persistence with a particular search was also largely influenced by the searcher's perception of the overall quality of result set retrieved. Respondents reported assessing relevance and validity on two intellectual levels simultaneously. On one level, the respondents' approach to determining the quality and relevance of a hit was purely 'rational' (Pharo and Jarvelin 2006), and involved skimming through the URL abstract provided by Google. On another level, the respondents' approach to determining relevance was 'heuristic', bringing into play the subject-knowledge and particular experience of the researcher in judging the 'respectability' of the source or organization hosting the page and in evaluating site-content, with a clear preference for information coming from a 'reputable' person or institution. This held true across the four domains both for junior and senior researchers:

> To be honest [assessing the quality of search results] is almost subliminal – looking for words and sites that you think would be respectable. Normally I would skim through the words that come up and then I would look at the Web address. If it was some kind of non-entity of a Non Governmental Organization, then I might ignore it, if it was the World Bank or the United Nations I might have a look. (CC01)

Ensuring the validity of primary data, e.g. statistics, was a particularly important concern for Terrorism researchers who felt that, owing to the highly sensitive nature of the issues they dealt with as well as the difficulties they faced in identifying 'legitimate' sources of data, any information collected from a search should be subjected to a stringent quality control process.

> ... [the problem is] most people don't sufficiently vet what they're looking at. I'm very, very careful about it, especially in a subject like mine where everything depends so upon subjectivity and perception, at least to some degree. (TM02)

In fact, the Terrorism researchers stressed the importance of following a two stage quality control process: in the first instance using their own judgment to determine what they felt was valid from within a list of search results, and then cross-checking the accuracy of the data by corroborating it with other sources of information, particularly with experienced colleagues in the field:

> ... corroboration is just as important when you're using a source off the Net as it is when you're using traditional media. If there's only one report on one particular site which said X did Y or is responsible, claimed responsibility, for doing this on a certain date, and you can't find anybody else who said this, even [if it's] in one of the most respected sources within that country, then you begin to worry that they've made a mistake or that somebody's trying to put false information into their account. You know...corroboration is extremely important in our field. (TM03)

It is important to bear in mind that the disparity between respondents' positive response to the Google representation of the domain-level information environment and what was identified as missing according to their reported use of online resources may have been due to the fact that they situated themselves at an early stage of information seeking, a stage at which Kuhlthau (1993) argues users are likely to hold a rather general standard of inclusion. Users tend to hold different relevance perceptions at different stages of information seeking. During the early stages of search formulation users tends to be more receptive to topically relevant items presented to them, whereas in the later stages following query formulation, the user tends to be more discriminating in identifying items only pertinent to their personal information need (Kuhlthau 1993).

14.6   Web-based Search Strategies

Though there were similarities in Web-search strategies across each of the four case study domains, there were also important differences. For example, while respondents reported using Google almost to the exclusion of all other generalist Internet search engines, the role that it played in their wider information environments varied considerably. In the HIV/AIDS and Internet and Society domains, for instance, Google is mainly used as what Beauvisage (2004) calls an "aide memoir", a locating tool for known sources. As one Internet and Society researcher noted:

> Very rarely would I put in a general query through Google – I think it [any query I do put in] would normally lead specifically to a policy article, newspaper or another article. I'm normally following up specific leads. (IS04)

The HIV/AIDS researchers, in particular, described quite distinct ways by which they found information and literature online, the predominant mode being Weblinks embedded in the body of email correspondence. These researchers tended to go to aggregated literature databases such as *PubMed* in the first instance, and then transferred their search to Google if they could not find the material they wanted:

> … if I had heard of a paper and could not access it through something like *PubMed* then I would do a Google search and try and find a Webpage for that author and see if they had a link to their paper. (HA01)

In response to the question whether they more often searched for people, topics or institutions, almost all researchers responded that they more often than not searched for a topic, looking for a specific information source. Occasionally, researchers looked for the home pages of people they had either met at conferences or whose work they were familiar with and wished to consult. This suggests that Web-based information seeking within the HIV/AIDS domain is driven by looking for known sources, rather than searching the Internet in an exploratory way.

In contrast, for researchers of Terrorism, Google plays a more central role in exploring the object of research and identifying relevant sources. This may be due to the amorphous, shadowy nature of the subject matter itself – Websites of terrorist groups and the message-boards, chatrooms and blogs associated with them are constantly being shut down by national intelligence agencies, only to resurface with new Web-addresses, and the only way to locate these and other sources like them is for researchers to 'excavate' resources across a range of resources and domain boundaries.

This varying role of Google was not solely contingent on domain, however, but also varied within domain according to what stage individuals were at in relation to a particular task. For example, while there was a core set of known Web-based resources within the HIV/AIDS domain, the following researcher also noted using Google as an exploratory tool:

> I think the thing is, when I am doing just general background research I tend to use Google more. If I am writing an article and I need to find specific information or in my mind I know that there's something out there on this topic that I haven't quite managed to track down, then I'll transfer to more specific journal site searches. (HA03)

The Climate Change researchers, used search engines both for exploratory searches as well as searching for specific information or datasets or literature on people's home pages. Like HIV/AIDS researchers, researchers of Climate Change mentioned sharing papers or links to papers via email as a common way of obtaining information:

> … I think they [other Climate Change researchers] are really good at sharing papers over email – if you ask for a paper you normally get it pretty promptly, or a link to it. (CC04)

One possible explanation for differential domain patterns in the role of Google and other Internet search engines as information seeking tools could be the extent to which important documents are scattered across domain boundaries (Bates 1996). The consequence of this for Web searching is that in low scatter fields, resources and sources can be found using a clearly circumscribed set of keywords and are likely to be produced by a limited number of dominant gate-keepers. Of the case studies, HIV/AIDS was the domain with the least scatter and this could explain why Google was used more as an 'aide memoir' than as an exploratory tool. Terrorism and Climate Change researchers on the other hand described their domains as scattered in terms of resources and respondents reported using Google for finding diverse sources more than in the other two case studies:

> Well, I've mentioned the World Bank, it's very important, but apart from that it's essentially very scattered. There are individual pages of bilateral and multilateral donors – the United Nations obviously, the International Energy Agency and specialized groups working on everything from renewable energy to national policies on cooking. (CC01)

Scatter also influences the degree to which directed searching, chaining or browsing will the most rewarding search technique (Fry and Talja 2007).

14.7   The Role of Gatekeepers

The characteristics and role of the predominant gatekeepers varied across each of the four domains. In this section we describe these differences and discuss their implications for degrees of 'winner-takes-all' on the Web.

The interview responses indicate a differentiated shift towards the decentraliza-tion of gatekeepers on the Internet. For example, in Climate Change 'hybrid research centres' produce and disseminate important sources; and policy or aca-demic research centres are key producers of information sources in Internet and Society research. Although not-for-profit organizations were key producers and disseminators of information and played an important gatekeeping role in the HIV/AIDS information environment, traditional gatekeepers such as publishers still maintain a central position in this domain because of the continued importance of peer-reviewed articles disseminated through discipline-centric aggregated data-bases such as *PubMed Central*.

The information environment of the Terrorism researchers was similar to that of the HIV/AIDS researchers in that, while non-governmental and not-for-profit organi-zations play a central role in disseminating primary information resources, publishers still had an enduring role as gatekeepers to academic research. In Terrorism, dissemination of research via books plays a major role in the scholarly communication system and still remains closely interrelated to the recognition and reward system. Research in Terrorism is of a sensitive nature, which may account to some extent for the sustained importance of the traditional gatekeepers such as publishers.

In contrast, the gatekeepers in the information environments of the Climate Change and the Internet and Society researchers were more decentralized. This meant that rather than access to information being coordinated by a predominant gatekeeper there were multiple gatekeepers providing specific resources in niche areas.

This variation in the characteristics and role of gatekeepers in the information environments of each of the four case study domains appears to be influenced by a number of domain-specific intellectual and social factors. This includes the types of data used in each domain, which, except for the *Terrorism* researchers, was primarily quantitatively oriented. For example, the Climate Change participants relied heavily on international and national statistics produced by The World Bank and the International Energy Agency; the Internet and Society researchers frequently used national statistics based on Internet surveys produced by academic research centres; the HIV/AIDS researchers cited national health statistics, such as those produced by the Health Protection Agency in the UK, as leading sources of information. For the Terrorism researchers, on the other hand, news sources and public speeches were a source of primary information, but there was also a heavy reliance on secondary sources such as academic publications.

There was also variation at the domain level in the extent to which researchers had developed practices to by-pass gatekeepers such as publishers and libraries. Amongst Internet and Society researchers, this was making full-text articles available on academic home pages:

> … it's getting more and more important to have a good homepage and I really like the way that people publish all their papers and so forth on the Internet. It's so helpful to go to somebody's home page and to know that everything is there. (IS02)

Whereas in the information environments of Climate Change, Terrorism and HIV/AIDS research, academic homepages have a much lower information valency. This variation may also be explained by the nature of each domain's Websphere (Fry 2006), in terms of the extent to which it is academically oriented or oriented towards not-for-profit organizations. Table 14.1 shows the top-level domains of the URLS in the Google representation for each domain. The representation of the academic domain (e.g. .edu and .ac.uk) is low within each of the case studies except for Internet and Society, whereas the .org domain accounts for the largest percentage of domains across HIV/AIDS, Climate Change and Terrorism.

The Climate Change and Internet and Society respondents reported mainly using the Web for finding policy documentation and survey reports. Thus, there was no alternate way of accessing this information other than the not-for-profit organizations with a national or international remit for producing such knowledge and data. Within Climate Change attempts had been made to centralize disparate sources across multiple organizations and institutions, but there had been difficulties in centralizing, integrating and maintaining scattered resources:

> There have been a number of attempts in the past to try and collate this, through a meta-site, but normally they are not successful because people don't put in enough effort to keep them updated. (CC01)

Interestingly, although publishers play a key dissemination and access role in HIV/AIDS and Terrorism, they are absent from the Google representation, which may reflect their low visibility in the wider domain Websphere.

14.8   Implications for Web Search

Where the information environment of a domain is highly-structured, well-organized and dominated by a limited number of gatekeepers search and other forms of information seeking are likely to also be structured, highly focused and predictable, as with the HIV/AIDS domain where researchers go to *PubMed Central* in the first instance using a well-defined set of keywords. In these cases, therefore, search is directed within a 'well-defined landscape'.

This contrasts with the information environments of the Terrorism and Internet and Society domains where resources are scattered across a diverse range of gatekeepers and domains. Consequently, concepts are often contested, which leads to more open-ended undirected searches and increased uncertainty with regard to the appropriate keywords to search. Rather than search being for a particular specialized concept it is often for individual researchers, institutions or general concepts. In these domains access to online resources is more likely to depend on the indexing algorithms of Internet search engines and the online presence of particular institutions, organizations, people and resources. We describe this type of information environment as 'undomesticated wilderness'. In short, the Websphere of a domain can be seen as a realm that in some domains is centrally structured around traditional gatekeepers, and in others more decentralized and fragmented across traditional and emergent gatekeepers. Access to sources of expertise in the online realm will be strongly shaped by this organization or lack of it.

For example, traditional gatekeepers with a high-degree of offline status, such as the major journal publishers, also contribute to this degree of organized-ness of the Websphere and shape the extent of Google's impact on 'winner takes all'. If, therefore, there are predominant centralized knowledge gateways within a domain's information environment, such as *PubMed Central* within HIV/AIDS, then Google mainly functions as a *facilitator* in accessing them. If, on the other hand, a domain's information environment is decentralized (Fry and Talja 2007) and the production of resources is fragmented across a range of different types of institutions and organizations e.g. academic, not-for-profit or commercial, Google becomes an *influential gatekeeper*. In terms of understanding the potential 'winner-take-all' effect on the Web it is therefore useful to identify more specifically *which* resources are concentrated online as well how new sources of information displace and complement those that have been traditionally used.

A different example, perhaps not of 'concentration' but rather of how access to expertise is shaped, is the degree to which fields are oriented to a national scientific, practitioner or lay-audience. The more nationally oriented a resource or producer is, the more likely it is to be marginalised by the current Internet search engines in popular use. This is particularly apparent when contrasting health-related topics, such as HIV/AIDS, as against more globally oriented topics such as Climate Change and Terrorism, though the U.S. bias of search results cuts across all four topics. Even if this bias does not relate directly to the extent of the well-organizedness of the Websphere it is nevertheless closely connected because 'organizedness' can be related to the degree of 'boundedness' of the information landscape.

14.9   Conclusions

Our qualitative interview findings corroborate the quantitative Webmetric results (Schroeder et al. 2005) that there is no uniform 'Winner-takes-all' effect in the use of online resources. Instead, there are different kinds of gatekeepers for the four topics we examined and for the types of information that are sought. We found the effect to be differentiated according to four factors: geographic orientation of knowledge domains; strength or weakness of networks of excellence; the scatter of material across disciplinary boundaries and the role of traditional gatekeepers. It is therefore important not just to identify a concentration or democratization effect, but rather to refine under what circumstances the search for expertise will be dominated by certain results and exhibit biases, and when, instead, researchers will be led to the resources they seek and to a variety of results. Particular characteristics of a domain's information environment will determine whether Google and other Internet search engines function as a *facilitator* or as an *influential gatekeeper*.

Web search engines, and Google in particular, thus exercise a gatekeeping function, at the same time that they enable researchers to find their way in the new online environment. But this environment can be a well-organized landscape or a less-well charted wilderness. As the production and use of online resources continues to grow, it will become increasingly important whether search can find its way through these different types of landscapes. For topics such as those examined here, which in some way cross the boundaries of established disciplines, there is the additional question of the extent to which online resources will transcend or reconfigure established bounds of expertise. Such a shift will necessitate libraries and publishers – not to speak of researchers and institutions that produce and use material online - to re-align their strategies for organizing services and content accordingly.

References

Adams A, Blandford A (2005) Digital libraries' support for the user's information journey. Proceedings of the 5th ACM/IEEE-CS joint conference on digital libraries 2005, Denver, CO, USA, June 7–11, pp 160–169

Adams A, Blandford A, Lunt P (2005) Social empowerment and exclusion: a case study on digital libraries. ACM Transactions on Computer–Human Interaction, 12.

Barabasi A (2003) Linked: the new science of networks. Perseus Books, New York

Bates MJ (1996) Learning about the information seeking of interdisciplinary scholars and students. Library Trends 45: 155–164

Beauvisage T (2004) A semantics of users' paths through the web. Unpublished PhD, University of Paris X: Nanterre, Paris (translated by Van Couvering, Web Behaviour: Search engines in context, draft paper)

Becher T, Trowler P (2001) Academic tribes and territories: intellectual inquiry and the culture of disciplines (2nd ed.). Open University Press, Milton Keynes

Caldas A (2005) On the origins of the web species and complexity. Paper presented to the New Approaches to Research on the Social Implications of Emerging Technologies Workshop, Oxford, 15–16 April

Van Couvering E (2006) Web behaviour: search engines in context. Available at: http://personal. lse.ac.uk/VANCOUVE/. Accessed 3 August 2006

Dahl R (1989) Democracy and its critics. New Haven, CT: Yale University Press.

Dutton WH, Gillet SE, McKnight LW, Peltu M (2003) Broadband Internet: the power to reconfigure access. Forum discussion paper no. 1, Oxford Internet Institute, August 2003

Fallows D (2005) Search engine users: Internet searchers are confident, satisfied and trusting – but they are also unaware and naïve. Report of the Pew Internet and American Life Project. Available at: http://www.pewInternet.org/pdfs/PIP_Searchengine_users.pdf. Accessed 3 August 2006

Fry J (2006) Studying the scholarly web: how disciplinary culture shapes online representations. Cybermetrics, 10. Available at: http://www.cindoc.csic.es/cybermetrics/vol10iss1.html. Accessed 3 August 2006

Fry J, Talja S (2004) The cultural shaping of scholarly communication: explaining e-journal use within and across academic fields. In: ASIST 2004: Proceedings of the 67th ASIST Annual Meeting 41. Medford, NJ.: Information Today

Fry J, Talja S (2007) The intellectual and social organization of academic fields and the shaping of digital resources. Journal of Information Science 33: 115–137

Granka LA, Joachims T, Gay G (2004) Eye-tracking analysis of user behavior in www-search. Proceedings of the 27th Annual International ACM SIGIR Conference on Research and Development in Information Retrieval, pp 478–479

Hindman M, Tsioutsiouliklis K, Johnson J (2003) Googlearchy: how a few heavily-linked sites dominate politics on the web. Available at: http://www.princeton.edu/~mhindman/googlearchy–hindman.pdf. Accessed 7 February 2006

Hjørland B, Albrechtsen H (1995) Toward a new horizon in information science : domain-analysis. Journal of the American Society for Information Science 46: 400–425

Jansen BJ, Spink A (2006) How are we searching the world wide web? a comparison of nine search engine transaction logs. Information Processing and Management 42: 248–263

Johnson DE, Case DO, Andres J, Allard SL, Johnson NE (2006) Fields and pathways: contrasting or complementary views of information seeking. Information Processing and Management 42: 569–582

Kuhlthau CC (1993) Seeking meaning: a process approach to library and information services. Ablex, Norwood, NJ

Merton RK (1988) The Matthew effect in science II, Isis 79: 606–623

Mote LJB (1962) Reasons for the variation of information needs of scientists. Journal of Documentation 18: 169–175

Palmer CL, Neumann LJ (2002) The information work of interdisciplinary humanities scholars: exploration and translation, Library Quarterly 72: 85–117.

Park HW, Thelwall M (2005) The network approach to web hyperlink research and its utility for science communication. In Christine Hine (Ed.) Virtual methods: issues in social research on the Internet. Berg, Oxford: 171–181

Pennock DM, Flake GW, Lawrence S, Glover EJ, Giles CL (2002) Winners don't take all: characterizing the competition for links on the web. Proceedings of the National Academy of Sciences 99: 5207–5211

Pew Internet and American Life Survey (2005) Search engine users: Internet searchers are confident, satisfied and trusting – but they are also unaware and naïve. Available at: http://www. pewInternet.org/PPF/r/146/report_display.asp. Accessed 12 July 2006

Pharo N, Jarvelin K (2006) Irrational searchers and IR-rational researchers. Journal of the American Society for Information Science and Technology 57: 222–232

Schneider SM, Foot KA (2002) Online structure for political action: exploring presidential websites from the 2000 American election, Javnost (The Public) 9: 43–60

Schroeder R, Caldas A, Mesch G, Dutton W (2005) The world wide web of science: reconfiguring access to information, First International Conference on e-Social Science, Manchester 22–24 June, Available at: http://www.oii.ox.ac.uk/research/project.cfm?id=22. Accessed 6 March 2007

Solomon P (1999) Information mosaics: patterns of action that structure. In Wilson, T., and Allen, D.K. (Ed.) Exploring the contexts of information behaviour (pp. 150–175). UK. London: Taylor Graham

Spink A, Wolfram D, Jansen BJ, Saracevic T (2001) Searching the web: the public and their queries. Journal of the American Society for Information Science and Technology 52: 226–234

Thelwall M (2006) Interpreting social science link analysis research: a theoretical framework. Journal of the American Society for Information Science and Technology 57: 60–68

Thelwall M, Vaughan L, Björneborn L (2005) Webometrics. Annual Review of Information Science and Technology 39: 81–135

Törmä S, Vakkari P (2004) Discipline, availability of electronic resources and the use of Finnish national electronic library – FinELib. Information Research 10 Available at http://informationr. net/ir/10-1/paper204.html. Accessed 13 July 2006

Tuominen K, Talja S, Savolainen R (2003) Multiperspective digital libraries: the implications of constructionism for the development of digital libraries. Journal of the American Society for Information Science and Technology 54: 561–569

Vakkari P, Talja S (2005) The influence of the scatter of literature on the use of electronic resources across disciplines: a case study of FinElib. In: A. Rauber et al. (Eds.) ECDL 2005, LNCS 3652, pp 207–217

Walsh JP, Bayma T (1996) Computer networks and scientific work. Social Studies of Science 26: 661–703

Wang P, Berry MW, Yang Y (2003) Mining longitudinal web queries: trends and patterns. Journal of the American Society for Information Science and Technology 54: 743–758

Whitley R (2000). (2nd ed.) The intellectual and social organization of the sciences, Oxford: Clarendon Press.

15
Conceptual Models for Search Engines

D.G. Hendry and E.N. Efthimiadis

Summary Search engines have entered popular culture. They touch people in diverse private and public settings and thus heighten the importance of such important social matters as information privacy and control, censorship, and equitable access. To fully benefit from search engines and to participate in debate about their merits, people necessarily appeal to their understandings for how they function. In this chapter we examine the conceptual understandings that people have of search engines by performing a content analysis on the sketches that 200 undergraduate and graduate students drew when asked to draw a sketch of how a search engine works. Analysis of the sketches reveals a diverse range of conceptual approaches, metaphors, representations, and misconceptions. On the whole, the conceptual models articulated by these students are simplistic. However, students with higher levels of academic achievement sketched more complete models. This research calls attention to the importance of improving students' technical knowledge of how search engines work so they can be better equipped to develop and advocate policies for how search engines should be embedded in, and restricted from, various private and public information settings.

15.1 Introduction

Search engines are remarkable for their mediating power: Every day, millions of people speak through their writing, while millions of others search for this "speech" with their queries. Popular quantitative and demographic measures (Lenhart et al. 2004; Media Metrix 2004) show that search engines are an important cultural phenomenon, matching searchers' queries with producers' content. The popular press, over the last several years, has created an impressive groundswell of public interest in search engines – how they work and the cultural phenomena surrounding them. Search – surprisingly given its dusty, technical roots – has become fashionable. In turn, search has shifted interest in such important civic issues as universal access, privacy rights, informed consent, and one's autonomy to pursue one's own interests to a new space – the Internet. Perhaps the most significant long-term implication of search engines is how they have raised these issues, which have been dormant, and how they prompt society to address them.

A. Spink and M. Zimmer (eds.), *Web Search, Springer Series in Information Science and Knowledge Management 14.*
© Springer-Verlag Berlin Heidelberg 2008

The networked infrastructure that enables information services like Google is an *artificial world* (Simon 1996), which presents people with a menagerie of new concepts, intricately interrelated. To list just a few: Web pages, keywords, meta tags, hyperlinks, caches, Web servers, robots.txt, file permissions, search engines, rankings, URLs, spiders, users, content providers, advertisers, spam, spammers, search-engine optimizers, tags, log files, and PageRank ™. While human-made, this is not a neat world. Indeed, many important relationships between elements are hidden and the intricacy of the overall system is largely due to localized technological improvement. The protocol for Web cookies is a classic example that illustrates how a seemingly straightforward technical protocol can have significant, unanticipated consequences on public policy in such important areas as privacy and informed consent (Friedman et al. 2002). To discuss the merits of such a technical protocol on privacy and similar values, one must draw upon technical knowledge for the protocol. Nevertheless, like the natural world, we engage this artificial world without complete understanding or even being aware of its underlying complexity.

However, when we encounter a phenomenon that triggers our interest or when we encounter a barrier that prevents us from obtaining a goal, we may ask a question that can only be answered by investigating the intricacies of this artificial world. Consider, for example, this barrier: "When I type my name into Google, why does my Web page not appear within the results on the first page?" To answer this question, we might follow a process of deductive thinking and draw on established concepts and principles to propose an explanation. From this explanation, we might then pursue a course of action to overcome the barrier. Alternately, in order to address the problem, we might seek the advice of experts and consider their explanations in light of our current understanding. Finally, we might follow a more inductive process and gather data related to the phenomenon and attempt to identify a general pattern. Of course, the rigor associated with each of these modes of inquiry will vary. Often, the process will be quick and ad hoc and sometimes it will be based on incorrect or only partially correct facts. Nevertheless, like a scientist seeking to understand the natural world, a person who seeks to understand the artificial world of search engines will appeal to his or her existing technical knowledge.

The question we address in this chapter is: What is the nature of this technical knowledge held by students of information science? We assert that knowledge of basic technical concepts for search engines is an important kind of scientific literacy. This assertion follows from the position that a healthy democracy requires a scientifically literate public where people understand basic scientific constructs such as "The Earth revolves around the Sun once each year", which can be assessed by closed and open questions in telephone surveys (Miller 1998). Certainly, technical knowledge about how a search engine works is needed in order to both search effectively, as well as to teach others how to search. This technical knowledge is also necessary to participate in higher level debates, such as participating in civic dispute about search engines, as well as advocating for their proper use. At the same time, it is important to acknowledge the social constructivist position, in which people learn by creating interpretations that are based on their past experiences and their current interactions with the world. In the context of public policy disputes concerning the environmental health of a river basin, Roth and Lee (2002), for example, show how scientific literacy can be constituted in a social setting of intense dialog between people of various backgrounds. Analogously, we expect that serious public dialog about search engines, involving people of varied backgrounds, would enable people to express knowledge that is not available to them when completing a survey over the telephone. We take the view, in short, that the ability for a single person to generate explicit facts about how search engines work is the only one kind of knowledge about them. Nevertheless, in this work we focus on just this form of knowledge. As educators, our goal is to take measure of students' knowledge of search engines so that we can provide better instruction and be more effective teachers.

In the next section, we develop the argument that the public discussion of search engines centers at the fuzzy junction of culture and technology. Indeed, we show that the popular press serves an important role for educating people about how search engines work and for identifying social consequences of their operation. Then, we review the literature on mental models for search engines, showing that the literature has focused on users' understandings for particular kinds of search systems. Not addressed to date are people's understandings for search at the cultural level; yet, this is clearly needed as search engines have moved from well-bounded settings, such as a library's catalog, to an information network that pervades home, work and play. Next, we report the results of an exploratory experiment where we ask students to draw sketches of how search engines work. A content analysis of the sketches reveals a tremendous diversity of approaches for conceptualizing search engines, and yet, on the whole, students have relatively weak models for how search engines actually work. Finally, we discuss the implications of this data for educators in information science.

15.2 Background

15.2.1 Everyday Reasoning about Internet Search-Engines

We begin by considering the popular activity of *Googling people*. In an episode of the popular and edgy HBO series *Sex and the City* we hear:

> Unidentified Woman #1: ... ridiculous. And according to my new best friend, Google.com ...
> Unidentified Woman #2: You Googled him!
> Unidentified Woman #1: ... the man has dated every woman in New York from 19 ...
> (Edwards, 2004, April 13).

Taking up the ethics of Googling people, *the Ethicist*, a weekly column in the New York Times Magazine, begins with a reader's question: "My friend went on a date last week and 'Googled' the man when she got home .... What do you think about using Google to check up on another person?" (Cohen 2002, December 15). And, continues:

> I'm for it ... Had your friend labored all afternoon at the courthouse checking equally pub-lic information on her date, she'd have crossed the border between casual curiosity and stalking. Her Googling, however, was akin to asking her friends about this fellow – offhand, sociable and benign. ... By calling an act "checking up" on someone, you make typing someone's name into a search engine sound devious and sinister. But that is less a consequence of malevolence than of its novelty ... As more and more people routinely Google their blind dates, nobody will feel uneasy doing so.

On the other side, some people seek as many Google hits as possible to demon-strate their social standing: "Guys all over town are on the phone saying 'I bet I can get more Google hits than you' ... It's become this ridiculous new power game" (Hochman 2004, March 14). With these two quotations, we see in uncommonly compact form how search engines can lead to important ethical questions and, what's more, influence cultural values at a remarkable pace.

At the same time, these and other newspaper pieces on *Googling people* beg many questions about the underlying operation of search engines: Why use Google and not some other engine? Who can you find through Google? How is information about people collected by Google? How reliable is the informa-tion? What responsibility does Google have for its *credibility*? How is it shared? How are queries about people processed? Does Google track search-ers' interests in people? Answers to such questions are important because they often inform conversations about information access, dissemination, and privacy.

An illustrative case is the phenomenon known as *Google bombing*, or more generally as *link bombing*, where arbitrary mappings between precise phrases and targeted Web pages are manufactured by a coordinated group of pranksters. For example, a politically motivated link bomb was created for the phrase *miserable failure*, which was linked to President George W. Bush's official biography by approximately twenty bloggers. This small citation network was enough to boost the weight of the ranking to first place. Of course, the phrase *miserable failure* is nowhere to be found on the page itself. How, then, is this connection possible? Only with a fairly sophisticated understanding of how search engines work, can we arrive at an understanding of this quandary.

In a series of articles, the popular press attempted to explain the Google bomb phenomenon, assuring readers that this was not a political statement by Google itself (Hansell, 2003, December 8; McNichol 2004, January 22). The important role of these articles played has been to provide people with accurate conceptual models for how search engines work, including the algorithm that causes Google bombs, known as PageRank (Brin and Page 1998). These articles cover to some degree such topics as fetching content over the network, document parsing, term frequency analysis, citation analysis, and so on. In short, search engines raise important social, political, and commercial concerns that can often best be addressed, at least in part, by invoking and reasoning with technical abstractions.

Our claim, then, is that everyday questions concerning search engines lead to technical questions about their underlying computational processes and data structures. To further this claim, consider the following scenarios, drawn from articles in the popular press, and reflective of the general cultural conversation regarding search engines.

Example 1: Consider a mother who publishes stories and photographs about family outings on a 'hidden' page on their Internet Service Provider Website. While she has not been able to find her family's page by searching Google with her family's name and other (common) words and phrases found on her site, she nevertheless wonders if Google, to anthropomorphize, knows about the page and if there is anything she can do to make sure that Google does not find it. On the other hand, the popular press has reported that *Googledorks*, also known as Google hackers, seek out supposedly private documents by discovering holes in *digital gatekeepers* (Noguchi 2004, February 9). These hackers, taking advantage of Google's exhaustive crawling and extensive index of sites, develop knowledge for terms, file types, and other features that turn up putatively private documents. While an owner of a document can request that it be removed from Google's index, it is likely that he or she won't think of exercising this option until after the privacy of the document has been compromised, at which point it is often too late. However, for the mother to fully understand her question about the privacy of her family's Website, she must in turn understand such technical minutia as spiders, directory permissions, robots.txt files, the notion of 'informal technical protocols', and so forth.

Example 2: A landscape architect, who knows that potential clients often 'Google her name', in order to look for information about her past projects. Thus, she would like the link to her home page to appear on the first page of results. A knowledgeable friend has told her that the *keywords meta-tag*, a protocol for associating keywords with pages, is an ineffective technique, but she doesn't understand why. To explain why this is, we must begin by modeling the relationship between information providers and search engines, which is adversarial. Then, we must examine how keywords are extracted from Web pages, how words are normalized, how weights that indicate the importance of keywords are calculated, and so on (Belew 2000; Liddy 2001). The adversarial stance that is generally taken between the producers of content and search engines is needed in order to appreciate why these various techniques are needed and thus why associating keywords with meta-tags is usually ineffective. A collaborative stance, where content producer and a search engine cooperate in the spirit of fairness, leads to a different set of implications.

Example 3: A high school teacher suspects a student of plagiarism and attempts to verify that a passage from the essay is not original by typing a couple of suspicious word choices from the passage into Google. She is not impressed with her search results and wonders if there are better approaches to searching for plagiarized text. In order for the teacher to devise a better search strategy, she must have, at the very least, some understanding of the probability of matching word phrases, stop words, exact match queries, and so on. Indeed, responding to this need, new companies have recently formed to commercialize specialized approaches for detecting plagiarism (e.g., www.turnitin.com).

Example 4: A business analyst notices that the following queries generate unexpected hit counts: *water* (97,800,000 hits), *skiing* (7,160,000) *water skiing* (2,440,000), *water OR skiing* (14,100,000), and *skiing OR water* (13,900,000).[153] He wonders about the logic underlying this simple experiment: Shouldn't the expression *skiing OR water* yield more results than *water* alone, and shouldn't *water OR skiing* and *skiing OR water* yield identical hit counts? Perplexed that the *OR* operator does not work as expected (i.e., the commutative property of the disjunction operator does not hold) and that the sizes of the result sets are illogical, he questions his understanding of Boolean logic and wonders what rules Google follows. As this example illustrates, even experts, without proprietary information, cannot answer certain kinds of operational questions that emerge from the ordinary use of search engines.

Example 5: A marketing manager is dismayed when her company's Web site ceases to appear on the first page of Google. She has heard that the *Google dance* has reduced the relevance of her site. That is, Google has computed new relevance information that has caused changes in how results are ranked. Further, she has heard that nothing can be done except to buy keywords from Google. Companies that sell search engine optimization services, meanwhile, have promised her that their techniques can improve the relevancy of her site to particular queries. But, the practices followed for such companies, such as *link farms*, can run afoul of Google's guidelines, leading to genuine confusion in the minds of information providers over the fairness of various publishing and linking practices (Totty and Mangalindan 2003).

Example 6: An article in the New York Times reports that before submitting a pair of *chandaleer earrings* to eBay, the owner checked the spelling of *chandaleer* on Google (Schemo 2004, January 28). She found 85 hits and assumed the spelling was correct and submitted the item. The article reports that "She never guessed … that results like that meant she was groping in the spelling wilderness. Chandelier, spelled right, turns up 715,000 times." On the other hand, others troll eBay listings, looking for items that are spelled incorrectly because items that are misspelled have lower bidding activity and therefore they generally have lower prices. Indeed, it is remarkable that lexical errors and simple word choices can have such significant commercial consequences (Gleick 2004, March 21). Perhaps, greater awareness of how words are harvested and processed by Google would have enabled this person to detect her lexical error.

Each of these scenarios demonstrates how interaction with a search engine can be facilitated with a little technical understanding. Sometimes the necessary technical knowledge is in the public domain. For example, while the *robots.txt* file can be used to communicate areas of a site that should be visited, it does not guarantee that spiders will respect this informal protocol. In other cases, the technical knowledge is closely held, proprietary information and without it, it is virtually impossible to develop an accurate model for what is going on. For example, the

---

[153] In January 2004 these hit counts were produced by Google in response to the queries.

unexpected result set sizes for the queries concerning 'water skiing' appear to be caused by probabilistic methods for estimating result set sizes. Even this is speculation. Search engines do not publish information about their algorithms in order to keep themselves competitive. Perhaps it is nothing more than a temporary error – who can tell?

Of course, this lack of technical knowledge does not prevent people from hypothesizing about the operational mechanisms of search engines that lead to particular phenomena. On the one hand, people show great resourcefulness in trying to predict how a search engine functions, as can be readily observed in many online discussions. For example, the newsgroup, google.public.support.general, which is located at www.google.com, is filled with questions and answers, sometimes speculative and sometimes plain wrong, about how search works. At www.googlewhack. com, search fanatics share and discuss queries that return one and only one result. By studying these special-case queries, these searchers claim that it is possible to reverse engineer some of the methods Google employs to filter results. This knowledge, if accurate and durable, is commercially valuable because it can lead to approaches for defeating the filters and promoting a given Web page's rank. Consultants at firms that promise *search-engine optimization* (i.e., creating Web pages that appear high on Google search results) draft intricate models of Google's ranking process and test them by running empirical studies, tracking patent applications, job postings, and so on (e.g., see www.webworkshop.net/florida-update. html). It seems likely that this cycle of escalating competitive intelligence will continue for some time. On the other hand, it is in the search engine's best interest to not disclose information that leads to practices that artificially improve the ranking of pages or that divulge information that might be exploited by competitors. Indeed, it is in the search engines' best interest to present a biased conceptual model for its operations, leading people to perform behaviors that favor the search engine. The relationship between these two positions is hence adversarial: Outside stakeholders seek a full understanding of a search engines' operation, yet to protect its intellectual property, and to satisfy its operational goals, a search engine must be highly selective in what it reveals about itself.

15.2.2   Metaphors and Mental Models for Search

Consider these neologisms from the above scenarios: Google hits, Google bombs, Google dance, search engines, link farms, spiders. From this list, we see evidence of explanatory metaphors being used to conceptualize search, as well as to prompt discussion about search engines in a given cultural milieu. Lakoff and Johnson (1980) show that metaphors are pervasive in everyday speech in order to support reasoning by using a source domain (*flies like an arrow*) to explain a target domain (*time*); indeed, they argue that metaphors are a fundamental tool to how we structure and conceptualize the world and our lives within it. While the above neologisms suggest dramatic technical mechanisms, alone they do not always tell the whole story. While *spider* is suggestive of an entity that creeps across a Web of pages, and suggest the presence of pests that owners might want to be rid of, other metaphors make sense only when you understand the underlying technical functional operation.

Consider, for example, the more complex concept *link bomb* (example given in the Introduction), which relies on the concrete domain of planted, physical bombs to explain the abstract domain of link bombs. Just as a bomb must be manufactured, packed with explosives, and set, so too must a citation network be constructed by linking a set of pages with a keyword trigger that ultimately point to the target page). Just as a bomb has a time-delay fuse which is triggered by some event, so too is time required for a search engine to process the citation network and be triggered by a keyword. Just as a bomb needs to be hidden to have its intended sudden impact, so too must the citation network be hidden. Just as persistent detective work is often marshaled to find hidden bombs, so too must search engines actively seek to detect manufactured citation networks. As with all metaphors, however, "bomb" is an imperfect mapping between a relatively more concrete source domain and a more abstract target domain (e.g., mapping the concepts of a *physical bomb* to the concepts of a *link bomb* on the Internet). For one, *link bombs* seem to be generally benign (no one dies or gets injured because of them). Indeed, they are by and large unnoticeable, except in the most publicized examples (as in the case of Mr. Bush's biography). Yet, pernicious effects can occur.[154] In sum, this metaphor encapsulates a significant amount of technical detail, but the metaphor in itself does not present a rigorous technical analogue that enables a person to understand the relationship between a source domain (*bomb*) and its target domain (*impacts of manufactured citation networks*).

This discussion leads to an obvious set of questions: What understandings and implications do people draw out of such metaphors related to search engines? How do these understandings initially develop and how do they then evolve over months and years? How are these understandings used to reason about individual and social consequences of search engines? How can technologies and educators best intervene to clarify the information issues surrounding search-engines? One approach for addressing such questions is to draw upon the theoretical notion of mental models (Gentner and Stevens 1983).

In the literature on Human-Computer Interaction, the term "mental model" is often used informally and without consistency; therefore, this construct can appear to lack analytic usefulness (Payne 2003). The term, which originated in psychology in the 1940s (Johnson-Laird 1983), appeals to the observation that over time, people develop understandings for the behaviors of other people, natural systems, and

---

[154] An example is that the query Jew returns anti-Semitic material. According to Google the term Jew brings up anti-Semitic material because, in general, anti-Semitic sites frequently employ the word Jew and not other words such as Judaism, Jewish, or Jewish people. After explaining the technical subtleties, an explanatory note reads: "The only sites we omit are those we are legally compelled to remove or those maliciously attempting to manipulate our results" (Google, April 30, 2004).

human-made artifacts. People, in short, learn. Then, when necessary this knowledge is used to anticipate future events to some probability and actions are selected that are believed to result in desired outcomes, to explain the reasons for the occurrence of observed phenomena, and so on. In addition, the term "model" entails the idea that one's knowledge about a given system is in some sense formal, that is, accurate and complete, thus allowing a person to identify the initial parameters of their model, simulate it in their heads, and calculate a set of consequences. For example, the operation of an elevator might be represented as a set of location states (above-floor, below-floor, and on-floor) and movements (moving-down, moving-up, stopped). With this understanding of an elevator and the starting condition (above-floor-and-moving-down), people, assuming they are waiting in a lobby and that the elevator is operating correctly, can anticipate when the elevator will arrive. Thus, in the most basic sense, a mental model allows a person to predict future events on the basis of an initial set of parameters.

Norman (1983) introduced some distinctions concerning mental models. He observed that to understand how a person interacts with a target system, called t, it is necessary to have a description of the system. He called this description a "conceptual model", labeled $C(t)$. The mental model of the system, labeled $M(t)$, is the long-term knowledge of the system. He noted that an analyst's conceptualization of a person's mental model, $C(M(t))$, will only be an approximation of $M(t)$. Thus, the manner in which an analyst elicits a person's mental model and, indeed, the manner used to describe users' models is an important consideration. Finally, Norman (1983) introduced the term "system image" to refer to the outer surface of the system, the displays, controls, help documents, and so on that inform users about the system and help users develop mental models. Ideally, a system image supports the development of a user's mental model that is congruent with the designer's conceptual model for the system. But, of course, this ideal is often not reached and, as we shall see, people typically hold only rudimentary approximations of the designer's conceptual model.

In a separate line of research, Johnson-Laird (1983) used the term "mental model" to label a cognitive architecture that enables people to perform deductive reasoning. Unlike the conceptualization of "mental models" found in Gentner and Stevens (1983), which focus on the long-term knowledge for how things work, Johnson-Laird's conceptualization hypothesizes a specific mechanism of working memory which enables people to infer valid conclusions. With deductive reasoning tasks, people are presented with a set of facts and are required to deduce a correct conclusion. The classic example is a syllogism, which takes one of a small number of forms. The simplest of the forms is:

All people like search engines
X is a search engine
Therefore, all people like X.

Johnston-Laird's theory describes how deductive reasoning tasks, such as the above *modus ponens* (if p then q, p therefore q) and *modus tollens* (if p then q, not q, therefore not p), are performed by people. The theory explains, for example, why *modus tollens* is more difficult and takes longer to perform as well as why it produces more erroneous deductions, than *modus ponens*. A general conclusion of this and other research in psychology is that such mental logic is universally difficult for people to perform because of how the human mind works. In sum, these two conceptualizations of mental models – Norman's knowledge-oriented perspective versus Johnston-Laird's short-term memory mechanism perspective – address different levels of analysis (Payne 2003 for careful analysis of the claims made of mental models). Both types have advanced our understanding for how people understand and use information retrieval systems. Next, this literature is briefly reviewed.

Borgman (1985, 1986) was the first to inquire into people's mental models – as conceptualized by Norman (1983) – for information retrieval systems. (Work preceding Borgman's seminal studies took a strongly cognitive perspective to understanding the nature of search and to derive insights for how systems could better support; for example, see Belkin et al. 1982; Ingwersen 1996) The systems investigated by Borgman were library catalogs that allowed people to enter Boolean expressions that formally specified information needs. As part of the study, she prompted undergraduate student participants to explain how these electronic catalogs worked. She found that participants had very weak models for how an electronic catalog worked even for participants who were given an explicit model of an electronic catalog and Boolean search expressions in pre-study training. In addition, she found that some participants from the undergraduate student population of the study had great difficulty writing simple Boolean expressions involving just one operator. She conjectured that the differences were due to differences in individual cognitive factors. In support of this conjecture, Greene et al. (1990) showed that higher scores on tests measuring the ability to reason correlated with a higher percentage of correct Boolean expressions. The search tasks were very similar to Borgman's study. The difference between the best and worst performers was very large at approximately 10% versus 90% correct solutions. The authors also showed, however, that this difference could be eliminated, enabling all participants to score at the 90% level, by replacing the query language with a query -by-example dialog, which enabled users to select exemplars of desired results. Thus, this study showed that the difficulties associated with generating correct Boolean expressions could be predicted by differences in individual cognitive factors but, more importantly, could be significantly reduced by changing the "system image" (Norman 1983) for querying. Other work has also sought to represent Boolean query languages through visualizations and guided user-interface dialogs that are intended to reduce the cognitive difficulties associated with Boolean expressions (Spoerri 1993; Topi and Lucas 2005; Young and Shneiderman 1993).

Taking a different approach, Internet search engines have largely supplanted Boolean searching by deploying complex algorithms for best-match keyword search. Boolean queries are typically available in advanced mode if at all (and even when offered, as seen in the example given previously in this chapter, they may not work as you would expect them to). In general, Internet search engines, with their short input fields and one-button operation, make the value proposition:

You enter some words. Your words will be analyzed and matched against billions of documents. Only the best documents will be returned. Amazing – isn't it?

Under this oracle-like system image, the complexity of the system is hidden behind a vague description of the most straightforward pattern of interaction. With Web-based search engines, the vexing problem that plagues typical interfaces to library resources, which is thoroughly reviewed and analyzed by Borgman (1996), are addressed with a radical simplification of the query and results. When considering the external forces that act upon Web search – such as the complexity of the Internet's infrastructure, the diversity of the target audience and their information needs, the diverse motivations of the content providers, and a competitive landscape where the costs assumed by users to switch between engines is very low or entirely absent – this vagueness of operation is actually a virtue. Yet, it does beg the question: Does presenting a richer conceptual model of the underlying matching process improve the ability of searchers to find documents and, if so, for what kinds of information needs?

Koenemann and Belkin (1996) sought to answer this question by varying the degree of visibility and control of an underlying best-match retrieval engine, which also offered relevance feedback. They report that the interface with the greatest degree of visibility and control enabled users to achieve better retrieval effectiveness, and participants reported stronger positive feelings for these interfaces, in terms of usability and trust. These findings, at least for the specialized system and document collection used in this study, illustrate that by improving the visibility of the matching and retrieval process, participants could develop more accurate mental models of the system, and thus use it to a higher degree of effectiveness. Muramatsu and Pratt (2001) examined peoples' understandings for how popular Web search engines transform and match queries against documents. They observed that search engines process queries in quite different ways and that, for optimal results, one must formulate queries differently for each search engine used. For example, some search engines treat two word queries with an implied AND while others assume an OR. Some engines remove stop words while others do not. Some engines are sensitive to term order while others are not, and so on. Muramatsu and Pratt (2001) asked the question: Do users understand these operational differences? In order to answer this question, they presented 14 participants (profiles not reported) with representative query transformations and probed participants for their understandings of the search results. For example, they asked participants to explain why the query "to be or not to be" returned zero results for a particular search engine. Only two of the 14 participants were able to invoke some approximation of the notion of stop words, which explain this phenomenon. In general, they found that participants have weak mental models for query transformation. They, in turn, conjecture that users' mental models could be improved with an interface that makes the transformation visible; however, they also carefully note that they have no evidence that by improving the visibility of how queries are processed the overall search process is improved.

Other work has elicited understandings for Web search in naturalistic environments. Fidel et al. (1999) studied the information-seeking behavior of high school students, and reported that students had strikingly naïve understandings of Web-based search. One student, for example, said: "There's like a master program or something and everyone just puts information in, and it can be sent out to all the computer systems that hook up to it" (p. 27). They also report that the high school students of their study had expectations that everything is available on the Web. Slone (2002) interviewed library users at the library aiming, in part, to describe the mental models that people new to the Web employ when searching and browsing. Her data shows that while people had largely positive impressions of the Web, expressing ideas such as "everything is available" and "magical abilities." These participants also had vague understandings of search and employed naïve metaphors, and simplistic technical descriptions.

In all, these studies are fully consistent with the literature on mental models for devices, even simple devices: People have rudimentary, incomplete understandings for their functions. Second, logic-based query languages present a significant barrier in the information-seeking process and innovations in search interfaces have not been able to significantly lower this barrier. Third, while it seems that improvements in the visibility of the matching process might lead to better mental models, and in turn, improved searching, no framework for the specific factors concerning what to make visible and how has been proposed. Fourth, the mental models' orientation has not directly led to significant improvements in search interface design. Nevertheless, as argued in the previous section, knowledge of the operation of search engines can be important for understanding possibilities for expressing queries and understanding results. Thus, seeking to uncover how users' concepts of search engines lead to the expression and reformulation of queries is an important level of analysis.

Yet, broader levels of analysis also seem important. Search is no longer restricted to specialized systems for experts or to systems used by non-experts in well-defined settings (e.g., library catalogs). Rather, as we have seen, Web search engines have entered the everyday infrastructure of the general public. Thus, it is important to inquire into how people currently conceptualize how search engines work, and, even more, to inquire into how these homegrown mental models affect policy debates concerning search engines, as well as policy on the use of the Internet. Search engines, in short, are at the intersection of renewed civic-technological disputes, and they present new demands on the public's understanding of science and technology (Miller 1998).

Insofar as we know, no one has investigated the "folk theories" for how search engines work. This term signals that one's mental models, which as we have seen, consist of a set of associated abstractions that enable explanation and prediction, have been shaped to a significant extent by social factors – friends, colleagues, and communities (Holland and Quinn 1987). Consider, for example, a study of mental models, where the investigator prompted participants for explanations of how their home thermostats work (Kempton 1987). Participants were found to understand how thermostats work via either the feedback theory (i.e., a thermostat is used to set a target temperature and the heating system turns itself on and off in order to hit that temperature) or the valve theory (i.e., a thermostat is like a gas peddle that regulates how much heat flows into the room). While participants that used the feedback theory to understand the thermostat, rarely adjusted it, those who used the valve theory tended to adjust the thermostat more frequently throughout the day. This work has been applied to the design of thermostats so that they match a given mental model and save energy. Now, turning to a domain more closely related to search engines, Payne (1991) asked people to explain how automatic bank machines functioned. In individual sessions participants were probed for their understanding of these machines by means of what-if questions such as: What happens to the card during the transaction? Why does it stay inside the machine? When analyzing the verbal protocols, he found a great diversity of explanations concerning the how the computational processes were decomposed and related and the roles of various storage devices (e.g., bank card, local teller machine, and centralized data bank).

The participants in studies of mental models are often non-specialists. Comparing their understanding of devices against expert models provides a method for exploring how information is imparted through specific devices or cultural sources. In turn, by examining the difference between people's understandings and the original conceptual model, one can seek to change the system image in order to clarify the conceptual model and hence improve the usability of the system. Moreover, the models that specialists hold are also worthy of investigation especially when specialists from different backgrounds need to communicate across disciplinary or institutional boundaries. An interesting example of this kind of a conceptual model for Web search has been created by Matt Leacock, a visual designer (Brown 2001). This conceptual model represents the search process with approximately 60 concepts and 100 relationships between these concepts. The model is divided into five conceptual zones and the concepts and relationships are very carefully laid out. To see the complete model in its entirety requires that it be printed on a 36 in. by 36 in. poster. An elided version, consisting of 20 concepts has also been published (Wurman 2001: 158). The aim of these complex models was to externalize a complete map of how a complex, enterprise-critical search system functioned. To produce the model, Leacock interviewed individual members of product groups and developed a composite model of how people understood the search system. This model was posted in public locations along with a red pen to encourage annotations and revisions. He found that no single person understood how the system operated but that by developing a complete model and placing it in public forums he was able to make the complexity of the system visible. This enabled people to communicate better, despite shifting teams and priorities, as well as differences in technical perspective (Brown 2001). Thus, the manner in which people tell stories about search and externalize their knowledge of search is an interesting type of technical communication.

15.3 Exploratory Study

To examine how people conceptualize Web search we decided to prompt students to draw sketches of how they thought search engines work. Then, we performed a content analysis of the resulting body of material. In Norman's terms (see previous section) this method elicits conceptual models, $C(M(t))$, from non-experts. We make no claims concerning how these models are put to use when reasoning about search engines in specific problem-solving or conversional contexts; in fact, for most participants this is likely the first time that they expressed their understanding for search-engines in any form. Furthermore, it is important to note that participants varied in their level of ability and comfort to draw sketches in a short period of time. The task, in short, was quite demanding. We decided on this form of expression because sketching is an expressive, open-ended form of communication, allowing people to stress what is important to them through both drawings and words.

Participants in this work were students at various levels of academic achievement in Information Science, ranging from freshman with undeclared majors to Ph.D. students in Information Science. This participant group is an interesting population to study for two reasons. First, as a group we can expect a diversity of experiences with Web search engines. Some students in Information Science, especially at the graduate level, will have had opportunities to develop their knowledge for search and to explain search to other people. Other students will have limited or no formal training in search but can be expected to have a high level of exposure to and interest in search engines. Thus, these students provide a population of users with a broad range of experience of search. Certainly, we expected graduate students to reflect the upper bound of knowledge. In any case, because of these students' level of educational accomplishment, generally high use of the Internet and search, and specific area of interest (Information Science), one would expect that this sample would have a relatively high-level knowledge. Second, as instructors of classes on Database and Information Retrieval systems, we were extremely interested in both the technical and folk knowledge that our students held for search systems. Thus, collecting this data, analyzing it, and reflecting upon it have also served a very practical need: to enable lively classroom discussions about Web search and to orient us to our students' understanding of how search works.

This exploratory study, in sum, addresses four research questions: 1) What concepts do people include and emphasize in their conceptual models; 2) What misconceptions are found in these models? 3) What visual forms do people use to express their understanding of search engines? 4) What metaphors and technical terms are used? Following the existing literature, we hypothesized that the models would reflect only a rudimentary understanding of search engines and that participants with greater levels of academic accomplishment in Information Science would produce more nuanced conceptual models with more correct concepts. Preliminary findings of this research were presented in Hendry and Efthimiadis (2004) and Efthimiadis and Hendry (2005).

15.4   Method

15.4.1   Instructions

At the top of a blank 8 × 11 in. paper sheet, undergraduate and graduate students at the University of Washington were instructed to draw and label a sketch explaining how a search engine works. Students were given approximately 10 minutes to complete the task at the beginning of a regularly scheduled class. The exact instructions and time available to complete the task varied because different moderators collected data in different classes. A sample of 232 sketches was collected in the spring and autumn of 2003.

15.4.2 Participants

The student participants ($N = 232$) were from the following academic levels: 1) Freshman taking their first college-level course; 2) Juniors and Seniors pursuing an undergraduate degree in Information Science; 3) Fulltime students pursuing a master's degree in Library and Information Science; 4) Working professionals pursuing a two-year executive degree in Information Management; and 5) Fulltime students pursing a doctorial degree in Information Science. For this analysis, student participants were assigned to the following three groups: 1) Undergraduate-freshman ($n = 53$); 2) Undergraduate-informatics ($n = 95$); and 3) Graduate-information-science ($n = 84$). While these categories represent three general levels of academic achievement, the demographic profiles for the participants within these groups are heterogeneous, especially for the second two categories, with broad ranges in ages, work experiences, and educational achievement.

15.4.3 Reference Model of Internet Search Engines

In order to analyze the sketches, a conceptual model for search was chosen as a reference point. This model drew upon standard textbook components of search engines (Belew 2000; Liddy 2001) and identified the major conceptual components of any generic search engine. The model divides search into three phases, indexing, searching, matching, each of which contains its own processing components, as follows:

A. INDEXING: Processing documents so they can be retrieved later

1. *Content:* The search engine accesses documents, such as Web pages.
2. *Spidering/Crawling:* The search engine fetches Web pages
3. *Parsing:* Words from Web pages are extracted and analyzed in some fashion
4. *Inverted-index-creation:* An index that maps words to Web pages is created
5. *Link-analysis:* The search engine analyzes the linking structure among Web pages
6. *Storage:* Web pages and indexes are stored at the search engine

B. SEARCHING: Users formulate a query and inspect results

7. *User:* A person interacts with the search engine
8. *User-need:* A 'need' triggers a user to perform a search
9. *Query:* An interface is used to submit a query to a search engine
10. *Results:* The output from a search-engine are a list of Web pages

C. MATCHING: Queries are matched against Web pages

    11. *Query processing:* Keywords and operators are extracted from the query
    12. *Matching:* Words from the query are matched against words in Web pages
    13. *Accessing-inverted-file:* Keywords are used to access the inverted file
    14. *Ranking:* A ranked ordering of Web pages is created

In the analysis below, this model is used as a baseline instrument to assess the completeness of the participants' conceptual models.

15.5   Results

Figures 15.1–15.7 show seven sketches () that are representative of the full sample of 232 sketches. Notably, these sketches – and the full sample – reveal a tremendous diversity of approaches for explaining the operation of search engines. Figure 15.1 is noteworthy for employing multiple metaphors while maintaining compositional coherence and Fig. 15.2 is noteworthy for employing both symbolic and representational elements while also maintaining compositional coherence. Sometimes, metaphoric imagery or idiomatic symbols are used; for example, a cloud is often used to depict the Internet and a cylinder is often used to depict an information store (e.g., see Figs. 15.1 and 15.2).

Figure 15.3, one of the most detailed and complete sketches in the sample, is an extreme example where, in a reversal of typical roles, the visual language

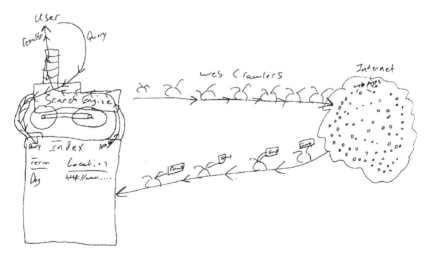

Fig. 15.1 Sketch of search engine illustrating the use of various metaphors, including a mechanical engine, complete with drive-train between wheels and a smoke stack, that performs the matching process, a cloud of particles indicating Websites on the Internet, and spiders that leave the search engine empty-handed and return with terms. In addition, the inverted file, user, query, and results are depicted

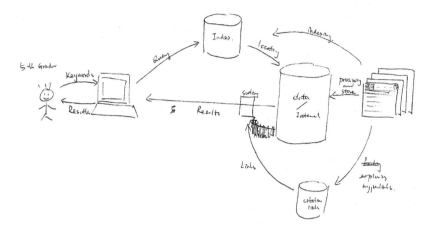

Fig. 15.2 Sketch of search engine illustrating the use of idiomatic symbols including cylinders for data stores, stick figure for users, computer monitor and keyboard client computer, and Graphical User Interface window for content. The processing steps are depicted with labeled lines between data stores and system inputs and outputs. This sketch illustrates an uncommon degree of coherence

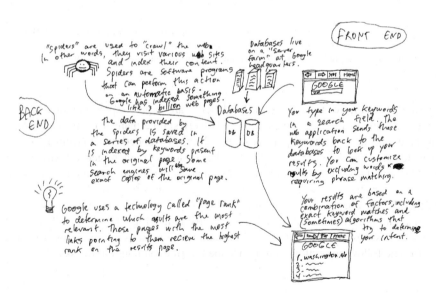

Fig. 15.3 Sketch of search engine that reveals a significant technical maturity, including an explanation of PageRank, approximate size of the WWW, and the complexity of determining a ranking of pages. The sketch segments the process into the front-end and back-end components. The use of visual symbols and user interface representations is noteworthy because to a large degree this visual language supports the written annotations – the reverse of many sketches. Finally, the light bulb, suggesting innovation and intelligence, draws attention to PageRank, a distinguishing characteristic of Google's matching algorithm

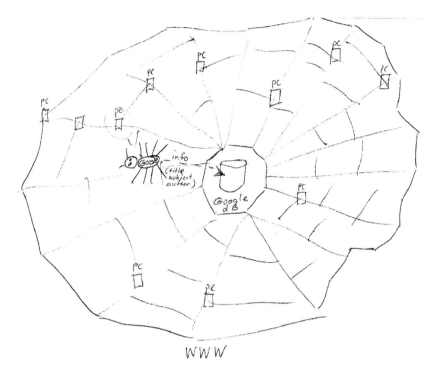

Fig. 15.4 Sketch of search engine illustrating the centrality of search with the Google DB at the center of a neatly organized Web of connections between PC computers. The Google spider crawls the Web, sending back information in the form of title, subject, and author

clarifies the narrative text. Some of the sketches are largely representational, and in such cases metaphors are depicted in a relatively simple manner or, for example, a query dialog and results display is sketched and the underlying machinery is not depicted (e.g., see Figs. 15.5 and 15.7). Other sketches are more general where box-and-line symbols are used to identify information types and communication pathways, such as those between client and server computers (e.g., see Fig. 15.2). None of the 232 sketches, however, employed a formal notation for representing systems, such as an Entity-Relationship modeling. Finally, unlike Figs. 15.1 and 15.2, many of the sketches depicted only a few concepts and relationships (e.g., see Figs. 15.5 and 15.6). The following sections summarize the information found in the sketches.

15.5.1 Concept Analysis

To assess the overall presence of search concepts in the sketches, each of the sketches was coded for concepts in the normative model presented above. As can be seen in even the small sample of eight sketches, these concepts manifest themselves

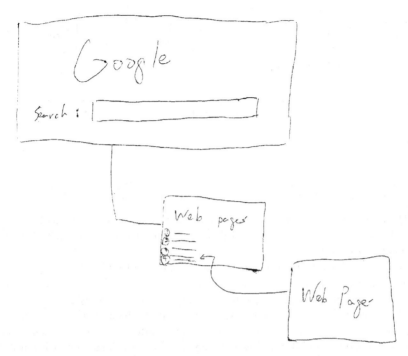

Fig. 15.5 Sketch of a search engine that illustrates the user interface. The first screen is recognizable as the Google input form for its use of whitespace and results pages shows a ranked list of Web pages

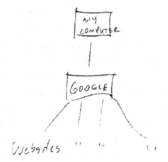

Fig. 15.6 Sketch of search engine that distinguishes between the client and server components and that indicates Google links to web sites

in numerous and different ways. For example, a query concept might be depicted as a box labeled 'query', as an input field and submit button, or as an annotation such as 'enter your keywords here'. Figures 15.1 and 15.5 each depict a query but in different styles. In this analysis, each of these manifestations of the concept would be counted.

Fig. 15.7 Sketch of search engine that illustrates that a client machine communicating with the world and returning results

The process for coding the sketches followed these steps:

1. The normative model was documented and a group of four coders, including the authors of this chapter, discussed this model and developed a common understanding for its concepts.
2. Working independently, the coders coded a sample of four sketches by inspecting each sketch and making a judgment for the presence or absence of each of the 14 concepts. Below, we call these binary judgments "votes".
3. The coders met to review each others' votes and discuss any differences in judgment. After three rounds of independent voting followed by group discussion, it was decided that the sketches were being coded in a sufficiently consistent fashion that the whole sample could be analyzed.
4. Working independently, each coder inspected each of the 232 sketches for the 14 concepts. This resulted in 12,992 votes for the presence or absence of concepts (4 coders × 14 concepts × 232 sketches).

The votes were analyzed for intercoder reliability by computing the percentage of agreement between each pairwise combination of the four coders for all 12,992 votes ($M = 0.84$, $N = 6$, $SD = 0.02$). At first glance, this may suggest a relatively high degree of agreement. But, in fact, these numbers overestimate the intercoder reliability because percentage agreement does not correct for cases where there is agreement by chance. This is especially important in this analysis because, as we shall see, the likelihood that a concept will be absent from a sketch is much higher than the likelihood that it will be present. Cohen's kappa statistic corrects for chance and is used extensively in the evaluation of intercoder reliability in medicine and content analysis. Unlike percentage agreement, which is rather liberal, Cohen's kappa is a rather conservative measure. This is because kappa accounts for the differences in the distribution of values across the categories for different coders and only gives credit for agreement beyond the distributions of values in the marginals (Lombard et al. 2002: 592). Cohen's kappa was calculated for each pair of coders (kappa = 0.57, $N = 6$, $SD = 0.04$). In general, this level of agreement is considered as moderate level of agreement beyond chance (Landis and Koch 1977: 165). Consensus on calculating, reporting, and interpreting intercoder reliability is lacking in the literature on content analysis, an especially important method of analysis in studies of media use and human-to-human communication (Lombard et al.

2002). Nevertheless, given the complex nature of the data and its overall pattern, we believe that a sufficient level of reliability is obtained when the following cut-offs are made: 1) if 3 or 4 votes inclusive, concept present; and 2) if 0–2 votes, concept absent. Using these cut-offs, the votes were counted to determine the presence-or-absence status of each concept in each sketch. This transformed data is used in the analysis below. It is also important to note that the intercoder agreement vary across concepts. For example, the coders could more reliably identify the presence or absence of the concept *query* than they could for the concept *accessing-the-inverted-file* because *query* is a simpler concept.

Figure 15.8 presents the frequency distribution of concepts across all sketches, showing that a sketch contains on average about 4.5 concepts ($SD = 3.0$) with a low of 0 concepts ($n = 25$) and a high of 13 concepts ($n = 2$). Examples of sketches with 0 concepts are written notes such as "I don't know" and "Magic" and uninterruptible sketches such as one depicting an octopus, a stickman exchanging documents, or sketches of cartoon characters that seem to be processing information generally

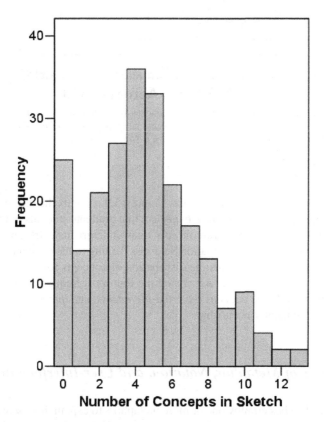

Fig. 15.8 The frequency distribution of number of concepts depicted in sketches ($N = 232$). On average, 4.5 concepts ($SD = 3.0$) are depicted in each sketch with a low of no concepts ($n = 17$) and a high of 13 concepts ($n = 1$)

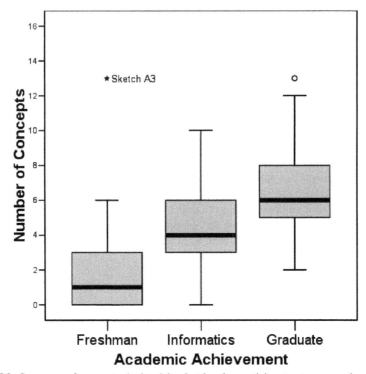

Fig. 15.9 Summary of concepts depicted in sketches by participant category, undergraduate-freshman (*Mdn* = 1.0, *SD* = 2.3, *n* = 53), under-graduate-informatics (*Mdn* = 4.0, *SD* = 2.4, *n* = 95), and graduate students (*Mdn* = 6.0, *SD* = 2.5, *n* = 84)

but lacked any identifiable explanations. Figure 15.9 presents the data collected by student group, showing, as might be expected, that graduate students in Information Science are able to depict more concepts than undergraduate freshmen or other undergraduate students in Information Science. Turning to the concepts depicted in the sketches, Fig. 15.10 presents the distribution of concepts found in the sketches with *query, results, content* and *user* being the four most frequently occurring concepts and *user need, link analysis, inverted-file-access*, and *query processing* being the four least frequently occurring.

15.5.2 Use of Metaphor, Notation, and User-Interface Imagery

Many of the sketches employ one or more metaphors to explain how search engines work, with, for example, Fig. 15.1 making a visual play on the metaphor *engine*. Figures 15.1, 15.4, and 15.7 are typical of the metaphors found in the sketches.

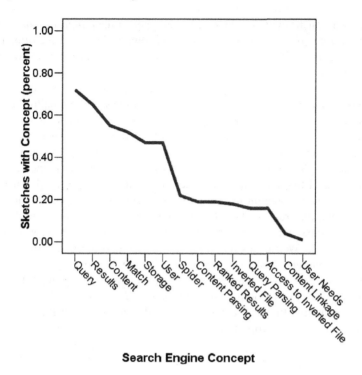

Search Engine Concept

Fig. 15.10 Summary of the 14 concepts depicted in all sketches ($N = 232$)

Images of *clouds* (e.g., see Fig. 15.1) and the *earth* (e.g., see Fig. 15.7) were commonly used to suggest the vast, undifferentiated yet ultimately connected and contained nature of the Internet. *Spiders, crawlers,* and *Webs* were used to illustrate the process of discovering and fetching content. *Books, bookshelves, store rooms,* and *card catalogs* were used to represent information stores or to indicate a degree of information organization. *Computers* were often given *arms, faces, smiles* and other anthropomorphic features to indicate such notions as agency and intelligence. *Gnomes, bots, robots, brains, stick-figure dogs* and other agents were used to suggest autonomous action and intelligence. *Eye glasses, magnifying glasses,* and *eyes* were used to suggest that the search process is about looking. *Radio towers,* an *orbiting satellite,* and a *bridge* were used to indicate all encompassing communication. A *message in a bottle* was used to suggest the challenge of finding relevant information. *Stick-figure people* with raised arms or *scoring a goal* with a foot were used to suggest successful searches. See Hendry (2006) for a detailed qualitative analysis of the conceptual metaphors that were employed in the sub-sample of sketches depicting algorithmic processes.

Turning to notation, many of the sketches contain symbols that represent a type of information and process. The symbol *cylinder* is frequently used to represent the storage of data. Figure 15.2, for example, depicts Web pages as a neat pile of documents that is in turn transformed into three different types of data: *indexes*, *data/Internet*, and *citation data*. *Monitors* and *keyboards*, as shown in Fig. 15.7, are often used to represent computers. It was more common, however, for participants to draw box-and-line diagrams with labeled inputs, outputs, processes, and data stores. For example, the concepts *user*, *search-engine*, and *database* are represented with labeled boxes and connected with directed lines. Many sketches employ subtle differences in notation to signal differences. For example, solid and dotted lines are sometimes used to signal a firm versus tenuous relationship between two artifacts, and symbols, such as circles and squares, are sometimes used to signal different types of entities. While such subtle differences occur frequently in the data, rarely is the meaning of the notational differences explicitly stated or used consistently. Finally, it was very common for participants to employ a mix of notation, meta-phoric imagery, and representation within the same sketch. For example, Figure 15.3 uses *cylinders* and *towers* to represent data and server farms, representational *boxes* to represent Web pages for query and result, and the image of a *spider* to represent the computational concept of "spidering" and "crawling." In Fig. 15.7, an image of the *world* is used to associate a query with a result that are both depicted as computers. As a metaphor, the image of the *world* was also used to refer to multiple ideas, including the geographic spread of the Internet as well as a repository of information at global proportions.

15.5.3 Misconceptions

The sketches also reveal a variety of misconceptions. Regarding information structure and organization, some sketches depict an Internet where a full list of Websites can be readily enumerated or an Internet that is an organized collection of Websites. Some participants gave search engines a privileged position to information: Google is often depicted at the center of the Web, and sometimes Google is even shown to, or at least implied to, directly link to Websites (see Fig. 15.6). Some participants depicted information as residing inside a search engine with, for example, Web pages arranged on bookshelves or pre-computed search results waiting to be retrieved and presented. Some sketches suggested an automatic categorization process where items found by a spider, for example, are sorted into categories by a computational process; other times, participants depicted human intervention, where people make selections based on editorial and legal standards during the indexing process. Meta tags were often denoted as a source for the indexing process, although search engines treat these terms with great care. Concerning the search process, some participants suggested collaboration amongst Web search engines: one engine asking for results from another engine, or a hierarchy or engines with Google at the center and other commercial services subsumed by it on a secondary tier. Some participants depicted de-centralized algorithms where Google initiates a search by asking a second tier of computers, which, in turn, ask a third tier. Concerning the matching process, participants often illustrated naïve sequential letter-by-letter matching algorithms (akin to regular expressions for matching) or vaguely expressed notions of indexed-based lookup.

15.6 Discussion

The main finding of this exploratory study is that students in this sample produced mostly rudimentary conceptual models for how search engines work. Even Graduate students in Information Science were, in general, only able to describe a few concepts within their sketches, and these were often the most obvious concepts (e.g., query and results). Undergraduates and freshman in Information Science produced sketches with still fewer concepts. A second finding is that the sketches reveal a great diversity of approaches for expressing a conceptual model. Some sketches proposed algorithms, illustrating successive transformations of data. Others were highly representational, showing iconographic depictions of such things as results, queries, and communication networks. Still others relied on the metaphoric language available, such as spiders and Webs. In sum, students seem to know relatively little about how search engines work and they describe what they know in very different ways.

Thus, this study follows the pattern of much of the literature on mental models. As Norman puts it: "... most people's understanding of devices they interact with is surprisingly meager, imprecisely specific, and full of inconsistencies, gaps, and idiosyncratic quirks" (1983: 8). Indeed, as we saw earlier, this is the main conclusion of previous studies of people's understandings of search. This study reproduces these findings in the current technical milieu. The instrument used in this study – drawing a conceptual model in a short period of time for a very complex system – is admittedly demanding, and the results likely underestimate students' knowledge, which would otherwise be expressed more robustly in situated or diagnostic settings. Nevertheless, in general, we believe that students' performance on this task should be much higher if the conceptual knowledge for how search engines work was a basic component of technical literacy. Without this knowledge students are ill-equipped to engage in topics associated with search engines and, indeed, to teach others about search engines – an activity that many students of information science programs will engage in during their careers. This argument for knowing the central concepts of search engines, moreover, applies to non-student populations as well, including everyday users of the Internet who, as recounted above in the stories from the popular press, often understand search as a perplexing phenomenon.

Assessing people's knowledge for search engines can be seen as a special case of the general problem of *civic scientific literacy* (Miller 1998), that is, having sufficient competence with science to understand public policy debates that center on science and technology. The argument is that a healthy democracy requires a scientifically literate citizenry; otherwise, citizens will be poorly equipped to influence public policy in such matters as nuclear power, reproductive technologies, global warming, and so on. Thus, an important goal is to measure the scientific literacy of a population for the purposes of benchmarking and garnering support for public education in science and technology, for making cross-cultural comparisons, and so on. Survey instruments of open- and closed-end questions that measure a person's knowledge for the standard of scientific inquiry and the knowledge of scientific vocabulary have been developed. These instruments, with the appropriate sampling procedures and statistical analysis, are claimed to produce a durable, meaningful measure of populations' scientific literacy (Miller 1998). This approach, it is important to note, privileges knowledge in the head. And, as a result, it has been attacked for not accounting for the situated, collective development and application of scientific knowledge, especially when technological issues play out in social contexts (Roth and Lee 2002). For now, we put this dispute aside and simply note that both positions have merit.

Next, we turn to the question of how best to intervene to improve the public's knowledge of search engines. One observation is that it is important to equip people with conceptual knowledge for search engines that can be put to use in different problem situations. Of course, the application of this conceptual knowledge may require other forms of knowledge that are specific to the problem setting (Borgman 1996). A second observation is that the conceptual knowledge of search is not localized to a well-bounded setting or system. Rather, it is distributed amongst a diverse number of sub-systems that make up the artificial world of the Internet, including Web servers, browsers, Internet protocols, search engine operations, and so on. Thus, approaches to explaining Web search engines will have to take into account the full complexity of the Internet, networking, fiber optics, etc. Below, we organize approaches of intervention into three categories:

1. Models and simulations of search engines;
2. Forums for discussing search engines;
3. Contextually relevant explanations.

15.6.1 Models and Simulations of Search Engines

Halttunen (2003) and Halttunen and Jarvelin (2005) seek to teach students about search engines by developing a constructive learning environment, called the Information Retrieval Game, which allows students to develop skills and conceptual knowledge for how search works. With this learning tool, students perform searches against a test collection and are given specific feedback on the quality of their searches. Thus, this approach helps students to develop specialized skills in searching. In contrast, to this pedagogically-centered approach are specialized tools, largely designed for programmers, for visualizing search processes. The Luke tool (Luke 2004), for example, allows programmers to inspect the search indices, query processing, and matching process for the Lucene search engine; indeed, in our teaching experience, it has proven to be quite effective for helping novice programmers learn the Lucene Application Programming Interface. For students in a library and information science program, Efthimiadis (2003) has developed the IR Toolbox, an experiential teaching tool for learning about information retrieval systems (Efthimiadis & Freier, 2007). Through hands on interaction, the IR Toolbox helps students develop their conceptual model of search engines by exploring, visualizing, and understanding IR processes and algorithms without needing to program. In a sequential fashion, the IR Toolbox presents the following processing steps: a) Document analysis (e.g., tokenizers, stemmers, stop lists), b) Indexing (e.g., ability to browse inverted file and extract statistics), c) Searching (e.g., ability to enter queries and select weighing algorithms such as IDF, TF-IDF, OKAPI), d) Evaluation (e.g., evaluate results using the TREC evaluation software and associated collections, presenting recall-precision tables and graphs). The IR-Toolbox uses Lucene as its underlining search engine. Students can interact with the IR Toolbox at different levels of complexity on individual or group exercises that help them understand the different IR processes and build a more detailed conceptual model of search engines.

For a more general audience, a viable approach would be to develop specialized simulations of the operation of Web search engines. These simulations would present conceptual models of Web search, and allow people, especially non-specialists, to visualize search engine processes, focusing particularly on the issues of Internet search. This approach would be an elaboration of the models often presented in the popular press – perhaps; the best analogue would be an interactive science-center museum exhibit for explaining a complex process. A further step would be to give people the ability to construct their own search engines though an end-user programming environment which allowed them to visualize and refine their work (Fischer et al. 2004; Hendry 2006; Hendry and Harper 1997).

15.6.2 Forums for Discussing Search Engines

A second, complementary approach would be to develop a forum for discussing search engines. The root concept would be to create an open, constructive place that supports learning about how search engines work for everyone. From this root concept, we propose the following three general requirements. First, the forum should be run by a neutral organization that does not give preference to any particular search engine. This is important because, as we have seen, it can be in the search engine's interest to misinform its audience so that people tend to behave in ways that are commercially advantageous. This requirement is derived from the relationship between search engines and content producers, which, as discussed previously, is fundamentally adversarial. Second, experts in search need to participate in the forum. They need to help guide the conversations as good teachers do, correct misinformation, add nuance to conjectures and speculations, propose "experiments" that clarify how search engines work, and explain when and why firm conclusions cannot be drawn. Third, and perhaps most of all, the forum needs to track and clarify the public policy disputes related to the use and development of search engines. It seems inevitable that as search engines undergo technological advancement, value-oriented issues centered on fair access to information, autonomy to pursue one's own interests, information credibility, and others will become important to the public (Friedman and Kahn 2003). The forum we have in mind would seek to educate the public through collective participation, allowing experts and non-experts to engage in serious dialog. In short, the forum would enable inquiry into the science and technology of search to be socially grounded. Insofar as we know, a forum with these aims does not exist, but however utopian this may sound, it would be of great benefit to the public if it did exist!

15.6.3   Contextually Relevant Help

The final approach for helping people to develop a robust conceptual model for how search engines work is to enable people to probe the operation of a search engine in a highly situated fashion. This, of course, is easier said than done as the lack of meaningful help messages, in general, and of context sensitive help, in particular, has dogged retrieval systems since the seventies. During the eighties there was an effort to include context sensitive help in front-end systems and expert intermediary systems with varied levels of success (see Efthimiadis, 1990, for a detailed literature review). The explosion of end-user search, on CD-ROM products and the Web, during the nineties shifted attention to other issues with no satisfactory solution to the problem. Research in this area includes work by Gauch and Smith (1993), Oakes and Taylor (1998), and more recently by Jansen (2005).

Our design ideas differ from the implicit suggestions that search engines make to users. These query refinements are not consistently correct and, in addition, require that the user could recognize them as well as distinguish them from sponsored results.

Triggered by some kind of breakdown, we therefore envision users being able to engage in meaningful interaction with the search engine, either by receiving system prompted context sensitive help, or by entering a diagnostic mode where they could ask questions about the problematic interaction or the problematic operation of the search engine. For example, if a person's home page does not appear on the first page, the user could ask a search engine to explain why this happened in the context of a particular query and set of results. In such a situation, the influence of query keywords, keywords on links, and page-to-page citation patterns could, in principle, be presented to users. Given the interests of the search engine, however, the searcher would do well to be skeptical. Obviously, such functionality would be used only rarely by those who are trying to understand the inner working of search engines. Nevertheless, being able to systematically explore and diagnose in the context of actual searching a particular query and set of results could provide a strong learning environment if the search engine were willing to disclose key information.

15.7 Conclusion

Search and culture are entwined in a dynamic dance. It is clear that people develop conceptual models for how search engines work, and, as this and previous studies have shown, these models are relatively weak. Less clear, however, is how educators, reformers, and activists can intervene effectively to improve the public's understanding of search. Yet, it seems clear that as search becomes even more embedded in our lives, value-oriented questions about the responsible and fair use of search will become more and more important. The adversarial relationship between content providers and search-engines is a transformative change in search that will be reckoned with for many years to come. In summary, the problem of search is one aspect of a larger question regarding the public's understandings of science and technology, of civic scientific literacy. Miller (1998: 220) says: "It is important to learn more about the magnitude and dynamics of [informal learning resources and processes] and about adults' selection of and trust in various kinds of communications [such as libraries, newspapers, magazines, television shows, and museums]". Quite right.

Acknowledgements We would like to thank Kreg Hasegawa for a very thorough review of a draft of this manuscript, Peyina Lin, Kristene Unsworth, and Hui P. Yang for help in conducting a content analysis of the sketches, and John LaMont who helped track down citations.

References

Belew RK (2000) Finding out about: a cognitive perspective on search engine technology and the WWW. Cambridge University Press, Cambridge

Belkin NJ, Oddy RN, Brooks HM (1982) ASK for information-retrieval: 1. background and theory. Journal of Documentation 38: 61–71

Borgman CL (1985) The user's mental model of an information retrieval system. Paper presented at the Proceedings of the 8th Annual International ACM SIGIR Conference on Research and Development in Information Retrieval (pp 268–273, June 5–7). Montreal, Quebec, Canada

Borgman CL (1986) The user's mental model of an information retrieval system: an experiment on a prototype online catalog. International Journal of Man-Machine Studies 24: 47–64

Borgman CL (1996) Why are online catalogs hard to use? Lessons learned from information-retrieval studies. Journal of the American Society for Information Science 37: 387–400

Brin S, Page L (1998) The anatomy of a large-scale hypertextual search engine. Paper presented at the 7th International World Wide Web Conference. Retrieved July 1, 2004, from http://wwwdb.stanford.edu/~backrub/google.html

Brown, DR (2001) SuperModeler: hugh dubberly. Gain: AIGA Journal of Design for the Network Economy, 1: 1–8. Retrieved, June 1, 2004, from http://gain1.aiga.org/pdf/profile.pdf

Cohen R (2002, December 15) Is googling okay? New York Times Magazine, p 50

Edwards B (2004, April 13) Morning edition: search engine wars, Part II. (Radio Broadcast). Seattle, National Public Radio, KUOW

Efthimiadis EN (1990) Progress in documentation: online searching aids: a review of front-ends, gateways and other interfaces. Journal of Documentation 46: 218–262

Efthimiadis EN (2003–2007) The IR toolbox. Available at http://irtoolbox. ischool.washington.edu

Efthimiadis EN, Freier NG (2007) IR-Toolbox: an experiential learning tool for teaching IR. In: Proceedings of the 30th Annual International ACM SIGIR Conference on Research and Development in Information Retrieval (Amsterdam, The Netherlands, July 23–27, 2007. SIGIR'07, ACM Press, New York

Efthimiadis EN, Hendry DG (2005) Search engines and how students think they work. In: Proceedings of the 28th Annual International ACM SIGIR Conference on Research and Development in Information Retrieval (Salvador, Brazil, August 15–19, 2005). SIGIR '05. ACM Press, New York, NY, pp 595–596. http://doi.acm.org/10.1145/1076034.1076145

Fidel R, Davies RK, Douglas MH, Holder JK, Hopkins CJ, Kushner EJ, Miyagishima BK, Toney CD (1999) A visit to the information mall: web searching behavior of high school students. Journal of American Society for Information Science 50: 24–37

Fischer G, Giaccardi E, Ye Y, Sutcliffe AG, Mehandjiev N (2004) Meta-design: a manifesto for end-user development. Communications of the ACM 47: 33–37

Friedman B, Kahn PH Jr (2003) Human values, ethics, and design. In: Jacko JA and Sears A (eds), The human–computer interaction handbook (pp 1177–1201). Mahwah, NJ: Lawrence Erlbaum Associates

Friedman B, Howe D, and Felten E (2002) Informed consent in the Mozilla browser: implementing value sensitive design. In: Proceedings of the 35th Annual Hawaii International Conference on System Sciences (HICSS '02) Vol 8 (January 7–10, 2002). Washington, DC: IEEE Computer Society. Retrieved July 15, 2005, from www.hicss.hawaii.edu/HICSS_35/HICSSpapers/PDFdocuments/OSPEI01.pdf

Gauch S, Smith J (1993) An expert system for automatic query reformulation. Journal of the American Society for Information Science 44: 124–136

Gentner D, Stevens AL (eds) (1983) Mental models. Hillsdale, NJ: Erlbaum

Gleick J (2004, March 21) Get out of my namespace. New York Times Magazine: 44–49

Greene SL, Devlin SJ, Cannata PE, Gomez LM (1990) No IFs, ANDs, ORs: a study of database querying. International Journal of Man–Machine Studies 32: 303–326

Halttunen K (2003) Students' conceptions of information retrieval: implications for the design of learning environments. Library and Information Science Research 25: 307–332

Halttunen K, Jarvelin K (2005) Assessing learning outcomes in two information retrieval learning environments. Information Processing and Management 41: 949–972

Hansell S (2003, December 8) Foes of bush enlist google in group prank. New York Times, p C.8

Hendry DG (2006) Sketching with conceptual metaphors to explain computational processes. In: Proceedings of IEEE Symposium on Visual Languages/Human-Centric Computing 2006, September 4–7, 2006, Brighton, UK (pp 95–102). IEEE Computer Society Press

Hendry DG, Efthimiadis EN (2004) Students' mental models of information retrieval systems. In: Proceedings of the American Society for Information Science and Technology, ASIST'04, Providence, Rhode Island, November 13–18, 2004. 41: 580–581. http://dx.doi.org/10.1002/meet.1450410186

Hendry DG, Harper DJ (1997) An informal information-seeking environment. Journal of American Society of Information Science (Special Issue on Human–Computer Interaction) 48: 1036–1048

Hochman D (2004, March 14) In searching we trust. New York Times, p 9.1

Holland D, Quinn N (eds) (1987) Cultural models in language and thought. Cambridge University Press, New York

Ingwersen P (1996) Cognitive perspectives of information retrieval interaction: elements of cognitive IR theory. Journal of Documentation 52: 3–50

Jansen BJ (2005) Seeking and implementing automated assistance during the search process. Information Processing and Management 41: 909–928

Johnson-Laird PN (1983) Mental models: towards a cognitive science of language, inference, and consciousness. Harvard University Press, Cambridge, MA

Kempton W (1987) Two theories of home heat control. In: D. Holland and N. Quinn (eds) Cultural models in language and thought (pp 223–242) Cambridge University Press, New York

Koenemann J, Belkin NJ (1996) A case for interaction: a study of interactive information retrieval behavior and effectiveness. In: Proceedings of the SIGCHI Conference on Human Factors in Computing Systems: Common Ground (pp 205–212). ACM Press

Lakoff G, Johnson M (1980) Metaphors we live by. The University of Chicago Press, Chicago

Landis J, Koch G (1977) The measurement of observer agreement for categorical data. Biometrics 33: 159–174

Lenhart A, Horrigan J, Fallows D (2004) Content creation online: Pew Internet and American Life Project. Retrieved 1 June 2004 from http://www.pewInternet.org/pdfs/PIP_Content_Creation_Report.pdf

Liddy E (2001) How a search engine works. Searcher 9(5). (Also Retrieved 1 June 2004 from http://www.infotoday.com/searcher/may01/liddy.htm)

Lombard MJ, Snyder-Duch J, Bracken CC (2002). Content analysis in mass communication: assessment and reporting of intercoder reliability. Human Communication Research 28: 587–604

Luke (2004, 1 June) Lucene Index Toolbox. Retrieved 1 June 2004 from http://www.getopt.org/luke/

McNichol T (2004, January 22) Your message here. New York Times, p G.1

Media Metrix (2004) Press Release, RESTON, Va. March 19, 2004. Retrieved 1 June 2004 from http://www.comscore.com/press/release.asp?press=443

Miller JD (1998) The measurement of civic scientific literacy. Public Understanding of Science 7: 203–223

Muramatsu J, Pratt W (2001) Transparent queries: investigating users' mental models of search engines. Paper presented at the Proceedings of the 24th Annual International ACM SIGIR Conference on Research and Development in Information Retrieval, New Orleans, LO

Noguchi Y (2004, February 9) Online search engines help lift cover of privacy. Washington Post, p A01

Norman DA (1983) Some observations on mental models. In: Gentner D, Stevens A (eds) Mental models (pp 7–14). Hillsdale, NJ: Lawrence Erlbaum Associates

Oakes MP, Taylor MJ (1998) Automated assistance in the formulation of search statements for bibliographic databases. Information Processing and Management 34: 645–668

Payne S (1991) A descriptive study of mental models. Behaviour & Information Technology 10: 3–21

Payne S (2003) Users' mental models: the very ideas. In: Carroll JM (ed) HCI models, theories, and frameworks (pp. 135–156). Morgan Kaufmann, New York

Roth W-M, Lee S. (2002). Scientific literacy as collective praxis. Public Understanding of Science 11: 33–56

Schemo J (2004, January 28) Online auctions, misspelling in ads often spells cash. New York Times, p A1

Simon H (1996) The Sciences of the artificial (3rd ed). MIT, Cambridge, MA

Slone D (2002) The influence of mental models and goals on search patterns during web interaction. Journal of the American Society for Information Science and Technology 53(13):1152–1169

Spoerri A (1993) InfoCrystal: a visual tool for information retrieval & management. Paper presented at the Proceedings of the Second International Conference on Information and Knowledge Management (pp 11–20). New York: ACM Press

Topi H, Lucas W (2005) Mix and match: combining terms and operators for successful web searches. Information Processing and Management 41: 801–817

Totty M, Mangalindan M (2003, February 26) As google becomes web's gatekeeper, sites fight to get in. Wall Street Journal, p A11.1

Wurman RS (2001) Information anxiety 2. Que, Indianapolis, IN

Young D, Shneiderman B (1993) A graphical filter/flow representation of boolean queries: a prototype implementation and evaluation. Journal of American Society for Information Science 44: 327–339

16
Web Searching: A Quality Measurement Perspective

D. Lewandowski and N. Höchstötter

Summary The purpose of this paper is to describe various quality measures for search engines and to ask whether these are suitable. We especially focus on user needs and their use of Web search engines. The paper presents an extensive literature review and a first quality measurement model, as well. Findings include that Web search engine quality can not be measured by just retrieval effectiveness (the quality of the results), but should also consider index quality, the quality of the search features and Web search engine usability. For each of these sections, empirical results from studies conducted in the past, as well as from our own research are presented. These results have implications for the evaluation of Web search engines and for the development of better search systems that give the user the best possible search experience.

16.1 Introduction

Web search engines have become important for information seeking in many different contexts (e.g., personal, business, and scientific). Research questions not answered satisfactorily are, as of now, how well these engines perform regarding user expectations and what measures should be used to get an overall picture of search engine quality. It is well known that search engine quality in its entirety cannot be measured with the use of traditional retrieval measures. But the development of new, search engine specific measures, as proposed in Vaughan (2004) are not sufficient, either. Search engine quality must be defined more extensively and integrate factors beyond retrieval performance such as index quality and the quality of the search features.

One aspect neglected is the user himself. But to discuss and judge the quality of search engines, it is important to focus on the user of such systems, too. Better performance of ranking algorithms or providing additional services does not always lead to users' satisfaction and to better search results. We focus on the Web search engine user behaviour to derive strategies to measure Web search engine quality. Additionally, quality assurance is an important aspect to improve customer satisfaction and loyalty. This is fundamental to protect market shares and revenues from

A. Spink and M. Zimmer (eds.), *Web Search, Springer Series in Information Science and Knowledge Management 14.*
© Springer-Verlag Berlin Heidelberg 2008

adverts. Furthermore, quality measurement helps to identify potential improvements of search engines.

We are sure that only an integrated approach to quality measurement can lead to results usable for the development of better search engines. As with information retrieval, in general, we find a paradigm shift from the more technical (document-oriented) perspective to the user-oriented perspective (Ingwersen and Järvelin 2005). Our goal in this chapter is to define the scope of our perspective in comparison to other approaches and to give a literature overview of quality measurements for search engines. We will also focus on each individual factor stated in studies dealing with user interaction with search engines and user expectations to search engines. The integrated approach of user and technical aspects shows that there are many possibilities but they are not widely adopted yet.

Our chapter first gives an overview of studies conducted to derive quality measures and to present the state of the art. The other focus in this section lies on user surveys and analyses to give an anticipation of what users really do by placing search queries. In Sect. 3 we give a general conspectus of parameters we deduced from our literature research and explain them shortly. In Sect. 4 we show empirical results that reflect the current quality standard by our individual measures of search engines. In the last section we summarize our findings and give potential strategies to improve search engines.

Many of the empirical findings stem from our own research conducted over the past years. Our integrated view on search engine quality measurement is reflected by the different research areas of the authors.

16.2   Related Studies

In this section, we will discuss studies dealing with search engines in the given context. The two areas relevant for extensive search engine quality measurement are the concept of information quality in general and its transfer to search engines as a technical background, and user studies to see what happens at the front-end. Each will be discussed under a separate heading.

16.2.1   Search Engine Quality

Referring to information quality, one usually appraises information on the basis of a single document or a set of documents. Two perspectives have to be differentiated: Firstly, information quality in the production of a database which means, how documents or sources have to be appropriately selected and secondly, information quality of the results retrieved by a certain IR system.

While the latter can be easily applied to Web search engines, the assurance of the quality of databases is more difficult. The approach of the major search engines is to index not only a part of the Web, but as much as possible (or as much as reasonable under economic aspects). Only certain fractions of the Web (such as Spam sites) should be willingly omitted from the database. While in the production of databases the process of selecting documents (or sources of documents) can be seen as an important quality aspect, in the context of search engines, this process is reassigned to the ranking process. Therefore, classic judgements for the selection of documents from a library context do not fit to search engines. Only specialized search engines rely on a selection of quality sources (Websites or servers) for building their indices.

An important point is that quality measurement of search results give only limited insight into the reliability and correctness of the information presented in the document. Popular examples are documents from Wikipedia, which are often highly ranked by search engines. But, there seems not to be an agreement of experts whether Wikipedia content is trustworthy or not. For a normal user, there is only a limited chance of scrutinising these documents. In this context, perceived information quality is more a matter of trust. Within the wider context of search engine evaluation, it is possible to build models completely based on trust (Wang et al. 1999), as explained later on.

When discussing quality of search results, one should also keep in mind how search engines determine relevance. They mainly focus on popularity (or *authority*) rather than on what is commonly regarded as quality. It should be emphasized that in the process of selecting documents to be indexed by engines and in the ranking process as well, no human reviews are involved. But a certain bias can be found inherent in the ranking algorithms (Lewandowski 2004b). These rate Web pages (apart from classic IR calculations) mainly by determining their popularity based on the link structure of the Web. The basic assumption is that a link to a page is a vote for that page. But not all links should be counted the same; link-based measures take into account the popularity of the linking page itself and the number of outgoing links, as well. This holds true for both of the main link-based ranking algorithms, Google's PageRank (Page et al. 1998) and HITS (Kleinberg 1999).

Link-based measures are commonly calculated query -independent, i.e., no computing power is needed to calculate these measures at the moment users place their search queries. Therefore, these measures can be applied very fast by the ranking process. Other query -independent factors are used as well (see Table 16.1 and for a detailed discussion Lewandowski 2005a). Here, the important point is that the process of ranking Web pages evolved from a query -document matching, based on term frequency and similar factors, to a process where several quality measurements are also taken into account.

Link-based algorithms are of good use to push some highly relevant results to the top of the results list. This approach is oriented towards the typical user behaviour.

Users often view only a few results from the top of the list and seldom process to the second or even third page of the results list. Another problem with the calculation of appropriate result lists is the shortness of search queries. Therefore, most ranking algorithms prefer popular pages and the presence of search terms in anchor

Table 16.1 Query-independent ranking factors (taken from Lewandowski 2005a)

Directory hierarchy	Documents on a higher hierarchy level are preferred
Number of incoming links	The higher the number of incoming links, the more important the document.
Link popularity	Quality/authority of a document is measured according to its linking within the Web graph.
Click popularity	Documents visited by many users are preferred.
Up-to-dateness	Current documents are preferred to older documents.
Document length	Documents within a sudden length range are preferred.
File format	Documents written in standard HTML are preferred to documents in other formats such as PDF or DOC.
Size of the Website	Documents from larger Websites (or within a sudden size range) are preferred.

texts. Although the general user rarely uses advanced search features, this does not make them unnecessary or useless. On the one hand, there are special user groups like librarians or information professionals who conduct complex searches. On the other hand, while there is a majority of queries that can be successfully formulated without the use of advanced search syntax, one knows from his or her own searching behaviour that at least *sometimes* one needs to use operators or other advanced features. Users who have some background in the field they are searching use more often phrase searches. Users who know how search engines work also apply operators and phrase search more frequently.

With a reasonable amount of search features users are able to influence their search queries and with that the quality of returned results. When the user is able to construct more complex queries, it will be easier for the engine to return relevant pages. A discussion of features provided by different search engines can be found in Lewandowski (2004a). The topic will be discussed later in detail.

16.2.2   User Perspective

There are two main empirical directions regarding user perspectives. One direction is represented by laboratory studies and surveys or by a combination of both. The other direction stands for the analysis of search engine transaction logs or the examination of live tickers published by search engines. Some search engines have a 'live ticker' or 'live search' enabling one to see the current search queries of other users (e.g., http.//www.lycos.de/suche/livesuche.html). This possibility is also often called 'spy function'. We will give a short overview of both regarding user behaviour to derive parameters for quality measurement. Table 16.2 shows the advantages and disadvantages of the different methods mentioned.

In surveys, users are sometimes directly asked which disturbing factors they notice by using Internet search engines. They also give a subjective view from the

Table 16.2 Methods for obtaining data on search engine users' behaviour

Method	Advantages	Disadvantages
User survey	Users express themselves, demographics are available, detailed questions are possible	Users lie, they try to "look better", dependent on formulation of queries and interviewer (if present)
Laboratory studies	Detailed interactions are observable, often combined with a user survey for demographics	Very small samples, expensive, time consuming, not representative
Live ticker inquiry	Large samples of search queries, special search feature usage is also available, time-dependent analysis of search queries	No information about sessions (reformulation, topic changes, search queries per session), no demographics
Transaction log analysis	Detailed information about searching behaviour by search session analysis, time-dependent analysis of search queries	No demographics, data set is often tampered by robots

users perspective on what special search features and other offers they use and know in search engine interfaces. Another possibility is to ask questions about their knowledge of the functionality of search engines, since users with different knowledge levels show a different searching behaviour (Schmidt-Maenz and Bomhardt 2005). In most cases, laboratory studies are only based on small samples and are for that reason not representative. It is also possible that subjects feel observed and try to search in a more professional way by using more operators or search features. One of the best and most representative ways to get user data is the analysis of transaction logs or data collected in live tickers. The problem is that there is no additional knowledge of the user himself.

The study of Machill et al. (2003) consists of two parts, namely a telephone survey with 1,000 participants and a laboratory study with 150 subjects. They show in their survey that 14% of search engine users definitely use advanced search features. Only 33% of respondents know that it is possible to personalize search engine interfaces. The title and the description of recommended Web pages are very important for users to evaluate the result lists. Users dislike results that have nothing in common with the search query submitted before (44%). Another 36% decline of so-called dead links. Machill et al. (2003) concluded their results with the remark that Web search engine users want their searches to be rewarded with success, a quick presentation of results, and clearly designed result screens. Hoelscher and Strube (2000) showed that experts and newbies show different searching behaviour. Hotchkiss found different groups of searching behaviour regarding the proceedings of the examination of result screens. Furthermore, users prefer organic results to sponsored listings.

Analyses of search engine transaction logs show a similar searching behaviour. Table 16.3 gives an overview. Most studies were based on the Excite search engine (Jansen 2000; Spink et al. 2000; Spink et al. 2001; Spink and Jansen 2004; Spink et al. 2002). Others are conducted using logs from Altavista (Silverstein et al. 1999; Beitzel et al. 2004), and AlltheWeb (Jansen and Spink 2003, 2006) as obtained by a Spanish search engine BIWE (Buscador en Internet para la Web en Español (Cacheda and Viña 2001)). Hoelscher and Strube (2000) analyzed a query log of Fireball, a German search engine. Zien et al. (2000) observed the Webcrawler live ticker over a 66 days period. The year and length of observation period is given in Table 16.3. Additionally, we extract most important results to get the users' perspective such as the number of search queries and the average length of search queries. We also analyse the percentage of complex search queries and in particular the percentage of phrase search, and the percentage of search sessions where only the first result screen is evaluated, too.

It is obvious that search queries are very short. Secondly, a remarkable part of search queries consist of only one term. With some exceptions the usage of Boolean operators is very small. The usage of phrase search is one of the most common ways to narrow search queries. Users commonly only examine the first result screen. These facts demonstrate that search engine users formulate their queries very intuitively and they do not try hard to evaluate every result in the list. The first two Excite studies (Excite 1 and Excite 2) and the BIWE log reveal that only a few users use special search features. This portion is 0.1% (Excite 1), 9.7% (Excite 2), and 0.2% (BIWE).

These extractions from user surveys and studies show that search engine users definitely have factors which disturb them and that they do not adopt all offered services such as special search features, possibilities to personalize search engines, or operators. Surveys are a good way to ask the user directly what he likes or dislikes while interacting with search engines. But surveys can become problematical when users get the illusion of a perfect search engine. For that reason the interpretation of search engine transactions logs is an objective way to see defective and non-adopted features or services. This helps to derive strategies for a user-friendly design or to design services that will be adopted by the user. With this in mind, we will give examples of interaction points between the user and search engines that could cause users' disconfirmation. Additionally, we give examples of how to evaluate these interaction points and already realized improvements.

16.3   Search Engine Quality Measurement

In this section, we focus on the quality indicators for search engines. We are aware of the fact that more factors exist than we describe in each subsection. But we regard the selected factors as the most important ones. Other factors could be considered in further studies while they are omitted, here, for the clarity of the overview.

Table 16.3 Overview of studies based on logs and some results

Search engine	Excite 1	Excite 2	Fireball	Altavista 1	Excite 3	Web-crawler	BI WE	Allthe Web 1	Excite 4	Allthe Web 2	Altavista 2
Year of observation	1997	1997	1998	1998	1999	2000	2000	2001	2001	2002	2002
Length of observation period	1	1	31	43	1	66	16	1	1	1	1
Number Search Queries	51,473	1,025,908	16,252,902	993,208,159	1,025,910	50,538,653	105,786	451,551	1,025,910	957,303	1,073,388
Average length of queries	38,750	38,750	38,899	38,809	38,809	38,779	38,869	38,809	38,870	38,778	38,962
Percentage of one term queries	–	62.6%	–	25.8%	29.8%	22.5%	–	25.0%	29.6%	33.0%	20.4%
Complex queries	15.9%	9.3%	2.6%	20.4%	10.9%	35.6%	8.6%	4.3%	11.3%	4.6%	27.3%
Phrase Search	6.0%	5.1%	–	–	5.9%	10.4%	3.6%	0.0%	5.9%	0.0%	12.1%
Only 1st result screen (%)	58.0	66.3	–	85.2	69.9	–	67.9	54.1	84.6	76.3	72.8

16.3.1   Retrieval Measures

Retrieval measures are used to measure the performance of IR systems and to compare them to one another. The main goal for search engine evaluation is to develop individual measures (or a set of measures) that are useful for describing the quality of search engines. Retrieval measures have been developed for some 50 years. We will give an overview of the main retrieval measures used in IR evaluation. It will be shown that these measures can also be used for search engine evaluation, but are of limited use in this context. Therefore, Web-specific retrieval measures were developed. But a set of measures that can be used for getting a complete picture of the quality of search engines is still missing.

General Retrieval Measures

The retrieval performance of the IR system is usually measured by the "two classics", precision and recall.

Precision measures the ability of an IR system to produce only relevant results. Precision is the ratio between the number of relevant documents retrieved by the system and the total number of documents retrieved. An ideal system would produce a precision score of 1, i.e. every document retrieved by the system is judged relevant.

Precision is relatively easy to calculate, which mainly accounts for its popularity. But a problem with precision in the search engine context is the number of results usually given back in response to typical queries. In many cases, search engines return thousands of results. In an evaluation scenario, it is not feasible to judge so many results. Therefore, cut-off rates (e.g. 20 for the first 20 hits) are used in retrieval tests.

The other popular measure, the so-called recall, measures the ability of an IR system to find the complete set of relevant results from a collection of documents. Recall is the ratio of the number of relevant documents retrieved by the system to the total number of relevant documents for the given query. In the search engine context the total number of relevant documents refers to all relevant documents on the Web. As one can easily see, recall cannot be measured, in this context. A proposed solution for this problem is the method of pooling results from different engines and then measuring the relative recall of each engine.

Precision and recall are not mathematically dependent on each other, but as a rule of thumb, the higher the precision of a result set, the lower the recall and vice versa. For example, a system only retrieving one relevant result receives a precision score of 1, but usually a low recall. Another system that returns the complete database as a result (maybe thousands or even millions of documents) will get the highest recall but a very low precision.

Other "classic" retrieval measures are fallout and generality (for a good overview of retrieval measures see Korfhage 1997). Newer approaches to measure the goodness of search results are

- Median Measure (Greisdorf and Spink 2001), which takes into account the total number of results retrieved. With median measure, it cannot only be measured how positive the given results are, but also how positive they are in relation to all negative results.
- Importance of completeness of search results and Importance of precision of the search to the user (Su 1998). These two measures try to employ typical user needs into the evaluation process. It is taken into account whether the user just needs a few precise results or maybe a complete result set (while accepting a lower precision rate). For the purpose of search engine evaluation that focuses on the user, these two measures seem highly promising.
- Value of Search Results as a Whole (Su 1998), which is a measure that seems to correlate well with other retrieval measures regarded as important. Therefore, it can be used to shorten the evaluation process and make it less time and cost consuming.

In the information science community, there is an ongoing and lively debate on the best retrieval measures. But unfortunately, there is a lack of current and continuous evaluation of search engines testing different measures.

Web-Specific Retrieval Measures

Quite early in the history of search engines, it became obvious that for the evaluation of these systems, Web-specific retrieval measures should be applied. In this section, we present the most important ones. They all have in common that they are used in experimental research and they are not widely used in real evaluations. Some empirical tests were applied in the development of these measures, but there are no larger evaluations, yet, that compare their use to that of other measures.

- *Salience* is the sum of ratings for all hits for *each* service out of the sum of ratings for *all* services investigated (Ding and Marchionini 1996). This measure takes into account how well all search engines studied perform on a certain query.
- *Relevance concentration* measures the number of items with ratings of 4 or 5 [from a five-point relevance scale] in the first 10 or 20 hits (Ding and Marchionini 1996).
- *CBC ratio* (MacCall and Cleveland, 1999) measures the number of content-bearing clicks (CBC) in relation to the number of other clicks in the search process. A CBC is "any hypertext click that is used to retrieve possibly relevant information as opposed to a hypertext click that is used for other reasons, such as the 'search' click that begins a database search or a 'navigation' click that is used to traverse a WWW-based information resource" (p. 764).
- *Quality of result ranking* takes into account the correlation between search engine ranking and human ranking (Vaughan 2004: 681).
- *Ability to retrieve top ranked pages* combines the results retrieved by all search engines considered and lets them be ranked by humans. The "ability to retrieve

top ranked pages" measures the ratio of the top 75% of documents in the results list of a certain search engine (Vaughan 2004).

But every quality measurement dealing with Web-specific retrieval measures has to be combined with user strategies. In reality, users only examine the first result screens (see Table 16.3), they do not even use search features or operators to really interact with search engines. (Hotchkiss et al. 2004) defined different search types. The normal search engine user corresponds to the "Scan and Clickers". They only watch the top results, sometimes also paid listings. They decide very quickly to visit a page after reading the short description texts and URLs. Machill et al. (2003) also observe subjects who try to get good answers after very short questions. Regarding these annotations, it is important to think about retrieval measures that deal with this user specific searching behaviour. If a user always watched the first three results, only, the best search engine would be the one returning the most appropriate pages within those first results. How do retrieval measures comply with the search engine users' search strategies?

16.3.2   Toward a Framework for Search Engine Quality

As already can be seen from the web-specific retrieval measures, search engine quality goes well beyond the pure classification of results in relevant or non-relevant ones. The relevance judgements may be the most important point in the evaluation of search engines, but surely not the only one.

A framework for measuring search engine quality was proposed in Xie et al. (1998) and further developed in Wang et al. (1999). The authors base their model on the application of the SERVQUAL (Service and Quality) model (Parasuraman et al. 1988) on search engines. As this is a completely user-centred model, only the *user perceived* quality can be measured. The authors apply gap analysis to make a comparison between expectations and perceived performance of the search engines, but do not weight the factors observed.

The model clearly lacks the system centred model of IR evaluation. It is interesting to see that according to this investigation, one of the main points in search engine evaluation ("Search results are relevant to the query ") does not differ greatly from engine to engine.

Contrary to such user-centred approaches is the "classic" system approach, which tries to measure the performance of information retrieval systems from a more "objective" point of view. Saracevic (1995) divides the evaluation of IR systems into two broad categories with three levels each:

- System-centred evaluation levels: Engineering level (e.g., hardware or software performance), input level (coverage of the designated area), and processing level (e.g., performance of algorithms).
- User-centred evaluation levels: Output level (interaction with the system, feedback), use and user level (where questions of application to given problems and

tasks are raised), and social level (which takes into account the impact on the environment).

Saracevic concludes that results from one level of evaluation do not say anything about the performance of the same system on the other levels of evaluation and that "this isolation of levels of evaluation could be considered a basic shortcoming of all IR evaluations" (p. 141).

In our opinion, this also applies to the evaluation of search engines. Only a combination of both, system and user-centred approach can lead to a clearer picture of the overall search engine quality.

There are several points of contact between users and search engines that can cause user discontent. The first and obvious point is the front-end of search engines. Next will be additional services that should help users to perform their search sessions. As shown above, special search features, personalization possibilities and operator usage are possible to control over transaction logs. Geoghegan (2004) gives five measures to compare search engine usability. He compares five major search engines by relevance of results, speed of result list calculation, the look of the input window and result list, and the performance of results based on a natural question. We suggest four main measures to check search engine quality out of the users' perspective.

- Interface design: structure of search engine Web pages and the presentation of the results. The input window should be structured in a clear way without over-whelming advertising. The result lists have to separate organic results from sponsored links. A different colour will be helpful.
- Acceptance of search features and operators: Which functions are accepted by users? Do they use operators? Do users personalize their preferred search engine?
- Performance of search engines: The speediness of result list presentation is one important point. Also intuitive and very short search queries should yield serious results. So-called dead links and spam have to be avoided.
- User guidance: Newbies need help to formulate adequate search queries, phrase searches, or complex searches. It is also helpful to give users some hints how search features work and what to do with them. A short introduction in search engine technology is recommended, too.

Taking both into account, the system approach and the user-centred approach, we propose another quality framework that considers more objective measures as well as the user perspective. Therefore, we expand the quality framework first proposed in Lewandowski (2006c) to four sections as follows:

- Index Quality: This points to the importance of the search engines' databases for retrieving relevant and comprehensive results. Measures applied in this section include Web coverage, country bias, and up-to-datedness.
- Quality of the results: This is the part where derivates of classic retrieval tests are applied. As can be seen from the discussion on retrieval measures above, it should be asked which measures should be applied and if new measures are needed to satisfy the unique character of the search engines and their users. An additional measure that should be applied is, for example, the uniqueness of

search results in comparison to other search engines. It is worth mentioning that users are pretty satisfied by finding what they search for. The subjects in the laboratory study conducted by Machill et al. (2003) admit that they are very pleased with search results and also with their favourite search engine. In the survey conducted by Schmidt-Maenz and Bomhardt (2005), 43.0% of 6,723 respondents very often found what they wanted and another 50.1% often. The question is if users could really evaluate the quality of results. Users are not able to compare all recommended Web pages. Sometimes 1,000,000 results are listed. It is more probable that they only think they find what they want since they do not even know what they could find in other results.

- Quality of search features: A good set of search features (such as advanced search), and a sophisticated query language is offered and works reliable.
- Search engine usability : This gives a feedback of user behaviour and is evaluated by user surveys or transaction log analyses. This will give comparable parameters concerning interface design. Is it possible for users to interact with search engines in an efficient and effective way? Is the number of search queries and of reformulations in different search engines lower? It is also of importance which features are given to assist users regardless if they are beginners or professionals in using search engines. Users search in a very intuitive way (Schmidt-Maenz and Koch 2006).

All in all, the user should feel comfortable using search engines. Since users currently have not developed all necessary skills to handle search engines in the best way their usage should be intuitive and simple. In addition, users should get every support whenever it is useful or required. It has to be possible that users enhance their searching behaviour by using additional services and features to get the best recommendations of Web pages as possible.

16.4 Empirical Results

In this section, we will present studies dealing with search engine quality and the behaviour of search engines users. The combination of these two research areas shows that there is a research gap in the user-centred evaluation of search engines. While there are a lot of studies dealing with single points, there is no study (or series of studies) focussing on an overall picture of search engine quality from the user perspective.

16.4.1 Index Quality

Search engines are unique in the way they build up their databases. While traditional IR systems are usually based on databases manually built by human indexers from selected sources (e.g., from journals or books within a certain subject area), search engines have to make use of the link structure of the Web to find their documents by crawling it. It is a big challenge to build up and maintain an index generated by Web robots. A good overview is given in Risvik and Michelsen (2002).

The quality of the index of an individual search engine can be regarded in several ways. At first, the index should be comprehensive (i.e. cover a large portion of the Web). While the overall comprehensiveness is important, a search engine with a good overall coverage is not necessarily the best for every area of the Web. For example, a user searching for German language content will not be satisfied if the search engine with a general Web coverage of maybe 80% does not include German documents at all or just to a small degree. Therefore, country bias in search engine databases is an important point in research.

The third important index quality factor is the up-to-datedness of the databases. The Web is in constant flux, new documents are added, older documents disappear and other documents change in content. As can be seen from Schmidt-Maenz and Koch (2006), to a large amount, users search for current events and actual news stories. In addition, the number of incoming links changes in a similar manner. Web pages concerning a current topic will achieve more incoming links, when this page is of importance. When the event will not longer be of interest anymore, the number of inbounds decreases again (Schmidt-Maenz and Gaul 2005). Such queries (to give one example) can only be "answered" by search engines with an up-to-date index.

Index Sizes and Web Coverage

An ideal search engine would keep a complete copy of the Web in its database. But for various reasons, this is impossible. Many searches return lots of results, often thousands or even millions. Keeping this in mind, one could ask why a search engine should take the effort to build indices as large as possible and not just smaller ones that would fit the general users' queries.

A large index is needed for two purposes. The first case is when the user wants a comprehensive list of results, e.g., to become familiar with a topic. The second case is obscure queries that produce just a few results. Here, the engine with a bigger index is likely to find more results.

In Table 16.4 the distribution of search terms is listed. Independent of search engines observed most search queries appear only once. Around 60% of all unique search queries appeared only once. Regarding all search queries including their recurrences, only 7.9% appeared once. With this in mind, it is maybe not important to have the largest but the most specialized index. It is also of interest to have the possibility to calculate results for very specialized and seldom queries rather than for those that are very popular. We have to stress that users only view the first two or three pages. For popular search queries, it is sufficient to list the most popular pages on the first result page. Search engines like Google already prefer pages such as the ones from Wikipedia.

Table 16.4 Appearance of search queries (Schmidt-Maenz and Koch, 2006)

ID		Search queries which appeared exactly...					
		once	twice	3 times	4 times	5 times	>5 times
Fireball	Absolute	10,480,377	3,024,799	1,330,798	738,817	461,185	1,956,093
	Percentage GN	7.9	4.6%	3.0	2.2	1.7%	80.6
	Percentage NN	58.3	16.8%	7.4	4.1	2.56%	10.9
Lycos	absolute	17,618,682	4,727,513	2,022,780	1,124,878	773,026	3,055,487
	Percentage GN	9.3	5.0%	3.2	2.4%	2.1	78.2
	Percentage NN	60.1	16.12%	6.9	3.8%	2.6	10.4
Met spinner	absolute	732,429	224,171	107,354	65,866	42,021	115,021
	Percentage GN	17.9	11.0	7.9%	6.4%	5.1	51.7
	Percentage NN	56.9	17.4	8.3%	5.1%	3.3	9.0

But the index sizes do not seem to be as important as reported for example in the general media. What makes them such a popular measure is the simplicity of comparison. But the mere sizes don't reveal that much about the quality of the index. A search engine could have, e.g., a large amount of spam pages in its index. Index size is just one measure that is only of importance in relation to other measures.

Search engine sizes are sometimes compared with one another on an absolute basis. But that says nothing about how big they are in relation to the total of the Web. Therefore, Web coverage should be taken into account. Studies dealing with the size of the Web often also investigate on the ratio covered by the search engine. Therefore, both types of studies are discussed together in this section.

There are three ways to get numbers for the discussion about the size of the Web and search engine coverage:

- *Self-reported numbers.* Search engines sometimes report their index sizes to show that they increased in size and/or have the largest index.
- *Overlap measures.* Based on the overlap of search engines, the total size of the Web indexed by all search engines is measured. A limitation of this method is that it omits all pages that are found by none of the search engines under investigation.
- *Random sampling.* Random samples are taken and tested for availability. A total number of available Web pages are calculated from the sample and all pages available are tested against the search engines.

The following paragraphs will give an overview of the most important studies using the different methods.

A comparison based on the self-reported numbers can be found on the SearchEngineWatch.com Web site (Sullivan 2005). The site offers information on the evolution of search engine sizes from the early days on until 2005. Unfortunately, the major search engines do not report their index sizes anymore. Furthermore, while such a comparison is nice to have, it does not say anything about the Web coverage of the indices. In addition, for such comparisons, one has to trust the search engines in giving the correct number. As some studies showed, self-reported numbers can be trusted from some search engines, while others are highly exaggerated (Lewandowski 2005b).

The most important studies determining the Web size and the coverage by search engines on the basis of overlap are Bharat and Broder (1998) and Lawrence and Giles (1998).

Bharat and Broder use a crawl of a part of the Web to build a vocabulary from which queries are selected and sent to four major search engines. From each result set (with up to 100 hits), one page is selected at random. For each Web page found, a "strong query" is built. Such a "strong query" consists of eight terms that should describe the individual documents. These queries are sent to the search engines studied. Ideally, only one result should be retrieved for each query. But there could be more results for various reasons: The same page could be reached under different URLs, and there could be near-identical versions of the same page. The method proposed can deal with this problem and should find the page searched for even if it is indexed by one search engine under a different URL than in the other search engine. From all pages found, the authors calculate the coverage ratio for all search engines. The results show that search engines in general have a moderate coverage of the Web with the best engine indexing 62% of the total of all pages, while the overlap of all engines is extremely low with just 1.4% at the end of 1997. Based on the data, the total size of the Web is estimated at 200 million pages.

The study from Lawrence and Giles (1999) is based on 575 queries from scientists at the NEC Research Institute. From the result sets, the intersection of two search engines under consideration is calculated. The total size of the Web is calculated based on the overlap between the known total index size of one search engine (HotBot with 110 million pages) and the search engine with the second-biggest index, AltaVista. The result is an estimate of the total size of the Web of 320 million pages and coverage of search engines from three to 34%.

While the total size estimates and the ratio of Web coverage differ in both studies presented, both show that (at least in 1997/1998) search engines were nowhere near complete coverage of the Web and that the overlap between the engines is rather small. This leads to the conclusion that meta search engines and/or the use of another search engine in case of failure could be useful.

The most current overlap study is from Gulli and Signorini (2005). They use an extended version of Bharat and Broder's methodology and find that the indexable Web in 2005 contains at least 11.5 billion pages. Search engine coverage of the data set (which consists of all pages found by at least one engine) lies between 57% to 76% for the four big search engines (Google, Yahoo, MSN, Ask).

The most prominent study using random sampling to determine the total size of the Web is the second study from Lawrence and Giles (1999). The basis is a set of random generated IP addresses which are tested for availability. For each of the IPs generally available, it is tested whether it is used by a public server (i.e., a server that hosts pages indexable by a search engine). Based on 3.6 million IP addresses, 2.8 million servers respond in the intended way. From these, 2,500 are randomly chosen and their contents are crawled. From the average number of pages per server of 289, the authors determine the size of the indexable Web to about 800 million pages. Search engine coverage is tested with 1,050 queries. NorthernLight, the search engine performing best, covers only 16% of the indexable Web. All engines under investigation cover only 42%.

All Web size and search engine coverage studies reported have in common that they focus on the indexable part of the Web, or *Surface Web*. But this is just a part of the Web in its entirety, the rest consisting of the so-called *Invisible Web* or *Deep Web*.

In short, the Invisible Web is the part of the Web that search engines do not add to their indices. There are several reasons for this, mainly limited storage space and the inability to index certain kinds of content.

There are two main definitions of the Invisible Web, and in this chapter, we do not need to distinguish between the terms Invisible Web and the Deep Web. Both terms are widely used for the same concept and using one or the other is just a matter of preference. We use the established term Invisible Web.

Sherman and Price (2001) give the following definition for the Invisible Web: "Text pages, files, or other often high-quality authoritative information available via the Web that general-purpose search engines cannot, due to technical limitations, or will not, due to deliberate choice, add to their indices of Web pages" (Sherman and Price 2001, p. 57).

This is a relatively wide definition as it takes into account all file types and includes the *inability* of search engines to index certain content as well as their *choice* not to index certain types of contents. In this definition, for example, Spam pages are part of the Invisible Web because search engines choose not to add them to their indices.

Bergman (2001) defines the Invisible Web (or in his words, the Deep Web) much more narrowly, focusing on databases available via the Web, he writes: "Traditional search engines cannot "see" or retrieve content in the deep Web – those pages do not exist until they are created dynamically as the result of a specific search."

Bergman estimates the size of the Invisible Web to be 550 times larger than the surface Web. Given that the size of the surface Web was estimated to one billion pages at the time the study was conducted, Bergman says the Deep Web consists of about 550 billion documents.

But, as Lewandowski and Mayr (2006) found, these size estimates are far too high, because of two fundamental errors. First the statistical error of using the mean instead of the median calculation and second his misleading projection from the database size in GB. When using the 85 billion documents from his Top 60 (which forms the basis of all further calculations), one can assume that the total number of documents will not exceed 100 billion because of the highly skewed distribution (for details, see Lewandowski and Mayr 2006). Even though this estimation is based on data from 2001, it seems that the typical growth rate of database sizes (Williams 2005) will not affect the total size to a large extent.

Further research is needed for the distinction between the Visible and the Invisible Web. In the past years, we saw the conversion of large databases into HTML pages for the purpose of getting indexed in the main Web search engines. Although this is mainly done in the commercial context, other vendors such as libraries followed this approach with varying degrees of success (Lewandowski 2006b). Further research on this topic is needed because today nobody knows to what extent database content is already available on the surface Web.

The interest of the search engines in indexing the Invisible Web seems just moderate. There is an attempt from Yahoo to index parts of the commercial Invisible Web (Yahoo Subscriptions; http://search.yahoo.com/subscription) as well as some specialised search engines for Invisible Web content (e.g., http://turbo10.com/). But as of yet, no real integration of larger parts of IW content into general search engines was achieved.

Country Bias

In the process of crawling the Web, there is a certain index due to the starting points chosen and the structure of the Web, as well. Highly linked pages have a better chance to be found by the engines than pages from the "periphery" of the Web. The Web was modelled as having a "bow-tie" structure by Broder et al. (2000). But pages in the centre of the Web (the "Strongly Connected Core") are of a higher probability to be older and – regarding the growth structure of the Web – from the U.S. (Vaughan and Thelwall 2004).

But for users not from the U.S. it is important that content in their native languages and from their native countries can be found in the search engines. It is astonishing that there is (at least to our knowledge) just one study dealing with country bias. Especially in the European context with the many languages spoken across Europe, there should be a focus on this topic.

Vaughan and Thelwall (2004) ask for the coverage of Websites from different countries in three major search engines. Countries investigated are the U.S.A., China, Singapore, and Taiwan. The countries are chosen in a way that it can be differentiated between bias due to language factors and "real" country bias. Selected sites both from the U.S. and from Singapore are in English, while sites both from China and Taiwan are in Chinese. The search engines chosen are Google, All the Web and AltaVista.

There are two main research questions: 1. What ratio of the Websites is indexed in the search engines? 2. What ratio of documents within these Websites is indexed by the search engines?

While the first question asks for the ratio of servers from a certain country known by a search engine, the second question asks how deep a certain search engines digs within the sites of a certain country.

All sites chosen for investigation are commercial sites from a random sample (based on IP numbers) from the chosen countries. A research crawler was used to index all sites as deeply as possible. Each page found was checked with the chosen search engines for availability in the indices.

The main result was that the coverage of the sites differs enormously between countries and search engines, as well. As expected, the U.S. sites received the best coverage with 80–87% according to the search engine. Sites from China had coverage from 52% to 70%, while the ones from Singapore reached between 41% and 56%, and the ones from China between four and 75%.

There were large differences in the depth of indexing, too. From U.S. sites, on average, 89% of the pages were indexed, while this number was only 22% for China and only 3% for Taiwan.

Regarding these results, the assumption that Chinese language Websites are not indexed as well as English language Websites due to properties of the Chinese language must be rejected. The same low indexing ratio is shown for English language sites from Singapore. The authors come to the conclusion that disadvantage for these sites must stem from the link structure of the Web.

This study gives indication of a heavy country bias in the search engines indices. We see it as important that similar studies should be conducted because of two reasons: Firstly, the results are now some years old and it can only be guessed that they are still valid today. Secondly, a larger country basis should be investigated. Keeping in mind the discussion in Europe whether a genuine European search engine should be built in competition to the dominating U.S. search engines and the discussion about the usefulness of country-specific search engines, we see an urgent need for studies investigating the country bias for at least a selection of European countries.

Up-to-Datedness

Up-to-datedness is a threefold problem for search engines. Firstly, up-to-datedness is important in keeping the index fresh. Secondly, up-to-datedness factors are used in the ranking of Web pages (Acharya et al. 2005; Lewandowski 2006a). And thirdly, up-to-datedness factors could play an important role in Web based research (Lewandowski 2004c). This section only deals with the first aspect, while the last one will be discussed later.

Ke et al. (2006) give a good overview of the problems for search engines resulting from Web dynamics. Crawling and indexing problems resulting from Web dynamics from a commercial search engine's point of can be found in Risvik and Michelsen (2002).

A study by Ntoulas et al. (2004) found that a large amount of Web pages is changing on a regular basis. Estimating the results of the study for the whole Web, the authors find that there are about 320 million new pages every week. About 20% of the Web pages of today will disappear within a year. About 50% of all contents will be changed within the same period. The link structure will change even faster: About 80% of all links will have changed or be new within a year. These results show how important it is for the search engines to keep their databases up to date.

But, there are just two (series) of studies discussing the actual up-to-datedness behaviour of the major search engines.

Notess conducts studies on the average age of Web pages in the search engines' indices. In the latest instalment, Notess (2003) uses six queries to analyse the freshness of eight different search engines (MSN, HotBot, Google, AlltheWeb, AltaVista, Gigablast, Teoma, and Wisenut). Unfortunately the author gives no detailed information on how the queries were selected. For each query all URLs in the result list are analysed which meet the following criteria: First, they need to be updated daily. Second, they need to have the reported update information in their text. For every Web page, its age is put down. Results show the age of the newest page found, the age of the oldest page found and a rough average per search engine. In the most recent test (Notess 2003), the bigger search engines such as MSN, HotBot, Google, AlltheWeb, and AltaVista have all some pages in their databases that are current or one day old. The databases of the smaller engines such as Gigablast, Teoma, and Wisenut contain pages that are quite older, at least 40 days.

When looking for the oldest pages, results differ a lot more and range from 51 days (MSN and HotBot) to 599 days (AlltheWeb). This shows that a regular update cycle of 30 days, as usually assumed for all the engines, is not used. All tested search engines have older pages in their databases.

For all search engines, a rough average in freshness is calculated, which ranges from four weeks to seven months. The bigger ones obtain an average of about one month except for AltaVista of which the index with an average of about three months is older.

Notess' studies have several shortcomings, which mainly lie in the insufficient disclosure of the methods. It is neither described how the queries are selected, nor how the rough averages were calculated. The methods used in the described study were used in several similar investigations from 2001 and 2002. Results show that search engines are performing better in indexing current pages, but they do not seem to be able to improve their intervals for a complete update. All engines have quite outdated pages in their index.

Lewandowski et al. (2006) use a selection of 38 German language Web sites that are updated on a daily basis for their analysis of the update frequencies of the major Web search engines. Therefore, the cache copies of the pages were checked every day within a time span of six weeks. The search engines investigated were Google, Yahoo and MSN. Only sites that display their latest update date or another currently updated date information were used because Yahoo doesn't display the date the cache copy was taken.

The analysis is based on a total of 1,558 results for every search engine. The authors measure how many of these records are no older than 1 or even 0 days. It was not possible to differentiate between these two values because the search engines were queried only once a day. If there had been a search engine that updated pages at a certain time of the day it would have been preferred to the others.

Therefore, it was assumed that a page that was indexed yesterday or even today is up-to-date in the cache.

Google handed back most of the results with the value 1 (or 0). The total number of 1,291 records shows that 82.86% of the Google results were no older than one day. MSN follows with 748 (48.01%). Yahoo contains 652 (41.85%) one or zero days old pages in its index.

Also, the arithmetic mean up-to-datedness of all Web pages was calculated. Again, Google hands back the best results with an average age of 3.1 days, closely followed by MSN with 3.5 days and Yahoo is behind with 9.8 days. The use of the median instead of the arithmetic mean presents a different picture in which the competitors are closer together: Google and MSN have a median of 1 while Yahoo has a median of 4 days.

Another important point is the age of the oldest pages in the indices. While Google as well as Yahoo have several pages in their indices that were not updated for quite a long time, only MSN seems to be able to completely update its index within a time-span of less than 20 days. Since the research only focussed on Web pages that are updated on a daily basis, this cannot be proved for the complete index. Further research is needed to answer this question. But on the basis of the findings it can be conjectured that Google and Yahoo, which both have outdated pages in their indices, will perform even worse for pages that are not updated on a daily basis.

To summarise the findings, Google is the fastest Web search engine in terms of index quality, because many of the sites were updated daily. In some cases there are outliers that were not updated within the whole time of the research or show some noticeable breaks in their updating frequency. In contrast to that, MSN updates the index in a very clear frequency. Many of the sites were updated very constantly. Taking a closer look at the results of Yahoo, it can be said that this engine has the worst update policy.

16.4.2 *Retrieval Effectiveness*

As already mentioned before, there are several difficulties measuring retrieval effectiveness. The studies discussed below follow a system approach to evaluation. Therefore, the real user behaviour is not represented adequately in the settings. Users only use short search queries and place in average only 2.1 queries per session (Ozmutlu et al. 2003). More than 40% of sessions exist only of one search query (Spink and Jansen 2004). Machill et al. (2003) show that users only place search queries consisting of only one term and they are possibly as effective as users who formulate and reformulate longer and complex queries. In consideration of these facts, it is inevitable to measure retrieval effectiveness with user searching behaviour in mind.

Furthermore, the different query types used in search engines are not taken into account. From the now classic distinction between navigational, informational and transactional queries (Broder 2002), usually, only informational queries are used for evaluation purposes.

According to Broder, with *informational queries*, users want to find information on a certain topic. Such queries usually lead to a set of results rather than just one suitable document. Informational queries are similar to queries sent to traditional text-based IR systems. According to Broder, such queries always target static Web pages. But the term "static" here should not refer to the technical delivery of the pages (e.g., dynamically generated pages by server side scripts like php or asp) but rather to the fact that once the page is delivered, no further interaction is needed to get the desired information.

Navigational queries are used to find a certain Web page the user already knows about or at least assumes that such a Web page exists. Typical queries in this category are searches for a homepage of a person or organization. Navigational queries are usually answered by just one result; the informational need is satisfied as soon as this one right result is found.

The results of *transactional queries* are Websites where a further interaction is necessary. A transaction can be the download of a program or file, the purchase of a product or a further search in a database.

Based on a log file analysis and a user survey (both from the AltaVista search engine), Broder finds that each query type stands for a significant amount of all searches. Navigational queries account for 20–24.5% of all queries, informational queries for 39–48% and transactional queries for 22–36%.

For the further discussion on retrieval tests, one should keep in mind that these only present results for a certain kind of queries, whereas the ranking approaches of some search engines are explicitly developed to better serve navigational queries (Brin and Page 1998), also see Lewandowski (2004b).

With respect to quality of the results, there is a vast amount of literature on the evaluation of the retrieval effectiveness of search engines (Ford et al. 2002; Griesbaum et al. 2002; Leighton and Srivastava 1999; Machill et al. 2004; Singhal and Kaszkiel 2001; Wolff 2000). Because of the constantly changing search engine landscape, older studies are mainly interesting for their methods, but provide only limited use in their results for the different search engines.

For the purpose of this chapter, we will discuss two newer studies (Griesbaum 2004; Véronis 2006), from which we will derive our demand for expanded tests on retrieval effectiveness. The most interesting result from these studies, in our opinion, is that the results of the different engines have converged within the last years. This supports our demand for a more extensive model for quality measurements.

Griesbaum's 2004 study continues research begun and uses methods developed in Griesbaum et al. (2002). Three search engines (Google, Lycos and AltaVista) are tested for relevance on a three-point scale. Results are judged either as relevant, not relevant or not relevant but leading (through a hyperlink) to a relevant document.

The study uses 50 queries and the first 20 results are judged for each query and search engine. Results show that the differences between the three engines investigated are quite low. Google reaches a mean average precision of 0.65, while Lycos reaches 0.60 and AltaVista 0.56, respectively. The complete precision-recall graph

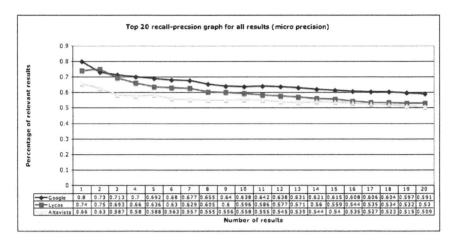

Fig. 16.1 Top 20 recall-precision graph for all results (taken from Griesbaum 2004)

is plotted in Fig. 16.1. These results are out-dated in that they do not describe the search engine landscape as of 2006. Major changes have occurred since the accomplishment of the study. But what the results clearly show is that the relevancy scores of the different engines tend to converge.

Véronis (2006) measures the retrieval effectiveness of six search engines (Google, Yahoo, MSN, Exalead, Voila, Dir.com) as of December, 2005. Here, these queries concern 14 topic areas with five queries each selected by student evaluators. Results are limited to the French language. For each query and search engine, the first ten results are evaluated. A six-point relevance scale (from 0 = worst to 5 = best) is used and some additional criteria are recorded.

Results show that neither of the engines tested receives a good overall relevance score. The author concludes that "the overall grades are extremely low, with no Web search engine achieving the 'pass' grade of 2.5" (Véronis 2006). The best Web search engines are Yahoo and Google (both 2.3), followed by MSN (2.0). The other (French) Web search engines perform worse with 1.8 for Exalead, 1.4 for Dir. com and 1.2 for Voila.

Looking at the relevance graph for the top 10 results (Fig. 16.2 one finds confirmation for the convergence of the results at least of the three major Web search engines.

The convergence of the relevance based on the precision measure leads us to the conclusion that, at least, the major search engines perform comparable on standard informational search queries. Other query types were not tested in either of the studies reported.

We think that there are differences between the retrieval effectiveness of the different Web search engines. But it seems that the precision of the first X results is not the best measure to compare search engines with one another. Therefore, retrieval tests applying other/new and Web-specific measures should be developed.

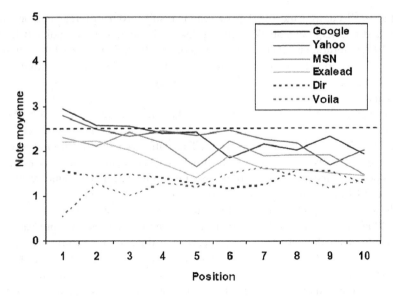

Fig. 16.2 Top10 recall-precision graph for all results (taken from Véronis 2006)

Unfortunately, such retrieval measures are only developed on an experimental basis (see above) and there is no larger initiative working on this topic yet.

16.4.3 Uniqueness of Search Results

Regarding the uniqueness of Web search engines, we have to distinguish between the uniqueness of the databases (defined by their overlap, see above) and the uniqueness of the search results (up to a certain cut-off rate). Two Web search engines based on the completely same index could deliver a completely different order of the results based on their ranking algorithms. This is an important point in Web-based research. The result sets tend to be overwhelmingly large, so that it is impossible for the user to look through all pages of the results list. Therefore, it could be useful to compare the top 10 or so results from different Web search engines to get different views on the same topic.

An important factor for the user is the uniqueness of the results of the different Web search engines (Spink et al. 2006; Véronis 2006). If switching the Web search engines brings different results, this is a good option if one does not find what was intended. In addition, the difference of the results is highly important for the discussion about the problems of a monopoly (or oligopoly) on the Web search engine market.

Studies discussing the overlap of search results from different engines were conducted to a large extent. We will not discuss in detail earlier studies (Chignell et al. 1999; Gordon and Pathak 1999; Nicholson 2000; Schwartz 1998). These all find little overlap between the Web search engines' results, but these findings are now of limited use because of the constantly changing Web search engine landscape.

A newer study focussing on the topic is the one by Spink et al. (2006). Search engines covered are Ask Jeeves, Google, Yahoo and MSN. For each Web search engine, the first 10 results are considered. The authors say that this limitation on the first page of results corresponds well to the user behaviour because users seldom go beyond the first page. The study also takes into account organic results and sponsored listings, but we will only report results for the organic listings.

The study is based on two sets of queries from April, 2005 (10,316 queries) and July, 2006 (12,570 queries). For every query, the top 10 results from each Web search engine are downloaded. The comparison is done automatically using a direct comparison of the URLs. This approach is somehow problematic because of identical content under different URLs, where the search engines omit all but one URL for duplication (Bharat and Broder 1998). This affects the results, and so we think that the actual overlap between Web search engines is higher than the numbers given in the results of studies just comparing URLs.

Spink et al. (2006) find that 84.9% of all hits are just listed by one search engine, while 11.4% by two, 2.6% by three and only 1.1% by all Web search engines considered. The authors conclude that "using a single Web search engine only for a query means that a user misses exposure to a range of highly ranked Websites that are provided on the first page of results retrieved to any query " (p. 1,385). This may be true, but for a user not only the changing of the Web search engine, but also clicking the next button on the first results page to retrieve more results could be useful. Further research is needed that takes into account more results from each Web Search engine and applies a comparison between results that goes beyond the mere comparison of URLs.

In Véronis' study (2006), the overlap of the top 10 results is also measured on the URL basis. He finds that the overlap between every two Web search engines is very low, ranging from 2.9% to 25.1%. Interestingly enough, the pair Google / Yahoo produces the highest degree of overlap.

16.4.4   Quality of the Search Features

This section discusses results from studies concerning the comparison of the power of the command languages and advanced search features, but also on the operational reliability of these.

There is no shortage of comparisons of search engine features and commands (Hock 2004; Notess 2006; Ojala 2002). Early Web search engines such as AltaVista adapted their search functionality from classic online databases, which usually offer a wide range of operators and search functions. Later instalments are more oriented towards the average user who is not interested in advanced search. Nevertheless, search features and operators are necessary for conducting serious Web-based research. A discussion of search features that should be offered by search engines and the degree to which they are applied in the major search engines is given in Lewandowski (2004a). Unfortunately, the comparison of the search engines itself is hopelessly outdated. The reader here is referred to Notess' (2006) compilation in table form.

From a comparison of Web search engines and online databases, Othman and Halim (2004) can show how limited the search functionalities in search engines are in general. Even the functions regarded as common (i.e., five of the databases/search engines investigated offer this function) are only in part applied in the search engines.

A problem with search features that is often overlooked is their operational reliability. While there are functions clearly without any problematic potential (such as restriction to the top level domain), other functions that are relatively easy to apply do not work properly in some major search engines (e.g., Boolean OR in Google; Notess, 2000). With trickier functions it is, to a large degree, unclear how well they work in different search engines. Such features are the language restriction, searching for related pages, content filters, and the date restriction.

This last feature is, to our knowledge, the only one of them systematically studied, as of yet. In a study testing the ability of Web search engines to determine the correct date of Web documents, Lewandowski (2004c) finds that the major search engines all have problems with this task. He uses 50 randomly selected queries from the live ticker of the German Web search engine Fireball, which are sent to the major search engines Google, Yahoo and Teoma. These engines were selected because of their index sizes and their popularity at the time of the investigation. All searches were done twice: once without any restrictions, and once with a date-restriction for the last six months. For each query, 20 results were examined for date information. The study reveals that about 30–33% of the pages have explicit update information in their content. This information was used to compare the non-restricted with the date-restricted queries.

The number of documents from the top 20 list that were updated within the last six months was counted and was defined as the up-to-datedness rate. The proportion of these documents, out of all the documents, was defined as the up-to-datedness rate. The corresponding sets of documents retrieved by the simple search, as well as by the date-restricted search, were calculated. The up-to-datedness rates for the simple search are 37% for Teoma, 49% for Google, and 41% for Yahoo. For the date-restricted search, the rates are 37% for Teoma (which means no improvement), 60% for Google, and 54% for Yahoo. Taking this into consideration, even Google, proved to be the best search engine, in this test fails in 40% of all documents. All in all, the study shows that the tested search engines have massive problems in determining the actual update of the documents found. But this data could be very useful for the indexing and even the ranking process (Lewandowski 2006a).

The study recommends using information from several sources to identify the actual date of a document. The following factors should be combined: server date, date of the first time the document was indexed, metadata (if available), and update information provided in the content of the page.

16.4.5 Search Engine Usability

With respect to the users' searching behaviour, we use findings from our online survey conducted in 2003 (Schmidt-Maenz and Bomhardt 2005), and other studies concerning search engine users. Additionally, we have observed the live tickers of three different search engines (Fireball (FB), Lycos (L), and Metaspinner (MS)), since Summer 2004 (Schmidt-Maenz and Koch 2005, 2006). In our live tickers observed, the list could be updated automatically by refreshing those pages by use of a program. With that, we collected a nearly complete list of search queries performed on these engines during our observation period. Table 16.4 shows the most important results concerning interaction points between search engines and users.

We have analyzed these longitudinally and simultaneously collected observation data based on different search engines. As a consequence, we have a representative view of what searching persons do, since we have comparable data sets regarding observation length, time, and method. The results of all three observed search engines are similar, for that reason it is assumed that these patterns will be the same for other engines, too.

The following results show how users interact with search engines regarding different parameters that reflect search engine usability.

Interface Design

Interfaces of search engines have only one dimension, but there are different groups of search engine users which have different needs (Hotchkiss et al. 2004). Most searching persons only evaluate the result listings very quickly before clicking on one or two recommended Web pages (Hotchkiss et al. 2004; Spink and Jansen 2004). Google has a very clear input window, while Yahoo! is overloaded by adverts and news (Geoghegan 2004). Paid placements are often not clearly separated from the organic lists. They highlight those links with very light background colors (e.g., Google) or give only hints written in very small and slightly coloured letters (e.g., Altavista). That's why users often cannot differentiate between those two or have the feeling that the link they clicked on could be a paid listed link. Additionally, it is important to present only a few results (10 to 15) since search engine users are not willingly to scroll (Hotchkiss et al. 2004).

Additionally, search engines have to provide features to help users to specialize their search queries. Especially advanced users apply operators and features.

Every major search engine provides advanced search features except Excite (Fauldrath and Kunisch 2005).

Acceptance of Search Features and Operators

Search queries are very short and do not show any variations over a longitudinal period. German search queries are, on average, a little bit shorter than English queries since in German word compositions are used instead of words stringed together. Nearly half of the search queries contain only one term. Regarding search terms that occur nearly every day (Schmidt-Maenz and Koch 2006) one finds many operators used inappropriately and fillers such as "in" or "for". This shows how intuitively online searching persons formulate their queries.

The results from studies mentioned above could not be confirmed, here, since only operators presented at the beginning such as ' + ', ' − ' or the phrase search used relatively frequently. But altogether, the usage of operators accounted for less than 3% of all search queries observed. The phrase search was the most frequent form to arrange search queries in a complex way. Here, search queries with phrases were 2.1% for Fireball, 2.4% for Lycos, and 2.5% for Metaspinner (Schmidt-Maenz and Koch 2005).

In the Live Ticker, the German search engines Fireball and Metaspinner also show the selected search area in addition to the current search queries. The search for German pages, only, is selected most frequently. This results from the fact that this area is a pre-adjusted standard in both search engines. In more than two thirds of all search queries, users do not personalize their search by using such features. People in the context of our Internet survey also told that they do not personalize their favourite search engines according to their needs. That means that, all in all, search features such as operators are not accepted. To tell the truth, John Q. Public does not even know how to use operators or what to do with search features.

Performance of Search Engines

The most disliked factor in search engine result lists are Web pages that are optimized to high rankings in result lists, only, and are therefore of little value to the user, and other pages that do not fit the search queries performed (24.4% of 2,014) and advertisement pages (21.4% of 2,014). We think that Internet users often do not know whether they click on paid or organic results. In Machill et al. (2003) respondents said that they are unsatisfied with results of which nobody knows whether they are paid. A high percentage of respondents (76.6% of 6,133) do not think about personalization possibilities of their preferred search engines. These results show that it is possible to evaluate the search engine usability by user surveys. Responders also find what they were supposed to. But the quality of results found is unclear. 70.8% of 6,722 responders very often return to the search engine, instantly, when they do not find what they want on a recommended Web page.

User Guidance

Internet users commonly do not know how search engines work. We asked five general questions about search engines, such as "Is the following statement correct? Meta search engines have their own index". But only 44.2% of 5,944 interviewees were able to answer four or five of these questions correctly. We also find that users with more correct answers use significantly more operators (Schmidt-Maenz and Bomhardt 2005). We show by our results that users, generally, don't understand search engines (Table 16.5). Considering this, it is important to have a clear and simple search engine interface to improve the usability of search engines.

Help functions are provided by most search engines, but it is always a very small button (Google, Yahoo !). Fauldrath and Kunisch (2005) stated that only 57% of examined search engine have a help page, which is easy to find. In most cases this is titled with "all about …" instead of a precise anchor text, such as "help". It is also hard for beginners to know what they are looking for. A general description of what search engines definitely do is missing. Only 71% of major search engines give some help on how to process a search session.

Another point to improve user guidance is to give additional information to the ranked pages. Here the title of the documents, a short description, and the URL are helpful. Every search engine provides this information. But it is also interesting for users to see when last changes were made on the recommended page, or similar search terms are given. Some 71% of major search engines provide temporal information and only 29% suggest similar terms (Fauldrath and Kunisch 2005).

16.5   Conclusions

Today, nobody knows the real performance or accuracy of search engines. There are several studies dealing with a single aspect of quality measurement, but none that tries to evaluate search engine quality as a whole. There was a lack of an overview of empirical results and of quality measures to be used. Our measurement perspectives initiate the discussion about the important matter of search engine quality. With this, it is possible to enhance transparency and diversity on the search engine market.

Table 16.5 Empirical results of the observation of three different search tickers (Schmidt-Maenz 2007)

ID	Year	Days	# Search queries	Avg. length	1-Term queries (%)	Complex queries (%)	Phrase search (%)	Search feature (%)
FB	2004	399	132,833,007	1.8	50.1	<3.0	2.1	65.8
L	2004	403	189,930,859	1.7	51.9	<3.0	2.4	–
MS	2004	314	4,089,731	1.8	48.4	<3.0	2.5	87.9

We showed that there definitely is a gap between the performance of search engines and user needs, respectively capabilities. Regarding user searching behaviour, there are several possibilities, which could be improved. Our assumption is that users do not know how to best interact with search engines. For that reason help functions have to be offered so that more intuitive users also can learn to handle Internet search engines. The next point is the presentation of search results. Search engine should clearly separate paid listings from organic results. User should also get the possibility to learn about the functionality of search engines. Users search often in an intuitive way, for that reason Web search engines should give accurate results based on very short or very specialised Web search queries.

Some questions are still open. What does the European country bias of search Engines look like? How large is the intersection of Web search engines regarding more than the first results page? Which design of Web search engine user interfaces will be best suitable for the users' needs? Our next steps will be to give answers to these questions.

Our search engine quality parameters will help to conduct quality studies to compare different search engines with the same measures. This will again help users to decide which search engines they will prefer to use.

Another important point in the future will be to enlighten users about how search engines work, what they really do and how to use them.

Most research deals with very special parameters to measure search engine quality and the user behaviour is often completely omitted. In this chapter, we introduced a comprehensive approach to measure both, search engine quality with all technical aspects and with aspects from the users' perspective.

Our further research will be to conduct such a comprehensive study by comparing search engine quality of the major Web search engines. Here, we will include user surveys and laboratory studies.

References

Acharya A, Cutts M, Dean J, Haahr P, Henzinger M, Hoelzle U, et al. (2005) Information retrieval based on historical data. USA

Beitzel S, Jensen C, Chowdhury A, Grossman D, Frieder O (2004) Hourly analysis of a very large topically categorized web query log (pp. 321–328). Paper presented at the ACM SIGIR Conference on Research and Development in Information Retrieval, Sheffield, UK. ACM Press

Bergman MK (2001) The deep web: surfacing hidden value. Journal of Electronic Publishing 7

Bharat K, Broder A (1998) A technique for measuring the relative size and overlap of public web search engines. Computer Networks and ISDN Systems 30: 379–388

Brin S, Page L (1998) The anatomy of a large-scale hypertextual web search engine. Computer Networks and ISDN Systems 30: 107–117

Broder A (2002) A taxonomy of web search. SIGIR Forum 36: 3–10

Broder A, Kumar R, Maghoul F, Raghavan P, Rajagopalan S, Stata R, et al. (2000) Graph structure in the web. Retrieved 15.4.2006, from http://www.almaden.ibm.com/webfountain/resources/GraphStructureintheWeb.pdf

Cacheda F, Viña Á (2001) Understanding how people use search engines: a statistical analysis for e-business. 1: 319–325. Paper presented at the e-2001 E-Business and E-Work Conference and Exhibition

Chignell MH, Gwizdka J, & Bodner RC (1999) Discriminating meta-search: a framework for evaluation. Information Processing and Management, 35(3), 337–362

Ding W, Marchionini G (1996) A comparative study of web search service performance. Proceedings of the 59th American Society for Information Science Annual Meeting (pp. 136–142): Learned Information

Fauldrath J, & Kunisch A (2005) Kooperative Evaluation der Usability von Suchmaschineninterfaces. Information: Wissenschaft und Praxis, 56(1), 21–28

Ford N, Miller D, Moss N (2002) Web search strategies and retrieval effectiveness: an empirical study. Journal of Documentation 58: 30–48

Geoghegan T (2004) Search wars: which is best? from news.bbc.co.uk/2/hi/uk_news/magazine/4003193.stm

Gordon M, & Pathak P (1999) Finding information on the World Wide Web: the retrieval effectiveness of search engines. Information Processing & Management, 35(2), 141–180

Greisdorf H, Spink A (2001) Median measure: an approach to IR systems evaluation. Information Processing and Management 37: 843–857

Griesbaum J (2004) Evaluation of three German search engines: Altavista.de, Google.de and Lycos.de. Information Research 9

Griesbaum J, Rittberger M, Bekavac B (2002) In: R. Hammwöhner, C. Wolff and C. Womser-Hacker (Eds.), Deutsche Suchmaschinen im Vergleich: AltaVista.de, Fireball.de, Google.de und Lycos.de (pp. 201–223). Paper presented at the Information und Mobilität. Optimierung und Vermeidung von Mobilität durch Information. 8. Internationales Symposium für Informationswissenschaft. UVK

Gulli A, Signorini A (2005) The indexable web is more than 11.5 billion pages (pp. 902–903). Paper presented at the Special Interest Tracks and Posters of the 14th International Conference on World Wide Web, Chiba, Japan

Hock R (2004) The latest field trip: An update on field searching in web search engines. Online (Wilton, Connecticut), 28(5), 15–21

Hoelscher C, Strube G (2000) Web search behavior of Internet experts and newbies (pp. 337–346). Paper presented at the 9th International World Wide Web Conference

Hotchkiss G, Garrison M, & Jensen S (2004) Search Engine Usage in North America, A Research Initiative by Enquiro. Retrieved 16.3.2006, from www.enquiro.com

Ingwersen P, Järvelin K (2005). The turn: integration of information seeking and retrieval in context. Springer, Dordrecht

Jansen BJ (2000) An investigation into the use of simple queries on web IR systems. Information Research 6

Jansen BJ, Spink A (2003) An analysis of web documents retrieved and viewed (pp. 64–69). Paper presented at the 4th International Conference on Internet Computing

Jansen BJ, Spink A (2006) How we are searching the world wide web? a comparison of nine search engine transaction logs. Information Processing and Management 42: 258–263

Ke Y, Deng L, Ng W, Lee DL (2006) Web dynamics and their ramifications for the development of web search engines. Computer Networks 50: 1430–1447

Kleinberg JM (1999) Authoritative sources in a hyperlinked environment. Journal of the ACM 46: 604–632

Korfhage RR (1997) Information storage and retrieval. Wiley, New York

Lawrence S, Giles CL (1998) Searching the world wide web. Science 280: 98–100

Lawrence S, Giles CL (1999) Accessibility of information on the web. Nature 400: 107–109

Leighton HV, Srivastava J (1999) First 20 precision among world wide web search services (search engines). Journal of the American Society for Information Science 50: 870–881

Lewandowski D (2004a) Abfragesprachen und erweiterte auchfunktionen von WWW-auchmaschinen. Information Wissenschaft und Praxis 55: 97–102

Lewandowski D (2004b) Bewertung von linktopologischen Verfahren als bestimmender Ranking-Faktor bei WWW-Suchmaschinen, Wissensorganisation und gesellschaftliche Verantwortung. 9. Tagung der Deutschen ISKO (Wissensorganisation 2004). Duisburg, Germany

Lewandowski D (2004c) Date-restricted queries in web search engines. Online Information Review 28: 420–427

Lewandowski D (2005a) Web searching, search engines and information retrieval. Information Services and Use 18: 137–147

Lewandowski D (2005b) Yahoo – Zweifel an den Angaben zur Indexgröße, Suche in mehreren Sprachen. Password 20: 21–22

Lewandowski D (2006a) Aktualität als erfolgskritischer Faktor bei Suchmaschinen. Information Wissenschaft und Praxis 57: 141–148

Lewandowski D (2006b) Suchmaschinen als Konkurrenten der Bibliothekskataloge: Wie Bibliotheken ihre Angebote durch Suchmaschinentechnologie attraktiver und durch Öffnung für die allgemeinen Suchmaschinen populärer machen können. Zeitschrift für Bibliothekswesen und Bibliographie 53: 71–78

Lewandowski D (2006c) Zur Bewertung der Qualität von Suchmaschinen. In: J. Eberspächer and S. Holtel (Eds.), Suchen und Finden im Internet (pp. 195–199). Heidelberg: Springer

Lewandowski D, Mayr P (2006) Exploring the academic invisible web. Library Hi Tech 24: 529–539

Lewandowski D, Wahlig H, Meyer-Bautor G (2006) The freshness of web search engine databases. Journal of Information Science 32: 133–150

MacCall SL, Cleveland AD (1999) A relevance-based quantitative measure for Internet information retrieval evaluation (pp. 763–768). Paper presented at the Proceedings of the American Society for Information Science Annual Meeting

Machill M, Neuberger C, Schweiger W, Wirth W (2003) Wegweiser im netz: qualität und nutzung von suchmaschinen. In: M. Machill and C. Welp (Eds.), Wegweiser im Netz. Gütersloh: Bertelsmann Stiftung

Machill M, Neuberger C, Schweiger W, Wirth W (2004) Navigating the Internet: a study of German-language search engines. European Journal of Communication 19: 321–347

Nicholson S (2000) Raising reliability of Web search tool research through replication and chaos theory. Journal of the American Society for Information Science, 51(8), 724–729

Notess GR (2006, 22.5.2006) Search Engine Features Chart. Retrieved 16.3.2006, from http://www.searchengineshowdown.com/features/

Notess GR (2003) Search engine statistics: freshness showdown. Retrieved 4.1.2005, from http://www.searchengineshowdown.com/stats/freshness.shtml

Ntoulas A, Cho J, Olston C (2004) What's new on the web? the evolution of the web from a search engine perspective. Paper presented at the Thirteenth WWW Conference, New York, USA

Ojala M (2002) Web search engines: Search syntax and features. Online (Wilton, Connecticut), 26(5), 28

Ozmutlu H, Spink A, Ozmutlu S (2003) A study of multitasking web search (pp. 145–148). Paper presented at the International Conference on Information Technology: Computers and Communications

Page L, Brin S, Motwani R, Winograd T (1998) The pagerank citation ranking : bringing order to the web. Retrieved 24.7.2006, from http://dbpubs.stanford.edu:8090/pub/1999–66

Parasuraman A, Zeithaml VA, Berry LL (1988). SERVQUAL: a multiple-item scale for measuring consumer perceptions of service quality. Journal of Retailing 64: 12–40

Risvik KM, Michelsen R (2002) Search engines and web dynamics. Computer Networks 39: 289–302

Saracevic T (1995) Evaluation of evaluation in information retrieval (pp. 138–146). Paper presented at the SIGIR'95, Seattle, CA. ACM Press

Schmidt-Maenz (2007) Untersuchung des suchverhaltens im web – Interaktion von Internetnutzern mit Suchmaschinen, Dr. Kovac Verlag, Hamburg

Schmidt-Maenz N, Bomhardt C (2005) Wie suchen onliner im Internet? Science Factory/Absatzwirtschaftb 2: 5–8

Schmidt-Maenz N, Gaul W (2005). Web mining and online visibility. In: C. Weihs and W. Gaul (Eds.), Classification – the ubiquitous challenge (pp. 418–425): Springer

Schmidt-Maenz N, & Koch M (2005) Patterns in Search Queries. In D. Baier, R. Decker & L. Schmidt-Thieme (Eds.), Data Analysis and Decision Support (pp. 122–129). Heidelberg: Springer

Schmidt-Maenz N, Koch M (2006) A general classification of (search) queries and terms (pp. 375–381). Paper presented at the 3rd International Conference on Information Technologies: Next Generations, Las Vegas, Nevada, USA

Schwartz C (1998) Web search engines. Journal of the American Society for Information Science and Technology, 49(11), 973–982

Sherman C, Price G (2001) The invisible web: uncovering information sources search engines can't see. Information Today, Medford, NJ

Silverstein C, Henzinger M, Marais H, Moricz M (1999) Analysis of a very large web search engine query log. ACM SIGIR Forum 33: 6–12

Singhal A, Kaszkiel M (2001) A case study in web search using TREC algorithms (pp. 708–716). Paper presented at the 10th International Conference on World Wide Web, Hong Kong

Spink A, Jansen BJ (2004) Web search: public searching of the web (Vol. 6). Dordrecht, Boston, London: Kluwer Academic.

Spink A, Jansen B, Ozmutlu H (2000) Use of query reformulation and relevance feedback by excite users. Internet Research: Electronic Networking Applications and Policy 19: 317–328

Spink A, Ozmutlu S, Ozmutlu H, Jansen B (2002) U.S. versus european web searching processes. Journal of the American Society for Information Science and Technology 53: 639–652

Spink A, Wolfram D, Jansen B, Saracevic T (2001) Searching the web: the public and their queries. Journal of the American Society for Information Science and Technology 52: 226–234

Spink A, Jansen BJ, Blakely C, & Koshman S. (2006). A study of results overlap and uniqueness among major Web search engines. Information Processing & Management, 42(5), 1379–1391

Su LT (1998) Value of search results as a whole as the best single measure of information retrieval performance. Information Processing and Management 34: 557–579

Sullivan D (2005) Search engine sizes. Retrieved 24.7.2006, from http://searchenginewatch.com/showPage.html?page=2156481

Vaughan L (2004) New measurements for search engine evaluation: proposed and tested. Information Processing and Management 40: 677–691

Vaughan L, Thelwall M (2004) Search engine coverage bias: evidence and possible causes. Information Processing and Management 40: 693–707

Véronis J (2006) A comparative study of six search engines. Retrieved 15.3.2006, from http://www.up.univ-mrs.fr/veronis/pdf/2006-comparative-study.pdf

Wang H, Xie M, Goh TN (1999) Service quality of Internet search engines. Journal of Information Science 25: 499–507

Williams ME (2005) The state of databases today: 2005. In: Gale Directory of Databases (Vol. 2, pp. XV–XXV). Detroit, Mich.: Gale Group

Wolff, C. (2000) Vergleichende evaluierung von such- und metasuchmaschinen, 7. Internationales Symposium für Informationswissenschaft (ISI 2000) (pp. 31–38). Universitätsverlag Konstanz, Darmstadt, Germany

Xie M, Wang H, Goh TN (1998) Quality dimensions of Internet search engines. Journal of Information Science 24: 365–372

Zien J, Meyer J, Tomlin J, Liu J (2000) Web query characteristics and their implications on search engines: Almaden Research Center

Part V
Conclusion

17
Conclusions and Further Research

A. Spink and M. Zimmer

17.1 Introduction

Until recently, most scholarly research on Web search engines have been technical studies originating from computer science and related disciplines. The preceding chapters reveal, however, the growing interest – and importance – of studying Web search from a variety of disciplinary approaches. Significant progress has been made to understand Web searching from within social, cultural, and philosophical perspectives, to utilize political, legal, and economic theories, and to place Web searching within information behavioral frameworks.

This final chapter provides a summary of the insights and conclusions presented in *Web Search: Multidisciplinary Perspectives*, illuminating both interconnections and disagreements among its contributors. We also propose new directions for future research to ensure continued progress in the multidisciplinary understanding of Web search.

17.2 Web Search Engine Bias

In the opening chapter of this book, Alex Diaz brings many of the social and cultural critiques commonly applied to traditional media systems to bear on Web search engines, arguing that decisions over content, advertising policies, and consolidation in the industry as a whole undermine the oft-touted promise of search engines to improve deliberative discourse in contemporary society. Diaz is most concerned with incentives for dominant search engines such as Google to "hypercommercialize content and to *bias* results in a self-interested manner" (emphasis added). For Diaz, and the community of scholars he draws from, instances of such bias – whether by mainstream media companies or Web search engines – represent a threat to democracy and the free and open access to information it demands.

Van Couvering's contribution appears to provide evidence of the kind of industry consolidation Diaz fears. With a few large firms forming an oligopoly within the search engine industry, it seems increasing likely that economic interests might take precedent over any desire to create more "egalitarian" search engines to serve the public good. In Chap. 8, however, Eric Goldman suggests that the marketplace will provide sufficient mechanisms to ensure that search engines support the values society deems important – including, presumably, the democratic ideals envisioned by Diaz. Further, Goldman argues that bias in search engines is both necessary and desirable to help relieve users of unnecessary clutter in their results. As the market pushes search engines to improve, Goldman argues, "the most problematic aspects of search engine bias [will] largely disappear."

Given this range of perspectives and concerns regarding search engine bias, the need for additional research seems obvious. Studies must be undertaken to identify not only possible instances of bias in search engines, but also to measure its effects on both a user and societal level. Only when armed with such additional data can we begin to address the normative dimensions of the bias itself.

17.3   Search Engines as Gatekeepers

Diaz and Van Couvering clearly are concerned about how the current state of the Web search engine industry might work against the maintenance of the liberal ideals of freedom from bias and access to knowledge. Their concern is that – given economic incentives – Web search engines might suppress some particular content in favor of other pieces of information. These reflect concerns of Web search engines as information gatekeepers. Hess's contribution approaches a similar concern, but from a different direction. Rather than focusing on market consolidation and other economic forces that might create a bias in Web search engine results, Hess considers the formal structure of Web search engines themselves, and concludes that by relying on search engines, the rhizomatic nature of the Internet is reduced to simple and convenient "tracts" – to the detriment of knowledge formation. While for different reasons, Hess shares concerns with Diaz and Van Couvering that Web search engines might become powerful gatekeepers of information, threatening the political and liberal promises many held for the Internet. Similarly, Hinman outlines some of the ethical problems that arise when search engines become "intellectual gatekeepers " which not only act as gatekeepers to information, but increasingly play a "central role in the constitution of knowledge itself." And Fry, Virkar and Schroeder provide necessary empirical evidence of the powerful gatekeeping roles Web search engines can take.

One of Hinman's central criticisms of Web search engines is their opacity: the public cannot know precisely how they work and must simply trust the search companies to not exhibit bias or act as gatekeepers to the detriment of knowledge acquisition. Future research, then, must focus on reducing this opacity and bring clarity to how Web search engines work, identifying whether any gatekeeping functions exist. While we are aware of some gatekeeping functions of search engines, such as Google's complicity with China's desire to censor certain search results, the extent to which gatekeeping might occur in versions of Web search engines that exist in more open societies must be explored in more detail.

17.4 Values and Ethics of Search

Concerns over bias and gatekeeping point to the ways in which Web search engines have particular value and ethical implications for society. One key value in liberal democratic societies is equal access of all citizens to information and opportunities for, as the U.S. Declaration of Independence puts it, "life, liberty, and the pursuit of happiness." Martey's contribution reveals, however, the ways in which Web searching might compromise the pursuit of these values. When relying on Internet search tools to find employment, women typically confront gendered notions of both the Internet itself as well as the jobs themselves. As a result, Martey suggests women are disadvantaged and disincented from using Web search tools in order to advance their employment situations.

Zimmer also explores the value and ethical dimensions of Web searching, focusing on the privacy and surveillance aspect of the drive for the "perfect search engine." He reveals the ways in which users are compelled to provide details of their personal and intellectual activities in order to enjoy the (perceived) benefits of Web searching. Considering Hinman's brief mention of government's ability to trace a person's search histories, the ethical implications of the widespread collection of one's search activities are significant.

These studies of the value and ethical dimensions of Web searching merely scratch the surface of this vital area of research. Additional work needs to take place to not only understand conceptually what values are at play with Web searching, but also how user's search activities actually impact values and ethics in the real world.

17.5 Design of Web Search Engines

Zimmer's discussion of the privacy and surveillance threats of the perfect search engine concludes with a call for the "value-conscious design " of Web search engines to try to mitigate their value and ethical consequences. Yet understanding the full implications of various designs of search engines remains elusive. An important first step towards gaining an appreciation of possible design variables is to study how users themselves view the technical design of the search tools they rely on. Hendry and Efthimiadis move us closer to this goal with their detailed study of users' perceptions and conceptual models of search engines. Combined with Lewandowski and Schmidt-Maenz's suggestions for improved quality measurements of Web search engines, we can begin to take steps towards improved design of these vital online information tools.

Continued work, then, must be performed to hone our ability to not only understand the technical design variables and possibilities of search engines, but also our ability measure the performance and affects of various design solutions.

17.6 Legal Constraints and Obligations

Redesigning Web search engines to mitigate against some of the concerns noted above is not the only solution. Legal and regulatory frameworks could also be constructed to ensure Web search engines do not contain bias, for example, or to protect women from being disadvantaged from their use. If we consider the complex picture Dutta and Brodie paint regarding users search activities for health information – clearly a subject matter of broad public interest – one could envision the creation of laws or regulations to ensure Web search engines provide accurate and unbiased access to health information. Similarly, Zimmer's concerns with privacy and surveillance of search engine records could be partially absolved if laws were passed limiting search engine's abilities to collect user data. Goldman, however, argues against any attempt to regulate the search industry, and instead insists that the marketplace will ensure users needs are adequately fulfilled and rights are properly respected. Determining which approach is best requires further study and debate.

Legal constraints and obligations can take a different form in the realm of Web searching. Fitzgerald and his colleagues present a very useful summary of the copyright issues that quickly arise with the rise of Web search engines, especially in light of the desire to scan and index contents of thousands of printed books (as discussed in Hinman's chapter). The impact Web searching will have on the dominant copyright paradigm in contemporary society will, undoubtedly, gain further attention.

17.7 Cognition and Information Behavior

Knight and Spink highlight the need to understand Web search from an information behavior perspective. Further research is needed to model and situate Web search within the everyday information behavior of individuals. Dutta and Brodie highlights the need for research to develop an integrative model of online health information behavior to help people understanding the health outcomes associated with new communication technologies.

17.8 Integration Across Various Perspectives

One of the key directions identified by chapter authors for Web research is the integration of various approaches to develop an integrated Web search framework. An integrated perspective for Web search seeks to create a more holistic understanding of Web search that takes into account the various contexts in which human-Web system interaction takes place. This book highlights the need for a more integrated understanding of Web search from the perspective of various scientific disciplines. No integrative framework presently exists. However, an integrated approach has the potential to yield a more holistic theoretical and cognitive understanding that will assist our understanding of the Web search phenomena.

17.9 Final Thoughts

This book provides an overview of new directions in Web search research from a broad social science, philosophical, and information science perspective. The field of Web search is vast, international, interdisciplinary, and dynamic with great potential to impact the everyday lives of people worldwide as they increasingly need to interact with Web search infrastructures. This book is not an historical or exhaustive overview of all the research areas that are important for the future of Web search studies. Web search, as a research issue, crosses from the quite technical areas of computer science to the cognitive sciences, and as we have highlighted in this book, to the social and information sciences. We hope that our book will stimulate further interdisciplinary dialogue to facilitate the development of Web search research.

Index

A

access to knowledge 67, 70, 73, 75, 119, 256, 344

advertising 11, 13, 15, 20, 21, 22, 23, 24, 25, 26, 29, 42, 43, 70, 71, 87, 88, 92, 107, 110, 116, 119, 153, 156, 179, 184, 185, 186, 192, 193, 195, 196, 197, 198, 202, 203, 257, 319, 343

algorithm 11, 15, 19, 29, 30, 41, 42, 44, 45, 67, 69, 71, 72, 74, 75, 123, 125, 126, 127, 129, 130, 131, 136, 137, 139, 154, 157, 161, 195, 209, 216, 223, 255, 272, 280, 283, 286, 293, 300, 301, 303, 309, 311, 318, 331

AltaVista 183, 185, 193, 195, 225, 226, 323, 325, 327, 329, 332

Amazon.com 42, 44, 46, 47, 71, 112

America Online 14, 21, 26, 77, 83, 87, 178, 180, 185, 193, 194, 195, 202

Ask.com 25, 28, 71, 124, 195, 201, 332

AskJeeves 21, 203

autonomy 78, 277, 304

B

Battelle, John 85, 91

bias 5, 6, 11, 16, 17, 18, 19, 20, 23, 24, 25, 26, 27, 29, 30, 59, 71, 83, 121, 122, 126, 127, 128, 129, 130, 131, 137, 218, 240, 264, 267, 272, 273, 283, 311, 319, 321, 325, 326, 337, 343, 344, 345, 346

Brin, Sergey 82

C

censorship 5, 74, 156, 170, 277

channel complementarity 237, 241, 244

China 74, 75, 92, 103, 104, 117, 118, 135, 136, 137, 143, 146, 147, 180, 325, 326, 344

commercialization 6, 27, 35, 70

computer mediated communication 36, 152

consolidation 6, 11, 24, 25, 27, 28, 178, 181, 196, 343, 344

consumer behavior 71

cookie 35, 41, 42, 45, 46, 47, 70, 78, 81, 86, 87, 88, 278

copyright 6, 73, 88, 103, 104, 105, 106, 107, 108, 109, 110, 111, 112, 113, 114, 115, 116, 117, 118, 119, 346

D

dataveillance 6, 77, 78, 80, 81, 83, 91, 92, 93

deliberative democracy 11, 12, 42

deliberative media 11

democracy 5, 11, 12, 13, 15, 16, 18, 22, 23, 25, 29, 30, 35, 37, 44, 47, 48, 135, 136, 138, 144, 145, 147, 173, 344, 345

Democratic deliberation 145

design 7, 17, 21, 28, 53, 55, 78, 79, 82, 92, 94, 95, 140, 151, 170, 206, 209, 221, 223, 244, 249, 250, 288, 289, 304, 306, 314, 319, 320, 334, 337, 345, 346

digital divide 45, 48, 236, 237, 248

directory 21, 137, 151, 153, 154, 155, 156, 158, 161, 162, 170, 182, 187, 188, 195, 197, 281

dual processing 237, 241, 244

E

e-commerce 190, 192, 194

epistemology 37, 39, 40

ethics 5, 6, 23, 67, 81, 83, 279, 280, 344, 345

Excite 4, 25, 182, 184, 185, 187, 188, 189, 190, 191, 193, 194, 314, 335

F

Foucault, Michel 79, 80, 93

G

gatekeeper 6, 11, 15, 20, 49, 68, 69, 151,
    153, 249, 255, 258, 270, 271, 272,
    273, 281, 344
gatekeeping 35, 151, 270, 273, 344, 345
gender 4, 36, 51, 52, 53, 54, 55, 58, 59, 60,
    61, 62, 63, 88, 226, 231, 236
Google 5, 11, 15, 16, 17, 18, 19, 20, 21, 22,
    23, 24, 25, 26, 27, 28, 35, 41, 42, 43,
    44, 45, 48, 69, 70, 71, 73, 74, 77, 78,
    82, 86, 87, 88, 91, 92, 93, 94, 103, 107,
    108, 109, 111, 112, 113, 114, 116, 117,
    118, 119, 29, 124, 126, 130, 135, 136,
    137, 143, 144, 146, 147, 152, 153, 154,
    155, 156, 158, 161, 167, 170, 178, 179,
    180, 181, 182, 195, 196, 197, 198, 199,
    201, 202, 203, 255, 256, 257, 258, 260,
    263, 264, 265, 266, 267, 268, 269, 271,
    272, 273, 278, 279, 280, 281, 282, 283,
    293, 294, 295, 300, 311, 321, 323, 325,
    327, 328, 329, 330, 332, 333, 334, 336,
    338, 343, 344
Google bomb 280
Googlearchy 132, 154, 158, 161,
    169, 173

H

health information seeking 6, 235, 236,
    237, 242, 243, 244, 245, 246, 250
hegemony 35
Herfiendhal-Hirshman Index 25
Human-Computer Interaction 284
hypertext 39, 40, 41, 45, 47, 224, 225, 317

I

information behavior 6, 53, 209, 210, 212,
    219, 223, 224, 228, 229, 230, 231,
    232, 346
information environment 138, 209, 210,
    211, 212, 215, 216, 217, 223, 224,
    232, 255, 256, 258, 264, 265, 266,
    268, 270, 272, 273
information network 279
Information retrieval 182, 209
information retrieval 6, 73, 182, 286, 303,
    310, 318
information science 3, 38, 182, 256, 274,
    278, 279, 301, 303, 317, 347

information seeking 3, 4, 6, 51, 52, 53, 54,
    55, 62, 78, 82, 83, 91, 93, 136, 138,
    141, 182, 209, 210, 211, 212, 213,
    215, 216, 217, 219, 220, 225, 226,
    228, 229, 230, 232, 235, 236, 237,
    238, 239, 240, 242, 243, 244, 245,
    246, 249, 250, 252, 255, 257, 259,
    268, 269, 272, 287, 288, 309, 338
intellectual property 73, 103, 283
interface 51, 57, 58, 62, 78, 82, 91, 92, 93,
    140, 195, 209, 220, 267, 286, 287,
    288, 291, 293, 295, 320, 336

K

keywords 21, 44, 91, 128, 129, 139, 141, 144,
    153, 155, 159, 225, 260, 261, 264, 265,
    267, 270, 272, 278, 281, 282, 295, 304

L

library 5, 68, 74, 136, 224, 258, 262, 279,
    286, 287, 288, 303, 311
link structure 14, 44, 137, 311, 321, 326

M

Microsoft 19, 21, 23, 25, 28, 35, 41, 42, 43,
    44, 46, 74, 77, 158, 167, 168, 178, 180,
    182, 195, 198, 199, 201, 202, 203, 323,
    327, 328, 330, 332
Mill, John Stuart 12, 16, 144, 145, 146,
    147, 148

P

Page, Larry 82, 86
PageRank 11, 15, 16, 17, 19, 26, 27, 29,
    44, 45, 126, 136, 137, 139, 278,
    280, 293, 311
paid placement 21, 22, 83
Panopticon 79, 80
perfect search engine 77, 78, 83, 85, 86, 93,
    94, 314, 345
Personalized search 130
personalized search 29, 88, 92, 121
Pew Internet & American Life Project 3, 82
philosophical 5, 38, 343, 347
political economy 5, 43, 44, 83, 177, 179,
    198, 201
portal 15, 21, 26, 28, 187, 189, 190, 192, 193,
    194, 195, 198, 199, 201, 263
privacy 5, 6, 45, 72, 78, 81, 83, 87, 94, 98,
    250, 277, 278, 280, 281, 345, 346

profile 71, 81, 90, 93, 287, 291
profiling 72, 88, 113, 157, 169, 171, 172,
    193, 194
protocol 278, 281, 282
public policy 142, 261, 278, 279, 301, 304
public sphere 4, 7, 37

R
ranking 15, 19, 44, 69, 71, 73, 74, 123, 124,
    125, 126, 127, 129, 130, 131, 133, 154,
    155, 157, 173, 195, 257, 266, 278, 280,
    283, 293, 309, 311, 317, 326, 329, 331,
    333, 335, 339
regulation 29, 74, 94, 129
rhizome 6, 35, 36, 37, 38, 39, 40, 41, 45, 46,
    47, 48, 344

S
search engine quality 309, 310, 318, 319, 320,
    336, 337
search history 47, 181, 222
search query 4, 19, 73, 85, 86, 87, 109,
    125, 130, 136, 139, 140, 141, 151,
    153, 155, 156, 157, 159, 166, 167,
    168, 169, 184, 218, 219, 222, 224,
    225, 226, 228, 230, 258, 268, 286,
    287, 288, 291, 292, 294, 295, 297,
    298, 300, 301, 302, 304, 311, 313,
    314, 316, 317, 318, 320, 323, 327,
    328, 329, 330, 332, 333
selective processing 237, 241, 244

server log 78, 86, 87, 88
social science 217, 256, 261, 263, 347
spam 278, 319, 322
spider 116, 284, 294, 300
surveillance 6, 72, 77, 78, 79, 80, 81, 93, 238,
    345, 346

T
textual analysis 6, 35, 41, 42
trust 5, 12, 67, 75, 83, 267, 287, 305, 311,
    322, 344

U
usability 287, 289, 309, 319, 320, 334, 335,
    336
uses and gratifications 237, 238, 241

W
Web crawlers 155, 158
Wikipedia 46, 49, 68, 311, 321
World Wide Web 27, 37, 39, 68, 69, 75, 185

Y
Yahoo 21, 23, 25, 26, 28, 30, 35, 41, 42,
    43, 44, 47, 74, 77, 118, 119, 155,
    158, 168, 177, 178, 180, 182, 184,
    185, 193, 196, 197, 198, 199, 201,
    202, 203, 323, 325, 327, 328, 330,
    332, 333, 334, 336